Fetal Positions

Fetal Positions

*Understanding Cross-National Public
Opinion about Abortion*

AMY ADAMCZYK

OXFORD
UNIVERSITY PRESS

Oxford University Press is a department of the University of Oxford.
It furthers the University's objective of excellence in research, scholarship,
and education by publishing worldwide. Oxford is a registered trade mark of
Oxford University Press in the UK and in certain other countries.

Published in the United States of America by Oxford University Press
198 Madison Avenue, New York, NY 10016, United States of America.

© Oxford University Press 2025

All rights reserved. No part of this publication may be reproduced, stored in a retrieval system, transmitted, used for text and data mining, or used for training artificial intelligence, in any form or by any means, without the prior permission in writing of Oxford University Press, or as expressly permitted by law, by license or under terms agreed with the appropriate reprographics rights organization. Inquiries concerning reproduction outside the scope of the above should be sent to the Rights Department, Oxford University Press, at the address above.

You must not circulate this work in any other form
and you must impose this same condition on any acquirer.

Library of Congress Cataloging-in-Publication Data

Names: Adamczyk, Amy, 1974- author.
Title: Fetal positions : understanding cross-national public opinion
about abortion / Amy Adamczyk.
Description: [New York] : [Oxford University Press], [2025] |
Includes bibliographical references and index. |
Identifiers: LCCN 2024038479 (print) | LCCN 2024038480 (ebook) |
ISBN 9780197761052 (paperback) | ISBN 9780197761045 (hardback) |
ISBN 9780197761076 (epub) | ISBN 9780197761083
Subjects: LCSH: Abortion—Public opinion—Cross-cultural studies. |
Abortion—Religious aspects—Cross-cultural studies. | LCGFT: Cross-cultural studies.
Classification: LCC HQ767 .A38 2025 (print) | LCC HQ767
(ebook) | DDC 362.1988/8—dc23/eng/20241210
LC record available at https://lccn.loc.gov/2024038479
LC ebook record available at https://lccn.loc.gov/2024038480

DOI: 10.1093/9780197761083.001.0001

Paperback printed by Integrated Books International, United States of America
Hardback printed by Bridgeport National Bindery, Inc., United States of America

For Clarence

Contents

List of Figures	viii
List of Tables	x
Acknowledgements	xi

Introduction	1
1. Religion and Abortion Attitudes	24
2. The Role of Economics and Education in Shaping Public Opinion about Abortion	65
3. Democracy, Laws, and Policy in Shaping Abortion Views	91
4. Gender Equality, Social Movement Activity, and Race for Understanding Views about Abortion	123
5. Communism, Confucianism, Cultural Values, and Survey Challenges for Understanding Abortion Attitudes	159
6. Investigating Cross-National Abortion Behavior and Its Relationship with Attitudes	199
Conclusion	237

Appendix A: WVS Analysis	254
Appendix B: Newspaper Analysis	265
Appendix C: Additional Indicators	273
Appendix D: Abortion Rate Analysis	275
Bibliography	278
Index	311

List of Figures

Figure 0.1. Map Presenting Abortion Disapproval Levels across the World — 5

Figure 0.2. Predicted Probabilities for Explaining Whether Abortion Is Illegal, except for Extreme Reasons — 8

Figure 1.1. Marginal Values for Abortion Disapproval by Personal Religious Affiliation — 38

Figure 1.2. Marginal Values for Abortion Disapproval by Individual and Country Religious Importance — 45

Figure 1.3. Proportion Catholic within a Country for Explaining Abortion Disapproval — 51

Figure 2.1. Scatterplots of the Relationship between GDP per Capita and Mean Levels of Education for Explaining the Percentage That Disapproves of Abortion in Each Society — 77

Figure 2.2. Marginal Values for Abortion Disapproval by Three Levels of Combined GDP per Capita and Mean Societal-Levels of Education — 78

Figure 2.3. Marginal Effects for the Interaction between Education and Economic Development and Four Levels of Personal Religious Importance for Explaining Abortion Disapproval — 89

Figure 3.1. Marginal Values for Individual Abortion Disapproval by a Country's Democracy Status and Abortion Policy — 94

Figure 3.2. Changes in Attitudes about Abortion over Time in China, Neighboring Countries, and the United States — 107

Figure 3.3. Percentage of Articles in Each Theme and Claimsmaker Category across Countries and English-Language Newspapers — 114

Figure 3.4. Marginal Percentage of Articles That Include Various Themes and Claimsmakers in English-Language Articles That Mention Abortion by Country's Freedom Score — 116

Figure 4.1. Marginal Values for Abortion Disapproval by Three Levels of Country-Level Gender Inequality — 131

Figure 5.1. Marginal Values for Abortion Disapproval by Country's Communist History — 166

LIST OF FIGURES   ix

Figure 5.2. Marginal Differences in Attitudes between Residents Living in Societies with and without Confucian Histories before and after Mean Levels of Religious Importance Are Included   180

Figure 5.3. Differences between Confucian and Non-confucian Nations in Conservative Values   184

Figure 5.4. Scatterplots of Abortion Disapproval for Three Different Cross-National Data Collections   197

Figure 6.1. Marginal Values of Statistically Significant Variables for Examining the Model-Estimated Annual Average Abortion Rates for Unintended Pregnancies per 1,000 Women, 2015–2019   204

Figure 6.2. Marginal Values for Country Abortion Rates at Three Different Country Levels of Gender Inequality and GDP/education before and after Including the Unintended Pregnancy Rate   206

Figure 6.3. Processes That Explain the Influence of Religion on American Women's Risk of Aborting First Pregnancies   222

Figure C.1. Legal Changes to Abortion Legislation between 1994 and 2022   248

Figure C.2. Changes in Abortion Disapproval over Time for the World's Ten Most Populous Countries   250

List of Tables

Table 5.1. Individual and Country-Level Values for Understanding Abortion Disapproval ... 171

Table 6.1. Logistic Regression Analysis of the Factors Increasing Abortion Risk for Women across Individual Countries using Data from The Demographic and Health Surveys ... 216

Table A.1. Societies Included in World Values Survey Analysis ... 254

Table A.2. Descriptive Statistics of Variables Included in Models Using World Values Survey Data ... 255

Table A.3. Mixed Models for Explaining Abortion Disapproval ... 259

Table A.4. Additional Analyses Examining the Interactions between Personal Religious Importance and GDP/Mean Education and Country Religious Importance and Gender Inequality for Understanding Abortion Disapproval ... 262

Table A.5. Mixed Models Examining the Independent and Joint Influences of Country Levels of Education and GDP on Abortion Disapproval ... 264

Table B.1. Newspapers and Countries Included in the Analysis ... 266

Table B.2. Descriptive Statistics for Variables Included in the Analysis ... 267

Table B.3. Multilevel Mixed-Effects Logistic Regression Models Examining the Country-Level Factors Shaping the Odds That Abortion Is Discussed in the Context of Key Themes and Claimsmakers ... 271

Table C.1. Additional Indicators Considered for Explaining Survey Respondent's Abortion Disapproval in Multivariate Mixed Models ... 273

Table D.1. Ordinal Least Squares Regression Models Examining of the Cross-National Factors Shaping Rates of Unintended Pregnancy and Abortions of Unintended Pregnancies ... 276

Acknowledgements

Several important people and organizations provided support that made this book possible. First, I want to acknowledge the funders. A Jack Shand Research Award from the Society for the Scientific Study of Religion provided a small grant to travel to China and conduct the interviews. A global pandemic got in the way of physical travel, but the funds were used to pay for translators, subject compensation, transcription services, and other related costs. The Professional Staff Congress-City University of New York Research Award Program provided release time and funding for a research assistant. The John Jay College of Criminal Justice Office for the Advancement of Research Faculty Scholarship Program paid for a laptop. Professor Yu Wang from Duke Kunshan University connected me with scholars willing to be interviewed, which eventually led to a large and varied sample. Professor Liqun Cao also provided guidance and support in arranging interviews. Professor Jing-Bao Nie, who wrote the only other book on Chinese abortion views, *Behind the Silence*, encouraged me to conduct this study and offered insight into the Chinese context and practical advice about how to move forward.

Fetal Positions relies heavily on information from forty expert interviews from China and the United States. They contributed invaluable insight into the processes shaping views within each country. Yen-Chiao (Angel) Liao and Samuel translated these discussions and helped recruit Chinese participants. Dr. Liao also transcribed the Chinese interviews, coded themes, and managed the paperwork and payment in China. Tzu-Ying (Michelle) Lo, Lindsay Lerner, Jewel Warner, and Mike Hourahan helped code interviews, gather literature, and prepare initial presentations. Also, Lindsay and Michelle helped to edit the text, as did my long-time friend and collaborator, Jacob Felson. I am also thankful to my editor, James Cook, for supporting the project, and to the anonymous reviewers, who provided invaluable feedback.

xii ACKNOWLEDGEMENTS

While I was researching *Fetal Positions*, I gave birth to my baby, Clarence. This book would never have been completed without high-quality and reliable childcare. I owe the Children's Center at John Jay College of Criminal Justice, their director, Linda Soleyn, his major teachers, and their assistants for caring for my young son. Knowing that Carmen Leon, Mercedes Maldonado, and Robyn Bailey were keeping Clarence safe, helping him grow, and loving him as their own made it possible for me to focus on writing this book. Finally, Donald Morisette, my life-partner, has supported this project from the beginning, listening to early ideas, thinking through the findings, coaching me on related presentations, and encouraging me to finish.

Introduction

In July 2022, the US Supreme Court stunned America when they overturned *Roe v. Wade*, which for nearly fifty years had guaranteed women a constitutional right to an abortion. Major protests followed. While some states had trigger laws in place that made abortion illegal, others scrambled to enact legislation that clarified their stance. The decision was shocking because most Americans (61%) supported a woman's right to obtain an abortion.[1] People on the left lamented the loss and vowed to change the law and provide a safe haven for women who wanted abortions. Conversely, many religious Americans celebrated. Some conservative activists have referred to abortion as a "silent holocaust,"[2] equating it to what happened to Jews in Nazi Germany. Thus, for some, the decision was a major moral victory.

Like the United States, other countries have also experienced contentious discussions about abortion. In Brazil, for example, abortion is permitted only in cases of rape or incest or to save a pregnant woman's life.[3] In 2022, a ten-year-old pregnant girl found herself in a Brazilian courtroom asking for permission to obtain an abortion on the grounds of rape. The judge asked whether she could stand to be pregnant a little longer so that she could give the child up for adoption "instead of letting him die—because it is already a baby, a child."[4] Leaked video of the hearing divided residents. Historically, most Brazilians have identified as Catholic, but Pentecostalism is the country's fastest-growing Christian religion. Religiously engaged Catholics and Pentecostals are especially opposed to abortion.[5] Brazilian doctors who perform illegal abortions can be sentenced to four years in jail.[6] Since the 1970s, when many other nations began permitting abortion during the first trimester, Brazilian feminists have been fighting to legalize abortion. However, like residents of other South American countries, over

---

[1] Delaney, "Roe v. Wade Has Been Overturned. What Does That Mean for America?"; Ziegler and Tsai, "How the Anti-Abortion Movement Used the Progressive Playbook to Chip Away at Roe v. Wade."

[2] Powell, *Abortion the Silent Holocaust*.

[3] Human Rights Watch, "Women's Human Rights: Abortion in Brazil."

[4] Lopes, "A 10-Year-Old Rape Victim Sought an Abortion. A Judge Urged."

[5] Ogland and Verona, "Religion and Attitudes toward Abortion and Abortion Policy in Brazil."

[6] Human Rights Watch, "Women's Human Rights: Abortion in Brazil."

2   FETAL POSITIONS

65% of Brazilians disapprove of abortion,[7] which has major implications for women who may need or want them and for society more generally.

While abortion is often a contested issue, in several countries it is not a major subject of public discussion or disapproval. Many residents in very liberal northern European societies may view abortion as a settled issue. Since the 1970s, abortion has been allowed within gestational limits in countries like Sweden, Norway, and Finland, and there is relatively little political debate about its legality. Likewise, in China, it may seem that abortion is not especially divisive. As one of the Chinese researchers I interviewed for this book explained, "I don't think this is a controversial issue. . . . There is really a long history for the one-child policy. So, abortion services are widely available and are usually safe." As I explain in Chapter 3, the Chinese are not as liberal as many might think. Moreover, the government would squash any passionate public discussion on this topic.

In this book, I investigate why views on abortion vary so considerably across the globe, what factors affect those perspectives, how those views are associated with laws and policies, and the ways attitudes have evolved within specific countries. I also analyze the forces shaping cross-national abortion rates and personal abortion decisions and the pathways through which personal and country characteristics have an effect. Finally, I unpack the evolution of abortion regulation in the United States and China.

Survey data from 88 societies and over 200,000 people form the backbone of this book. However, surveys intentionally obscure the role of unique histories and cultures in shaping attitudes. To overcome this limitation, I conduct a comparative case study analysis of China and the United States, where I conducted dozens of interviews with people who could offer insight into the public's views. The United States and China have massive populations, housing roughly 22% of the world's population. As such, they are major forces of economic, political, and cultural power. With vastly different levels of religious belief, democracy, and abortion-related policies, as well as diverse economic transitions, these nations provide fascinating points of contrast. They also share some meaningful similarities. Additional insight is drawn from an analysis of abortion discourse in newspapers from forty-one countries. I also draw on examples from several other countries to illustrate key ideas.

---

[7] See Figure 0.1.

Feelings about abortion play a major role in whether people are willing to talk about it, obtain an abortion for themselves, or help others get one. The ease with which a woman can access abortion services has important consequences for her health, career, economic trajectories, the well-being of her other children, relationships with her partners, and so forth. Even in China, where abortion has been legal since 1956, many women still view it as a deeply personal issue, only to be discussed with close family and friends. As one of the professors I spoke with explained, "Very few students would be open to talking about [getting an abortion]. Most of them would just keep it private. So, for most of them it's a very private personal matter. And it's probably very shameful."

Public opinion about abortion also has country-wide implications. Across the world, many women work outside of their homes, making major contributions to their country's economies, civic organizations, religious communities, and political institutions. Many are also the primary caretakers for their children.[8] Poorer countries tend to have a stronger division of labor, with women more likely to act as caretakers and men to be responsible for supporting their families financially. However, even in rich nations, such as those located in North America and Western Europe, women shoulder a disproportionate amount of caretaking duties.[9] The decision to bring more children into the world can contribute to a stronger division of labor between men and women.[10] Abortion, attitudes, access, and fertility control can also shape who residents see in positions of economic and political power and whether they believe that their country is in grave moral danger.

What Explains Massive Differences in Attitudes about Abortion?

Significant differences in abortion views among people living in North America, Europe, the Global South, and East Asia illustrate the diversity of perspectives across the world. Figure 1.1 shows a map of the world that indicates differences in abortion support. The figure relies on data from the last three waves of the World Values Survey (WVS) and includes the majority of

---

[8] Ferrant, Pesando, and Nowacka, "Unpaid Care Work: The Missing Link in the Analysis of Gender Gaps in Labour Outcomes."

[9] Gromada and Richardson, "Where Do Rich Countries Stand on Childcare?"

[10] Samman, Presler-Marshall, and Jones, "Women's Work: Mothers, Children and the Global Childcare Crisis."

4   FETAL POSITIONS

the world's population. Lighter gray indicates where abortion has the greatest acceptance. Across much of Europe, less than 25% of people believe that abortion is never justified. With these data, the United States appears quite liberal, with less than 25% of residents reporting that abortion is never justified. Conversely, attitudes become more conservative in Latin America, East Asia, and especially Russia, where between 25% and 50% of people say that abortion is never justified. Individuals living in countries like Brazil, Colombia, Ghana, Indonesia, and Iraq have some of the most conservative views, with more than 65% of residents reporting that abortion is never acceptable.

Why are there such large differences in public opinion about abortion around the world? Part of the answer involves how national characteristics shape people's attitudes. Public opinion about abortion is not randomly distributed across the globe. Rather, patterns can be found across nations. For example, Catholicism has historically dominated Latin America, though more recently Evangelical Christian faiths have been growing. The Catholic Church's hierarchical structure and cultural and political dominance has elevated its vocal condemnation of abortion. Indeed, in Catholic-majority countries like Poland, Brazil, and Colombia, many residents report that religion is important and that abortion is problematic. Conversely, while France and Spain have strong historical connections to the Catholic Church, the proportion who believe that religion is important is much lower and attitudes more liberal.

Aside from organized religion, other factors matter as well. Figure 0.1 shows that residents of Nigeria, Ghana, Ethiopia, and Zimbabwe strongly oppose abortion. These nations are all located in Africa, which includes some of the poorest societies in the world. In 2021, Ethiopia had an average gross national income per capita of about $890, which classifies it as a low-income country.[11] The proportion of Ethiopians who disapprove of abortion is especially high (74%). Ethiopians also have high levels of religious belief, with 86% reporting that religion is very important. The overlap between various country characteristics, such as income and religious importance, makes it difficult to easily ascertain what is truly driving abortion disapproval. Using the appropriate statistical techniques, the sophisticated analyses presented in this book help to untangle these relationships, isolating the major forces shaping public opinion about abortion around the world.

[11] World Population Review, "Poorest Countries in the World 2022."

Figure 0.1 Map Presenting Abortion Disapproval Levels across the World

Notes: Respondents were asked whether abortion is always justified, never justified, or something in between. This map presents the average weighted percentage of residents within each country reporting that abortion is never justified, which is the most disapproving category.

Source: WVS, waves 5, 6, and 7

6 FETAL POSITIONS

To understand people's views about abortion, personal characteristics (e.g., gender, age, education, income, and religious beliefs) matter. Studies done within individual countries have found that people who are older, less educated, and feel that religion is important are more likely to view abortion as problematic.[12] These relationships appear across most countries. Hence, more religious people living in the United States tend to be more opposed,[13] as are more religious people residing in Britain,[14] Turkey,[15] and Mexico.[16] Thus, these individual characteristics are relatively constant across the world.

While both individual and country-level attributes shape people's feelings about abortion, societal forces are more likely to provide insight into why support for abortion varies so substantially across the world. Sociologists discuss the influence of country or macro forces on individuals' attitudes as the "macro-micro link".[17] The basic idea is that along with personal characteristics (e.g., gender, age, and personal religious beliefs) country or macro factors can also affect people's attitudes and understandings. Whereas micro influences reflect the role of personal characteristics in affecting opinions, macro factors refer to the influence of larger structural forces (e.g., economics and democracy) and culture (e.g., religion) in shaping people's views.

Macro forces are especially intriguing because they can influence individuals' attitudes over and above their personal characteristics. For example, some countries have much higher overall levels of religious belief than others. As I discuss in Chapter 1, religion plays an especially powerful role in shaping abortion attitudes. When a high proportion of religious people live in the same geographical area, their religious beliefs generate a unique power. One of sociology's forefathers, Emile Durkheim, referred to this as "*sui generis*," or an effect over and above its component parts.[18] The energy created from collective religious beliefs can shape cultures and structures

[12] Adamczyk, Kim, and Dillon, "Examining Public Opinion about Abortion;" Jelen and Wilcox, "Causes and Consequences of Public Attitudes toward Abortion."

[13] Adamczyk and Valdimarsdóttir, "Understanding Americans' Abortion Attitudes,"

[14] Clements, "Religion and the Sources of Public Opposition to Abortion in Britain."

[15] Fidan, Alagoz, and Karaman, "Liberal Sexual Morality, Religion, and Attitudes toward Abortion in Turkey."

[16] Tuman, Roth-Johnson, and Jelen, "Conscience and Context."

[17] Coleman, "Social Theory, Social Research, and a Theory of Action"; Liska, "The Significance of Aggregate Dependent Variables and Contextual Independent Variables for Linking Macro and Micro Theories."

[18] Durkheim, *Suicide: A Study in Sociology*, 1897; Durkheim, *The Elementary Forms of Religious Life*, 1912.

within nations. As a result, even residents who are not religious may find their abortion views shaped by the surrounding religious culture and its influence on institutions such as healthcare, government, and education.

Other country characteristics, such as economic development, can also influence public opinion, even after accounting for individual attributes like personal income. Drawing on ideas from cultural sociology, I argue in Chapter 2 that as nations develop, cultural values tend to shift per overall levels of education and economic development. As a result, even relatively poor people are likely to develop attitudes consistent with values such as individualism, self-expression, and independence, similar to those found in richer countries. In other words, wealthy and poor people living in affluent societies are likely to be similarly influenced by the values fostered by economic development, leading them to support abortion.

Previous studies have investigated how a nation's culture (e.g., religion) and structures (e.g., laws and policies, government structure) shape individual views and actions.[19] When people feel strongly about a particular issue, their attitudes can also drive laws and policies. This is the process through which individual preferences become collective action. In 2018, Ireland voted to repeal its highly restrictive abortion law. At the time, 66% of residents supported overturning it. Through a constitutional referendum, which has been described as a form of "direct democracy," the Irish took collective action to change their nation's abortion law.[20] Government legislation can also have the opposite effect. In Chapter 3, for example, I explain that decades after China instituted its one-child policy, the Chinese have become more disapproving about abortion, possibly in response to the draconian policy. The research presented in this book follows prior work in examining the macro and micro forces that shape individuals' attitudes, how strong feelings about abortion can lead to political action, and the ways that legislation can shape public opinion.

Figure 0.2 presents the effect size of abortion attitudes in shaping laws across countries relative to other meaningful forces. Abortion is illegal in about 41% of countries in this sample, which includes eighty-eight nations and represents the vast majority of the world's population. Public opinion

---

[19] Coleman, "Social Theory, Social Research, and a Theory of Action"; Adamczyk, *Cross-National Public Opinion about Homosexuality*; Finke and Adamczyk, "Cross-National Moral Beliefs: The Influence of National Religious Context"; Scheepers, Te Grotenhuis, and Van Der Slik, "Education, Religiosity and Moral Attitudes."
[20] Suiter, "Deliberation in Action—Ireland's Abortion Referendum."

has a significant and meaningful effect; countries with a high proportion of disapproval have a probability of 0.55 of abortion being illegal under most circumstances. But when the proportion who find it problematic is low, the probability of abortion being illegal drops to 0.22. Abortion attitudes are moderately correlated with laws and policies. Other forces, such as democracy, communism, economic development, and education, are also important. The proportion of Catholics also matters, as does the overall level of religious importance. Indeed, the latter is so highly correlated with disapproval that the statistical model underlying the estimates in Figure 0.2 cannot include both measures (i.e., religious importance and abortion attitudes).

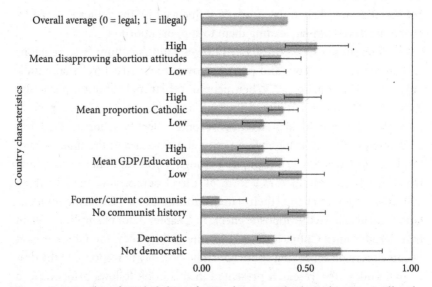

Figure 0.2 Predicted Probabilities for Explaining Whether Abortion Is Illegal, except for Extreme Reasons (e.g., rape, incest, danger to the mother's life or health, and fetal viability) (N = 88 societies)

Notes: The figure is based on a logistic regression analysis of country-level data that includes only these variables. The model's log odds are abortion disapproval (2.58*), proportion Catholic (37.17**), mean GDP/education (.370), communist history (0.02**), and democracy (0.03*), where the constant is 0.005 and the pseudo R-squared is 0.57. High and low estimates of religious importance, Catholic proportion, and GDP/education are based on one standard deviation above and below the mean. Two standard deviations were considered and then the confidence intervals would not overlap. However, some of the estimates would have fallen outside the sample range. A separate analysis showed that the proportion Muslim is not statistically significant. Other ways of measuring abortion legality were considered, but the coding presented here, which distinguishes between legal on demand during the first trimester versus all others, is theoretically and statistically meaningful. The overall average is the mean across the 88 societies. The data were collected on the countries included in the larger analysis. I also found that overall religious importance is highly significant for shaping abortion policy. However, it is so highly correlated with abortion disapproval (.73) that I am unable to include them both in the model.

Source: WVS, waves 5, 6, and 7

INTRODUCTION   9

While the public's preferences often inform laws and policies,[21] there are important instances of misalignment where residents' views do not mirror legal proscriptions. As noted above, China's one-child policy is an important exception. Likewise, in 2022, the United States Supreme Court ruled that the US Constitution did not confer the right for a woman to have an abortion,[22] which overturned the 1973 *Roe v. Wade* decision that allowed it. The ruling was especially surprising because the majority of Americans (61%) thought that abortion should be legal in all or most circumstances.[23] In the United States, academics and journalists[24] have pointed to the power of social movements, in this case the religious right, in positioning preferred US government officials to act in ways consistent with the minority's views. Countries have unique histories and influences. My analysis of the factors shaping cross-national abortion disapproval considers not only dominant trends across nations but also important deviations and outliers.

Much sociological research has been devoted to examining macro and micro forces shaping attitudes.[25] However, many of the studies done on abortion attitudes have been conducted within individual countries, focusing on personal characteristics or the influence of smaller contexts, such as counties.[26] In the United States, for example, there have been two meta reviews of research on Americans' abortion attitudes.[27] Social scientists have also conducted studies in specific European,[28] Latin American,[29] Asian,[30] and African[31] countries on abortion disapproval.

Despite the importance of public opinion about abortion and the attention given to it within individual nations, cross-national analyses of attitudes

---

[21] Brooks, "Abortion Policy in Western Democracies."

[22] "19-1392 Dobbs v. Jackson Women's Health Organization."

[23] Hartig, "About Six-in-Ten Americans Say Abortion Should Be Legal in All or Most Cases."

[24] Delaney, "Roe v. Wade Has Been Overturned. What Does That Mean for America?"; Ziegler and Tsai, "How the Anti-Abortion Movement Used the Progressive Playbook to Chip Away at Roe v. Wade."

[25] Scheepers, Te Grotenhuis, and Van Der Slik, "Education, Religiosity and Moral Attitudes"; Adamczyk, *Cross-National Public Opinion about Homosexuality*; Finke and Adamczyk, "Cross-National Moral Beliefs: The Influence of National Religious Context"; Stack, Adamczyk, and Cao, "Survivalism and Public Opinion on Criminality."

[26] Adamczyk and Valdimarsdóttir, "Understanding Americans' Abortion Attitudes."

[27] Jelen and Wilcox, "Causes and Consequences of Public Attitudes toward Abortion"; Adamczyk, Kim, and Dillon, "Examining Public Opinion about Abortion."

[28] Clements, "Religion and the Sources of Public Opposition to Abortion in Britain."

[29] Tuman, Roth-Johnson, and Jelen, "Conscience and Context"; Ogland and Verona, "Religion and Attitudes Toward Abortion and Abortion Policy in Brazil."

[30] Lee et al., "Cross-Cultural Research on Euthanasia and Abortion"; Nie, *Behind the Silence*.

[31] Rominski et al., "Attitudes toward Abortion among Students at the University of Cape Coast, Ghana"; Mosley et al., "Abortion Attitudes among South Africans."

10 FETAL POSITIONS

across dozens of countries have been lacking. A few journal articles,[32] including one of my own,[33] have examined the factors shaping views in 70 societies, but this is the first book-length treatment of public opinion about abortion around the world.

Even within sociology, where several of the discipline's forefathers (e.g., Max Weber, Emile Durkheim, Karl Marx) devoted attention to studying macro properties such as religion, researchers have been reticent to examine cross-national attitudes about abortion. Part of the problem relates to difficulties in obtaining cross-national public opinion data. Additionally, when several countries are compared at once, scholars tend to diminish the role of their unique histories and cultures in shaping attitudes. By combining survey data with a large analysis of newspaper articles, case studies from China and the United States, and multiple examples from other countries, the research presented in this book provides insight into larger trends across the globe and unique forces (e.g., China's one-child only policy and the United States being both highly religious and wealthy) shaping public opinion.

While limited research attention has been devoted to attitudes, scholars have investigated cross-national variation in abortion laws and policies,[34] which are important because they can influence abortion access and women's reproductive health. Information on laws and policies is easier to obtain than attitudinal data. Every country has a national law regarding abortion, and organizations like the Guttmacher Institute[35] and the Center for Reproductive Rights[36] have made this information publicly available. Collecting public opinion data across the globe requires asking tens of thousands of people about their personal thoughts and feelings, which is logistically complicated. However, as I explain below, some publicly available databases include this information. Merging attitudinal data with information on laws and policies, as well as abortion rates, presents an especially rich source of information for understanding the relationships between them around the world.

---

[32] Fernández, Valiente, and Jaime-Castillo, "Gender Balance in the Workforce and Abortion Attitudes"; Loll and Hall, "Differences in Abortion Attitudes by Policy Context and between Men and Women in the World Values Survey."

[33] Adamczyk, "Religion as a Micro and Macro Property."

[34] For an excellent analysis of cross-national abortion legislation, see Sommer and Forman-Rabinovici, *Producing Reproductive Rights*.

[35] Guttmacher Institute, "An Overview of Abortion Laws."

[36] Center for Reproductive Rights, "The World's Abortion Laws."

Scholars have also been hesitant to study public opinion topics where the meaning of questions may be interpreted in various ways, which is especially likely in cross-national studies where cultures, languages, and histories vary considerably. Nevertheless, public opinion research has been evolving. Increasingly, scholars are examining particularly complicated subjects such as same-sex relationships[37] and prostitution.[38] Abortion is an issue that most people can easily understand and render an opinion about. The research presented here joins prior work in investigating the factors that give rise to and are affected by public opinion about abortion.

Mixed Methods and Cross-National Research

The research presented in this book uses several different types of information to understand the factors shaping abortion policies, risk, and public opinion. The different data and methods include an analysis of cross-national and within-nation survey and institutional data, interviews conducted in the United States and China, and an examination of newspaper portrayals of abortion around the world. Below I describe the various forms of data and methodology and why I selected China and the United States as case study countries.

Much of the public opinion data in this book are taken from the WVS, which includes information on 88 societies from more than 200,000 people. The WVS has the largest number and greatest diversity of nations. Moreover, since they began collecting data, WVS survey administrators have regularly asked respondents how they feel about abortion, specifically whether they think it is justified. Cross-national survey data can be expensive and challenging to collect because of language differences, government opposition to some questions (e.g., democracy, same-sex relationships), logistics in administering surveys, and concern that respondents will not respond truthfully. Aside from the WVS, there are only two other ongoing efforts to gather cross-national data across a wide range (i.e., over forty countries) of economically and regionally diverse nations and

---

[37] Adamczyk, *Cross-National Public Opinion about Homosexuality*; Adamczyk and Pitt, "Shaping Attitudes about Homosexuality"; Scheepers, Te Grotenhuis, and Van Der Slik, "Education, Religiosity and Moral Attitudes."

[38] Stack, Adamczyk, and Cao, "Survivalism and Public Opinion on Criminality."

12 FETAL POSITIONS

ask about people's feelings regarding abortion.[39] These surveys are the International Social Survey Programme (ISSP) and Pew's Global Attitudes Project.

Compared with these other surveys, the WVS includes the largest number of societies and has data for some nations going back to 1981 when the first wave was collected.[40] For the cross-national analysis of public opinion, I rely on data from the fifth, sixth, and seventh waves, which include almost 85% of the world's population.[41] These data also provide information on a range of useful individual-level characteristics, including gender, religious importance and affiliation, education, age, income, views about other sex-related issues (e.g., same-sex relations, prostitution), and values and beliefs about other relevant issues. Information on country characteristics is drawn from a diverse array of sources, including the World Bank, the United Nations, the Association of Religion Data Archives, and the Center for Reproductive Health. Finally, the Guttmacher Institute provides estimates on cross-national abortion rates, the Demographic and Health Surveys program provides survey data on abortion decisions in seven countries, and the National Longitudinal Study of Adolescent Health provides insight into the factors shaping young American women's abortion decisions.

I use mixed-modeling statistical techniques to assess the forces most likely to influence cross-national abortion views. These methods account for clustering, where people living in the same country are more similar to each other than two residents from different nations. With these analyses, I aim to confirm or reject theoretically informed explanations for the factors most

---

[39] Because of these difficulties, early cross-national researchers devoted their survey efforts to studying rich nations with high overall levels of education and strong research infrastructures. These countries were largely located in the Global North (i.e., North America and Europe) where Christianity dominates and most nations are democratic and wealthy, limiting the findings' relevance to societies with these characteristics. As noted above, to adequately assess the factors shaping views about abortion, we need survey data from people from a wide range of different backgrounds (e.g., Buddhist, Hindu, Islam, Jewish, Protestant, Catholic) so that they can be compared. Moreover, to assess the influence of societal cultures and structures, data from diverse countries are required.

[40] The ISSP also has high-quality cross-sectional longitudinal data. But it includes many more economically developed nations, making them less desirable for understanding views across a diverse range of countries. The Pew Research Center also asks a question about abortion, but they seem to only have done this once, and their sample of countries is not nearly as big or diverse as the WVS. There are a handful of regionally based survey collections, such as the European Values Survey, European Social Survey, Eurobarometer, and Latinobarometer, that include questions about abortion. Because much time, energy, and money goes into collecting these cross-national data, survey administrators make them available to the public to maximize the number of people who will analyze the data.

[41] "WVS Database."

likely shaping cross-national attitudes. Instead of identifying unique individual or historical factors, my goal here is to explain broad patterns across dozens of countries. Statistical tests, which tend to be more conservative than other techniques (e.g., case studies) for making empirical generalizations, are used to support or refute hypothesized relationships.[42]

While a large macro-level quantitative analysis can provide insight into how individual and country-level properties shape attitudes, it cannot explain how these patterns emerged, how they are manifested within nations, or the ways that they affect residents. Moreover, the findings from cross-national quantitative survey data can be overly abstract. I therefore draw on a comparative case study of China and the United States to better understand the processes shaping cross-national public opinion.

In contrast to quantitative survey data, case studies provide much more detail in the form of "thick description" and include a lot of the complexity that survey methods intentionally exclude. Additionally, they tend to focus on specific laws and policies (i.e., one-child only), particular people (e.g., President Trump), and certain organizations and movements (e.g., the religious right). A case study approach is ideal when there are just a few countries to examine. When there are more than two or three comparisons, the complexities become too numerous, making it challenging to compare.[43]

To gather and combine the quantitative data, case studies, and newspaper articles, I used an explanatory sequential design, which proceeds with successive phases of data collection.[44] First, the quantitative data were examined to establish the major factors shaping differences across nations. Next I collected the newspaper data[45] in forty-one countries. Finally, I conducted interviews in the United States and China, drawing on the cross-national survey and newspaper analyses to develop the questions. Once all the data were collected, findings from one source would sometimes prompt me to

---

[42] Ragin, *The Comparative Method.*

[43] Ragin.

[44] Creswell et al., "Advanced Mixed Methods Research Designs"; Creswell, *Research Design: Qualitative, Quantitative and Mixed Methods Approaches.*

[45] For the newspaper analysis, my research team and I hand coded over 800 articles for the 1-year period of 2018. As I describe in more detail in Chapter 3 and Appendix B, we isolated every newspaper article that mentioned the term "abortion" and then coded it according to several different claimsmakers and themes. We then employed mixed-modeling techniques to examine how newspaper and country characteristics (e.g., religion, democracy, abortion laws, and economic development) shape the odds that various themes and claimsmakers would appear.

14 FETAL POSITIONS

further examine evidence from another. Hence, while the data collection proceeded sequentially, the analyses and writing phases were not always consecutive.

China and the United States as Case Study Countries

To better understand the forces shaping cross-national views about abortion, I chose China and the United States as case study countries. I conducted dozens of interviews in these nations, scrutinized secondary research and surveys, and reviewed newspaper articles as well as laws and policies. As noted above, the findings from the quantitative analysis helped inform my selection of China and the United States. As I show in the first four chapters, religion, economic and educational development, democracy, communism, and gender inequality are major forces shaping cross-national support for abortion. I wanted case study countries that could provide insight into the processes shaping these forces, which these countries can. Additionally, China and the United States are two of the three most populous nations in the world. Together, they constitute roughly 22% of the world's population. As such, they have a powerful global social, economic, and political impact.

As I discuss in Chapter 1, religion is an important factor shaping residents' abortion views in many countries.[46] The United States is similar to many other nations in having high levels of religious belief, with 53% of people reporting that religion is very important.[47] Likewise, it is dominated by Christian religious traditions where many leaders proscribe abortion. While dozens of studies have gathered information on religious belief in the United States and other Christian-dominated countries,[48] we know much less about religion in China. Indeed, there are major challenges for assessing what religion means to the Chinese, how many religious people live there, and the number of Christians relative to other religious adherents.[49]

---

[46] Jelen and Bradley, "Abortion Opinion in Emerging Democracies"; Jelen, "The Subjective Bases of Abortion Attitudes"; Jelen and Wilcox, "Causes and Consequences of Public Attitudes toward Abortion"; Adamczyk, Kim, and Dillon, "Examining Public Opinion about Abortion."

[47] Pew Research Center, "The Age Gap in Religion around the World."

[48] Adamczyk, Kim, and Dillon, "Examining Public Opinion about Abortion"; Jelen and Wilcox, "Causes and Consequences of Public Attitudes toward Abortion."

[49] Pew Research Center, "Measuring Religion in China."

One concern relates to differences between monotheistic and polytheistic religions. Followers of monotheistic traditions, like Christianity and Islam, typically believe in just one God who is omnipresent and powerful, making very clear demands. Conversely, polytheistic faiths (e.g., Buddhism, Taoism, and Hinduism) usually have multiple Gods and permit worship of more than one. Like other East Asian nations, China is dominated by Buddhism and local traditional beliefs, including Confucianism and ancestral worship. Researchers have found that polytheistic religions are not as successful at eliciting follower's devotion and persuading them to abide by specific demands.[50] Hence, when researchers ask people about the strength of their religious beliefs, Christians and Muslims tend to report higher levels than Buddhists.[51] Likewise, because many Christian religious leaders have made abortion a central issue, Christians who say that religion is important are usually more opposed.[52]

The government has also made it difficult to study religious belief in China. Officially, China is an atheist state and Communist Party members are not supposed to believe in or practice any religion.[53] There is concern that religion could function as an alternative to communism, undermining government loyalty. The Chinese constitution technically allows for religion. However, the government has employed various tactics to make religious practice difficult. For example, the government defines religion and only allows five of them (Buddhism, Daoism, Islam, Catholicism, and Protestantism).[54] Other religions are technically illegal, including popular religions that blend Daoism, Buddhism, and other elements and attract the majority of Chinese believers. Likewise, religious entities must officially register, and the government can close them if they are not operating correctly.

By conventional measures, the majority of Chinese are atheist. Survey data show that only about 3% of Chinese report that religion is very important.[55] However, 33% of Chinese also say that they believe in Buddha and/or a bodhisattva.[56] Likewise, a substantial minority (26%) of Chinese

---

[50] Stark and Finke, *Acts of Faith*.

[51] Evans et al., "Buddhism, Islam and Religious Pluralism in South and Southeast Asia."

[52] Adamczyk, Kim, and Dillon, "Examining Public Opinion about Abortion."

[53] Human Rights Watch, "Religious Repression in China."

[54] United States Department of State, "2022 Report on International Religious Freedom: China (Includes Hong Kong, Macau, Tibet, and Xinjiang)."

[55] Pew Research Center, "The Age Gap in Religion around the World."

[56] Pew Research Center, "Measuring Religion in China."

16 FETAL POSITIONS

burn incense at least a few times a year.[57] In China, this practice typically involves making a wish to a deity (e.g., Buddha), signaling hope in divine intervention. The polytheistic forms of Chinese religious belief and government opposition make assessing Chinese respondents' religious belief for understanding abortion disapproval challenging. Throughout this book, I present survey analyses using traditional measures of religious belief. In many countries, conventional assessments of religious importance are meaningful for understanding abortion disapproval. However, these standard measures are unlikely to capture religion's role in countries like China. The interviews therefore offer pertinent information about how religion may shape abortion views in China.

The United States and China also differ in their levels of economic development, democracy, and abortion-related policies, providing additional points of comparison, though there are also some key similarities as well. China has an authoritarian political system and limits public discourse, controls internet access, and censors the media.[58] Conversely, the United States has one of the oldest modern democracies and has a relatively high democracy score.[59] Nevertheless, in 2022 the US Supreme Court handed the authority to make abortion illegal to individual states, eliminating legal abortion access across many regions. Likewise, while the United States is a rich country (GDP per person = $59,800), China is by no means poor (GDP per person = $18,200).[60] However, they differ in terms of the pace that they underwent industrialization and modernization processes. Whereas the United States took close to a century to undergo this development change, China went through the process at a breakneck pace—in about thirty-five years.[61] In its quest for economic improvement, China's Communist Party implemented the one-child policy, which has major ramifications for abortion views.

Throughout this book, I talk at length about the one-child policy because it is vital for understanding how many Chinese see abortion. The policy may have also influenced WVS survey responses. China's survey data show a clear decrease in support for abortion over time (see Chapter 3), when

---

[57] Pew Research Center.

[58] Jiang, Min. "Authoritarian Informationalism: China's Approach to Internet Sovereignty"; Stockmann and Daniela. *Media Commercialization and Authoritarian Rule in China*.

[59] Freedom House, "Countries and Territories Global Freedom Index."

[60] Index Mundi, "GDP—per Capita (PPP)—Country Comparison."

[61] Jiahong, and Ryder, "The Chinese Experience of Rapid Modernization: Sociocultural Changes, Psychological Consequences?"

other nations in the region were experiencing natural fertility declines. In the 1970s, China enacted the one-child policy, which limited most couples to one child. The population was very large at that time, and the government was concerned that it could not support everyone. Some couples were exempt from the policy (e.g., various ethnic minorities, some rural families, handicapped firstborn), but most residents had to pay a large fine and their jobs could be in jeopardy if they had more than one child. Likewise, undocumented children that resulted from subsequent births could encounter major challenges in securing education and employment.[62] In some regions of China, the policy was implemented in particularly harsh ways, including the monitoring of menstrual cycles and forced abortions.[63]

In 2016, the Chinese government changed the one-child policy so that couples could have up to two children. By then, the policy had existed in some form for thirty-five years. An entire generation of Chinese had grown up without siblings. China's fertility rate had also plummeted, as it had in surrounding East Asian Confucian societies. In 2021, the Chinese government began allowing couples to have up to three children. The one-child policy repeatedly came up in my interviews. Those discussions provide an important comparison to the US interviews, in which respondents were much more concerned about the opposite policy—losing abortion access, which happened in many states in 2022.

Who Did I Interview?

Between 2020 and 2022, I conducted forty interviews in the United States and China. The people with whom I spoke had jobs or participated in activities that offered insight into how residents from their respective countries saw abortion. These are "expert interviews"; the respondent is treated "as a guide who possesses certain valid pieces of knowledge and information" and can enlighten the researcher on "objective" matters.[64] The interviewees included journalists, professors, researchers, religious leaders, doctors, civil servants, and social movement activists from both sides of the abortion debate. I conducted twenty-three interviews with experts in China, twelve with US residents, and five additional ones with people who had insight

[62] Liao, "The One-Child Policy."
[63] Fong, *One Child*.
[64] Bogner and Menz, "The Theory-Generating Expert Interview," p. 46.

18 FETAL POSITIONS

into both countries. Because it is rarely discussed in the academic literature, news, or even social media, researchers know relatively little about Chinese views on abortion.[65] I therefore completed more interviews in China than in the United States, which has been the source of dozens of studies that could inform my analysis.[66] The conversations, which often included an interpreter, lasted about an hour. All respondents were offered the equivalent of a $30 gift card, which almost every American accepted, but only half the Chinese did.[67]

Using a theoretical sampling approach,[68] respondents were initially selected based on their research interests (e.g., professor), job (e.g., doctor), or position within their organization (e.g., religious leader, journalist). After the first eight interviews, I focused recruitment efforts on groups (e.g., religious officials) and people who had views that were not initially well represented (e.g., pro-life supporters). Within a snowball sampling approach, respondents are asked to help identify other potential subjects. Because the quantitative analysis of WVS data provided insight into the individual and country characteristics related to abortion attitudes, my initial discussion questions flowed from the survey findings. However, as the interviews continued, the inquiries were further revised to address emerging ideas.

I intended to interview everyone in person. But in early 2020, the world experienced a global pandemic and so foreign travel became nearly impossible. In particular, China imposed strict rules about who could enter and instituted a long quarantine period. I was unable to obtain the necessary travel documents. Even if I had, internal movement within China was severely restricted, making face-to-face interviews impossible. The United

[65] An important exception is Nie, *Behind the Silence*. His research was conducted in the 1990s when the one-child policy was strongly enforced.

[66] The following are meta reviews done on attitudes in the United States: Jelen and Wilcox, "Causes and Consequences of Public Attitudes toward Abortion"; Adamczyk, Kim, and Dillon, "Examining Public Opinion about Abortion."

[67] The process for giving a gift card in the United States was straightforward, simply requiring me to enter the interviewee's email address to have it sent. In China, I encountered major problems in purchasing gift cards and ultimately used Taboo, which is similar to Amazon.com in the United States. But, to process them the website required more information from respondents, including their mailing addresses, which many subjects were hesitant to provide. They may have been concerned that the Chinese government would attempt to trace them, but more likely the process of providing all the information was too onerous and the small amount of $30 in the form of a gift card was not worth it. Additionally, many Chinese respondents seemed especially interested in talking with me because I was a researcher from the United States, which likely seemed less novel in the United States, which is my home country.

[68] Ligita et al., "A Practical Example of Using Theoretical Sampling throughout a Grounded Theory Study"; Coyne, "Sampling in Qualitative Research. Purposeful and Theoretical Sampling; Merging or Clear Boundaries?"

States also had restrictions, and residents were strongly urged to limit in-person interactions. During this period, talking over the phone, through Zoom, and other forms of electronic communication (e.g., WhatsApp, Face-Time) became more common for everyone. Initially, I was going to focus my study on subjects in Beijing. But because I was no longer meeting people in person, I was able to speak with residents all across China and the United States.

China's government restricts internet access and limits freedom of the press.[69] How did people respond to an American researcher who wanted to talk through WeChat about abortion attitudes? In many countries, abortion is a controversial topic that people are reluctant to discuss. But the Chinese expressed little hesitancy. As I was about to begin the interviews, I spoke with a social scientist who had done a lot of research in China. When asked whether I would have any problems finding people to interview, he explained that in China abortion is not a controversial issue. If I had wanted to ask about democracy or social movement activity, the response might be different, but not for this topic. Additionally, because the pandemic severely limited travel, live entertainment, and informal gatherings, the people I contacted seemed especially willing to talk. Perhaps they were a bit bored and this American researcher seemed intriguing enough.

The Chinese discussions were fascinating, especially compared to those from the United States. However, the two countries also shared a surprising amount of similarity. The interviews and analyses offer fresh and novel insight into our understanding of abortion attitudes across the globe.

Overview of Chapters

Below I present a brief outline of each chapter. Chapters 1 through 5 focus on the major characteristics shaping cross-national views. Chapter 6 shifts our attention from attitudes to abortion decisions. All the chapters draw on cross-national quantitative data and interviews conducted in China and the United States. Chapter 3 also includes a cross-national analysis of newspaper articles. Throughout the book, examples from other countries help illustrate key ideas and processes.

---

[69] Freedom House, "Countries and Territories Global Freedom Index."

20   FETAL POSITIONS

Chapter 1 examines religion's role in shaping public opinion about abortion around the world. Researchers have conducted most studies on public opinion about abortion in Christian-majority nations. In these countries, social scientists typically find that organized religion is a key factor shaping abortion views. People who say their religion is important are more likely to believe that abortion is problematic. When looking across the world and at different religions, I show that religion, as conventionally assessed, is still a driving force for abortion disapproval. I discuss different religious dimensions and the processes through which they shape support. I show that residents living in nations with higher levels of religious importance, like the United States, are more likely to have abortion views that are shaped by the religious culture surrounding them. Surprisingly, there are few differences across the major religions once religious importance enters the picture.

Special attention is given to the way that religion can inspire social movements or combine with nationalism, which happened in Poland, resulting in more conservative abortion legislation. In countries like China, where belief in organized religion is low, religion is rarely discussed as a power that drives residents to feel strongly about the rightness or wrongness of abortion. Conversely, American interviewees described religion as a force that can influence attitudes. Finally, while my Chinese respondents did not talk about religion shaping disapproval, they spoke about it as helping some women cope or rationalize abortion decisions, and as contributing to the valuing of male children over females. Chapter 5 also provides insight into the role of Confucianism. While China is typically described as a secular country, I show the ways ritual, faith, belief, and values shape residents' understandings of abortion.

Chapter 2 examines how money and education shape differences in attitudes. I explain how economic and educational development can shift cultural values, allowing for more tolerant perspectives. As a result, even people who are not personally wealthy or well educated are more likely to adopt liberal views. Special attention is given to China's one-child policy. Along with other developmental changes over the past fifty years, that policy has shaped how many Chinese think about abortion, childrearing, and the ideal family size. This chapter also discusses how overall levels of economic development and education condition the influence of religious importance on attitudes. Personal religious beliefs, as conventionally assessed on surveys, have a greater role in shaping disapproving attitudes in richer and more educated countries, when compared to poorer ones, offering important insight into current debates in well-developed nations. The chapter also includes a discussion about how personal social class influences views and the ways that education and income shape abortion attitudes specifically in China and the United States.

Chapter 3 examines how the government impacts views on abortion. Across the world, the ability to protest, discuss, politically organize, and vote are important for developing tolerance for new ideas and a willingness to publicly support individual rights. For understanding the abortion debate—both liberal laws that allow for abortion on demand and conservative attitudes that strongly discourage abortion support—democracy and the ideas it stimulates are key.

I begin Chapter 3 by unpacking the processes that democracy engenders, explaining how generic democratic values can affect attitudes and behaviors related to abortion. I then focus on the specific role of democracy in influencing abortion attitudes and policies, which are interrelated. Drawing on an analysis of over 800 newspaper articles from 41 countries that mention abortion, I show that the news in more democratic nations is more likely to talk about abortion from a range of different perspectives. Next, I discuss differences between the United States and China with regard to the role of democracy in forming public opinion and abortion-related policies. Finally, I explain how the media both influences democratic processes and encourages the exchange of information that can further aid tolerance.

Chapter 4 focuses on the roles of gender inequality and racial and ethnic differences in shaping abortion views. Across the world, gender inequality persists and affects the way many people view abortion. Even after accounting for gender, I show that residents from countries with higher levels of gender inequality are more opposed to abortion. Indeed, the relationship between gender equality and abortion access is so strong that these measures could serve as proxies for each other.

Drawing on Chinese and American interviews, I examine the various ways that gender inequality shapes abortion views. From there, I discuss the forces that gave rise to the overturning of *Roe v. Wade*, which removed American women's constitutional right to an abortion. A significant contributor was social movement activity that made abortion a critical issue for many conservative Americans who supported traditional family values and a gendered division of labor. In the United States especially, the intersections of race and gender have informed views on both sides of the debate.

22 FETAL POSITIONS

The chapter ends with a discussion about how racial and ethnic differences can shape abortion views.

Chapter 5 focuses on the remaining macro-level factors that contribute to cross-national abortion views and can be measured with available survey information. I show that two forces—communist history and Confucian culture—are especially important. Even though the Soviet Union collapsed in the early 1990s, the political system left an indelible mark on abortion attitudes and behaviors. Likewise, countries with Chinese or Confucian histories are unique from others in shaping residents' views. I dissect the many reasons for these differences.

I also show in Chapter 5 that personal values related to the family, sexual morality, and ending life are essential for understanding individual differences. But they do not contribute to cultural effects that influence most residents' abortion views over and above their personal values. Next, I examine more than two dozen additional country characteristics (e.g., fertility rates, economic inequality) that would logically seem related to abortion views but no longer have a statistical relationship once other factors are considered. Finally, I discuss the different dimensions of the abortion debate and how changing the questions we ask can affect survey findings. To assess the reliability of the WVS cross-national survey, the chapter ends with a comparison of abortion disapproval across three different international surveys.

In Chapter 6, we turn our attention to abortion behavior. Individuals are often interested in public opinion about abortion because it can shape related laws and abortion access, which, in turn, can affect lives. This final chapter investigates abortion behavior and its relationship with attitudes, laws, and other factors. I begin by examining the country-level forces associated with cross-national abortion rates. I show that neither legislation nor public abortion disapproval is significantly associated with rates. Rather, economic and educational development and gender equality are critical for decreasing abortion rates because they limit unintended pregnancies.

From there, the chapter examines the key characteristics associated with women's abortion decisions in a set of economically, politically, and religiously diverse countries. Using longitudinal data from young American women, I then trace the pathways through which personal religious beliefs shape abortion decisions. Next, I use interviews from the United States and China to investigate how stigma and shame connect to abortion behavior in these countries. Finally, I explain the circumstances and characteristics

INTRODUCTION 23

of the women whom the Chinese and Americans may think typically obtain abortions. I then compare this information to who actually gets them.

The Conclusion revisits this book's major ideas. It also considers where the world is headed from here. Using longitudinal data, I show that over time abortion laws have generally become more liberal. But this movement is neither straightforward nor linear. Focusing on the largest countries in the WVS sample, I show how attitudes have evolved over time and where they may be headed. Abortion laws in the Global North are moving in a progressive direction. But there are important exceptions. Moreover, the liberalization of attitudes is not straightforward. Given the history of the abortion debate, the pathway forward is likely to be bumpy, especially as new technological developments (e.g., in vitro fertilization, newborn survival at twenty-four weeks) and ways of understanding abortion emerge.

Let's begin!

Chapter 1
Religion and Abortion Attitudes

> Abortion is often discussed in some Western countries because they
> are Christian and they value the presence of a baby. But in China,
> maybe because they are influenced by the one-child policy, abortion
> is much more common.
>
> —Chinese social scientist

Researchers have conducted most of the studies on public opinion about abortion in Christian-majority nations. In these countries, social scientists typically find that religion is a key factor shaping disapproval. People who say that their religion is important are more likely to feel that abortion is problematic. When looking across the world and different religions, is religion still a driving force of abortion disapproval?

This chapter discusses the different dimensions of religion, as conventionally measured, and the processes through which they shape individual and societal attitudes. I dissect the statistical data showing that the importance people place on organized religion is the most significant measurable factor shaping abortion disapproval. I also demonstrate that residents who live in more religious nations, as assessed by overall levels of religious importance, are more likely to have abortion views that are shaped by the religious culture surrounding them. Surprisingly, there are few differences across the major religions once religious importance enters the picture. Special attention is given to the way that religion can inspire social movements or combine with nationalism to shape disapproval.

In countries like China, where typical measures of religious belief and engagement are low, religion is rarely discussed as a force that drives people to feel strongly about the rightness or wrongness of abortion. China is often described as an atheist country. However, as I discuss here and in Chapter 5, religion-related beliefs and practices still emerged in my interviews. They helped some Chinese women cope and justify an abortion, especially when they did not feel like they had much control over the decision, which was common during the one-child policy era. Religion also added to the valuing of male children over females, contributing to the nation's gender imbalance via abortion. This chapter opens with a discussion about the challenges in comparing and assessing personal religious attributes for understanding global attitudes.

Comparing and Assessing Religion and Abortion Attitudes

Abortion has been an important issue in many nations for decades. However, the extent of research on abortion attitudes varies considerably across the globe. In some countries, there have been relatively few studies. For example, in China very little research has examined the public's attitudes about abortion. However, in others—mostly those in North America and Europe—there have been dozens.[1] In the United States, there have been two major meta reviews of research on abortion attitudes.[2] Both of them find that religion is the most researched and consistent factor shaping public opinion.[3] As one review concluded, "Of all the social predictors of abortion attitudes, religion is generally considered to be the strongest."[4] Below I explore some of the differences in how religion is understood and practiced in the United States and China, which has relevance for other countries. I then explain the processes through which religious beliefs, as traditionally assessed, may shape attitudes.

The United States has a majority Christian population with a high proportion of people who say religion is very important (53%),[5] which is how belief has typically been measured. Not surprisingly, the Americans I interviewed regularly drew on religion to explain abortion disapproval and the divisive debate more generally. As a journalist at a pro-life magazine explained, "It just so happens that in the United States, a lot of values are dictated through a formal religious prism." When talking about differences between the United States and other nations, an American academic said, "I think

---

[1] Hanschmidt et al., "Abortion Stigma"; Rehnström Loi et al., "Health Care Providers' Perceptions of and Attitudes towards Induced Abortions in Sub-Saharan Africa and Southeast Asia"; Yam, Dries-Daffner, and Garcia, "Abortion Opinion Research in Latin America and the Caribbean."

[2] Adamczyk, Kim, and Dillon, "Examining Public Opinion about Abortion"; Jelen and Wilcox, "Causes and Consequences of Public Attitudes toward Abortion."

[3] In their review of 116 journal articles from the past 15 years conducted in the United States, Adamczyk et al. (2020) found that religion was the most researched factor associated with abortion disapproval.

[4] Jelen and Wilcox, "Causes and Consequences of Public Attitudes toward Abortion," 492.

[5] Pew Research Center, "The Age Gap in Religion around the World."

26 FETAL POSITIONS

that we're different in the sense that we already have this conservative baggage. Some of that is tied to a greater emphasis on Judeo-Christian religion in the US, which has been framed as primarily antiabortion." An editor at a pro-life magazine added, "I think Americans go to church and take religion more seriously." Finally, when asked what could shed insight on abortion views, a medical doctor commented, "I think the US is based on Christian values." Across the US-based interviews, religion was a consistent theme for understanding how residents felt about abortion. Indeed, every person interviewed mentioned the importance of religion in shaping attitudes.

In contrast to Americans, the Chinese have much lower levels of religious belief, as conventionally assessed.[6] As mentioned in the introduction, measuring religion across the globe can be especially challenging when examining both polytheistic and monotheistic religious traditions. Judaism, Christianity, and Islam are monotheistic religions with just one God who is omnipresent and powerful, making very clear demands. This God "asks" Muslims to pray five times a day, and many Christian religious leaders interpret God's commandment to regularly worship him, as attending services once a week. Conversely, polytheistic faiths (e.g., Buddhism, Taoism, and Hinduism) typically have more than one god, and followers may worship many. These gods or deities can be fickle. Sometimes they will respond to follower's requests, but other times they can be fairly distant. Moreover, their commandments are not always clear and consistent, moderating belief and religious engagement.

Researchers can easily use survey questions about religious engagement or belief to quantify religion for people from monotheistic traditions. For example, many Muslims believe that Allah asks them to pray five times a day. Hence, on surveys Muslims can calculate the number of times they pray and indicate how important religion is in their lives. Their God is clear about what is needed, and followers can thus self-report their engagement and belief. But, quantifying religious belief and participation may be harder for followers of polytheistic traditions, where demands are less routinized. Likewise, many people who connect with polytheistic religions, folk beliefs, and ancestral religions engage in practices as the need arises, further complicating measurement.[7] Finally, some governments, including China, strongly discourages religious belief and carefully regulate religion. Thus, reporting

---

[6] Pew Research Center.
[7] Hackett, "Is China a Religious Country or Not?"

high levels of personal religious belief or engagement on a survey supported by the Chinese government, which the World Values Survey (WVS) is, would not necessarily be in one's best interest.

Although religious belief, as conventionally measured, is typically low in China, when researchers use more meaningful measures to assess religion there, we do not see especially high levels of other types of engagement or belief. Nevertheless, the level is definitely higher than if we simply ask about strength of religious importance. About 3% of the Chinese report on the WVS that religion is very important[8] and according to the Chinese General Social Survey, just one in ten adults identify with a religion.[9] These survey questions are asking about religious belief in organized religion (i.e., the five religions officially recognized by the government). Conversely, 33% say that they believe in Buddha and/or a bodhisattva.[10] Likewise, a substantial minority (i.e., 26%) of Chinese report burning incense at least a few times a year,[11] which typically involve making a wish to a deity (e.g., Buddha), signaling hope in divine intervention.

Based on survey measures of formal religion (i.e., zongjiao), China is not religious, and the government officially classifies itself atheistic. Yet, many Chinese engage in practices that, broadly understood, would be considered religious. When I discuss religion's role for shaping abortion views, I draw on both dimensions. The available cross-national survey data rely on traditional measures of religious belief in organized religion. But the Chinese interviews at the end of this chapter reveal the roles of spirits, deities, and ancestral worship, which are important in other Asian countries as well.

Throughout my interviews, Chinese respondents were quick to note how little religion, as conventionally understood (i.e., weekly or daily prayer, rituals, attendance, or by asking how important it is), seemed to matter for shaping abortion attitudes. As one minister explained, "Most Chinese people wouldn't think that they had any religious faith." A Chinese-based academic added, "I don't think religion really influences a lot," and a second noted that "We don't really have a religion per se." When discussing major differences between the United States and China in abortion views, a Chinese professor put it this way, "In China, people usually don't have any religious faith at all. So, in Chinese society in general, when people are having abortions,

---

[8] Pew Research Center, "The Age Gap in Religion around the World."
[9] Hackett, "Is China a Religious Country or Not?"
[10] Pew Research Center, "Measuring Religion in China."
[11] Pew Research Center.

28   FETAL POSITIONS

they don't really have to deal with the guilt coming from religion." Whereas religion is a key factor in the abortion debate in the United States, Chinese respondents were clear about how little they thought religion, as traditionally understood (i.e., engagement with a major world religion), mattered for shaping attitudes and public discussions about abortion.

At the time I was writing this book, there was little research on religion and abortion views in China.[12] Likewise, only a few studies had examined abortion attitudes across multiple nations at once. When researchers have investigated cross-national relationships, they typically focus on wealthier societies, such as those found in North America and Europe.[13] Hence, we do not know the extent to which personal religious beliefs, as traditionally understood, are related to abortion attitudes in countries with different levels of economic development and religious cultures and traditions (e.g., Buddhism, Islam). Furthermore, some of the few studies that have examined a greater range of countries do not use the appropriate mixed-modeling techniques that account for within-and between-country variation, limiting our understanding of the findings.[14] Below I discuss the major processes through which personal religious beliefs and engagement may shape attitudes. I then use survey data and the proper techniques to test the influence of personal religious importance in shaping cross-national abortion disapproval.

How Do Personal Religious Beliefs Shape Attitudes?

Religious importance and engagement are likely meaningful religion dimensions for understanding abortion views across societies. Later in this chapter, I discuss the role of religious affiliation for examining disapproval. Around the world, people do not differ substantially in their level of disapproval

---

[12] The research that comes closest is Nie's excellent book *Behind the Silence*. Aside from the WVS, when I was writing this book, there were no surveys in China that asked about public opinion regarding abortion.

[13] Carol and Milewski, "Attitudes toward Abortion among the Muslim Minority and Non-Muslim Majority in Cross-National Perspective"; Halman and van Ingen, "Secularization and Changing Moral Views"; Jelen, O'Donnell, and Wilcox, "A Contextual Analysis of Catholicism and Abortion Attitudes in Western Europe"; Jelen and Wilcox, "Continuity and Change in Attitudes Toward Abortion."

[14] See for example, Jelen, "The Subjective Bases of Abortion Attitudes"; Jelen and Bradley, "Abortion Opinion in Emerging Democracies." Compared to residents of different nations, people within the same country are more likely to be similar to each other because they are shaped by some of the same societal characteristics. Hence, statistical techniques that take this clustering effect into consideration are needed.

based on affiliation with the major religions (i.e., Hinduism, Buddhism, Islam, Christianity, and Judaism). All of these religions have some proscriptions regarding abortion.[15] Some specific subgroups or religious denominations (e.g., Evangelical Christians) may be especially opposed to abortion, which may shape followers' attitudes. However, if we focus on adherence to the major religions and all of them find abortion problematic at some level, then strength of religious beliefs and engagement are likely more important for understanding disapproval. How might strength of personal religious beliefs and engagement shape attitudes? Below I explain how they can work through social learning and control processes to increase disapproval.

A key mechanism through which religion may shape abortion support is through social learning. Social learning theory argues that people acquire norms, ideas, and mores by observing, studying, and modeling the behaviors of others and by assimilating information in other ways (e.g., reading material, television, social media).[16] If they feel that religion is important, they are more likely to be physically involved with their faith. They will therefore be more likely to regularly attend religious services and classes, read religious texts, and participate with fellow congregants in other activities. Through these interactions, they will hear, read, and sense that abortion is problematic. They may also be more likely to talk directly with their pastor, imam, or spiritual master about abortion. As one Chinese religious leader explained, "For Buddhists, they talk about abortion a lot because it's against their religious faith. So maybe only if you are Buddhist and you care about it a lot [would religion affect abortion attitudes]." Likewise, as they spend time with other religious adherents, these people are likely to hear that it is problematic. Through these formal and informal learning opportunities, more religious people may assimilate the perspective that abortion is wrong.

While spending time with other religious adherents may increase contact with disapproving views, it can also decrease exposure to more positive perspectives about abortion. Religious adherents may be less likely than others to know someone who has gotten an abortion because these women may be reticent to share this information. Abortion is often distressing. Even in China, where belief in organized religion is low, abortion is still associated with stigma and shame. As one Chinese Christian pastor explained, it's not really about "faith" or "morality" but rather "there is social stigma."

---

[15] Jelen, "The Subjective Bases of Abortion Attitudes."
[16] Akers, *Social Learning and Social Structure*; Sutherland, *Principles of Criminology*.

30 FETAL POSITIONS

Many interviewees thought that few Chinese women would disclose their abortions to anyone other than their partner and select friends and family members. As one Chinese professor elaborated, "For most of them it's a very private, very personal matter. And it's probably very shameful." Because religious importance is higher in the United States, American women may be especially unlikely to talk about their abortions, limiting the likelihood that others will hear about their experiences.

Indeed, researchers have found that traditional religious beliefs can exacerbate the embarrassment and shame associated with abortion.[17] Even if a high proportion of women end their pregnancies, many people, especially religious adherents, may not think that they know anyone who has gotten one. As a result, they will have limited exposure to alternative perspectives[18] on abortion, including how the benefits (e.g., better mental and physical health, more time for other children, educational and career opportunities) might outweigh the costs. Therefore, religious followers may remain opposed.

Along with social learning processes, more religious people are likely to develop attachments to other religious adherents, which could further increase their disapproval.[19] This is the process of social control[20] through which individuals with strong relationships to others are likely to develop opinions that are consistent with their views.[21] By spending time and getting to know other adherents, religious individuals are likely to develop interpersonal connections, leading them to care more about what these people think. As a result of these relationships, more religious followers may be more likely to take their views about abortion seriously. Even if they were not initially opposed to abortion, over time they may adopt their religion's stance to maintain their sense of self and maximize the likelihood of good relationships with valued others.[22]

[17] Frohwirth, Coleman, and Moore, "Managing Religion and Morality within the Abortion Experience."
[18] Scheitle and Adamczyk, "It Takes Two"; Schwadel, "Individual, Congregational, and Denominational Effects on Church Members' Civic Participation."
[19] Scheitle and Adamczyk, "It Takes Two."
[20] Hirschi, Causes of Delinquency.
[21] For the application of these ideas to religion see, for example, Adamczyk and Palmer, "Religion and Initiation into Marijuana Use"; Adamczyk and Felson, "Friends' Religiosity and First Sex"; Adamczyk, "Socialization and Selection in the Link between Friends' Religiosity and the Transition to Sexual Intercourse."
[22] Kelman, "Interests, Relationships, Identities."

There are various ways through which personal religious beliefs and engagement could shape people's abortion views. One pathway (e.g., hearing about the problems with abortion from fellow religious adherents) is likely to strengthen others (e.g., reading religious literature that also disapproves). Additionally, social control and learning processes may reinforce each other by both providing information and motivating people to take it seriously through strong bonds. Finally, while one pathway (e.g., attending religious services) may increase exposure to negative views about abortion, it may also limit alternative and more positive perspectives. In the next section, I empirically examine the association between personal religiosity and disapproval.

Testing Personal Religious Beliefs and Abortion Views around the World

Previous research has found that religious importance, as traditionally measured, is a key characteristic shaping attitudes within nations in the Global North and Christian-majority countries. The analysis presented here provides insight into whether personal religious importance shapes attitudes around the globe and across different religions. Ideally, researchers would have access to a myriad of different religion measures to examine abortion support. However, religions differ in the emphasis they place on various dimensions (e.g., prayer for Muslims versus religious service attendance for Christians). Additionally, the available data includes very few religion questions. Hence, the following analysis focuses on the link between personal religious importance and abortion disapproval.

To examine the empirical relationship between religious importance and attitudes, I use data from the WVS. The WVS is one of the few databases that includes a wide range of different nations and asks respondents about their attitudes. By combining the last three waves of data, we have access to information on the views of over 200,000 people living in 88 diverse societies. I use these data and the appropriate mixed-modeling analysis techniques to examine the major factors shaping disapproval across the globe.

The following analysis provides insight into whether a typical measure of religious belief (i.e., religious importance) shapes global abortion views. However, it does not capture folk or ancestral beliefs, or Confucian values, which are further discussed at the end of this chapter. Likewise, in Chapter 5

32 FETAL POSITIONS

I do a deep dive into the potential role of Confucian cultures in shaping residents' abortion perspectives. For now, I focus on the influence of personal religious importance.

Table A.3 in Appendix A presents the results. Among the individual-level measures, personal religious importance, which is one of the few religion-related measures the WVS has, is statistically significant and has the biggest effect size for explaining attitudes.[23] Religious importance explains more variation in abortion disapproval around the world than gender, age, marital status, income, or education. Moreover, religious importance, as conventionally measured, matters substantially more than religious affiliation. Indeed, there are few statistically significant differences in the level of disapproval between people based on their religious affiliation (e.g., Islam, Christianity). Later in this chapter, I provide more insight into why personal religious affiliation has a small role in shaping attitudes.

Aside from religious affiliation and importance, the WVS does not consistently ask respondents many other questions about religion (e.g. prayer frequency), limiting our knowledge of how other religion-related variables connect to abortion attitudes.[24] However, if only a few measures are available for understanding disapproval across the globe, religious affiliation and importance are reasonable ones. Even monotheistic religions differ in the emphasis they place on various aspects of their faiths. While many Christian ministers, for example, encourage regular religious attendance, Islamic leaders do not place as much importance on it. Conversely, many Muslim adherents are dedicated to praying five times a day. Hence, religious importance may be more relevant than other measures, though as noted above, it may not be as meaningful for followers of polytheistic religions and ancestral beliefs.

The findings in Appendix A indicate that regardless of where in the world they reside, the strength of belief in organized religion matters in how individuals view the rightness or wrongness of abortion. When people feel that religion is important, it permeates their views about abortion as well as

---

[23] It can be difficult to compare effect sizes, especially across dummy, ordinal, and interval-level variables. Beta coefficients indicate that country and individual-level religiosity have the largest effect sizes. Marginal values and variance explained provide additional information. Marginal values are produced for all of the country-level variables presented in Appendix A, except population size, and can be found throughout the first half of the book in the form of figures. Appendix A provides a discussion about how effect sizes were measured and compared.

[24] Adamczyk, Kim, and Dillon, "Examining Public Opinion about Abortion."

related issues. When individuals do not feel that religion is especially important, other factors (e.g., education, income, marital status) likely matter more.

Causal Relationship between Religion and Abortion Attitudes

While religion is often described as a force that can "influence" attitudes, views about abortion can also "affect" religious importance, and affiliation. More religious people may be opposed to abortion because of their beliefs. Conversely, if their abortion views become more liberal, they could also switch their religion or adjust the amount of importance they place on it. Unfortunately, empirically establishing the correct causal direction between religion and abortion attitudes using cross-national survey data is very difficult. No cross-national surveys have the necessary information (i.e., within person changes) to assess the extent to which personal religious beliefs and affiliation precede abortion attitudes.

Even within countries with strong research infrastructures, few, if any, studies make it possible to ascertain the direction of the religion and abortion attitudes' relationship. Before writing this book, my research team and I conducted a mixed-methods review of every journal article published on Americans' abortion attitudes from the past fifteen years.[25] Of the 116 peer-reviewed journal articles examined, only 4% of them (i.e., 5 articles) used longitudinal data. None of them established that religion preceded abortion attitudes, as opposed to the opposite relationship.

While researchers have been unable to empirically show that attitudes likely follow religious beliefs, most social scientists agree that this is the correct direction.[26] Religious beliefs tend to form during childhood and adolescence.[27] Once religious preferences develop, only a relatively small proportion of people switch to a religion that is radically different from the one in which they were raised.[28] In places like the United States, the majority of Americans (71%) who were raised Christian follow it into adulthood.[29] In other parts of the world, such as Africa, the proportion remaining in their

---

[25] Adamczyk, Kim, and Dillon, "Examining Public Opinion about Abortion."
[26] Adamczyk, Kim, and Dillon.
[27] Smith, *Soul Searching*.
[28] Scheitle and Adamczyk, "High-Cost Religion, Religious Switching, and Health"; Sherkat, *Changing Faith*.
[29] Pew Research Center, "America's Changing Religious Landscape."

34 FETAL POSITIONS

parents' religion (i.e., Islam or Christianity) is exceptionally high, ranging from 95% to 100%.[30]

Regardless of their specific religion, parents' religious importance likely has a powerful role in their children's inclination to feel that religion is significant later in life.[31] Indeed, the relationship between children and parents' level of religiosity is so strong that some researchers have characterized it as "religious inheritance,"[32] whereby children inherit religious belief in the same way they receive other types of inheritances (e.g., houses) from their parents. Religious beliefs tend to develop at a young age before children understand much about sexual reproduction and pregnancy termination. Hence, we have good reason to think that religion provides a foundation for how many people feel about abortion.

While religious belief and affiliation likely "influence" attitudes, some people can and do change their views about religion and abortion[33] over time.[34] Additionally, other factors may also be at work. People who are more religious tend to have preferences that are consistent with antiabortion views. Hence, religion's influence on abortion disapproval may be confounded by other forces. For example, all the major religions encourage a traditional family structure with married parents. Multiple studies have found that individuals with strong traditional family orientations tend to be more opposed to abortion than divorced people.[35]

Most social scientists account for confounding elements in their statistical analyses using controls. I also control for factors like marital status, educational attainment, and income. The findings in Appendix A show that religious importance is clearly meaningful *after* considering these other factors. Nevertheless, the longitudinal data that could help us better test the causal relationship between religion and attitudes is unavailable. Hence, we cannot fully rule out the possibility that views about abortion shape religious beliefs. For some individuals, secular attitudes no doubt drive religious

[30] Pew Research Center, "Tolerance and Tension: Islam and Christianity in Sub-Saharan Africa."
[31] Bengtson, *Families and Faith*; Smith and Adamczyk, *Handing Down the Faith*.
[32] Myers, "An Interactive Model of Religiosity Inheritance."
[33] Woodruff et al., "Attitudes toward Abortion after Receiving vs. Being Denied an Abortion in the USA."
[34] Loveland, "Religious Switching"; Scheitle and Adamczyk, "High-Cost Religion, Religious Switching, and Health."
[35] Loll and Hall, "Differences in Abortion Attitudes by Policy Context and between Men and Women in the World Values Survey"; Carol and Milewski, "Attitudes toward Abortion among the Muslim Minority and Non-Muslim Majority in Cross-National Perspective"; Finke and Adamczyk, "Cross-National Moral Beliefs: The Influence of National Religious Context."

beliefs. But they are likely in the minority. The following section focuses on differences between specific religions.

Religious Affiliation

In addition to measures of religiosity (i.e., religious importance, prayer, service attendance), in many countries religious affiliation is important for understanding abortion views. However, differences between religious groups can be difficult to capture using cross-national survey data. Below I explain the challenges with assessing religious affiliation across the world and use WVS data to provide insight into how followers from the five world religions (i.e., Hinduism, Buddhism, Judaism. Christianity, and Islam) compare in their level of abortion disapproval.

All the major world religions (i.e., Islam, Catholicism, Protestantism, Hinduism, Judaism, and Buddhism) offer scriptural reasons to oppose abortion.[36] While some Muslim leaders have argued, for example, that the fetus does not have a soul until later in the pregnancy, women and children have a prominent place within the family and chastity is important, making abortion undesirable.[37] From a Hindu perspective, abortion may be problematic because it could disrupt family continuity and structure, and the fetus is seen as having a life that is distinct from the mother.[38] Some Buddhists oppose abortion because there is no distinction between an unborn and living fetus,[39] and abortion can be seen as killing life, having ramifications for the future.[40] Additionally, from a Buddhist perspective abortion may be seen as selfish and violating appropriate social roles for women.[41] For various reasons, the five major world religions offer reasons why followers might oppose religion. Religious leaders then construct a narrative about the extent to which abortion is problematic and hence should be a major issue of concern.

The Judeo-Christian faiths (i.e., Judaism, Catholicism, Protestantism) have received the most attention for how their leaders and constituents view abortion. Followers of Reform Judaism tend to have particularly liberal views across a range of sex-related issues (e.g., same-sex relationships,

---

[36] Jelen, "The Subjective Bases of Abortion Attitudes."
[37] Shapiro, "Abortion Law in Muslim-Majority Countries."
[38] Damian, "Abortion from the Perspective of Eastern Religions: Hinduism and Buddhism."
[39] Damian.
[40] Hongladarom, "Buddhism and Abortion."
[41] Flordia, "Buddhist Approaches to Abortion."

36 FETAL POSITIONS

premarital sex), including abortion. In the United States, which has the largest population of Jews outside of Israel, 83% believe that abortion should be allowed in most circumstances.[42] Conversely, Orthodox Jews, which constitute a very small proportion of the US Jewish population, are generally opposed, encouraging large traditional families.

Cross-national survey data do not typically distinguish between mainline (e.g., Episcopalians, Presbyterians, Evangelical Lutherans) and more conservative Protestant denominations (e.g., Southern Baptist, Missouri Synod Lutheran). But within individual countries, we find that mainline Protestants exhibit rather liberal views. For example, only 35% of mainline Protestants in the United States report that abortion should be illegal in all or most cases.[43] Conversely, affiliates of conservative Protestant or Evangelical denominations, have been clear in their condemnation of abortion, viewing it as a sexual morality issue and to a lesser extent, violating the life ethic.[44] Indeed, among those who adhere to Evangelical Protestant traditions in the United States, nearly twice as many say they oppose legal abortion as support it (63% to 33%).[45]

Among all the major religions, Catholic leaders have elicited some of the greatest attention regarding abortion.[46] The Catholic Church has drawn on the idea that all life is sacred and hence people should reject not only abortion but also euthanasia and capital punishment because these acts also end lives. Additional opposition has been grounded in concerns about sexual morality.[47] Abortion may be seen as part of a continuum of sexual morality issues, including homosexuality, sex outside of marriage, and birth control, of which the Catholic Church disapproves. Since the Catholic Church is centralized and has a hierarchical structure with the pope at its helm, it is able to deliver a fairly clear and consistent message regarding its disapproval. Other religious groups have either not been as unified or, like conservative Protestant denominations, have taken longer to realize and act on their mutual interests regarding abortion.[48]

---

[42] Masci, "American Religious Groups Vary Widely in Their Views of Abortion."
[43] Masci.
[44] Jelen, "Respect for Life, Sexual Morality, and Opposition to Abortion"; Williams, "The Partisan Trajectory of the American Pro-Life Movement."
[45] Masci, "American Religious Groups Vary Widely in Their Views of Abortion."
[46] Perl and McClintock, "The Catholic 'Consistent Life Ethic' and Attitudes toward Capital Punishment and Welfare Reform."
[47] Jelen, "The Subjective Bases of Abortion Attitudes," September 2014; Jelen and Bradley, "Abortion Opinion in Emerging Democracies."
[48] Williams, "The Partisan Trajectory of the American Pro-Life Movement."

Although the Catholic Church is officially opposed to abortion, many of its adherents do not abide by papal authority with regards to abortion or other sex-related issues (e.g., birth control)[49] Indeed, even though the Catholic Church is staunchly opposed to abortion, 48% of Catholic Americans, for example, think that it should be legal.[50] As I explain below, there are some good reasons for the disconnect between official Church doctrine and Catholics' views.

Unlike other religions, the Catholic Church does not have denominational subgroups. For other religions, like Protestants, if adherents do not like a given edict, activity, worship style, or even fellow congregants, they can switch to a different "brand" of the same religion. For example, if adherents prefer a Lutheran church that is more liberal than their current one, they might consider joining the relatively liberal Evangelical Lutheran Church of America. If there is not a more liberal Lutheran church nearby, they might think about joining an Episcopal Church, which is also liberal, has a similar worship style as the Lutheran Church, and may not have discernable liturgical differences. Conversely, Catholics cannot easily select a more liberal "brand" of Catholicism that is better aligned with progressive views.[51] Even attending a Catholic Church outside of one's designated parish is discouraged, and moving to a different Catholic Church would not lead to more liberal official views on abortion since the pope, who leads this hierarchically structured religion, is opposed. As a result, many people who are raised Catholic continue to affiliate as such even if they do not necessarily agree with the Catholic Church's official stance on a range of issues, like premarital sex, birth control, and abortion.[52] The more diverse perspectives among Catholics may dilute support for Catholic proscriptions regarding abortion.

Using data from the last three waves of the WVS, I examine individuals' disapproval about abortion by personal religious affiliation. While dozens of studies have examined religious variation within nations, this analysis will test for religious affiliation differences across the world. The mixed-modeling results, which accounts for a range of potential confounders, can be found in Appendix A. There are relatively few differences across the major religions. Figure 1.1 provides the marginal values for abortion disapproval by personal religious affiliation. When the confidence intervals

[49] D'Antonio, "The American Catholic Family"; D'Antonio, *American Catholics Today.*
[50] Masci, "American Religious Groups Vary Widely in Their Views of Abortion."
[51] Stark and Finke, *Acts of Faith.*
[52] Manning, "Women in a Divided Church."

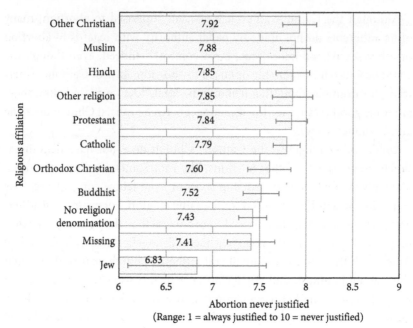

Figure 1.1 Marginal Values for Abortion Disapproval by Personal Religious Affiliation (Society N = 88; Individual N = 211,317)

Note: Marginal values are generated from the mixed-modeling results found in Appendix A, Table A.3, Model 8. All other variables in the model are held constant.

Source: WVS, waves 5, 6, and 7

overlap (i.e., the black lines), this means that the religious groups are not statistically significant from each other. Higher numbers indicate more disapproval.

As might be expected, Jews across the world are the most liberal with an average disapproval score of 6.83 (on a scale ranging from 1 = always justified to 10 = never justified). They appear even more supportive than people who did not declare a religion, though the difference between the two groups is not statistically significant (i.e., the black lines representing the confidence intervals overlap). With an average disapproval score of 7.52, Buddhists are fairly supportive as well, and more liberal on the abortion issue than Catholics, Protestants, Hindus, and Muslims. There are no differences among the remaining religious groups—Orthodox Christians, Catholics, Protestants, Hindus, and Muslims.

The analysis presented here focuses on the world's five major religions (i.e., Judaism, Christianity, Islam, Buddhism, and Hinduism). As noted

RELIGION AND ABORTION ATTITUDES   39

above, within individual countries, researchers have often found important differences among certain religious groups. For example, in the United States, clear distinctions exist in the level of disapproval between people who identify as mainline versus conservative Protestant or Evangelical, with the latter groups being particularly opposed.[53] Indeed, several of the people I interviewed referred to Evangelicals as a major driver of abortion disapproval in the United States. As one academic explained, "I've used the term Evangelical quite a few times. And I suspect their religious influence on these [abortion] policy issues is greater than any other factor." As one of the doctors who performs abortions in the US made clear, "Evangelical Christians have had a big say in abortion and how the government views abortion." Unfortunately, the few cross-national studies that survey individuals about abortion disapproval do not consistently ask about respondents' religious denomination (e.g., Evangelical) as opposed to their religion (e.g., Protestant). As a result, followers of different subgroups of a major religion (e.g., Shia and Sunni Muslim) may view abortion differently but are lumped together in the cross-national survey data.

The lack of difference among the major religions raises the possibility that the categories may be too broad to detect meaningful variation in attitudes about sex-related issues. However, other studies, which have used these same data, have found significant and substantial distinctions among religious affiliates for sex-related issues other than abortion.[54] Indeed, in my previous work on cross-national views about same-sex relationships[55] Muslims and Protestants were clearly more opposed than Jews, Buddhists and Catholics.[56] Using cross-national survey data, other researchers have found similar religion differences in disapproval for issues other than abortion.[57] The findings in Figure 1.1 suggest that for understanding abortion disapproval around the globe, there are just a few statistically significant distinctions across

---

[53] Bartkowski et al., "Faith, Race-Ethnicity, and Public Policy Preferences"; Ellison, Echevarria, and Smith, "Religion and Abortion Attitudes among US Hispanics"; Adamczyk and Valdimarsdóttir, "Understanding Americans' Abortion Attitudes."

[54] Finke and Adamczyk, "Cross-National Moral Beliefs: The Influence of National Religious Context"; Adamczyk and Pitt, "Shaping Attitudes about Homosexuality."

[55] The term "homosexuality" is the one used by the WVS on this issue and hence tends to be used by researchers who analyze these data.

[56] Adamczyk, Cross-National Public Opinion about Homosexuality.

[57] Hanneke van den Akker, van der Ploeg, and Scheepers, "Disapproval of Homosexuality"; Štulhofer and Rimac, "Determinants of Homonegativity in Europe"; Andersen and Fetner, "Economic Inequality and Intolerance."

40 FETAL POSITIONS

the major religions. Relative to religious affiliation, religious importance, as measured on surveys, is a more meaningful factor for understanding public opinion about abortion.

Country-Level Religious Forces

So far, this chapter has focused on religion's role in shaping personal attitudes, which is how people tend to see religious influences. Individuals are either more or less religious, which, along with other personal characteristics, shape the extent to which they view abortion as problematic. But religion can also influence people's attitudes through the larger religious contexts in which they live. Religious belief is not evenly distributed across the globe. Rather some parts of the world (e.g., Africa) have clusters of people with particularly high levels of religious belief. Other geographical areas (e.g., Western Europe, East Asia) are filled with residents who are less likely to report that religion is important on surveys. Residents may find that their views on abortion are shaped by the many more religious or secular people in their country.

In China, where survey measures on organized religion indicate that religious importance is low, I asked interviewees about the collective influence of religion in shaping abortion views. The response was clear—unless you belong to one of the religious minorities (e.g., Uyghur Muslims), religion, as traditionally understood, did not influence abortion attitudes. A Chinese-based university lecturer explained about the religion and abortion relationship, "Individually, maybe some people will be afraid of karma, but not as collective thinking. It's very different from the context in the U.S. where people might somehow share this kind of collective thinking—if I do this, then God will punish me or getting an abortion is regarded as something against the norm" A Christian Chinese youth minister noted, "For the general public, people are rarely affected by religion. It's mostly their own family cultures or the experiences they have throughout life that sort of shapes their attitudes towards abortion or family related issues." Another academic added that it may not even be appropriate to use the term "religion" in China, rather "It's just part of their daily life. It's really something more general that they believe in, but they wouldn't say it's a religion." In China, respondents felt that the religious culture, as understood as overall levels of religious importance or adherence to a specific religion, had little impact on personal views about abortion.

Perhaps not surprising, American interviewees had strong conviction that religion was powerful in shaping collective views about abortion. As one academic explained, "It's so interesting, I think religion plays a part of it, even for people that aren't religious. I think Christianity, especially in the US, is just so pervasive in our culture, even if you're not Christian yourself, like it's just so influential." A doctor who conducts abortions added, "This country was founded on religious freedom but is fairly conservative and has Judeo-Christian values that essentially run [through] everyone's moral compass. Finally, a journalist from an antiabortion organization highlighted the country's uniqueness, explaining that "part of it may be that the United States is an outlier among developed nations and that we are a more religious country." The reporter is correct that the United States has higher levels of religious belief, as conventionally measured, than most other rich Christian-majority nations. A high proportion of religious people can create a culture infused with religion that can affect everyone's attitudes.

Within sociology, researchers have given a great deal of attention to how macro structural and cultural characteristics shape individuals' attitudes and behaviors, especially religion's collective influence. The relationship between societal characteristics, like a nation's religious culture and individuals' attitudes is referred to as the macro-micro link.[58] Focusing on religion's macro effects, Emile Durkheim,[59] one of sociology's founders, explained that religion is a power that can strengthen and solidify the group, resulting in an effect that exists over and above the religious individuals that initially contributed to it. This is referred to as a "sui generis" effect. This would be the force that some interviewees described as "group thinking" or when Christianity is so pervasive that even if you are not religious, it still has an influence.

Many studies have examined religious contextual influences for shaping attitudes and behaviors, though research on country-level effects for understanding abortion disapproval is much more limited. A group or collective religious influence may emerge from very small groups, like friends and families, to counties, states, and nations. Even if people are not personally religious, researchers have found that if they have more religious friends, they are less likely to initiate premarital sex,[60] use marijuana,[61] and

---

[58] Coleman, "Social Theory, Social Research, and a Theory of Action"; Collins, "On the Microfoundations of Macrosociology"; Hazelrigg, "The Problem of Micro-Macro Linkage."
[59] Durkheim, "The Elementary Forms of Religious Life"; Durkheim, "Suicide."
[60] Adamczyk and Felson, "Friends' Religiosity and First Sex."
[61] Adamczyk and Palmer, "Religion and Initiation into Marijuana Use."

42 FETAL POSITIONS

participate in delinquent acts.[62] In this case, the group's high level of religious belief is having an influence, even though some participants may not
buy into the religion. Likewise, the religious context of schools, counties, and
states can shape attitudes and behaviors related to a range of gender and sex-
related issues, including feelings about same-sex relations,[63] gender views,[64]
abortion attitudes,[65] and the likelihood of obtaining an abortion.[66] Finally,
social scientists have found that the country religious context can influence
attitudes related to sexual morality[67] and same-sex relations.[68] In the next
section, I explain how the country's religious context could seep into the
abortion attitudes of its residents,

Processes through Which the Country Religious Context May Shape Attitudes

There are several pathways through which the country religious context
could shape residents' attitudes, regardless of their personal religious beliefs.
Below, I unpack these mechanisms. In the next section I then use WVS data
to empirically examine how the majority's religious conviction may affect
the views of others.

As discussed above, both social learning and control processes can help
explain the link between personal religious importance and abortion disapproval. Similar processes may also work to shape the attitudes of secular
and religious people alike in more religious nations. As the level of religious
importance within a country increase, even people who are not personally religious will have more interactions with religious adherents whose
views may subtly shape their attitudes, as well as limit exposure to alternative
perspectives.[69] In more religious countries, there are likely more interactions
with religious people in friendship groups, schools, organizations, and the

---

[62] Adamczyk, "Understanding Delinquency with Friendship Group Religious Context."

[63] Adamczyk, Boyd, and Hayes, "Place Matters: Contextualizing the Roles of Religion and Race for Understanding Americans' Attitudes about Homosexuality."

[64] Moore and Vanneman, "Context Matters."

[65] Adamczyk and Valdimarsdóttir, "Understanding Americans' Abortion Attitudes."

[66] Adamczyk, "The Effects of Religious Contextual Norms, Structural Constraints, and Personal Religiosity on Abortion Decisions."; Adamczyk, "Understanding the Effects of Personal and School Religiosity on the Decision to Abort a Premarital Pregnancy."

[67] Scheepers, Te Grotenhuis, and Van Der Slik, "Education, Religiosity and Moral Attitudes."

[68] Adamczyk, Cross-National Public Opinion about Homosexuality.

[69] Schwadel, "Individual, Congregational, and Denominational Effects on Church Members' Civic Participation."

local community. As a result of social learning processes[70] occurring through formal and informal interactions, everyone may adopt the views of the religious majority. Likewise, if people care about what others think, they may assimilate their attitudes through social control processes,[71] even if they are not personally religious.

Because the larger public is more opposed to abortion in more religious countries, businesses and organizations should also be more likely to support religious views. Likewise, the electronic and print media should mirror dominant perspectives. Several of the Chinese respondents I interviewed mentioned the many advertisements for "painless abortion." As one professor explained about China when they still had the one-child policy, "there's a lot of TV commercials or newspaper advertisements about painless abortions posted by all those hospitals. It is very common. And you can see them everywhere. . . So abortion is not an ethical issue at all." It would be rare to see these public advertisements in religious countries like the United States. Rather, it is much more common to see billboards on the highway that deliver prolife messages like "Black children are an endangered species"[72] and "The most dangerous place for an African American is in the womb,"[73] highlighting the higher abortion rate amongst Black women. With its higher levels of organized religion, as well as stronger democracy, which allows for nongovernment organizations, advocates have worked to shape the public's views through the US media.[74]

In more religious societies religious institutions may also take on more roles, providing social and state bureaucratic services, social activities, and political organizing.[75] Indeed, when religion is tightly linked to the government and other institutions (e.g., family) it can also have a "structural" effect. For example, when religion is tied to the state, it may infuse social services, like health care and welfare programs. When people partake of these services, they may find themselves interacting with religious officials. Likewise, in more religious countries, even atheists may have to engage religious institutions after their loved ones die and they lay them to rest. Similarly,

---

[70] Sutherland, *Principles of Criminology*; Akers, *Social Learning and Social Structure*.

[71] Hirschi, *Causes of Delinquency*.

[72] Luna, "Black Children Are an Endangered Species."

[73] Johnson and Williams, "'The Most Dangerous Place for an African American Is in the Womb': Reproductive Health Disparities."

[74] Rohlinger, *Abortion Politics, Mass Media, and Social Movements in America*.

[75] Nepstad and Williams, "Religion in Rebellion, Resistance, and Social Movements."

44 FETAL POSITIONS

when they have a child or get married they may have to register with a local religious organization that is providing a secular service.

Finally, it would seem that abortion legislation may be a key process through which the religious culture shapes attitudes. When people feel strongly about their religion, they are likely to lobby for laws and policies that reflect religion-inspired proscriptions. Sociologists refer to this as the micro-macro process through which individual action produces group properties,[76] like abortion-related laws and policies. In the United States, for example, counties that include more religious individuals are less likely to house abortion clinics, where the majority of abortions are conducted.[77] Once laws are in place, religious and secular residents alike may beocme less supportive of abortion, as the government has indicated its disapproval and informal norms against abortion are now supported by the legal structure. There is also more limited abortion access, leading fewer people to openly know women who have had them, and galvanizing stigma around abortion. Below, I test for a religious contextual effect on abortion disapproval.

Testing for a Country Religious Effect

Having provided the rational for how and why the religious convictions of others could shape attitudes, I use WVS data, to examine the role of the country religious context (i.e., overall levels of religious importance) in shaping residents' disapproval, after accounting for personal religious beliefs and a host of potential individual and country-level confounders. These findings appear in Appendix A, Table A.5, Model 2. They show that overall country religious importance has a statistically significant association with more disapproving attitudes, even after controlling for a range of other factors, including personal religious importance. In other words, people's views about abortion are shaped not only by their personal religious beliefs, but also that of their fellow residents.

How large is the country religiosity effect relative to personal religious importance? Figure 1.2 illustrates the effect sizes (i.e., marginal effects) for both personal and country levels of religious importance, after accounting for a range of other factors that might otherwise complicate the relationships.

---

[76] Liska, "The Significance of Aggregate Dependent Variables and Contextual Independent Variables for Linking Macro and Micro Theories."

[77] Adamczyk and Valdimarsdóttir, "Understanding Americans' Abortion Attitudes."

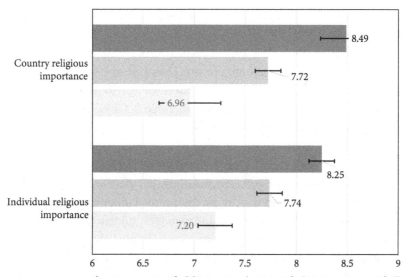

Figure 1.2 Marginal Values for Abortion Disapproval by Individual and Country Religious Importance (Society N = 88; Individual N = 211,317)

Note: Marginal values are generated from the mixed-modeling results found in Appendix A, Table A.3, Model 8. All other variables in the model are held constant.

Source: WVS, waves 5, 6, and 7

For someone living in a country with average levels of religious importance, their level of abortion disapproval is 7.72 on a scale where 10=never justified. In nations that are highly religious (i.e., one standard deviation above the mean), their disapproval score is 8.49. The effect of individual religious importance looks a little smaller (i.e., 8.24 for more religious people) than country religious importance. But, in a separate analysis, I found that the difference between the two religious measures is not statistically significant.

In Appendix A, Table A.3, Model 8, several additional country-level controls are included. The effect of country religious importance is by far the largest, followed by economic development and then a range of additional national-level characteristics like democracy and abortion policies.[78] For understanding why abortion attitudes vary so substantially across the world,

---

[78] This information was obtained (1) through a comparison of standardized coefficients, (2) by examining the amount of country-level variance explained (i.e., intraclass correlation) once each new macro-level variable was included from Appendix A, Table A.3 and (3) assessing marginal effects across the different national-level measures.

46 FETAL POSITIONS

a country's overall level of religious importance explains an important piece of the puzzle.

One potential pathway through which the country religious context could shape abortion is through national abortion laws. I am able to test whether or not higher levels of country religious importance lead to more disapproval through abortion being illegal. Appendix A, Table A.3, Model 8 includes the national abortion law, which is a dichotomous measure indicating whether or not abortion is allowed only in cases of rape, fetal abnormalities, or to save the life of the mother.[79] The indicator of conservative abortion laws and policies is statistically significant, meaning that more conservative abortion policies are associated with more disapproval among residents living in these nations. While laws have an independent influence, as can be seen in Model 8, the effect of country religious importance changes minimally when it is included. Laws and policies do not seem to be working through a nation's religious context to shape attitudes. Rather, the national religious context and abortion laws are having unique relationships with residents' abortion disapproval.

There are a couple of reasons why the religious context does not appear to shape attitudes via laws. In some countries, abortion legislation may have initially been established through religion-related forces (e.g., social movements, media) and over time transitioned, resulting in an independent effect on attitudes. Conversely, the religious culture and abortion-related laws may never have been that closely linked and could have arisen from other sources. Also, the correct causal order between abortion laws and attitudes is particularly unclear. Appendix A, Table A.3, Model 8 is conceptualized as laws shaping individuals' abortion attitudes. However, the opposite relationship—where laws arise from the public's feelings—is entirely feasible. When a large proportion of a country's residents feel passionately about a given issue, they may advocate for laws and policies that support their views.

The findings here show that the religious culture and abortion-related legislation are independently associated with attitudes. But these are general findings. Individual countries have unique histories. In some nations, country religious importance and abortion-related laws and policies may be

---

[79] In separate analyses, I also considered the influence of several other measures of abortion policies. But the abortion legal measure presented in Model 8 seemed to produce the clearest and most consistent results, given the laws in most countries (e.g., only three nations do not allow abortion under any circumstances).

closely linked. However, on average abortion policies and overall levels of importance placed on organized religion within countries around the world appear to have independent relationships with attitudes.

Moral Communities

The analysis above makes clear that the national religious context has an important role in shaping abortion disapproval. A number of studies within the sociology of religion have suggested that the surrounding religious context could heighten the effect of personal religious beliefs on views about behaviors that religion proscribes, including abortion. This is referred to as the "moral communities' hypothesis," which I explain and then empirically test below.

The moral communities' hypothesis, which builds off of Émile Durkheim's writings about religion,[80] was developed by American social scientists[81] to explain why religious beliefs were empirically associated with attitudes and behaviors that religion proscribes in some parts of the United States but not others. It posits that when religious adherents are around other religious people, their own beliefs are more likely to influence their behaviors.[82] From this perspective, personal religious beliefs are seen as having their greatest power when they are "turned on" by the presence of other religious followers, who work as meso or macro-level moderators. When individuals regularly interact with other religious people, their own religious beliefs may be ignited. Conversely, when these same individuals are in more secular environments and around fewer religious followers, their religious beliefs become a compartmentalized part of their lives and are less likely to shape their views. Is the moral communities' hypothesis relevant for understanding cross-national abortion disapproval?

The likelihood that religious contexts shape abortion attitudes may depend on the size or level of intimacy of the context being examined. Countries may be too large. In studying delinquency, researchers have found support for the moral communities' hypothesis when they focus on the

---

[80] Durkheim, *The Elementary Forms of Religious Life.*
[81] Stark, Kent, and Doyle, "Religion and Delinquency"; Stark, Doyle, and Kent, "Rediscovering Moral Communities."
[82] Stark, "Religion as Context"; Stark, Kent, and Doyle, "Religion and Delinquency"; Finke and Adamczyk, "Cross-National Moral Beliefs: The Influence of National Religious Context"; Regnerus, "Moral Communities and Adolescent Delinquency."

48 FETAL POSITIONS

religious context of friendship groups, high schools, and regions.[83] Several other social scientists have examined whether the country religious context heightens the influence of personal religious beliefs on disapproval of various moral or deviance issues (e.g., same-sex relations).[84] With one exception,[85] none of these studies have found that national religious contexts strengthen the relationship between personal religious beliefs and moral attitudes.

Does the national religious context heighten the effect of personal religious beliefs on abortion disapproval? I test for this relationship in Appendix A, Table A.4, Model 1. The interaction is not statistically significant, meaning that the link between personal religious beliefs and abortion disapproval does not depend on the national religious context. The reason there is no moderation or amplified effect may be due to countries being too larger or not-being-intimate-enough. Suppose the moral communities' effect occurs because face-to-face interactions with other religious people heighten the influence of one's personal religious beliefs. In that case, the religious context may need to be assessed at a fairly intimate level, like friendship groups. Countries may simply be too large to create a moral communities' effect. For understanding abortion disapproval, the national religious context appears to influence more secular and religious people alike, which is powerful!

Dominant Religion

Religious importance, as conventionally measured, clearly matters for understanding cross-national disapproval. Along with religious salience, most nations are historically connected to one of the five major religions (i.e., Hinduism, Buddhism, Judaism, Christianity, and Islam).[86] Does the dominant religious tradition within a country also shape individuals' abortion opinions? As I explain below, much like personal religious affiliation, the dominant religion is minimally related to attitudes. The exception is

---

[83] Regnerus, "Moral Communities and Adolescent Delinquency"; Stark, Kent, and Doyle, "Religion and Delinquency"; Stark, "Religion as Context."

[84] See for example: Finke and Adamczyk, "Cross-National Moral Beliefs: The Influence of National Religious Context"; Adamczyk, Cross-National Public Opinion about Homosexuality.

[85] Scheepers, Te Grotenhuis, and Van Der Slik, "Education, Religiosity and Moral Attitudes."

[86] The handful of countries that have a mixture of these religious faiths are often plagued by religious conflict. Hence, Nigeria which has larger proportions of both Christians and Muslims has seen a particularly high level of religious conflict.

Catholicism, which has a small, albeit statistically significant relationship with residents' abortion disapproval. In Chapter 5, I also show that countries with Confucian histories have less-supportive residents.

Researchers have examined differences between monotheistic and polytheistic religions to understand the strength of religious commitment and the likelihood of abiding by religious proscriptions and developing consistent attitudes. As noted previously, Hinduism and Buddhism, which celebrate many deities that mostly do not require exclusivity, are polytheistic. The Abrahamic religions (i.e., Islam, Christianity, Judaism) are largely monotheistic. Scholars have found that monotheistic religions generate higher levels of belief, in part, because they have a single demanding, jealous, and loving God who requires exclusive devotion.[87] Monotheistic faiths that are strict, making lots of demands of their members, can be especially successful at eliciting support and generating commitment.[88]

Among the major monotheistic religions, Islam and conservative Protestantism are typically considered stricter than others, generating high levels of religious belief, commitment, and engagement. Their adherents are also likely to disapprove of a range of sexual morality issues that at the national level has translated into laws that discourage women's free movement and produced draconian punishments for people convicted of same-sex relationships. However, as noted above, for individual survey respondents I found few statistically significant differences in abortion disapproval based on residents' religious affiliation.

In the global debate about abortion, the Catholic Church has been particularly vocal about its disapproval. Indeed, of all the major religions, Catholic leaders seem to be the most organized in opposing abortion across the world. Conservative Protestants have also been clear in their condemnation of abortion, but they do not have the same unifying structure as the Catholic Church. Additionally, conservative Protestant faiths have a substantial presence in only a handful of countries (i.e., Ghana, Zimbabwe, South Africa, Trinidad and Tobago, the United States, and Zambia).

---

[87] Stark and Finke, *Acts of Faith*.

[88] In might seem like strict religions would discourage people from joining because of the demands, but often the opposite happens. Adherents who give more to their religion are more likely to feel that they will receive the ultimate reward after they die. Additionally, religious organizations often try to provide interesting and fun activities for their adherents (e.g., ice cream socials, bowling night, potlucks), so members are likely to enjoy spending time with the group, which further strengthens bonds.

50   FETAL POSITIONS

Along with offering a clear and consistent message about the problems with abortion, in many countries the Catholic Church has had a powerful role in shaping abortion legislation[89] and impeding the development of more liberal reforms.[90] I examined whether the proportion of Catholics also shapes residents' abortion attitudes. These findings can be found in Appendix A, Table A.3, Model 6. The percentage of Catholics within a nation is associated with slightly more abortion disapproval, but *only* after several of the country and individual-level control variables are considered.

Figure 1.3 provides information on how people living in countries with low, medium, high, and very high levels of Catholicism feel about abortion. In countries where there are almost no Catholics and all other individual and country-level factors are held constant, the average abortion disapproval level is 7.59 (where 10 = never justified). However, in a country like Poland where 93% of residents adhere to the Catholic faith, the disapproval rises to 8.18.

The complicated relationship between the proportion of Catholics and abortion disapproval (i.e., the effect only appears after accounting for several other factors) is related to higher levels of religious importance in South America and to greater economic development in Europe. Catholic-majority nations are clustered in the Global North and Latin America. Many European countries (e.g., France, Spain, Portugal, Italy) are well developed and have especially low levels of religious belief and high proportions of Catholic affiliates. Conversely, many Latin American countries have stringent abortion legislation, moderate levels of religious belief, and also high Catholic proportions (e.g., Brazil). Because of the countervailing forces of economics and religious belief, the Catholic country effect only begins to emerge after accounting for economic and educational development and overall levels of religious importance, as well as other factors such as communist history and democracy. The statistically significant relationship between the proportion of Catholics and disapproval is consistent with other cross-national studies finding an association between Catholic history and stricter abortion legislation.[91]

[89] Forman-Rabinovici and Sommer, "An Impediment to Gender Equality?"
[90] Knill, Preidel, and Nebel, "Brake Rather than Barrier."
[91] Forman-Rabinovici and Sommer, "An Impediment to Gender Equality?"; Kozlowska, Béland, and Lecours, "Nationalism, Religion, and Abortion Policy in Four Catholic Societies"; Mishtal, *The Politics of Morality*; Hildebrandt, "What Shapes Abortion Law?"

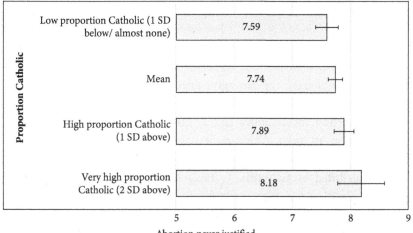

Figure 1.3 Proportion Catholic within a Country for Explaining Abortion Disapproval (Society N = 88; Individual N = 211,317)

Notes: Estimates are taken from Appendix A, Table A.3, Model 8. All other variables are held constant. Abortion legality is not included because it could create artificial relationships. Nevertheless, as shown in Model 9, it is still statistically significant and positive when the measure is included. The Catholic measure is skewed; the minimum range for proportion Catholic is zero, which is also one standard deviation below the mean. Conversely, on the high end the proportion Catholic extends to 95% in Poland, which is beyond 80% Catholic, which is two standard deviations above the mean.

Source: WVS, waves 5, 6, and 7

In a separate analysis, I also examined whether residents from countries with higher proportions of Muslims or concentrations of Pentecostals, Evangelicals, and conservative Protestants are more likely to disapprove. Neither the proportion Muslim nor higher concentrations of the latter groups[92] are statistically associated with abortion disapproval.[93] Likewise, relative to other religions, no major differences exist in abortion support between countries dominated by Islam or a mixture of Protestant faiths (i.e., conservative

---

[92] The WVS did not ask respondents whether they belonged to a conservative Protestant, Evangelical, or Pentecostal faith and hence I was unable to calculate the proportion who belong to these denominations. However, I was able to classify countries as having a wide range of Protestant faiths versus those that are dominated largely by mainline Protestant religions that are prevalent in Europe (e.g. Episcopal).

[93] There does not seem to be a moral communities' effect whereby a higher proportion of Muslims heighten the disapproving influence of Islamic religious affiliation on attitudes.

52 FETAL POSITIONS

and mainline Protestant religions and Catholicism, which can be found in Africa and the United States).[94] For understanding cross-national abortion disapproval, country-level measures of Islam and conservative Protestantism may be inconsequential, especially in light of religious importance, which appears to have the strongest effect size at both individual and country-levels.

The proportion of Catholics has a minor role to play in explaining global abortion attitudes. Although it is statistically significant, the proportion of Catholics has the smallest effect size among the country-level variables included in Appendix A, Table A.3. As noted above, Catholics are not more disapproving about abortion than other religious followers, suggesting that Catholic adherence per se is not producing the effect. Rather, the Catholic Church has been highly vocal on this issue. As I explain in the following section, with its hierarchical structure, the Catholic Church has had an outsized influence on the global abortion debate.

Abortion and the Catholic Church

While Catholic affiliation is unlikely to shape abortion views, in some societies the Catholic Church has had a meaningful effect on attitudes and on abortion-related policies. In countries with higher Catholic proportions, the Catholic Church is likely to have a greater influence on secular matters, including laws and policies, culture, nongovernment institutions, and so forth. Some of the Catholic Church's effect on policy may transfer to people's public opinion about abortion. As I discuss below, the Catholic Church may be especially successful at exerting its influence when a nation's identity is fused with Catholicism. Likewise, the Catholic Church has historically opposed abortion. This opposition has contributed to a pathway for other Christian faiths to advocate against pro-abortion legislation in some countries. This advocacy work may also shape residents' views, increasing disapproval.

---

[94] I coded all nations by their dominant religion using the Association of Religion Data Archive's Cross-National Socio-Economic and Religion Data. See also Adamczyk, "Religion as a Micro and Macro Property."

A country's social programs, like health insurance, childcare, and food assistance, may represent national values.[95] Scandinavian countries, like Sweden and Norway, for example, are often seen as exemplars of gender equality and family support. This is partially because they have policies like very long paid parental leave and free preschool that make the economic costs of having children more manageable.[96] In a similar way, abortion laws and policies may be viewed as expressing national norms and identities, which has happened in some Catholic-majority nations, like Poland and Ireland.

Although communist-era laws made abortion widely available, in 1993 Poland enacted some of the most restrictive abortion legislation in Europe. In 2020, the nation took another conservative step with a near total ban on abortion, permitting it only in cases of rape or incest or when pregnancy threatens the mother's health. Some researchers have argued that the reason it has such a restrictive law is related to a resurgence of Polish nationalism, linked to an emphasis on the family, following the fall of communism, as well as the enduring influence of the Catholic Church.[97] The strong relationship between the Catholic Church and national identity in Poland offers insight into how abortion opponents have successfully enacted stringent abortion laws in the name of religious norms by embedding them in claims about national identity.[98] The coupling of Catholic and national identity has created a conservative framework through which abortion in Poland is politically understood and negotiated.

Like Poland, Irish national identity has also been historically fused with Catholicism.[99] However, religious belief has been decreasing in Ireland. Over the past few decades, Ireland has experienced some of the steepest drops in religious belief and affiliation across the world. In 2005, 69% of people reported that they are "a religious person," but by 2011—just six years

---

[95] Béland and Lecours, *Nationalism and Social Policy.*

[96] Chzhen, Gromada, and Rees, "Are the World's Richest Countries Family Friendly?"

[97] Kozlowska, Béland, and Lecours, "Nationalism, Religion, and Abortion Policy in Four Catholic Societies"; Mishtal, *The Politics of Morality.*

[98] Kozlowska, Béland, and Lecours, "Nationalism, Religion, and Abortion Policy in Four Catholic Societies."

[99] Spain and Quebec are also majority Catholic societies, but they have had liberal abortion legislation. Scholars argue that Spaniards' and Quebeckers' national identity has been less fused with Catholicism. As a result, abortion rights have become more liberal at a quicker pace than in Poland and Ireland (see Kozlowska, Béland, and Lecours, "Nationalism, Religion, and Abortion Policy in Four Catholic Societies").

54 FETAL POSITIONS

later—the proportion had dropped to 47%.[100] In a 2018 landside, Irish residents voted to repeal the nation's near total ban on abortion. As a result, women could obtain an abortion during the first trimester.[101] This legal change may have been driven by a decline in religious belief and Catholic identity within the country.[102]

The Catholic Church has also had an important role in shaping political opposition to abortion through protest activities, which can also heighten abortion opposition. The Catholic antiabortion movement in the United States illustrates some of the Catholic-inspired logic for opposing abortion. The Catholic campaign against abortion legalization in the United States grew out of a concern for human life that was consistent with the principles of the New Deal welfare state, including taking care of the poor and disenfranchised. Even Jesse Jackson—a liberal Protestant and civil rights' activist—initially found the Catholic social justice argument persuasive because it was seen as an extension of his efforts to help poor people. As he explained in an article for the *National Right to Life News*, "Politicians argue for abortion largely because they do not want to spend the money necessary to feed, clothe and educate more people."[103]

Beginning in the 1970s, the Catholic-inspired perspective on abortion as a liberal right-to-life issue started being challenged because it conflicted with a different liberal view on abortion: a woman's right to equality and bodily autonomy. After the 1973 *Roe v. Wade* decision, which eliminated legal barriers to abortion during the first trimester, conservative Protestants began joining the antiabortion campaign. They transitioned the campaign's focus from human rights and dignity to preserving the moral order and battling the sexual revolution.[104] While conservative Protestants could allow for preserving the life of the mother and other important exceptions, like rape and incest, some researchers have argued that they were especially opposed to "abortion on demand" because of its association with "moral disorder, sexual licentiousness, and a disregard for unborn human life."[105]

Along with attitudes, the Catholic proportion within a country is associated with more conservative abortion policies (See Figure 0.2 in the

---

[100] WIN-Gallup International, "Global Index of Religiosity and Atheism."
[101] McDonald, Graham-Harrison, and Baker, "Ireland Votes by Landslide to Legalise Abortion."
[102] Central Statistics Office, "Religious Change."
[103] Jackson, "How We Respect Life Is the Over-Riding Moral Issue."
[104] Williams, "The Partisan Trajectory of the American Pro-Life Movement."
[105] Williams, p. 461.

Introduction). Some of the same processes linking the Catholic Church and abortion laws can also shed light on the role of the Church's power to shape attitudes, even as Catholic religious affiliation is minimally related. Residents may be less supportive of abortion in nations where national identity is closely aligned with the Catholic Church because opposition is consistent with religion-inspired national values. Likewise, in countries where the Catholic Church has been especially active in the pro-life movement, antiabortion discourse may also contribute to disapproval.

Buddhism, Taoism, Confucianism, and Folk Religions

Religion's influence on attitudes is clear in countries with high levels of belief in organized religion. However, when a nation of people report that organized religion is not important in their lives, does religion still enter discussions about abortion and, if so, how? This final section focuses on China and the ways that religion emerged in my interviews about abortion attitudes. The findings from China have relevance for other East Asian countries where researchers have also found that religious importance, as traditionally measured, is low.

Even though China has low levels of belief in organized religion,[106] the country has several important traditions, including Buddhism, Taoism, ancestral beliefs, and folk religions. Many of the Chinese I interviewed also spoke about the importance of Confucianism, a Chinese belief system focused on ethics and morality. In Chapter 5, I assess the role of Confucianism in shaping attitudes. As I explain below, only a minority of Chinese respondents felt that the beliefs (e.g., ancestral, folk) in their country had clear abortion proscriptions. Partially for this reason, Chinese women seemed better able to drawn on religion-inspired practices and beliefs to cope with unintended pregnancies and abortions than Americans. Throughout the Chinese discussions on religion and abortion, the one-child policy lingered in the background. It seemed to limit the extent to which religion could motivate disapproval. I discuss the policy briefly below before presenting the interview findings.

Because of concerns about high population growth, the Chinese government began implementing the one-child policy in the 1970s. The policy

---

[106] Pew Research Center, "The Age Gap in Religion around the World."

56 FETAL POSITIONS

reduced the number of children most couples could have to one. There were some exceptions, but for many residents, if they chose to have multiple children, they had to pay a large fine and government jobs could be jeopardized.[107] To help enforce the law, the Chinese state carefully monitored the fertility status of women and in some cases forced women to get abortions.[108] One of the unintended consequences of the law was that a disproportionate number of female fetuses were aborted. Likewise, many baby girls were given up for adoption.[109] In the early 2000s, the government made it illegal to detect a fetus's gender for nonmedical purposes.

Related to population decline, in the mid-2010s the Chinese government eliminated the one-child policy to permit most couples to have two children. In 2021, they changed the policy again to allow parents to have up to three kids.[110] When I spoke with respondents about religion's role in shaping abortion views, the one-child policy regularly emerged. Even though I was asking about the public's perspective, the respondents often drew on examples from friends, families, and others who got abortions during the one-child era, either because they wanted to or felt they had to. Although the following section focuses on religion, it would be difficult to divorce any contemporary discussion about abortion in China from the one-child policy.

An important feature of China is that its major religious traditions are polytheistic, meaning that there is belief or worship in more than one god, which may cross over into other beliefs (e.g., Confucianism). Not surprisingly, many interviewees spoke about the polytheistic nature of religion. As one female professor joked, "My family might think that we're Buddhist, but when we're really in trouble, we're going to just try everything . . . if becoming a Catholic will solve the problem we'll do it [laughs]." For many Chinese, different belief systems can easily intermingle, and monotheistic traditions that do not support the worship of other gods are novel.

Of the various religious traditions and beliefs found in China, Buddhism has perhaps the clearest abortion proscriptions. The most knowledgeable respondents, namely Buddhist leaders, thought that Chinese who strongly connected with the religion knew that Buddhism forbids abortion. As one monk explained, "So if the people believe in Buddhism, they rarely, rarely,

---

[107] Liao, "The One-Child Policy."

[108] Nie, *Behind the Silence*, 2005; Rigdon, "Abortion Law and Practice in China."

[109] Kaur, "Mapping the Adverse Consequences of Sex Selection and Gender Imbalance in India and China"; Zhu, Lu, and Hesketh, "China's Excess Males, Sex Selective Abortion, and One Child Policy."

[110] BBC, "China Allows Three Children in Major Policy Shift."

RELIGION AND ABORTION ATTITUDES   57

rarely do abortions. But we don't have surveys [to know for sure]." Nevertheless, the majority of Chinese may not think much about belief-inspired abortion proscriptions. The same monk explained that his mother had four abortions throughout her life. "But she didn't know much about religion until I became a Buddhist monk, and then I did a lot of rituals for her, for the souls of the four children. So, they can go to their next lives sooner." Hence, only once he became a monk did his mother think much about the link between religion and abortion. Similarly, when asked if some of the rituals a professor was describing might be related to religion, she explained, "I don't know. But, it is part of the local culture and how people in general would view these issues." Even well-educated interviewees did not necessarily know specific details related to beliefs and abortion.

When asked how religion was connected to abortion in China, many respondents focused on religion's role in helping women cope after obtaining one.[111] My study was not primarily focused on abortion behavior, which my respondents knew. However, the authoritarian government and history of the one-child policy created little space for public discussion about abortion. As a Buddhist monk explained, "The Chinese government basically dominates all people's views or ideas. So, they wouldn't allow people to have their own individual ideas about public issues at all." Like this monk, other Chinese were similarly cynical about the government, which I discuss in greater detail in Chapter 4.

Along with an authoritarian government, China does not have many of the nongovernment, nonprofit, or religious organizations that can effectively promote abortion-related legislation. The lack of these establishments may have further impeded public discussions about abortion. Talking about people's willingness to challenge the government, a researcher explained that Chinese people would "rarely fight the state on the grounds of abortion, fetuses, women's rights—absolutely no." For many Chinese, abortion was not an issue that drove people to publicly engage, which is a sharp contrast to the abortion-related mobilizing efforts in other parts of the world.

Many of the respondents I interviewed described the Chinese as highly practical about family planning, carefully calculating economic and career-related costs. Even for Chinese adherents of Judeo-Christian faiths, religion had a more limited role in energizing abortion disapproval. As one Chinese Catholic sister explained, "Even though cognitively they understand what

[111] Similar findings can also be found in Nie, *Behind the Silence*.

58 FETAL POSITIONS

the church says about abortion, in terms of their own decisions, they will prioritize other things first, such as their own financial situations, their own careers, etc." As I explain in Chapter 2, American and Chinese interviewees regularly mentioned practical considerations when talking about abortion. But in China, for close to three decades many residents had little choice over the number of children they could have because of the one-child policy. Hence, even if they were highly religious by Judeo-Christian or Muslim standards, publicly opposing the policy could have made their lives extremely difficult. Moreover, the state could make life very challenging for children who exceed the official family-planning limits. Hence, even more so than Americans, the Chinese were highly practical about when and if they had a child.

Despite organized religion's limited influence in driving public opposition, discussions about religion's role in managing the aftermath of an abortion offer valuable insight into how some Chinese thought about the belief and abortion relationship. Some of the Chinese interviewees spoke about how women who have abortions, regardless of the reason (e.g., one-child policy, genetic defects, unanticipated pregnancy), may experience a conflict within themselves, which religion could help mitigate. A male Chinese Christian youth minister explained, "Most women who had abortions, they usually have this kind of conflict. Most Chinese people are very kind-hearted and once they have this kind of experience, it becomes a thug. It becomes something really painful that they have to bury inside." A Buddhist monk added that most women would not talk about their abortion experience, but there is an exception, which "is when a woman has some regrets." A female bioethicist thought that most women "were actually traumatized by the abortion experience." Religion was discussed as a potential coping mechanism for those experiencing regret or conflict.

Among the interviewees who felt that women might feel bad about obtaining an abortion, they tended to see negative feelings as arising from concerns about karma, a fetus ghost, or bad luck. As one professor explained, "In southern provinces of China, people usually associate abortion with something bad, which could bring back consequences or bad luck for your own families, possibly affecting the bloodline of the whole family." A Buddhist monk added that you need to try and transform "the souls of the babies . . . [so that] they could have better lives, better luck for their next lives." A different monk explained, "So there are two kinds of ghosts, the good and the evil, and they [the aborted fetus] became the evil ones or the lost souls in the world.... [so you have to send] all these blessings to them and help them get rid of the condition that trapped them ... so that could be transferred to the next life sooner." The basic idea was that an aborted fetus might bring bad luck or cause problems for the woman and her family. Hence, something needs to be done.

For women who experienced abortion-related conflict, some coped by visiting temples and reciting prayers to "release the soul" and help the fetus move on. As mentioned by one Buddhist expert, "Women could read Buddhist text to send blessings to the child they aborted. So, the child's soul can go to the next life sooner. And they can also seek help from the temple or from the Buddhist Masters." Another added that through rituals "the souls of the babies can be transformed, and they could have better lives, better luck for their next lives." Likewise, one interviewee explained, "if you haven't done the ritual, then the aborted child might be in hell suffering." Most people felt that the rituals were effective and could relieve the abortion-related burden. "It's very direct and concrete. So, after they are done with the ritual, they think they have sent the child to the next life" (Buddhist monk). Many respondents felt that religion-related rituals and traditions were successful in helping women cope.

The use of religion-inspired mechanisms (e.g., rituals, prayers, temple visits) to manage negative feelings related to an abortion can be found in other religions as well. As a Chinese Catholic sister explained, if a Catholic woman regretted an abortion, then there are many ways to resolve such conflicts, "including confessions, therapy sessions with sisters, and volunteering, so you will feel like you are being helpful and contributing to the society instead of staying in the past with regrets." Even for Chinese Catholics, religion could be useful for easing negative abortion-related feelings.

In contrast to China, the religion-inspired disapproval of abortion in the United States likely limits the use of religion to cope with an abortion.[112] Indeed, religious American women report more self-judgment and perceive more community condemnation than their more secular counterparts.[113] As one US-based journalist explained to me, "I hear from women after the fact who have struggled or have miscarried in subsequent pregnancies. And they feel like God's punishing them for the abortion.... And then they feel guilty."

---

[112] Frohwirth, Coleman, and Moore, "Managing Religion and Morality within the Abortion Experience."

[113] Cockrill et al., "The Stigma of Having an Abortion"; Cockrill and Nack, "I'm Not That Type of Person."

60 FETAL POSITIONS

Participating in a behavior that religion is seen as proscribing in a highly religious country is likely to exacerbate negative feelings.

An undue emphasis on guilt is an important distinction in how the interviewees thought women in the United States versus China felt about abortion. Several respondents noted that in China it "is not a culture of guilt." As one academic explained, "[Chinese women] wouldn't feel guilty or feel morally judged when they went for abortion. Even during the 80s, throughout the 90s, when it's under the one child policy, when people were having abortions, they would think of very practical matters instead of ethical concerns." Another added, "In the United States, probably it's Christianity-based, faith-based society, so people are feeling guiltier about having abortion and it's very controversial." Interviewees thought abortion-related guilt was a bigger concern for American women than Chinese. If the Chinese feel that they have little choice in the decision, they may indeed feel more regret, disappointment, or sadness rather than guilt.[114]

In contrast to American respondents, the Chinese also spoke about justifying abortion on religious grounds. As one academic explained to me, a spirit has many opportunities to become human and if the conditions to have a child are not right,

> then it's actually a better decision to end it, so that the spirit [can] kind of wait for the next opportunity, which will be more optimal, and the world, is cruel. And so, as parents you are doing this child a service by not making their life so challenging after they're born.

Another Chinese interviewee, who had lived in both countries, told me that she had attended a US-based church where a woman testified about how she decided against an abortion, even though her doctor suggested it because of birth defects. "So, at that time, the decision was celebrated by a lot of elders in the church. But my peers and I, like our friends, we feel kind of hesitant, like we feel maybe it's not a good decision [to have this child with these genetic difficulties]." Although this Chinese respondent is Christian, she saw abortion as acceptable when life would otherwise be very challenging for the baby.

Throughout the interviews, the Chinese were very practical about abortion and religion. Part of this was related to the perceived costs of a child and

---

[114] But see also Nie, *Behind the Silence*. He found more discussions of guilt in interviews from the 1990s.

the one-child policy, which had only recently ended and loomed large in many of our discussions. As one professor explained about Chinese women, "I think there's a lot more grieving than guilt, because there's so much they can't control even in the circumstances where they make the decision." Reincarnation seemed to lend itself to a narrative that could justify ending a pregnancy, especially when many women felt like they had little choice.

The majority of women who obtain abortions in the United States are religious.[115] Some of them have publicly commented on how their faith helped them decide to get an abortion.[116] But, this is not a shared discourse. In fact, none of the US-based respondents mentioned the use of religion to directly justify an abortion. A final religion-related distinction between the United States and China, which can also be found in other countries, relates to gender, which I discuss in the following section.

Religion, Gender, and Abortion

In both China and the United States, gender was mentioned as a factor in the abortion debate that was related to religion and cultural beliefs (i.e., Confucianism). Respondents in both countries discussed concerns about others wanting to control women's bodies. In the United States, interviewees pointed to religious ideology as a motivating force. Some of the Chinese respondents also mentioned that the differential valuing of boys over girls, which has fertility-related repercussion, was grounded in Buddhism and traditional beliefs.

In many nations, the women's movement ushered in a new perspective on abortion. Even in the United States, as noted above, progressive public officials like Jessie Jackson were initially opposed to abortion because it challenged ideas about the right to life and the government's willingness to help minorities and poor people. As the women's movement gained momentum, the view that women have the right to equality and control over their bodies became a dominant liberal theme. Conversely, conservative perspectives on abortion were tied to religion and a gendered division of labor with women taking on more caretaking roles.

---

[115] Adamczyk and Felson, "Fetal Positions"; Jerman, Jones, and Onda, "Characteristics of US Abortion Patients in 2014 and Changes since 2008."
[116] Chorley, "I'm a Minister and a Mother—and I Had an Abortion"; Peters, "I'm a Christian Minister Who's Had 2 Abortions. Here's How Faith Informed Those Decisions."

62 FETAL POSITIONS

Before US federal abortion rights were overturned in 2022, survey research found that approximately half of all US residents (46%) viewed abortion as a moral issue.[117] More religious residents were especially likely to report that it is morally wrong.[118] An employee from a pro-life nonprofit explained religious conservatives' moral perspective on women who unintentionally become pregnant: "This woman made her bed and now she has to lie in it' type thing," and, "She should've just kept her legs closed." Similarly, a professor added,

> There's a lot of disrespect of women and a lot of distrust of women. And if women are in any way acting outside of very traditional roles. . . . then I think they will think the worst of them and sort of demonize them. . . . I think religion feeds that. I think it goes all the way back to the founding in Christianity, the founding myth of Adam and Eve, this idea of women to blame.

Related to this theme of control was the idea that women who unintentionally get pregnant are immoral or deficient in some way. If they do not follow religious proscriptions (e.g., premarital or extramarital sex), then an unintentional pregnancy may be seen as their fault.

While in the United States the idea of controlling females centered on restricting abortion, which Judeo-Christian beliefs are often interpreted as proscribing, in China it focused on others dictating the number of children a woman could have. As one female professor explained, "Chinese women's bodies never belong to themselves. They belong to their fathers, their husbands, and then the state, because the state tells you, you have one child, now you can have two." At the same time, some of the Chinese I interviewed felt that eliminating abortion was a greater threat to women's autonomy over their bodies than controlling the number of children. One Chinese journalist told me, "You know, it's not like in the US. It's not like whether it should be forbidden or not. If you say it should be forbidden, then I think a lot of Chinese feminists will say, OK, you force the women to be the tool of male power to produce children." Although it did not arise in my US-based interviews, I suspect that many Americans would feel that limiting the number of children could be just as controlling as outlawing abortion.

[117] Brenan, "Record-High 47% in U.S. Think Abortion Is Morally Acceptable."
[118] Pew Research Center, "Categorizing Americans' Religious Typology Groups."

A final way that gender inequality and religious and cultural values were connected in my interviews was in the valuing of boys over girls. One of the major repercussions of China's family-planning policy was the gender imbalance that it created, resulting in a disproportionate number of male babies relative to female ones. This has caused a range of issues, including challenges in finding potential wives, especially for men with lower incomes, increasing crime because men commit the majority, and riskier sex-related behaviors (e.g., commercial sex) for men.[119]

My interviews revealed that some of the origins for valuing males over females is grounded in traditional religious or Confucian ideals.[120] One Buddhist monk explained that some people feel "men are superior to women," which, he argued comes from both Buddhism and Confucianism. A female professor added, "It's Chinese traditional culture that values boys much more than girls that would be the major factor." Another Buddhist master added, "The view that boys are better than girls should be coming from traditional culture." Many Chinese respondents felt that religious, Confucian, and traditional beliefs were responsible for the differential valuing of boys over girls.

In contrast to the Chinese, none of my American interviewees mentioned religion and the valuing of male babies over female ones. An important reason why sex-selective abortions were rarely mentioned in the United States is partially because antiabortion organizations have focused on the preciousness of each fetus, regardless of gender. Moreover, there are no restrictions on the number of children Americans can have. Hence, couples can keep procreating until they get the gender balance they want.

Gender inequality emerged throughout the interviews. While some respondents thought that religious ideology was responsible, other felt that alternative forces were at work. Chapter 5 talks more specifically about how gender inequality shapes abortion disapproval and access. Chapter 6 shows that it can make abortion rates rise by increasing unintended pregnancies. This section has connected religion to gender inequality as it relates to controlling women's bodies and sex-selective abortions.

---

[119] Kaur, "Mapping the Adverse Consequences of Sex Selection and Gender Imbalance in India and China."

[120] Vu and Yamada, "The Legacy of Confucianism in Gender Inequality in Vietnam"; Vu and Van, "The View of Confucianism about the Importance of Men, Disregard for Women and Its Influence on Vietnam"; Gu, "Bargaining with Confucian Patriarchy."

Conclusion

This chapter focused on the roles of religious importance and affiliation in shaping cross-national understandings about abortion. Among the factors that can be measured with the WVS, religious importance is the most meaningful force driving disapproval. Because all the major religions have some proscriptions regarding abortion, the strength of belief matters more than the specific religion (e.g., Catholic, Islam). The role of religion in shaping views is powerful—even for residents who do not find belief in organized religion important but live in more religious countries. The beliefs of others can influence residents' views through media exposure, culture, policies, and interactions with religious adherents. When I statistically compare the sizes of the coefficients for country and individual religious importance for explaining abortion disapproval, I find that the sizes are similar. Other researchers have found strong support for the effect of personal religious importance in shaping disapproval within nations. My findings show that country-level religious importance effects may be just as powerful. The proportion of Catholics also has a small role in shaping cross-national views, enhancing the effect of national identity and activism to shape disapproval.

Belief in organized religion is low in China. Because of the restrictive family-planning policy, my interviews suggested that religious contextual forces were limited in how much they could influence views. Nevertheless, religion-related beliefs, rituals, and practices still emerged. Respondents spoke about how religion could help manage feelings of regret, justify the procedure, and discourage sex-selective abortions. Chapter 5 offers more insight into differences between Confucian and non-Confucian countries in abortion disapproval. Having established the importance of religion, in the next chapter I explain the role economics and education play in shaping attitudes toward abortion.

Chapter 2

The Role of Economics and Education in Shaping Public Opinion about Abortion

Western European countries have some of the highest levels of education and economic development in the world. They also allow for unrestricted abortion access though the first trimester, and residents have relatively liberal attitudes.[1] Conversely, African nations have much lower levels of educational attainment and economic development. Ninety-three percent of African women live in countries with restrictive abortion laws, and most residents disapprove of abortion. In Kenya, for example, abortion is allowed only to save the health or life of the mother.[2] Less than 30% of Kenyans strongly agree that women should have access to safe abortion services to terminate unwanted pregnancies.[3]

As individual and country characteristics, money and education are important for understanding why some residents are more opposed than others. Across nations, educational attainment and economic development can inform cultural values, which, in turn, can shape abortion support. Many African countries, for example, emphasize large families in part because children are more likely to contribute to the household's production.[4] Conversely, in richer nations families are smaller[5] and children are less likely to be valued for their economic contributions. Differences in cultural values offer valuable insight into why disapproval of abortion varies considerably across the globe.

This chapter begins by examining the relationship between social class and abortion support. I use World Values Survey (WSV) data to establish a link. Drawing on interview data, I then discuss how social class relates to abortion attitudes in China and the United States.

---

[1] Center for Reproductive Rights, "The World's Abortion Laws."
[2] Center for Reproductive Rights, "Kenya's Abortion Provisions."
[3] WVS, "World Values Survey Wave 7: 2017–2020."
[4] Nauck and Klaus, "The Varying Value of Children."
[5] The World Bank Data, "Fertility Rate, Total (Births per Woman)—Kenya."

66 FETAL POSITIONS

Next, I investigate how education and income as macro factors shape cultural values, allowing for more tolerant views. I show that even residents who are not personally wealthy or well educated are more likely to adopt liberal views in these societies. Special attention is given to China's one-child policy. Along with major changes in development over the past fifty years, the policy has shaped how many Chinese think about abortion, childrearing, and the ideal family size.

The chapter ends with an examination of how overall levels of economic development and education condition the effect of religion on attitudes. I show that personal religious beliefs have a greater influence on disapproving views in richer countries than in poorer ones. This finding offers insight into why abortion has remained a contentious issue in many well-developed societies.

Personal Education and Income in Shaping Abortion Disapproval

Research conducted within countries has found that social class matters for understanding abortion attitudes.[6] A handful of cross-national studies also suggest that income and education may be valuable for understanding public opinion.[7] Below I explain why income and education are important, even after accounting for other personal characteristics such as religious beliefs. I then test whether they can help explain abortion disapproval in a large sample of countries from across the globe.

Two key components of social class are education and income. While these characteristics are typically correlated, they may each have a unique relationship with abortion disapproval. Researchers have found that income, wealth, education, and class position can shape people's opinions on a range of issues.[8] Additionally, because it is associated with that of their parents, social class background can have an enduring effect on adult children's

---

[6] Adamczyk, Kim, and Dillon, "Examining Public Opinion about Abortion"; Petersen, "Religion, Plausibility Structures, and Education's Effect on Attitudes toward Elective Abortion."

[7] Loll and Hall, "Differences in Abortion Attitudes by Policy Context and between Men and Women in the World Values Survey"; Adamczyk, "Religion as a Micro and Macro Property"; Fernández, Valiente, and Jaime-Castillo, "Gender Balance in the Workforce and Abortion Attitudes."

[8] McCall and Manza, "Class Differences in Social and Political Attitudes in the United States"; Adamczyk, Kim, and Dillon, "Examining Public Opinion about Abortion"; Adamczyk, *Cross-National Public Opinion about Homosexuality.*

attitudes.[9] I begin by discussing why economics would matter before turning to education.

Prior research shows that people from working-class backgrounds tend to be more liberal about economic matters (e.g., economic redistribution) than those from the middle class.[10] Conversely, they are generally more conservative on social-cultural subjects like abortion and LGBTQ issues, even in countries with high levels of economic development.[11] To explain this relationship, some social scientists suggest that people with higher incomes feel more secure, bolstering their tolerance for complex and controversial issues.[12] Conversely, poorer individuals may be more concerned about having enough money to support themselves and their families. As a result, they may be more conservative about social issues that deviate from long-held beliefs. In the midst of uncertainty, traditional values can provide comfort and stability.

Related to concerns about security, people with lower incomes may also worry about economic threats from others, including women. The abortion debate is often framed as a women's rights issue. Legal abortion access provides women more freedom to pursue educational and career aspirations.[13] As a result, some working-class people may feel greater economic threat from women, just as they may from immigrants and other minorities.[14] In other words, they may feel that women who are better able to control their fertility may be more competitive, which could then threaten their own social class position.

Along with income, more educated people tend to have more liberal attitudes across a range of issues.[15] One way that education contributes to more supportive views is by introducing people to a greater variety of ideas and perspectives. It not only offers fundamental ideas but also teaches new ways

[9] Green, Palmquist, and Schickler, *Partisan Hearts and Minds*; De Graaf, Nieuwbeerta, and Heath, "Class Mobility and Political Preferences: Individual and Contextual Effects."

[10] Lindh and McCall, "Class Position and Political Opinion in Rich Democracies"; Lipset, *Political Man; the Social Bases of Politics.*

[11] Inglehart, *Culture Shift in Advanced Industrial Society*; Adamczyk and Liao, "Examining Public Opinion about LGBTQ-Related Issues in the United States and across Multiple Nations."

[12] Kunovich, "Social Structural Position and Prejudice."

[13] Upadhyay, Biggs, and Foster, "The Effect of Abortion on Having and Achieving Aspirational One-Year Plans."

[14] Haubert and Fussell, "Explaining Pro-Immigrant Sentiment in the U.S."; Andersen and Fetner, "Economic Inequality and Intolerance."

[15] Lindh and McCall, "Class Position and Political Opinion in Rich Democracies"; McCall and Manza, "Class Differences in Social and Political Attitudes in the United States"; Adamczyk, *Cross-National Public Opinion about Homosexuality.*

68 FETAL POSITIONS

of interpreting information. As people gain more education, they are likely to develop more nuanced ideas and understandings of the world, making them better able to reconcile inconsistencies and ambiguities.[16] Even if someone would not support abortion for themselves or their partner, education may contribute to the view that abortion is a personal choice about which the government should not have a say. More educated people may also be less likely to rigidly classify others, reducing the likelihood that they would make judgments that are shaped by irrational anxieties.[17]

Education's influence on civil liberties may also be important for understanding abortion support. Research has found that people with higher vocabulary scores are more supportive of the civil liberties of out-groups, such as communists and non-heterosexual individuals.[18] Education seems to foster cognitive sophistication and complexity.[19] More educated individuals may also be better at expressing feelings about those who differ from the norm,[20] drawing a distinction between their personal views about specific behaviors and whether a group that they do not personally like should have certain liberties. Because their own education likely aided their professional development, more educated people may also be more empathetic to women who need an abortion and how an unanticipated pregnancy could derail one's career.

Having provided the logic for why education and income matter for understanding abortion support, I test these relationships in a large sample of eighty-eight societies from around the world. These findings, which rely on WVS data, can be found in Appendix A, Table A.3. They show that even in the midst of other factors, personal income and education are associated with abortion attitudes. Specifically, richer and more educated individuals are more supportive of abortion. Moreover, even though income and education are correlated with each other, each factor is explaining unique variation in abortion disapproval. In other words, they are both important and at least partially operate through different processes to shape attitudes. The next section covers what the American and Chinese experts thought about these factors.

---

[16] Jackman and Muha, "Education and Intergroup Attitudes."

[17] Sniderman et al., "Values under Pressure: AIDS and Civil Liberties."

[18] Bobo and Licari, "Education and Political Tolerance Testing the Effects of Cognitive Sophistication and Target Group Affect."

[19] Ohlander, Batalova, and Treas, "Explaining Educational Influences on Attitudes toward Homosexual Relations."

[20] Chong, "How People Think, Reason, and Feel about Rights and Liberties."

The Roles of Education and Income in Shaping Views in the United States and China

Having provided the theoretical rationale and empirical evidence for why social class matters for explaining abortion attitudes around the world, I now turn to the Chinese and American interviews to better understand its influence on residents' views. Throughout the interviews, education and income regularly emerged as important topics. Because I was interested in talking with people who either had a stake in the abortion debate or would be able to provide insight, most of the interviewees had positions that required a college education, and many had advanced degrees.[21] At times they discussed how education and income might influence people's views. But more often they talked about how they personally saw educational, career, and economic aspirations shaping women's willingness to have children, as well as how those factors influenced people's ability to provide a child with the best life possible. Some American respondents also spoke about education's potential to shift feelings about the rightness or wrongness of abortion, which the Chinese did not mention. American interviewees were also more likely to discuss the financial and logistical challenges to obtaining an abortion, especially for poor and minority women. I discuss these findings below.

Because abortion is so politicized in the United States, some of the interviewees thought about the sort of information or education that might change people's minds about abortion. For example, an academic who did research on public opinion wondered if Americans understood that most women who get abortions already have kids; as some might think, "If you're a poor mom that can't afford a third, then I can support your abortion more than if you're a twenty-five-year-old who didn't use contraception and now doesn't want to deal with the consequences." A woman who was more opposed to abortion also thought that education on this issue might change views: "Probably over these next five to ten years [people will get] more education on this issue. And either the government's going to have to change its position as far as what it does or is going to have to leave this

---

[21] While the vast majority of interviewees had at least some college education, it is possible that people with less education had similar responses. However, the quantitative findings found in Appendix B make clear that across the world people with higher levels of education tend to be more supportive of abortion. In separate analyses focused only on China and the United States, I also found that more education was statistically associated with more abortion approval.

70 FETAL POSITIONS

issue alone." In contrast to the US-based interviews, in China there was little mention about trying to educate people or provide new information that might change minds. Compared to the United States, abortion access was not at risk in China when the interviews occurred. Likewise, the lack of public space for these discussions in China meant that people may not have been thinking about how to change someone's viewpoint.

In contrast to thinking about education as changing minds, in China one of the only ways that personal income and education were discussed in relation to abortion was in providing the resources to raise a child and maintain a satisfactory life. All of the Chinese experts and stakeholders I interviewed expressed empathy for individuals who may not have the resources to support an unanticipated pregnancy. As a Catholic sister explained, "In China nowadays the educational cost is really high, which is very different from my parents' or grandparents' generations. Back then it would be easier to have more kids and then just to raise them." A Buddhist monk noted, "But now in modern societies, the cost of raising a child has been really high. . . . So much for most families, if you have two children, then that's enough." Other Chinese respondents mentioned the opportunity costs that women had to consider: "their own quality of life, their right, and also their freedom," as a female professor explained. Another academic added, "[Having children is] much more constraining of women's self-development, self-care, everything." Every Chinese interviewee I spoke to discussed the various challenges (e.g., economic, educational, career, time, opportunity, etc.) of having children, many talking at length.

The one-child policy personally affected everyone in China in some way. My interviewees were also aware of the high childrearing, educational, and career-related costs.[22] As a result, many respondents thought that good timing and preparation were especially important before having children. A male pastor from China explained that for people his age there is a popular saying:

> If you bring a child into the world and you cannot give him or her a quality life, like a good education or living environment, and you cannot get him or her into good public schools, send him or her to college, then it is very irresponsible. . . . If you cannot guarantee or improve the life of the children, then don't let them come into the world. It is immoral.

[22] See also Zhou and Guo, "Fertility Intentions of Having a Second Child among the Floating Population in China."

In the same way that many religious people talk about the moral challenge of abortion, at least some Chinese felt that it is immoral to have a child for whom you cannot provide a good life.

American respondents also expressed empathy and understanding that women often need an abortion for financial reasons. Additionally, they were concerned that the public did not understand how difficult and costly it could be for some women to get them. The majority of my interviews were done in 2021, the year before *Roe v. Wade* was overturned in 2022, which made abortion illegal in several states. Even though it was still legal when we spoke, many respondents mentioned the financial and logistical obstacles to getting an abortion in some states. One interviewee who worked with a nonprofit that helped women obtain abortions explained the challenge: "Like if they don't have the money to pay for the Uber, how are they going to raise the $700? Because, of course, insurance and Medicaid do not pay for abortion. It's already inaccessible to some people, but in public opinion, if abortion is legal, then it's available." A doctor who performs abortions added, "We know that Medicaid patients tend to be lower income, tend to be people of color, yet in the majority of states, they don't have insurance coverage for abortions." Many respondents highlighted the precarious access poor and minority women had to getting an abortion.

In contrast to the Chinese interviewees, American respondents seemed to have a more nuanced understanding of who had abortion access and the fact that racial and ethnic minority women were more likely to need abortion services and may struggle to pay. A female doctor noted that "a lot of the controls around abortion in the US are very race based." In addition to abortion access, respondents mentioned concerns that certain segments of the public have racist abortion-related views. As one male academic explained, "I closely link sexuality and gender to race and the idea of the Quiverfull movement.[23] This idea is that if women go and get educated, they have fewer children. Then there are fewer white people, and white people lose political power. I think this is where anti-immigrant attitudes come in as well." A professor who was conducting abortion-related research told me that she asked Americans how they view women who need abortions. She

---

[23] The movement sees children as a blessing from God. Couples who are a part of the movement feel that God will not provide more children than they can handle. Blumberg, "What You Need To Know about the 'Quiverfull' Movement." There have been suggestions in the media that the movement is linked to racist ideas that white Christians in particular should have more children. Quivering, "Racism Drives Quiverfull—Nancy Campbell Really Fears Brown People."

72 FETAL POSITIONS

explained, "There's some quite racialized imagery that comes off the tip of people's tongues around inner-city poor places. Certainly, lots of signifiers of women of color." While the first professor discussed the racist view that white women should be discouraged from getting abortions to preserve the white race, the second academic wondered why survey subjects were inclined to think of black women as primarily getting abortions.

In the United States, many interviewees talked about who could access abortion services and whether access was evenly distributed, which no one felt it was. None of the Chinese respondents mentioned major challenges in obtaining an abortion, most likely because they were widely available. A more controversial issue in China may have been who is discouraged from having children either because they could not financially support additional children or because the government did not want them to have children.

As I was doing research for this book, there were several media stories about one Chinese ethnic population in particular: the Uyghurs. Some well-respected international news outlets suggested that the Chinese government was forcing them to obtain abortions to limit their population size.[24] But none of my Chinese respondents mentioned this group. Indeed, only one Chinese respondent, a professor, talked about the specific challenges for some groups of women (in this case, migrants). As she explained, "So in the factory workers' case, a lot of migrant workers are from rural areas, so they don't have enough access to education. . . . They don't have a good job to support themselves. So usually when they accidentally get pregnant, they will just abort the child." My interview questions did not specifically ask about fertility or population control and minority populations (e.g., Uyghurs, migrants) in China. Likewise, given the government's control of the media, many respondents may have had limited access to international news and thus the plight of the Uyghurs. Rather than specific groups of women (e.g., ethnic, immigrant, etc.), all the Chinese respondents talked about how many poorer families would essentially be denied the opportunity for larger families because of high personal, economic, and career-related costs.

---

[24] Associated Press, "Uyghur Exiles Describe Forced Abortions, Torture in Xinjiang"; Associated Press, "China Cuts Uighur Births with IUDs, Abortion, Sterilization."

THE ROLE OF ECONOMICS AND EDUCATION   73

Economic Development and Overall Levels of Education

In Chapter 1, I explained that religion can have micro and macro dimensions that shape abortion support. Similarly, income and education can also be conceptualized as societal forces that influence residents' attitudes, even after accounting for them as personal characteristics. Over the past 250 years, most countries in the world have undergone some level of industrialization and modernization, albeit at various speeds, timing, and duration. Researchers have found that as nations transform from traditional, rural, and agrarian societies to ones that are more urban, industrial, and rich, their cultural values (i.e., the values that residents generally share) tend to move in somewhat predictable ways.[25] The shift in cultural values provides insight into the link between rising education and economic development and views about abortion. Below I explain why we would expect richer and more educated nations to have more supportive residents than others. I then test these ideas using data from the WVS.

Several researchers (e.g., Geert Hofstede,[26] Shalom Schwartz,[27] and Ronald Inglehart[28]) have developed schemes to describe how modernization and economic development lead to changes in cultural value orientations, which can shape the views of most residents in a given country. The underlying basis of these ideas is that people's connections with each other and their environments shape cultural values. As their interactions and environments change, so too do their cultural value orientations.

In very poor countries, residents are likely to regularly encounter food and housing insecurity and unpredictable health and safety issues. These survival-related concerns can consume them.[29] On a daily basis, they may have to think about where to get food and shelter. They may worry about

---

[25] Inglehart and Baker, "Modernization, Cultural Change, and the Persistence of Traditional Values"; Marx, *Capital*; Schwartz, "A Theory of Cultural Value Orientations: Explication and Applications."

[26] Hofstede, *Culture's Consequences*.

[27] Schwartz, "A Theory of Cultural Value Orientations: Explication and Applications"; Schwartz, "National Culture as Value Orientations"; Schwartz, "A Theory of Cultural Values and Some Implications for Work."

[28] Inglehart, "Mapping Global Values"; Inglehart and Baker, "Modernization, Cultural Change, and the Persistence of Traditional Values"; Inglehart and Oyserman, "Individualism, Autonomy, Self-Expression. The Human Development Syndrome."

[29] Inglehart and Baker, "Modernization, Cultural Change, and the Persistence of Traditional Values."

74 FETAL POSITIONS

how to keep their children safe and whether they can attend school. They are likely concerned about whether or not they or their loved ones will be physically hurt.

Because they cannot easily pay for what they need, residents in less economically secure societies are more likely to rely on each other, reciprocating in kind. Their interconnectedness and dependency are reflected in cultural values that are likely consistent with what many have always known[30] and emphasize adherence to group norms and values.[31] If large families have always been valued, then abortion is more likely to be seen as problematic because it violates traditional norms. Furthermore, residents may feel that women's major societal contributions are producing and raising children, thereby reducing public support for elective abortion. In these societies, embracing social change can destabilize an already fragile social order, potentially causing massive disruptions and further economic insecurity.

As nations become richer, residents no longer have to rely so heavily on others because everyone has more money and lives are more predictable. They can pay for what they need, which can limit reliance on interpersonal connections. With less focus on survival, people's orientations evolve.[32] As they become more autonomous from their friends, family, and communities, many residents develop more specialized skills.[33] Additionally, when people are less dependent on the larger group, they are likely to cultivate unique interests. Modernization and industrialization give rise to a wide range of occupations, ideas, and values. People may begin to feel differently about what they can contribute to society (e.g., having children versus a career), think more about individual rights, and believe that women should control their own bodies. As a result, residents are likely to become more supportive of legal abortion.

Economic development is likely to shape the value orientations of everyone in society, rather than just richer and well-educated residents. As nations accumulate more resources, the government can raise the overall living standard. All children may then be able to attend primary and secondary school for free, and everyone may have access to high-quality and affordable healthcare. Women will have the option of giving birth in hospitals, physical

---

[30] Inglehart, Norris, and Welzel, "Gender Equality and Democracy."
[31] Schwartz, "A Theory of Cultural Value Orientations: Explication and Applications."
[32] Schwartz.
[33] Durkheim, *The Division of Labor in Society*.

infrastructure will improve, and most people will have access to functioning police and fire departments. Overall increases in economic development are likely to produce more stability and security for everyone. As a result, most residents are likely to develop more liberal views about a range of issues, including abortion.

As nations become richer, educational levels will also rise. Many of the same effects that education has for individuals can shape societies more generally. Hence, more educated countries are likely to offer a greater range of perspectives and ideas that are broadcast across media outlets (newspapers, magazines, television, online, etc.). Cultural institutions in these nations are likely to cater to more educated tastes, raising the diversity and sophistication of the ideas presented. Debates about controversial topics will be more readily engaged and less easily dismissed because a substantial number of residents are thinking in more complicated ways and are less prone to stereotypes and simplistic understandings.

When a substantial number of people are college educated, we would also expect more empathy and understanding for women who might want an abortion and how an unanticipated pregnancy could derail one's career. Likewise, richer and more educated societies will produce more medical professionals, strengthening the medical culture. When a nation has a substantial number of medical workers, their experiences and interests are likely to garner more attention. Many will want to avoid the public health costs associated with botched abortions, which are more common when it is illegal. At least some will also have a personal stake in abortion support because either they or their colleagues will want autonomy to make health decisions and advise women in need of an abortion.[34]

Using data from the last three waves of the WVS, Figure 2.1 presents a scatter plot of the relationship between abortion disapproval and gross domestic product (GDP) per capita and mean levels of education across countries. The correlation between GDP per capita and the proportion of people who say abortion is never justified is 0.54, indicating a strong association. In nations like Mali and the Philippines, where the GDP per capita is below $10,000, over 50% of residents say that abortion is never justified. Conversely, in rich countries like Norway and Switzerland, less than 15% of people say that it is never justified.

---

[34] Petersen, *Abortion Regimes.*

76 FETAL POSITIONS

A similarly robust relationship appears for mean levels of education and abortion disapproval. In societies like Burkina Faso, where the average resident has completed just primary or elementary school (i.e. 1.41), 64% of people report that abortion is never justified. In nations like the United States and Canada, where most residents have graduated from high school (i.e., secondary school), the proportion who say abortion is never justified drops to about 25%. Richer and more educated populations are also more likely to enact laws that allow for abortion on demand (see Figure 0.2 in the Introduction).

Figure 2.1 shows a positive correlation between increases in GDP and education and overall abortion disapproval. But this figure cannot tell us whether educational and economic development have independent associations with attitudes over and above residents' social class position. In other words, are richer and more educated people driving friendlier abortion attitudes? Or is everyone, regardless of income or educational background, more likely to support abortion in economically developed and more educated nations?[35] To further complicate matters, countries with higher levels of economic development tend to have lower levels of religious belief and more democratic governments. Does the societal effect of education and economics remain after accounting for other important societal influences?

Using the appropriate statistical techniques and data from eighty-eight countries, representing the vast majority of the world's population, I examine the influence of a combined measure of economic and educational development on abortion disapproval, while accounting for a host of other individual and country-level factors. The findings appear in Appendix A, Table A.3. Like personal educational attainment and income, I considered examining education and economic development as distinct societal factors. However, as dissected in Appendix A,[36] Table A5, the measures are so

---

[35] This process would be consistent with theories arguing that economic and educational development drive changes in cultural values, as opposed to personal preferences. See Schwartz, "National Culture as Value Orientations"; Hofstede, *Culture's Consequences*; Inglehart and Baker, "Modernization, Cultural Change, and the Persistence of Traditional Values."

[36] Table A.5 in Appendix A shows that when analyzed separately both GDP per capita and societal levels of education are associated with more abortion disapproval (i.e., $p < 0.05$ for a one-tailed test) in the multivariate context. But, when both measures are included in the same model, neither is statistically significant. The correlation between logged GDP and mean levels of education is high (0.55). The Cronbach's alpha, which measures internal consistency reliability, is also high for these two measures (7.10), suggesting that they may be assessing a similar dimension, or that it is difficult to unravel with a sample of eighty-eight countries and several other macro measures. I therefore combined standardized versions of the two variables. The combined measure is statistically significant, as shown in Appendix A, Table A.5, Model 4.

THE ROLE OF ECONOMICS AND EDUCATION 77

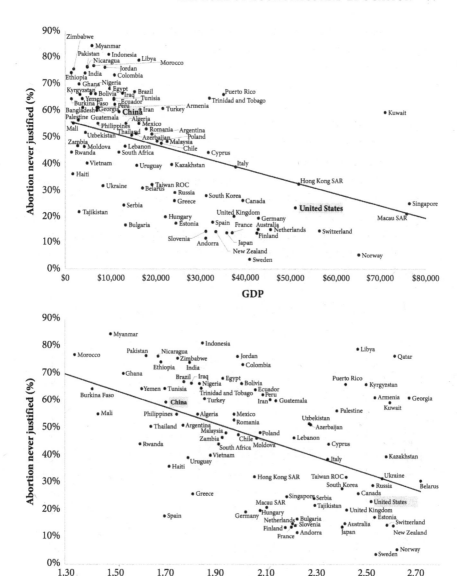

Figure 2.1 Scatterplots of the Relationship between GDP per Capita and Mean Levels of Education for Explaining the Percentage That Disapproves of Abortion in Each Society (N = 88)

Notes: Dots represent societies. For educational level, primary or less is the lowest level (1), followed by some secondary or high school (2), then secondary completed but not university (3), and finally, university completed (4). For GDP per capita, Qatar is not included because it is such an extreme outlier (GDP per capita= $140,000). The average level of abortion disapproval is taken from the weighted mean for the last three waves of the World Values Survey.

Source: WVS, waves 5, 6, and 7

closely related to each other and abortion attitudes that I could not easily disentangle them. Using the combined measure, I find that in more economically and educationally developed nations, residents are more likely to support abortion, even after considering personal income, education, and a host of other characteristics.

Figure 2.2 presents the marginal effects of a combined measure of GDP per capita and mean country levels of education for explaining abortion disapproval, after accounting for all other individual and country characteristics. Residents from societies with low mean levels of education and GDP have an average disapproval score of 8.11 on a scale ranging from 1 to 10, where 10 means abortion is never justified. Conversely, in richer and better educated countries, the average score becomes less disapproving, dropping to 7.36. These estimates account for a host of other national characteristics, such as democracy, population size, and communist history.

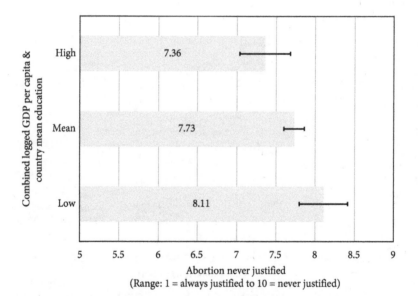

Figure 2.2 Marginal Values for Abortion Disapproval by Three Levels of Combined GDP per Capita and Mean Societal-Levels of Education (Society N = 88; Individual N = 211,317)

Notes: Marginal values are taken from Appendix A, Table A.3, Model 7 and based on two standard deviations above and below the mean. Abortion policy is not included in this model because holding it constant could lead to values that fall outside the normal ranges. But even when policy is included, the marginal values are very similar to those presented here.

Source: WVS, waves 5, 6, and 7

THE ROLE OF ECONOMICS AND EDUCATION   79

Even after controlling for other personal and societal factors, a statistically significant relationship remains between economic and educational development and disapproval of abortion. Within individual countries, one aspect of development (educational levels or economic development) may be more likely to shape attitudes. But across a wide range of countries, both measures account for similar variation in disapproval.[37]

The question that the WVS asks about abortion is not ideal. It does not consider the circumstances surrounding a potential abortion or whether people are asked about support for legal abortion versus their moral views—both of which can drive disapproval (see Chapter 5). However, very few cross-national studies include a large number of people and a range of nations at different levels of economic development that allow for adequate comparisons. Studies that use different survey questions have found that higher levels of development are associated with friendlier views about abortion and similar sexual morality issues,[38] as has research that uses a different set of nations.[39] Likewise, social scientists have shown that more developed nations tend to have more liberal abortion legislation (see also Figure 0.2 in the Introduction).[40] For examining abortion support, the WVS question provides adequate insight into public opinion about abortion across the world.

Economic and Educational Development and Attitudes in China

While most nations have undergone some development stages, they do not transition at the same time or pace. The majority of countries in the Global North went through major industrialization and modernization processes in the eighteenth and nineteenth centuries. England was one of the first to industrialize. Beginning in 1770, the share of English national income from agriculture fell from 45% to just 15% over a hundred-year period.[41] The United States came later to industrialization. But, like England, the

---

[37] See the intraclass correlations in Models 1 and 2 of Table A.5 in Appendix A.

[38] Scheepers, Te Grotenhuis, and Van Der Slik, "Education, Religiosity and Moral Attitudes"; Finke and Adamczyk, "Cross-National Moral Beliefs: The Influence of National Religious Context."

[39] Adamczyk, "Religion as a Micro and Macro Property"; Pitt, "'Thou Shall Not Kill.'" The survey measure on the justifiability of abortion is also correlated with laws about abortion.

[40] Hildebrandt, "What Shapes Abortion Law?"

[41] Cipolla, *Economic History of World Population*.

80   FETAL POSITIONS

proportion of Americans engaged in agriculture dropped from about 50% to less than 5% over a century.[42] More recently, nations have been undergoing developmental changes more quickly.

China is perhaps the premier example of a country that has recently undergone industrialization and modernization at a breakneck pace. Over the thirty-five-year period from 1978 until 2013, the proportion of China's population that worked in agriculture was cut in half, going from 70% to just 35%.[43] Below I explain the important role of China's quickly moving economic development and educational increases in shaping feelings about fertility, family size, and the quality life they desire for their children and themselves—all of which inform abortion views.

Many of the Chinese people I interviewed were fully cognizant of the changes their country had recently experienced. When asked about the forces shaping fertility-related attitudes, they often mentioned economic development and education as influencing abortion views, as well as ideal family size, childrearing desires, and sex education. As a Chinese Catholic nun explained, "So especially nowadays, we have this economic development consequence, because most of us are facing very high pressure in our job market [and if there is an] unwanted pregnancy, they have to get an abortion." Changing opportunities for women also accounted for new perspectives on marriage and deterred interest in having more children. A professor explained, "So now many more women are entering the labor force, and they don't have to depend on their marriages anymore. They don't have to feel like getting married and having children are the only options in their lives." Others talked about the major economic changes happening in both rural and urban areas. One interviewee even mentioned how new roads made it easier for people to travel to different cities in China, exposing residents to new ideas, places, and people. Not all the changes happening in China have resulted from development alone. But given the rapid economic growth and educational expansion the country has experienced in the previous fifty years, they are major contributors.

Because they are so interconnected and undergo processes of economic development and modernization at different speeds and times, countries that are further along can have outsized political power and economic, cultural, and media effects. Interviewees often mentioned Western influences

[42] Inkeles, "Industrialization, Modernization and the Quality of Life."
[43] "Global Agricultural Productivity Report: China's Agricultural Productivity Imperative."

THE ROLE OF ECONOMICS AND EDUCATION   81

when discussing how people in China gained more liberal views about pre-marital sex, family roles, and abortion. As one professor explained, "Chinese society developed so much in the last twenty years and [our parents] didn't know what was happening in other countries. The TV only had government news. But our generations, we have Internet, we have Twitter and Facebook, Google; we go abroad, and we go to other countries to meet people. We know what other people think." A Chinese nun added that because of economic collaboration with other countries, there are now a lot of foreigners; "So that also means some Western values really come to China." A journalist explained that younger generations now know English and can search online for information from other countries, which also influences their views. Many Chinese thought that social and traditional forms of media were accelerating liberal perspectives on women and the family.

Only part of the explanation for why the Chinese had limited media information two decades ago is related to economic development. The Chinese government has a history of closely monitoring[44] and censoring the media. Even today, access to information is still closely controlled by the government, though interviewees often spoke about getting around government censors to access online information.

Chinese interviewees sometimes discussed abortion using a women's rights lens, which is common in Western discourse. As one Chinese professor explained about the outcome of higher educational levels in China, there are "more women's rights discussions. So they will say, well, women should have their own reproductive rights in terms of this issue." A male minister from China added, "As they are getting more and more education, they would think that abortion is women's rights or it's just one of the individual rights." While viewing abortion as a women's right is a common liberal frame, Chinese women have had relatively easy access to abortion since 1957.[45] Moreover, the government's one-child policy made it challenging for many Chinese women to have more than one child,[46] severely limiting reproductive rights in a different way. Most of the Chinese I interviewed only

---

[44] Despite state censorship about some issues, respondents from different occupational backgrounds (e.g., civil service employees, academics, journalists, religious leaders, survey researchers, etc.) made clear that discussions about abortion were not something they felt the Chinese government was concerned about monitoring or restricting. Indeed, several noted that an American researcher asking about social movement activities, rather than about abortion views, would have been much more provocative than my study.

[45] Rigdon, "Abortion Law and Practice in China."

[46] Feng, Gu, and Cai, "The End of China's One-Child Policy."

82 FETAL POSITIONS

used the women's rights frame with regards to abortion. Given the history of the one-child policy and limited ability to challenge the government, many Chinese may only be able to apply the women's rights narrative to liberal abortion access, rather than to control over women's bodies more generally.

Although some exceptions applied to the one-child policy (e.g., ethnic minorities, rural residents, rich people), as noted previously, the policy was particularly draconian for many couples. Chinese residents who did not have permission to have a second child would have to pay a large fine that could cost several years' worth of wages and government jobs could be jeopardized.[47] A male Chinese Christian minister told me that growing up he had a friend whose nickname was "Six Thousand Dollars" because that is the massive fine his parents paid when they had him as their second child. Another respondent explained that in addition to lacking money for the fine, her parents only had one child because they were concerned that a second one would negatively affect their work positions. For a woman who had an unanticipated pregnancy that violated national policy, an abortion was often the only reasonable choice. In China, globalizing forces, especially from Western and highly developed nations, may have contributed to the underlying logic for viewing abortion as a women's right's concern rather than as a potential form of oppression the government could use to limit family size.

During the 1950s, China valued big families in part because much of the population was living in rural areas and children could help sustain family farms. But the overall population was especially large and quickly growing. As one interviewee explained, "We could not afford to feed all these people and find jobs for them." In the late 1970s, the Chinese government began implementing the one-child policy to help control the population size. During the same period, other Asia countries also had high birthrates.[48] However, they never took such drastic policy measures, and their fertility rates eventually decreased. Today, there is much debate about whether the one-child policy was necessary.[49] As one Chinese faculty member explained, "I think that if they never had that policy ever, I think the birthrate would finally go down like Korea and Japan. They never had that one-child policy. It's just, with the social development, with the financial issues, like with women getting into work [the birth rate decreased]."

[47] Liao, "The One-Child Policy."
[48] World Bank, "Fertility Rate, Total (Births per Woman)—East Asia & Pacific Data."
[49] Gietel-Basten, Han, and Cheng, "Assessing the Impact of the 'One-Child Policy' in China."

THE ROLE OF ECONOMICS AND EDUCATION   83

Researchers have found that higher levels of economic development are strongly associated with lower fertility rates.[50] As a result of industrialization and modernization processes, people move from rural areas where agriculture dominates to cities where children are no longer a work-related asset. Related to the shifting cultural values that these changes bring, parents increasingly want to give their children a high-quality life, including a strong education that will make them competitive and may produce a more fulfilling life. This is easier to do with smaller families and is referred to as the "demographic-economic paradox" (i.e., people in richer nations, who can most afford them, have fewer children).

Although Chinese parents today can have more kids, giving them all a very good life is more challenging because China is especially costly for raising children. A 2022 report found that China was the second most expensive among the countries examined for bringing up children.[51] A major reason for the high cost is the expense and limited availability of childcare and price of college. Until recently, preschools in China were mostly private. Likewise, compared to other countries, such as the United States, the Chinese are less likely to use student loans to fund college (thus burdening parents).

Across the Chinese interviews, respondents were clear and consistent in saying that the majority of Chinese parents are worried about giving their children the best life possible, which shaped how many parents thought about the ideal family size and the importance of abortion. In 2021, the Chinese government changed its family policy to allow couples to have up to three children.[52] But for many Chinese, the new policy did little to change their minds about the ideal family size. A Chinese Christian minister explained that the policy modification would have made it possible for him and his wife to have a second child, but they chose not to, and "the first and foremost reason is economics." He added that because raising a child is so expensive for people from his generation, "[if] they get pregnant, they will choose the abortion." A Chinese doctor who performs abortions noted, "[When women] choose whether or not have [a] third baby, they will most likely consider economic factors and then policy factors." Concerns about the affordability of children dominated discussions about abortion in China.

---

[50] Lesthaeghe, "The Unfolding Story of the Second Demographic Transition"; Panopoulou and Tsakloglou, "Fertility and Economic Development."
[51] Korea was the most expensive. Tappe, "Child Care Is Expensive Everywhere. But This Country Tops the List."
[52] BBC, "China Allows Three Children in Major Policy Shift."

84   FETAL POSITIONS

Many of the Chinese I interviewed saw themselves as liberal. They also thought that China had made a lot of economic and educational progress over the past thirty years. From a development perspective, the nation has advanced considerably. Consistent with research in cultural sociology, many cultural values have adjusted along with increases in economic and educational development. Respondents spoke about the role of development in shaping support for women's rights and abortion access. But they typically did not draw a connection between women's rights and fertility control. The one-child policy and authoritarian government limited some progressive views that might have otherwise emerged with economic and educational development.

Creating Space for "Options" in American Abortion Discourse

Like many Chinese respondents, Americans on both sides of the abortion debate spoke about the role of societal forces related to economics and education in shaping abortion views. However, an important point of contrast emerged in their divergent understandings of what choice meant, which I discuss in this section.

Similar to the Chinese, many Americans saw the educational or economic justification for having an abortion as connected to the values that development encourages: choice, freedom, and rights. As one professor explained, "A woman who makes a decision to have an abortion is making a decision that, like I'm going to invest in my life or my economic opportunity or I'm going to invest in a better economic reality for my existing children." Respondents generally thought that education and economics were important for liberalizing attitudes about abortion.

Like the Chinese, Americans were also concerned about the high expense of having children and the pressure to limit family size, which contributed to more progressive views. Many respondents thought that abortion gave women more control over their bodies and lives than they would otherwise have. However, in contrast to the Americans, Chinese interviewees were less likely to question the rationale for why women should abort an unplanned pregnancy. US respondents, especially those more opposed to abortion, were more likely to push back on the idea that getting an abortion is the ideal choice in this wealthy country. For example, one professor thought that economic development in the United States has led to a "throwaway culture," whereby people feel comfortable discarding things that should be valued, like fetuses. When discussing prenatal tests that detect abnormalities, he added that "we can discard [the embryos] without feeling too bad about it." In criticizing the idea that abortion is "a woman's choice," a respondent from a pro-life nongovernment organization (NGO) explained that "it's cheaper to fund abortion and birth control than it is to provide programming to those who are in low-income households." Another pro-life respondent from an NGO added, "In a perfect feminist utopia, a woman wouldn't have to choose between her career or her education and becoming a mother because a support system would be there for that." For this respondent, "feminism" includes having the economic and social support system to raise an unexpected child *and* still pursue educational and career goals.

Although many Chinese respondents empathized with the sense of loss an abortion could bring, they were more willing to accept abortion as a reasonable solution to the challenge of an unanticipated pregnancy. Part of their willingness to accept and adapt was no doubt related to the history of the one-child policy, which many accepted as necessary for the country's development, at least initially. The policy also meant that many of my interviewees did not have siblings and were quite comfortable with raising an only child. Additionally, as noted above, the Chinese government limits free speech and social movement activities, which may have added to their sense of resolution (see also Chapter 3). Conversely, in the United States, people were much more critical of the prevailing government, economic, and social support systems. Some were especially frustrated with pro-choice supporters who they felt reconciled themselves to the idea that abortion was a reasonable choice, rather than fighting for a better system that could help women keep unanticipated pregnancies. In the next and final section, I switch gears to discuss the moderating influence of development in shaping the link between personal religious beliefs and abortion attitudes.

Interrelationship between Personal Religious Importance and Development

In Chapter 1, I showed that religion has a powerful influence on abortion disapproval. In many countries, however, religious belief is declining, which

86   FETAL POSITIONS

some scholars have attributed to increases in education and economic development. Regardless of the specific mechanisms, religion is countries like the United States is indeed waning. Nevertheless, I make the case in this section that personal religious beliefs may have a stronger effect on abortion disapproval in richer and more educated countries because norms and values regarding a host of issues, including abortion, are less certain, increasing religion's relevancy. WVS data are then used to test these ideas.

Several theorists, including sociology's forefathers (i.e., Marx, Durkheim, and Weber) argued that as nations become more developed, religious belief would decline.[53] Studies have found a correlation between higher economic development and educational levels and lower religious engagement and belief.[54] However, among developed nations, the United States is an important outlier because it continues to house a high proportion of religious residents. Nevertheless, even there, religious faith and engagement are beginning to wane.

At the beginning of the twenty-first century, studies began trickling in to suggest that religious belief in the United States was declining.[55] From 1999 to 2020, the proportion of Americans who reported belonging to a church, synagogue, or mosque dropped from 70% to 47%, which is substantial.[56] Nevertheless, the United States continues to have much higher levels of religious belief than Western European countries. Additionally, the findings in Appendix A show that personal religious beliefs and national religious cultures influence abortion support, even after accounting for educational and economic development, as well as democracy and a host of other characteristics. Additionally, in countries like Poland and the United States, religion-inspired activism has been a major force in limiting abortion access, illustrating religion's ongoing relevance.[57] Hence, even though religious belief in some societies is declining, it is likely to remain a potent force for directing people's views about abortion.

While personal religious beliefs shape attitudes even after accounting for educational and economic development, some research has suggested that personal religious beliefs may have a greater influence on attitudes in more developed nations, offering novel insight into why abortion has remained

[53] Martin, *On Secularization*; Norris and Inglehart, *Sacred and Secular*.
[54] Pew Research Center, "The Age Gap in Religion around the World."
[55] Pew Research Center, "In U.S., Decline of Christianity Continues at Rapid Pace."
[56] Jones, "U.S. Church Membership Falls below Majority for First Time."
[57] Jacqueline Heinen and Stéphane Portet, "Reproductive Rights in Poland: When Politicians Fear the Wrath of the Church"; Williams, "This Really Is a Different Pro-Life Movement."

an important issue in these countries. Sociologists of religion have found that religion tends to have its biggest effect on attitudes toward behaviors that can be viewed as deviant or immoral, such as abortion, alcohol use, and same-sex relationships, where there is ambiguity in the larger culture about their acceptability. By contrast, personal religious beliefs have less of an effect on views related to murder or rape, where everyone is likely to think they are problematic. In the 1960s, sociologists of religion began to recognize this distinction and proposed the antiascetic hypothesis (i.e., a lack of self-discipline) to explain the phenomenon.[58]

The antiascetic hypothesis posits that when the government has put certain laws in place that govern behaviors, then there are likely to be strong values, norms, and beliefs associated with them as well. Because secular laws regulate these behaviors, personal religious beliefs are less likely to shape people's attitudes about their acceptability.[59] For example, in most countries it would be hard to find someone who thinks that murder should be legal. Thus, for the most part, there is no room for ambiguity that urges people to seek religious justification.

Conversely, when there is more ambiguity about the rightness or wrongness of a given issue, religious beliefs are more likely to play a role in shaping how they are viewed. When people feel that religion is important, they will be more engaged in their religion. As a result, they will get more exposure to information about the problematic aspects of various antiascetic behaviors, like drugs and alcohol use, sex outside of marriage, and same-sex relationships, which many religions discourage.[60] People who are not religious are less likely to regularly hear that these things are unacceptable because religious leaders, rather than secular authorities (e.g., government, laws, etc.), are primarily disseminating this information. Religious beliefs are more likely to shape behaviors and related attitudes that have been condemned explicitly by religion, even if the larger society does not find them particularly problematic. Consistent with the antiascetic hypothesis,

---

[58] Burkett and White, "Hellfire and Delinquency"; Hadaway, Elifson, and Petersen, "Religious Involvement and Drug Use among Urban Adolescents"; Tittle and Welch, "Religiosity and Deviance."

[59] Finke and Adamczyk, "Cross-National Moral Beliefs: The Influence of National Religious Context."

[60] Amy Adamczyk, "Understanding Delinquency with Friendship Group Religious Context"; Finke and Adamczyk, "Cross-National Moral Beliefs: The Influence of National Religious Context"; Amy Adamczyk and Cassady Pitt, "Shaping Attitudes about Homosexuality: The Role of Religion and Cultural Context"; Reisig, Wolfe, and Pratt, "Low Self-Control and the Religiosity-Crime Relationship."

88 FETAL POSITIONS

a number of studies have found that strength of religious belief tends to be related to the disapproval of deviant and sexual morality issues, like same-sex relationships, substance use, and premarital sex, as well as abortion.[61]

Based on the logic of the antiascetic hypothesis, personal religious importance should have a greater influence on abortion disapproval in countries with higher levels of educational and economic development. Nations that are richer and better educated should produce more ambiguity about the rightness and wrongness of a range of deviance and morality issues, including abortion. In these countries, residents are not tied so closely to the larger group, and there is a greater emphasis on self-expression and individualism. There may be a smaller proportion of religious people in richer and better-educated societies. However, religion may matter more in shaping adherents' views in these societies than others. Conversely, religious beliefs may be less directive in shaping attitudes about deviant and moral issues in less-developed countries where people are more ideologically connected to their families, friends, and communities. In these societies, religion will be one of many authority sources proscribing behaviors like abortion.

Drawing on data from the WVS, Figure 2.3 depicts the moderating influence of overall education and economic development on the relationship between personal religious beliefs and abortion disapproval. The analysis used to create Figure 2.3 is taken from Model 2 of Table A.4 in Appendix A, which shows a statistically significant interaction between a country's level of development and personal religious beliefs for explaining abortion attitudes. For residents from countries with lower overall levels of education and wealth, the difference in abortion disapproval for various levels of religious importance is fairly minimal. But for people in the richest and most educated nations, there are larger differences in the level of abortion support. In the poorest and least-educated countries, people who say religion is very important have a disapproval score of 8.47 on a scale ranging from 0 (abortion is always justified) to 10 (abortion is never justified). Residents who report that religion is not important at all have a score of 7.79—less than a one-point difference. Conversely, in countries with the highest levels of education and wealth (i.e., the United States and Western Europe), the most religious adherents (i.e., religion very important in life) have a disapproval

---

[61] Adamczyk, "Understanding Delinquency with Friendship Group Religious Context"; Finke and Adamczyk, "Cross-National Moral Beliefs: The Influence of National Religious Context"; Adamczyk, *Cross-National Public Opinion about Homosexuality*; Adamczyk and Palmer, "Religion and Initiation into Marijuana Use."

level of about 7.88. The least-religious people (i.e., religion is not at all important) in these countries have a score that is more than two points lower at 5.60.

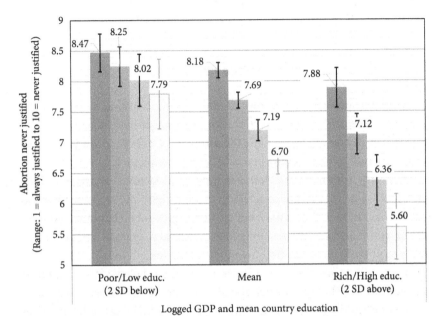

Figure 2.3 Marginal Effects for the Interaction between Education and Economic Development and Four Levels of Personal Religious Importance for Explaining Abortion Disapproval (Society N = 88; Individual N = 211,317)

Notes: Estimates are taken from Appendix A, Table A.4, Model 2. All other variables are held constant. Abortion policy is not included in this model to keep the value range realistic. But when included, the marginal values are very similar to those presented here.

Source: WVS, waves 5, 6, and 7

By combining ideas from the antiascetic hypothesis[62] and cultural sociology,[63] the findings here show that education and economic development boost the effect of religious importance. Personal religious beliefs are more strongly associated with abortion disapproval in more developed nations,

---

[62] Hadaway, Elifson, and Petersen, "Religious Involvement and Drug Use among Urban Adolescents"; Tittle and Welch, "Religiosity and Deviance."
[63] Inglehart and Baker, "Modernization, Cultural Change, and the Persistence of Traditional Values."

90   FETAL POSITIONS

which are more likely to be characterized by normative ambiguity.[64] Far from becoming irrelevant, in many rich and well-educated societies, abortion is a controversial issue for religious people. Abortion is likely to remain a divisive topic for religious adherents, especially in countries with high levels of economic development, where normative ambiguity is more prevalent.

Conclusion

This chapter focused on how money and education lead to more abortion support. Increasing wages and education often usher in changes to cultural values that trickle down to shape the attitudes of everyone within society. While overall levels of education and income explain much of the same variation in cross-national views, as individual factors they have unique influences. The survey findings also provide insight into why the abortion debate has remained so contested in richer and more educated nations. When norms and values are ambiguous, personal religious beliefs are more likely to provide direction for how people feel about abortion.

In both China and the United States, respondents believed that economic and educational changes affected abortion attitudes. Having been influenced by the one-child policy, as well as the particularly high cost of having children, Chinese respondents felt that most residents would think that abortion is useful in helping provide a "quality" life for themselves and existing children. Conversely, Americans were more likely to challenge the idea that abortion is a reasonable response to an unanticipated pregnancy and the high cost of having children. Additionally, American respondents were more cognizant of how the government may inadvertently restrict fertility-related options for poor and minority women.

---

[64] Halman and van Ingen also found that a greater diversity of perspectives in Western Europe, relative to Eastern Europe, led to a stronger relationship between church attendance and moral attitudes in Western Europe.

Chapter 3
Democracy, Laws, and Policy in Shaping Abortion Views

> No matter how popular social media is in China, I still think that public opinion is quite constrained. You don't hear a lot of different voices, even though the voices may not all come from the state. The voices are quite monotonous. That's how successful our government is.
>
> —Chinese researcher

Across the world, the ability to protest, discuss, politically organize, and vote have been important factors in determining the extent to which people can tolerate new ideas, stand up for rights, and be themselves in public. Democracy is closely related to people's willingness to engage in these activities and express themselves. To understand the abortion debate—liberal laws that allow for abortion on demand and conservative attitudes that condemn abortion—democracy and the ideas it engenders are key.

This chapter examines how governments influence views on abortion. I begin by unpacking the processes that democracy engenders, explaining how generic democratic developments can shape attitudes and behaviors related to abortion. I then focus on the specific role of democracy in influencing abortion attitudes and policies, which are interrelated. Drawing on an analysis of over 800 newspaper articles from 41 countries that mention abortion, I also show that in more democratic nations, newspapers are more likely to talk about abortion from a range of different perspectives, including gender equality, rights, religion, and morality. Next, I discuss the differences between the United States and China and the role democracy plays in forming public opinion and policies related to abortion. Finally, I examine how the media both shapes democratic processes and encourages the exchange of information that further contributes to tolerance.

Democracy's Influence

In democracies, citizens vote for officials who represent their ideas and concerns. Once elected, ideally these politicians will develop policies and laws that reflect the public's interest. In the United States, which has a strong democracy,[1] several respondents commented on its role in shaping the vibrant abortion debate.[2] As one professor explained, "Politicians have been able to leverage abortion because you have a lot of people who are willing to vote for candidates who are antiabortion." Since the public is seen as having a primary role in directing laws and policies, more democratic nations have outlets, like newspapers, social media, public forums, and other avenues, where people's views can be heard. Likewise, in democracies residents can collectively indicate their preferences through protest and social movement activities. An editor at a US-based pro-life journal explained, "Americans are invited all the time to advocate for what they believe in, and, we are a very right's conscious people, because that's how we were founded. And that's good and healthy." She saw Americans as concerned about preserving and defending the rights of individuals.

In democracies, residents are able to petition the government or even protest against it to get their views heard and their rights respected. Conversely, in less-representative societies, citizens are less likely to criticize the government or express views inconsistent with official policies because protesting may have legal consequences. China has a one-party communist dictatorship and routinely scores low on measures of democracy. When asked how the Chinese feel about various fertility-related restrictions, including the one-child policy, a Buddhist monk explained, "Even if people blamed the government, it would be a very private conversation. They wouldn't criticize the government in public." A Chinese Christian minister added that "[there is] an unspoken consensus among my colleagues that we won't on the pulpit say brothers, sisters do not get abortions. . . . And my guess is that because we have the one-child policy, which is kind of like a constitution." Although this religious leader was opposed to abortion because he felt it was "against the will of God," the power of China's non-democratic government kept him from preaching against it. Not only might residents

---

[1] Freedom House, "Countries and Territories Global Freedom Index."
[2] See also Halfmann, *Doctors and Demonstrators*.

DEMOCRACY, LAWS, AND POLICY IN SHAPING ABORTION VIEWS   93

fear legal consequences in less-democratic societies, but there may also be a lack of information and transparency.

Because democracies allow for greater access to different media and communication, residents have more exposure to ideas and perspectives that differ from the norm, which can encourage tolerance.[3] Likewise, well-run democracies embody ideals and standards for government behavior[4] (e.g., equality, fairness, impartiality, and the right to demonstrate) that can increase understanding of people who violate conventional behaviors. Indeed, researchers have found that residents from democratic nations have more supportive views about same-sex relationships, prostitution, extra-marital sex, and marijuana use.[5] We would therefore anticipate that people from democracies would also be less disapproving of abortion because they are aware of the wide range of circumstances that might require an abortion. Likewise, they should be less likely to view abortion through a single lens, like morality or religion. Finally, they should regularly witness their government acting in fair and impartial ways, establishing dominant norms of what is acceptable. Even people who have never gotten or who will never need an abortion may feel compelled to support abortion rights. Ideally, within democracies, residents should support the rights of others, leading to a culture whereby citizens' rights are less likely to be violated.

When examining dozens of countries worldwide, to what extent does democracy influence abortion attitudes? Figure 3.1 presents the marginal values of democracy in shaping abortion disapproval on a scale ranging from 1 to 10. These estimates are taken from Table A.3 in Appendix A. For the eighty-eight countries examined in this analysis, residents from societies with either a partial (i.e., anocracy) or full democracy have a value of 7.66. Conversely, people living in non-democratic nations (i.e., autocracies) have a score of 8.10, indicating greater opposition than residents from more democratic places.

Among the eighty-eight nations examined, the societies coded as non-democratic are Belarus, China, Palestine, Iran, Iraq, Jordan, Kuwait, Lebanon, Libya, Macau, Morocco, Qatar, and Vietnam. All others are designated as partial or full democracies. In a separate analysis, I also assessed whether there were statistically significant differences between partial versus

---

[3] Thompson, *The Democratic Citizen*.

[4] Guérin, Petry, and Crête, "Tolerance, Protest and Democratic Transition."

[5] Hadler, "The Influence of World Societal Forces on Social Tolerance. A Time Comparative Study of Prejudices in 32 Countries"; Adamczyk, *Cross-National Public Opinion about Homosexuality*.

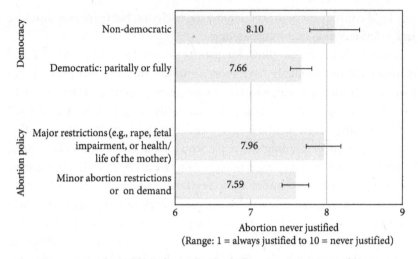

Figure 3.1 Marginal Values for Individual Abortion Disapproval by a Country's Democracy Status and Abortion Policy (Society N = 88; Individual N = 211,317)

Note: The United Nations' polity score captures the regime's authority spectrum. Each society was initially given a score ranging from −10 (hereditary monarchy) to +10 (consolidated democracy) on a 21-point scale. The UN then converted the scores into three regime categories: autocracies (−10 to −6), anocracies (−5 to +5), and democracies (+6 to +10). I further combined the anocracies (or semi-democracies) and democracies for a dichotomous outcome, as the major attitudinal division appears between non-democratic and all other countries. The countries that were coded as non-democratic were Belarus, China, Palestine, Iran, Iraq, Jordan, Kuwait, Lebanon, Libya, Macau SAR, Morocco, Qatar, and Vietnam. The abortion policy provides information on the different array of policies within each country. In a separate analysis, I examined how different types of policies and groups of policies were associated with abortion attitudes, finding that the clearest division is between the major and minor restrictions indicated here. Because some policies shifted over the time period being examined, the most consistent policy over the period is indicated. At the time in both the United States and Poland, abortion was legal. Marginal values are generated from the mixed-modeling results found in Appendix A, Table A.3, Model 8. All other variables in the model are held constant.

Sources: United Nations' polity score; WVS, waves 5, 6, and 7

full democracies. I did not find any differences. The key distinction seems to be between non-democratic nations and all others. Hence, even moving from a dictatorship to a partial democracy, which mixes democratic and autocratic features, leads to more supportive views.

Many societies coded as non-democratic have other characteristics that distinguish them, including a highly religious population. The analysis that produced the estimates in Figure 3.1 accounts for several potential confounding characteristics, including overall levels of religious belief, economic development, communist history, abortion policy, and population

DEMOCRACY, LAWS, AND POLICY IN SHAPING ABORTION VIEWS   95

size. Additionally, these findings control for differences in personal characteristics, like income, education, marital status, and gender.

As noted in the Chapter 2, increases in economic development and education can contribute to cultures that are more supportive of democratic values. As people become more secure, more resources become available to help others, and residents may have the funds to consider how they may support everyone within their country. Indeed, economic development may be only one pathway through which democratic ideals develop. However, the findings here show that even after accounting for economic-related development, democracy is meaningfully related to abortion support.

Other studies have found a correlation between democracy-related measures and more liberal policies and laws.[6] But, the findings in Figure 3.1 are some of the first to show the influence of democracy in shaping individuals' attitudes. Regardless of their personal attributes (e.g., religious belief, marital status, income, education, and age), residents in more democratic nations are more supportive of abortion than others. The democratic culture that pervades these countries shapes the views of all residents.

People living in countries with more robust democracies tend to have more liberal views about abortion. But other processes can complicate democracy's influence.[7] Likewise, the duration of democracy matters. Learning tolerance through democratic institutions and cultures takes time.[8] In more democratic societies, residents become more tolerant toward others, especially those they may not personally know or like, by engaging in democratic elections and learning about disputes over freedom and rights through the media. Many may also use democratic methods, like nonviolent protest, to challenge the government, and will witness their government uphold civil liberties and rights of unpopular groups.[9] A Chinese researcher who now lives in the United States drove home this point:

We rarely go to protests or sittings or demonstrations [in the United States], even for a lot of well-known movements, because it's something that was

[6] Minkenberg, "Religion and Public Policy Institutional, Cultural, and Political Impact on the Shaping of Abortion Policies in Western Democracies"; Hildebrandt, "What Shapes Abortion Law?"
[7] Halfmann, *Doctors and Demonstrators.*
[8] Hadler, "The Influence of World Societal Forces on Social Tolerance. A Time Comparative Study of Prejudices in 32 Countries"; Peffley and Rohrschneider, "Democratization and Political Tolerance in Seventeen Countries."
[9] Nelson, Clawson, and Oxley, "Media Framing of a Civil Liberties Conflict and Its Effect on Tolerance."

96 FETAL POSITIONS

absent in our culture as kids. We never experienced that when we were in China. So, we don't know how to do that.

Conversely, a pro-choice advocate from the United States lamented the high levels of Americans' engagement on both sides of the abortion debate: "There are abortion providers out there who grew up protesting abortion clinics because that's what their families did and that's what they were taught was the correct thing." Regardless of your side of the debate, democracy seems to encourage advocacy even as people shift sides.

Under the umbrella of democracy, several essential processes—policy, media, gender equality, and social movement activity—are relevant for understanding cross-national abortion attitudes. Below I discuss the interrelationship between policy and abortion views. I then move into a discussion about the media. Social movements and gender equality are also important for understanding how attitudes and policies are shaped. Chapter 4 discusses the important roles that gender equality and social movements play, especially in the United States, in shaping abortion attitudes, policies, and democratic engagement more generally.

Abortion Policy

An essential element of democracies is that residents select the people who represent them politically. Elected officials should be motivated to establish policies consistent with public preferences (i.e., policy feedback and responsiveness[10]). Because residents' perspectives shape laws and policies, when they have strong policy-related preferences they can advocate for officials to pass ones that are consistent with their views, urge politicians to appoint people (e.g., Supreme Court justices) who are likely to consider the majority's attitudes, and advocate for referendums where the public can directly vote on the issues of greatest concern.[11] If politicians do not listen, the public can oust them from office and elect others. Elected officials want to keep their jobs, money, and power. Hence, they are often magnifying glasses for the constituents who voted for them, and many politicians hold to the ideologies of those they represent. Below, I discuss the relationship

[10] Busemeyer, "Policy Feedback and Government Responsiveness in a Comparative Perspective"; Brooks and Manza, "Social Policy Responsiveness in Developed Democracies."

[11] Page and Shapiro, "Effects of Public Opinion on Policy"; Burstein, "Bringing the Public Back In."

between democracy and abortion laws and policies, showing their close correspondence.

Much research has examined the relationship between the public's atti-tudes and policies. To some extent, the alignment between public opinions and laws depends on the issue being examined. When residents have a lot of information on a given topic, can easily understand it, and is heavily invested, their views are more likely to align with policy. For many, abortion is highly salient because it can directly affect their health, career prospects, ability to care for other children, and family formation. For others, it may be seen as a relatively uncomplicated moral issue.[12] Although it varies substan-tially across regions and countries, of the roughly 121 million *unintended* pregnancies that occur each year worldwide, approximately 61% end in abortion.[13] Hence, many people will either obtain an abortion themselves or will have friends and loved ones who have, though abortion behavior does not always translate into more liberal views. In the political science literature, abortion is often described as morality politics because a large portion of the public has strong and uncompromising views.[14] As a morality issue, abortion often captures the attention of democratically elected official, bureaucrats, and interest groups. Indeed, the subject of abortion has dominated many political debates,[15] though not everywhere.

Research done within specific countries[16] has found that abortion laws and policies tend to align with public preferences about abortion. When examining dozens of countries across the world, what is the relationship between attitudes and laws? Using data from eighty-eight societies from the World Values Survey (WVS), which represents the vast majority of the world's population, I find that in the thirty countries with the most liberal attitudes (i.e., less than 33% of people say that abortion is never justified), all but one society (Andorra) permits abortion on demand. Conversely, in the twenty most conservative societies, where more than 66% of people say that abortion is never justified, only 25% of them allow for abortion on demand.

[12] Mooney, "The Public Clash of Private Values."

[13] Bearak et al., "Unintended Pregnancy and Abortion by Income, Region, and the Legal Status of Abortion."

[14] Mooney, "The Public Clash of Private Values"; Norrander and Wilcox, "Public Opinion and Policymaking in the States."

[15] Mooney and Lee, "Legislative Morality in the American States."

[16] In the United States, for example, within certain parameters set by *Roe v. Wade* states could decide how to regulate abortion, restricting the use of public funds to pay for them, enacting waiting period laws, and requiring parental consent for minors to obtain abortions. Many of these policies were decided through referendums, which tended to align with residents' views.

98   FETAL POSITIONS

The relationship is not perfect, but there is consistency between abortion attitudes and laws. Below I discuss the three major democratic processes (legislative, judicial, and referendum) through which abortion-related laws and policies are often implemented.

Until the end of the nineteenth century, abortion was criminalized throughout most of the world. By importing laws from their own countries, the colonizing empires of Britain, France, Portugal, Spain, and Italy were largely responsible for making abortion illegal throughout the world.[17] The national laws that many countries adopted in the late 1800s typically permitted abortion to save the mother's life. Because pregnant women were prone to complications that could result in death, this was a reasonable and common provision. The conditions that could meet this criterion were broad and included cardiovascular disease, tuberculosis, and even "pernicious vomiting."[18] Russia is considered the first modern state to legalize abortion, which it did in 1920. However, in 1936 Russia made abortion illegal again because Stalin believed that a more populous country would conjure greater power.[19] Other factors gradually emerged in Western countries that made abortion a debated issue.

Beginning in the 1960s, medical advances made it increasingly rare for a woman's pregnancy to endanger her life. More importantly, the burst of feminist-oriented social movement activity in the late 1960s and 1970s led to changing views about abortion as a women's rights issue, allowing females to enact more control over their bodies and lives. People who were opposed to abortion emphasized its moral dimension, framing abortion as a right to life for the unborn. The contemporary debate in many countries, especially Christian-majority societies, has focused on these competing notions of rights.[20]

The public's views about abortion can be a major driver of its legal status, with changes mostly taking place through legislative or judicial branches of government or by referendum.[21] Beginning in the 1960s, Denmark, France, and Britain enacted more liberal abortion-related laws and policies.[22] After heated debate in 1967, for example, Britain's parliament voted

[17] Berer, "Abortion Law and Policy around the World"; Brookman-Amissah and Moyo, "Abortion Law Reform in Sub-Saharan Africa."
[18] Glendon, *Abortion and Divorce in Western Law.*
[19] Ferris-Rotman, "Putin's Next Target Is Russia's Abortion Culture."
[20] Lovenduski, "Feminism and Western European Politics."
[21] Brooks, "Abortion Policy in Western Democracies."
[22] Brooks.

for the Abortion Act, which allowed women to obtain abortions from medical practitioners on certain grounds and regulated the tax-paid provision of abortions through the National Health Service. Similarly, in 1973 the US Supreme Court ruled that the Constitution conferred the right of a woman to have an abortion. When the same branch of government overturned *Roe v. Wade* in 2022, women no longer had a federal constitutional right to an abortion.[23] Instead, each of the fifty states was given the power to decide its own abortion-related laws. While some states moved to guarantee the right to an abortion in their constitutions, others banned abortion in almost all circumstances, including incest and rape.[24] Chapter 4 provides additional insight into the factors that gave rise to the recent legal change (i.e., *Dobbs v. Jackson*) in the United States.

The final democratic process through which abortion legislation tends to change is through referendum. Often referred to as direct democracy, referendums ask voters whether they approve of a specific type of legislation. In 1983, Ireland had a referendum on abortion that resulted in support for existing legislation that continued to make it illegal under almost all circumstances. Thirty-five years later, in 2018, the same referendum process legalized abortion, with 66% of residents voting to repeal the existing restrictive law.[25] Similarly, Switzerland and Italy used referendums to liberalize abortion-related laws and policies. At least with regards to abortion, which is a topic the public often knows, understands, and may feel passionately about, referendums on the legality of abortion tend to mirror public sentiment.[26]

Through legislative or judicial changes or referendums, abortion laws can become more liberal or conservative. In the United States, in 2022, the Supreme Court ruled that abortion is no longer a constitutional right, and in 2021 Poland's legislature made abortion illegal in most circumstances. But referendums in Ireland and Italy legalized abortion on demand. Just as abortion attitudes have become more supportive across the Global North since the 1970s, abortion-related laws and policies have generally become more liberal globally.[27] Hence, the conservative turn in Poland and the United States is unusual.

---

[23] "19-1392 Dobbs v. Jackson Women's Health Organization."
[24] Center for Reproductive Rights, "Abortion Laws by State."
[25] Suiter, "Deliberation in Action—Ireland's Abortion Referendum."
[26] Arceneaux, "Direct Democracy and the Link between Public Opinion and State Abortion Policy"; Brooks, "Abortion Policy in Western Democracies."
[27] Brooks, "Abortion Policy in Western Democracies."

100 FETAL POSITIONS

While in many countries abortion laws and policies are often the most important issue being discussed,[28] there are clear exceptions. In less-democratic societies, abortion may not be an important public opinion or legal issue because the state may not want residents' views informing abortion-related laws and policies. As a result, governments may limit the discourse surrounding it. As noted above, China has a one-party dictatorship whereby the Communist Party has a monopoly on power. Consistent with the non-democratic nature of China, many of the residents I interviewed seemed surprised by my question about whether the public thinks that abortion is acceptable. They could easily talk about how they thought women might personally feel about getting an abortion or the circumstances that might lead someone to obtain one. But there was much less discussion about the general rightness or wrongness of the issue.

One social scientist who conducts survey research in China said to me that there is no structure for the Chinese to think about the rightness or wrongness of abortion. There is no religious or moral framework, nor is there a strong women's rights perspective on the issue. As noted in Chapter 2, however, there may be some importing of various frameworks (e.g., feminist) from other countries for viewing abortion. He suggested that the major reason for the lack of public discussion about abortion is the non-democratic nature of the Chinese government, which has prevented alternative perspectives and interpretations of abortion through the media, social movements, and other forms of organizing and advocating, which would also expose people to a wider range of perspectives on the issue. Additionally, China has low levels of religious belief. As noted in Chapter 1, the dominant belief and value systems (i.e., Buddhism, Taoism, Confucianism) do not elicit high levels of commitment as traditionally measured and understood,[29] further limiting the likelihood that a religious framework would be used in abortion discussions.

On the other side of the spectrum, in June 2022 the US Supreme Court overturned a constitutional right to an abortion, which women had been guaranteed for the previous forty-nine years. The change was especially surprising because the majority of Americans were opposed to overturning the original *Roe v. Wade* decision. According to a national public opinion poll

---

[28] Jelen and Wilcox, "Causes and Consequences of Public Attitudes toward Abortion"; Adamczyk, Kim, and Dillon, "Examining Public Opinion about Abortion."
[29] Stark and Finke, *Acts of Faith.*

taken right before the ruling, 61% of Americans said that abortion should be legal in all or most cases.[30]

The US public does not directly elect Supreme Court justices. Rather the country's president appoints them, and once confirmed, the justices can remain in office for life. Although, the US government could codify a woman's right to an abortion, when *Roe v. Wade* was overturned, abortion-rights supporters had not elected enough congressional officials to change the law. A Chinese professor put it succinctly in explaining that in the United States "[abortion] became politicized because of the democratic process that needs to secure voters." As I detail in Chapter 4, pro-life advocates have been working for years to enact more stringent abortion laws and policies, in part by electing officials who support their agenda. With the 2022 *Dobbs v. Jackson Women's Health Organization* Supreme Court decision, individual states got to determine the legal status of abortion. While many states quickly added more supports for abortion, others made it illegal, with state responses largely determined by their constituents.

This section has focused on the relationship between attitudes and abortion laws and policies. While studies have found a link between them, the causal order and the processes connecting them can be ambiguous.[31] With referendums, for example, it may seem as though people's preferences are being enacted because they directly vote on the issue. But the threat of direct legislation can also keep policy-makers closely attuned to public desires. Or the fact that these countries have an institutional mechanism for direct legislation could indicate a tradition of responsive government.[32] While public opinion is likely to shape laws and policies, once created, laws and policies can take on a life of their own, influencing residents' attitudes because the state has now taken an authoritative stance and codified attitudes into law. Given the state's clear stance and the legal repercussions associated with violations, residents may develop attitudes consistent with legislative changes.

While the exact process and correct causal order between laws and attitudes may be unclear, survey data allow us to assess whether abortion laws have an independent relationship with public disapproval of abortion after

---

[30] Hartig, "About Six-in-Ten Americans Say Abortion Should Be Legal in All or Most Cases."

[31] Hildebrandt, "What Shapes Abortion Law?"; Loll and Hall, "Differences in Abortion Attitudes by Policy Context and between Men and Women in the World Values Survey."

[32] Arceneaux, "Direct Democracy and the Link between Public Opinion and State Abortion Policy."

102 FETAL POSITIONS

accounting for other key characteristics, (e.g., democracy and economic development). Do more democratic nations have more tolerant residents partially because of more supportive abortion-related laws? Or do democratic processes and abortion laws have unique associations with residents' attitudes?

Earlier in this chapter, I reported on the relationship between attitudes and laws without controlling for any other factors, like democracy. The analyses presented in, Table A.3 in Appendix A, Model 8, examines the relationship between individuals' attitudes and abortion laws, after accounting for a wide range of characteristics, including democracy. As this and other studies[33] have found, democracy and abortion laws are closely connected. More democratic nations are more likely to offer abortion on demand (within gestational limits) and have more supportive residents. The findings presented here also show that democracy and abortion laws have unique associations with public disapproval.

Figure 3.1 above provides more information on this relationship by presenting marginal values for the average attitude in countries by abortion laws after controlling for individual and country-level factors. In societies where there are major abortion restrictions and abortion is only allowed in cases of rape, fetal impairment, and to protect the life and health of the mother, the average abortion disapproval score is 7.96, where 10 equals never justified. Conversely, in countries where there are few restrictions or abortion is allowed on demand, the average resident is less disapproving with a score of 7.59. The coefficient effect sizes for democracy and abortion legislation are similar, meaning that they explain about the same amounts of variation in abortion attitudes. We do not know if more liberal abortion legislation is driving supportive views or if attitudes are affecting laws. However, we do know that a statistically significant inverse association exists between attitudes and policies that remains even after considering a wide range of other individual and country-level characteristics, including democracy.

This section has explored the relationship between abortion attitudes, laws, and democracy. All three of these factors are closely related. In the next section, I look at how these relationships play out in China, where lowdemocratic processes are limited.

---

[33] Brooks, "Abortion Policy in Western Democracies."

Family-Planning Laws and Policies in China

In China, abortion has been legal since 1956. Many of the respondents I interviewed seemed to believe that abortion was acceptable, even normative. As a Buddhist monk explained, "In terms of the Chinese government policies, they've never made it illegal. As a result, people just feel like, oh, this is a normal thing to do, and they don't feel like this is wrong." As noted previously, because of population constraints, China's authoritarian government began enacting the one-child policy in the 1970s, whereby most residents were permitted to have only one child. If they chose to have more, they had to pay a large fine, and if they had a government job, which many people did, it could be jeopardized.[34] As I explain below, when the Chinese spoke about abortion, the ramifications of the one-child policy often emerged as a policy force that shaped their attitudes and behaviors.

Several scholars have argued that as a result of fast-paced economic growth, China's birthrate would have shrunk even without the policy. They may be right.[35] Nevertheless, for my respondents, there was no doubt that the one-child policy directly affected fertility decisions. As one professor explained, "I am that generation of single child. And so my mother was forced to have one child because of that policy, and her mother was forced to have nine children by the state." Other respondents talked about coerced abortions. A Christian minister explained, "So they may enforce the one-child policy, which will lead to forced abortions in a more aggressive way." But, for many Chinese, the economic and career ramifications were often severe enough to dissuade them from having a second child. A faculty member explained that her parents did not have any more children: "Because my mom is working in the army, a doctor in the army, so it's a very serious thing [to have a second child]. And my dad is working in the government . . . . So my dad would have lost his job, and my mom might have too."

When the government put forth the one-child policy they could not solely rely on penalties (e.g., job loss, demotion, fines, the monitoring of menstrual cycles, forced abortions) to induce people to limit their family sizes. They also had to change people's views about abortion, turning it into something that was acceptable, even honorable. As one professor explained, around 1980 the state tried to destigmatize abortion "by telling people you're doing a good thing, you're helping the state by having an abortion." For the most

---

[34] Liao, "The One-Child Policy."

[35] Gietel-Basten, Han, and Cheng, "Assessing the Impact of the 'One-Child Policy' in China."

104 FETAL POSITIONS

part, she felt that they had been successful, though she also noted that "none of women's suffering and pain and emotional price were featured in those propaganda." Another faculty member added that "looking back, abortion has been normalized under the governmental policies, especially the family-planning policies." Despite personal misgivings about abortion, which many had, respondents largely thought that the state had successfully convinced the Chinese that abortions could reasonably be used to manage unplanned pregnancies.

In addition to the legality of abortion and the one-child policy, beginning in 2005 the Chinese government began implementing a policy that forbids couples from learning the child's gender before birth.[36] With the option of having only one child and the importance that many Chinese place on having a son,[37] some families aborted, abandoned, or gave up their daughters for adoption.[38] In response, the Chinese government enacted a policy that made determining the fetal gender illegal.[39] They also strongly encouraged the public to see the value of having girls. Officials rightfully anticipated that without the discrimination policy there would be a gender imbalance that would cause new problems.[40] Like the one-child policy, Chinese respondents seemed to think that the gender policy was effective. A Catholic sister living in China explained that no one is getting gender-selective abortions anymore, "and, in general, people also have this consensus; people are aware that this is against the law." A professor added, "The government really did a lot of propaganda in order to ensure people's daughters are okay as well as acceptable. So, I always think of no matter how we criticize the government, they were really trying to change people's opinion about a son and daughter." Hence, many interviewees thought the government's gender campaign had been successful.

After eliminating the one-child policy and allowing for two children, in 2021 the Chinese government changed its family policy again to allow couples to have up to three children.[41] Some respondents thought that the change would be effective in not only influencing behavior but also attitudes, making abortions less common and acceptable. As one professor explained,

[36] Zaugg, "Blood Smuggling in China."
[37] Chan et al., "Gender Selection in China: Its Meanings and Implications."
[38] See Chapters 1 and 4 for a larger discussion on the factors contributing to a greater valuing of boys over girls.
[39] Zhu, Lu, and Hesketh, "China's Excess Males, Sex Selective Abortion, and One Child Policy."
[40] Chan et al., "Gender Selection in China: Its Meanings and Implications."
[41] BBC, "China Allows Three Children in Major Policy Shift."

DEMOCRACY, LAWS, AND POLICY IN SHAPING ABORTION VIEWS 105

"The change in the policy definitely decreases abortions and [favorable] attitudes toward abortion." Another researcher affirmed this sentiment: "The public opinion will change if the policy has changed, and it will move toward abortion being less acceptable." Some respondents made clear that while they thought the general population might be persuaded by the government, they personally felt differently. One professor was deeply resentful of the government trying to control the population size with its policies: "Why do we have to listen to you? We're not your machine." When referring to the Chinese public, respondents often thought the government's aims were successful, but many had personal misgivings.

As the family-planning policy became more liberal, I was curious whether the change from the one-child policy to now allowing up to three children, especially within a relatively short time period, would cause Chinese residents to question the government's decision to limit women's fertility in the first place. A Chinese researcher who now lives in the United States told me that most Chinese would not think that "the government had been arbitrary or too totalitarian or caring too much or interfering too much." Rather, when the one-child policy was first enacted, "most of them would say, they lived in bad times, and right now we have better times." So, the government policy shifted accordingly. The same researcher went on to explain that the Chinese often distinguish between frustration with government policy and officials who enact orders. As she explained, criticizing government policy is very sensitive: "You can only say good things about it and complain about local officials who did not carry out the policy in the way it's supposed to [work]." She added that many Chinese may believe that "no policy is always good." But you can complain about local bureaucrats, who are "just bad apples who cannot make it right." Hence, if the Chinese are frustrated with government policies that people living in more democratic nations would find invasive, residents may displace their irritation or anger onto more politically acceptable culprits.

For the most part, respondents thought that through government policies Chinese citizens would adjust their attitudes and behaviors. As one respondent explained, "So everything surrounding having the baby or having an abortion would be related to the government. So most of the time they listen to the government." However, many interviewees also acknowledged people's agency and gave examples of how highly motivated citizens navigate around government policies. A graduate student elaborated, "The government has a firm affect through policy, but we, as citizens, have other

106   FETAL POSITIONS

approaches to just avoid it, to avoid being influenced by this policy." She went on to explain that in Guangdong Province almost every family has at least two children and "they are not afraid of fines or being punished" and that they will do some things to keep the government from finding out about additional children. I could not find any support for "most" Guangdong residents having two children. But, in 2021 it was the only Chinese province where the number of newborns exceeded one million, though it is also the largest province. During this period, the majority of provinces experienced a decrease in newborns, including Guangdong, which dropped 22% compared to 2017.[42]

Consistent with the graduate student's perspective about bypassing the government, another respondent explained that "there are people who have resources, and they have more kids. There are always gray areas and ways to get around things, so they are able to do it." Talking about the government's policy to limit gender selection, a professor added, "But in some cases you can bribe the doctor, you can fly to Hong Kong to do it and know it, because outside of China, you can [discover the gender]."[43] Respondents were clear that the Chinese are industrious and that the most-determined residents can circumvent restrictions.

While some Chinese found ways to have more children despite the policy, most thought that the public's views about abortion attitudes and behaviors would coincide with family-planning policy changes. Less clear was the extent to which the decrease in family size was a direct result of the policy or the natural inclination to have smaller families, as the nation became richer,[44] which, as discussed in the Chapter 2, China did at an incredibly fast pace.

While the relationships between family size, government policy, and economic development are unclear, the WVS has information on attitudes about abortion over time in China beginning in 1990. Hence, we can see how residents' attitudes are associated with family-planning adjustments and other societal changes over the decades. Figure 3.2 presents fluctuations

---

[42] Hui, "S. China's Guangdong No Longer Uses Birth Registration to Restrict Births; Moves Closer to 'Scraping All Restrictions.'"

[43] See also Zaugg, "Blood Smuggling in China."

[44] Lesthaeghe, "The Unfolding Story of the Second Demographic Transition"; Panopoulou and Tsakloglou, "Fertility and Economic Development."

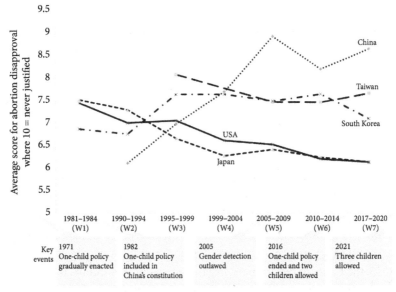

Figure 3.2 Changes in Attitudes about Abortion over Time in China, Neighboring Countries, and the United States

Note: Data are weighted to represent their populations. Taiwan, Japan, South Korea, and the United States provide comparisons for how attitudes have changed in China. Key events in China related to fertility are indicated at the bottom.

Source: WVS

in public opinion over time, along with those in some surrounding countries and the United States. China is one of the few countries where attitudes have become drastically more conservative. The figure illustrates the massive diversity of perspectives over time. My interviews and the work of others[45] also illustrate the great geographical variation within China.

In 1971, the government took its first steps toward the one-child policy. In 1982, the policy was included in China's constitution. By the early 1990s, almost a decade of babies had been born under the policy. For the most part, the Chinese were quite supportive of abortion, with an average score of 6.1, where 10 means never justified (see Figure 3.2). During this second wave of data collection in the early 1990s, the WVS surveyed only fifteen countries. However, these nations were diverse and from different regions

---

[45] Nie, *Behind the Silence.*

108 FETAL POSITIONS

of the world. The only country that appeared more liberal than China was Canada (not shown here), with a score of 6. From 1990 until 2007, the Chinese became substantially more opposed, with a score of 6.96 in 1995, 7.69 in 2001, and 8.91 in 2007. By 2007, China's average score (8.91) was now above the sample mean for this wave, which was 8.14. During this time period (2005–2009), the Chinese appeared more disapproving than people from Turkey, Ghana, Ethiopia, and Iran (not shown here), all of which have religiously conservative cultures.

By 2007, the one-child policy had been around for twenty-five years. An entire generation of Chinese had grown up without siblings. The fertility rates in China, as well as in neighboring Asian nations, had plummeted. When survey data were collected again in 2013 (i.e., wave six), Chinese attitudes had grown slightly more liberal, with an average score of 8.19. However, by 2018 they had again moved in a more conservative direction (8.63). In 2013, the Chinese government began approving exemptions that allowed for two children for families in which one parent was an only child. Finally, in 2016, the government abandoned the one-child policy.

Based on the more conservative turn attitudes took shortly before the one-child policy ended, it is possible that Chinese residents may have grown increasingly frustrated with the policy. By changing it, the Chinese government may have been responding accordingly to shifting public opinion, which is a negative policy feedback effect.[46] In the late 1970s, China was clearly facing a population crisis, which was going to undermine its growth unless the country could resolve it. But, over time the Chinese may have increasingly viewed the one-child policy as unnecessary because population growth was slowing in neighboring countries. Young men were encountering a shortage of wives. Likewise, without the assistance of a sibling, adult children faced heavy burdens in supporting their parents' aging generation.[47]

During the same time period, the WVS also collected public opinion data on abortion disapproval in Taiwan, Japan, and the United States. Attitudes in these countries have become more liberal over the same era. South Korea also has data from the same period as China. Beginning in the mid-1990s, public opinion in South Korea became more conservative. However, attitudes never became anywhere near as conservative as they became in China.

---

[46] Fernández and Jaime-Castillo, "Positive or Negative Policy Feedbacks?"
[47] Zhu, Lu, and Hesketh, "China's Excess Males, Sex Selective Abortion, and One Child Policy."

By the seventh wave of data collection in the late 2010s, South Koreans' disapproval score (7.09) was somewhat similar to what it was during the first waves (6.86). Conversely, China's score had gone from 6.11 to 8.64.

To better understand these findings, I asked my respondents if they thought that over time the Chinese may have become disillusioned with the one-child policy and the context in which abortion was experienced (i.e., common procedure, occasionally forced, etc.), prompting the government to change policies. Some interviewees were skeptical of any data (i.e., health or public opinion) produced by Chinese institutions. As one professor explained, "Number one, I don't trust any statistics coming from China, especially for things they are not proud of, like teenage pregnancies or abortions. I don't trust their numbers." Because the country is not democratic, she believed that government authorities would not publicly announce anything that made the country look bad. These statistics could have presented an unfavorable view. But, based on my research in China, no one seemed to be giving abortion attitudes much heed.

Another researcher, who collects public opinion data in China, thought that greater opposition over time may have been driven by rural residents. They may have become especially disgruntled with forced abortions, high penalties, and a desire to have more children that could help the family farm. Indeed, in my own analysis of China's WVS data, I found that people from less-populous areas were more likely than those in larger ones to oppose abortion, once other factors were considered. However, I did not find that rural residents became more opposed to abortion over time relative to urbanites. Rather, regardless of their community size, residents across China became more opposed over time.

China's WVS data could be flawed. The proportion of people from more rural versus urban areas fluctuates drastically over the five waves of Chinese WVS data. Nevertheless, in later survey waves (i.e., five, six, and seven) when opposition skyrocketed and then remained high, administrators surveyed high proportions of urban residents.[48] With many fewer people from more

---

[48] China's WVS data include a measure of the community where respondents live, but the distribution of residents varies considerably across the waves. During the seventh WVS Chinese wave, all respondents came from areas with 20,000 to 500,000 people. During the sixth wave, everyone came from areas with more than 100,000 people. In the fifth wave, everyone came from places with 5,000 to 500,000 people, with the average being 20,000 to 50,000. The fourth wave did not include information on community size. The third wave of data was fairly evenly distributed, and 78% of people in the second wave were from areas of 500,000 or more. The survey data note that this variable is an indicator of town size. However, the Chinese could have been liberal in their coding. For example,

110 FETAL POSITIONS

rural areas in later years, urbanities were well represented among those with high disapproval.[49]

When I was writing this book, researchers did not have access to any other surveys that assessed Chinese views about abortion. The WVS question asks about the extent to which abortion is "justified," which seemed liked an awkward term. I, therefore, had two native speakers review the Chinese translation. Both thought that the term "justified" had been adequately conveyed in the translation. The same term, as best translated, is consistently used in the WVS across all countries, making findings comparable.

Finally, some respondents indeed thought that over time the Chinese had become disillusioned, leading to more opposition. As one researcher whose specialty is China explained, "When people just start to reflect upon [abortion], then they realize, there are some issues there." He went on to say that other factors may have exacerbated people's negative feelings about abortion over time, including increased awareness of the aging population, the loss of female babies, that the policy was only ever meant to be temporary, a burgeoning interest in individual rights discourse, and so forth.

Although the validity of China's WVS data is unclear, interviews clarified the powerful impact of China's family-planning policies on respondents' attitudes and behaviors. The interviews also illustrated how residents managed policy changes coming from a non-democratic government. They are careful not to criticize the policy but may take issue with officials who implement it. Likewise, if they have the resources, they might try to circumvent it. The following section switches gears, focusing on the relationship between the media and the public's attitudes, which often have a reciprocal relationship with democracy.

Media, Democracy, and Attitudes

An important feature of democracies is that people can access information about their societies and elected representatives. The media often serves this

---

it could indicate the nearest large town. All analyses use WVS weights, which should make the data representative.

[49] The third wave of data include respondents from very small and large places. When I focus just on this wave in China, residents from more rural and suburban areas appear more opposed than those from large urban ones (i.e., a dichotomous variable), as we would expect. Likewise, if I combine all the waves that have the needed measures, I find that people from more rural areas are more opposed. In later waves, many fewer rural people were included. Hence, even when residents from more populous areas are a major part of the sample, over time everyone in the sample appears, on average, highly opposed to abortion.

purpose. Television, newspapers, books, magazines, music, and the internet make it possible for dialogue and exchange of ideas. This information can help the public confirm that their political interests are being served and politicians can learn about their preferences.[50] In democracies, the media should be independent from the government so that it can function unimpeded by the state.[51] When people have access to various perspectives in the media and there are multiple types (e.g., television, magazines, newspapers) that are not created by the government, media outlets can better support democratic processes. Exposure to vast and varied information can contribute to a diversity of views, encouraging more liberal attitudes. Below I discuss the important role of the media in shaping public opinion, as well as the media reflecting residents' views. Drawing on a cross-national analysis of over 800 hand-coded newspaper articles from over 40 countries, I examine the role of democracy in shaping the different themes and claimsmakers used when abortion is discussed around the world. Following this section, I explain how Chinese and American respondents saw the role of democracy in shaping media discourse about abortion.

The media has been described as a nation's "collective consciousness"— expressing the values within a given society.[52] The professionals who help create the media typically live in the same culture as their constituents. They are aware of their audiences,[53] producing different kinds of news for various groups.[54] Researchers have found that when residents' attitudes change, media portrayals tend to adjust.[55] Since media producers are sensitive to their constituents, residents' perspectives on abortion and how the media frames them often correspond. For example, research done on portrayals of women in South African newspapers from 1978 to 2005 found that when abortion was highly restrictive, newspapers were more likely to talk about "innocent mothers" who needed abortions for medical reasons.[56] Conversely, when abortion legislation became more liberal, newspapers were more likely to use the term "patient" to describe a woman who needed

[50] Blumler and Coleman, "Democracy and the Media—Revisited."

[51] Center for Democracy, and Governance. *The role of media in democracy: A strategic approach.* Center for Democracy and Governance, Bureau for Global Programs, Field Support, and Research, US Agency for International Development, 1999. https://2017-2020.usaid.gov/sites/default/files/documents/2496/200sbc.pdf.

[52] Edelstein, *Comparative Communication Research.*

[53] Scudson, *The Power of the News.*

[54] Barker, "Cultural Influences on the News Portrayals of the Iraq War by Swedish and American Media."

[55] Pan, Meng, and Zhou, "Morality or Equality?"

[56] Macleod and Feltham-King, "Representations of the Subject 'Woman' and the Politics of Abortion."

112 FETAL POSITIONS

an abortion. Once it was legal, newspapers no longer needed to be as sympathetic in talking about women who obtained them.

While the media may represent the public's views, the media can also shape public opinion. Early researchers thought that the media had a potent influence on people's attitudes and behaviors.[57] We now know that the media's effect is neither as simple nor as strong as originally thought. Nevertheless, the media is still seen as having a potentially important role in shaping views, especially those related to abortion.[58] For example, a twelve-month study done on US-based cable news programs on Fox News, CNN, and MSNBC found that the conservative Fox News was the most likely to include abortion segments and was more likely than the other more liberal programs to contain inaccurate information about abortion,[59] which could have ramifications for viewers' understanding.

The extent to which people have access to political rights and civil liberties should shape the presence and types of discussions found in the media. In countries with higher levels of democratic freedom, we would expect more abortion-related discourse that includes coverage of political protest and social movements, as well as laws and policies surrounding abortion. In democratic countries, political protest and social movements should be permitted and may even be normative and encouraged. But the media should also be more likely to report on these activities because state censorship is minimal, even in countries where people are protesting the government itself. Likewise, when abortion is mentioned in the media, there should be more discussion about laws and policies, as well as government officials, as the media provides a forum for citizens to debate controversial topics. Finally, in more democratic nations, residents should be exposed to a wider range of viewpoints, including more conservative perspectives and those from religious leaders. Hence, nations with stronger democracies should be more likely to publish news that mentions abortion-related social movement activities, protests, legislation, morality, and religion.

How does democracy shape the media portrayals of abortion across nations? To answer this question, my research team and I hand coded 810

[57] Lowery and DeFleur, *Milestones in Mass Communication Research.*
[58] Purcell, Hilton, and McDaid, "The Stigmatisation of Abortion"; Pruitt and Mullen, "Contraception or Abortion?"
[59] Kann and Tulbert, "Right-Wing Media Are Filling a Void of Abortion-Related Coverage with Misinformation."

English-language articles from 80 newspapers[60] in 41 diverse societies that mentioned abortion over the 1-year period of 2018. See Appendix B for more information about the newspapers, descriptive statistics, and multivariate models.[61] We aimed to have newspapers from a diverse array of countries from different regions and levels of economic development, democracy, and religious cultures. We focused on English-language articles because our small research team did not know all of the languages across this diverse array of countries. For each society, we tried to code two different newspapers to increase diversity. Whenever possible, we selected English-language newspapers that were not government-run.

Every newspaper article was hand coded for both associations and different types of claimsmakers. Associations are the themes or frames that are used when abortion is discussed. If the news media referred to religion (e.g., God, Catholicism, Sunday morning worship) while mentioning abortion, then "religion" would be considered an association. Claimsmakers are people (e.g., religious leaders, activists, government officials) who make assertions about a given topic, idea, or individual, in this case abortion, and try to persuade readers to define or respond to a social condition as a social problem.[62] Claimsmakers have a lot of power to shape discourse and thus the news. If a religious leader, for example, is quoted as discussing something related to abortion or mentioned in the context of the article, then they would be considered a claimsmaker. Based on previous research and analysis, we coded several different themes (i.e., social movement and protest, laws and policy, morality, and religion) and claimsmakers (i.e., social movement, government, and religious).

Figure 3.3 provides information on the proportion of articles that used each theme and claimsmaker. By far, the most popular theme was laws and policies (77%), followed by social movement and protest activities (27%), and then morality (19%) and religious themes (16%). Claimsmakers closely tracked themes, with 69% of articles mentioning government officials, followed by 23% including social movement claimsmakers, and only 9% having religious authorities.

---

[60] Whenever possible we coded twenty-five articles for each country over the one-year period. When there were fewer than twenty-five, we used all of them. But, when there were more, we drew a random sample of twenty-five. We had two coders code every article, and when there were disagreements in their coding, we had a third person be the tiebreaker.

[61] See also Adamczyk and Lerner, "Synthesizing the Global English-Language Abortion Narrative."

[62] Loseke, *Thinking about Social Problems.*

114 FETAL POSITIONS

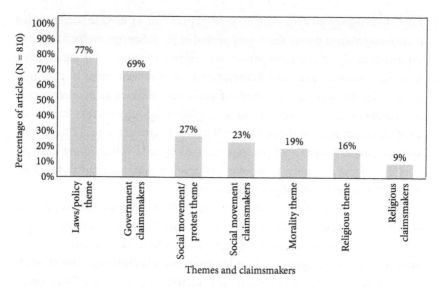

Figure 3.3 Percentage of Articles in Each Theme and Claimsmaker Category across Countries and English-Language Newspapers (Country N = 41; Newspaper N = 80; Article N = 810)

Note: Each article could have multiple themes and claimsmakers, which is why the percentages do not add up to 100%.

Source: Original set of handed coded newspaper articles

My primary aim was to assess the influence of democracy in shaping the likelihood that certain themes or claimsmakers were included when abortion was mentioned. However, I also examined several other country-level forces, including economic development, overall levels of religious importance, the religious culture, and abortion laws/policies.[63] By using a three-level logit model, I implemented the proper analysis technique to account for the greater likelihood of articles from the same country and paper being more likely to have similar themes and claimsmakers (see Appendix B). I also controlled for several potentially confounding factors (e.g., GDP per capita, abortion laws, religious importance, daily publication, English usage, online versus print only).

Figure 3.4 presents marginal percentages that provide insight into the influence of democracy in shaping newspaper portrayals when abortion is mentioned in the English-language press (see Appendix B for full results).

---

[63] I also accounted for whether English was the dominant/official language, which minimally impacted the results, as well as whether the newspaper was published daily (or only online).

Regardless of the specific category (e.g., morality, religion), newspaper articles could have mentioned abortion in positive or negative ways. The extent of democracy within a country, which was the most consistent country-level force across the themes and claimsmakers, was measured with a freedom score that assesses political rights and civil liberties (i.e., higher numbers indicate more freedom).[64] Countries with more rights and liberties (i.e., one standard deviation or more above the mean) include Canada, Taiwan, Finland, Germany, Ireland, Japan, and the United Kingdom. The nations with low scores (i.e., one standard deviation or more below the mean) were China, Iran, Saudi Arabia, Vietnam, Zimbabwe, Thailand, Turkey, Uganda, and Egypt.

Figure 3.4 accounts for all other factors and uses the appropriate analysis techniques. The bar chart shows that countries with fewer rights and liberties are *less* likely to have newspaper articles about abortion that mention religious claimsmakers (4%), morality or other moral issues (8%), social movement claimsmakers (15%), social movement/protest activities (19%), government claimsmakers (54%), and laws and policies (64%). Conversely, in nations with high democracy scores, the proportion with these same themes increases an average of 23 percentage points. Specifically, in societies with high levels of rights and liberties, 19% mention religious claimsmakers, 40% morality themes, 34% social movement claimsmakers, 36% social movement/protest activities, 82% government claimsmakers, and 88% laws and policies.

The interesting thing about these results is that countries with more freedom are more likely to mention abortion in the context of social movement and protest activities, which is consistent with notions of democracy. They are also more likely to discuss religious claimsmakers and morality. Indeed, for all the themes and claimsmakers examined, the morality theme effect size is the largest (see Appendix B, Table 3, Model 7). People living in nations with more civil liberties and rights are more likely to hear about abortion in the context of morality than are residents from countries with fewer civil liberties and rights.

In a separate analysis, I also examined how freedom scores, which was the way democracy was measured in this study, influenced the number of different themes and claimsmakers each article had. The average number

---

[64] Freedom House, "Countries and Territories Global Freedom Index."

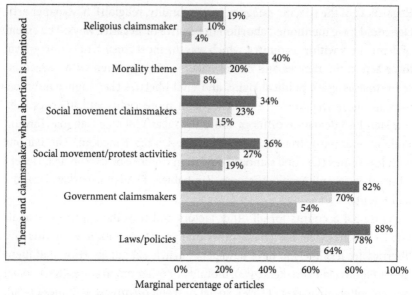

Figure 3.4 Marginal Percentage of Articles That Include Various Themes and Claimsmakers in English-Language Articles That Mention Abortion by Country's Freedom Score (Country N = 41; Newspaper N = 80; Article N = 810)

Note: Marginal percentages are generated from information found in Appendix B. The 2020 freedom score was taken from Freedom House, which rates people's access to political rights and civil liberties. The values selected for the freedom score were one hundred for nations with many rights and liberties (top of the scale) and twenty-seven for few of them (bottom of the scale). These values were selected because they were within the range of values for the countries used in the analysis. Two standard deviations would have fallen outside of the range for the sample.

Source: Original set of handed coded newspaper articles

of themes (ranging from 0, which means no themes related to morality, religion, social movements/protest, or abortion laws/policies, to 4, which means four different themes), was 1.40, after accounting for all other factors. But for countries with low freedom scores, the average number of different themes for each article was 1.02. For nations with high freedom scores, the number increased to 1.78. A similar relationship appears for claimsmakers, with a greater diversity found in more democratic nations.[65] The number of different themes and claimsmakers could be related to overall levels of education,

---

[65] Using a mixed regression model with articles nested within papers nested within countries and controlling for all individual and country-level factors found in Appendix B, the overall average number of different claimsmakers was 1.01. Each article could have from zero to three different

with richer nations having higher levels. But this factor was considered and had no statistically significant effect on the number of diverse themes. These findings illustrate the power of democracy in presenting a diversity of frames and claimsmakers in discussions about abortion.

What do these conversations about abortion that include various themes and claimsmakers look like? In countries with high levels of civil rights and liberties, newspaper discussions often focused on protest activities and engagement with various pro-life and pro-choice movements. For example, the *Helsinki Times* reported that its Finish minister of foreign affairs (i.e., Timo Soini) sparked controversy by marching in a National March for Life in his visit to Ottawa, Canada. Likewise, an article from *The Japan Times* talked about the organizing of plaintiffs in a case asking for government compensation related to the now-defunct Eugenic Protection Law. The law was established in 1948 to prevent eugenically inferior offspring and utilized abortions and sterilization.

As noted above, the majority of articles (77%) mentioned laws and policies when abortion was discussed. These articles tended to focus on laws and policies within the nations included in the study, as well as reports on changes abroad. The *China Daily*, for example, interviewed a medical administrator about the challenges the hospital's ethics committee faced in deciding whether to allow a late-term abortion (i.e., after twenty-eight weeks). Grounding the committee's decision-making process within the guidelines of China's abortion policy, he explained, "The parents' attitude plays a key role because a child's birth is not necessarily a good result if the parents' desire to save the baby is not strong." The pro-government Saudi Arabian newspaper *Al Riyadh* only mentioned abortion-related laws and policies from other countries, like Ireland, Poland, and the United States. In 2018, all three countries were building toward major legislative changes and attracting international press attention. For this authoritarian nation, Saudi Arabia's *Al Riyadh* did not mention its own conservative laws and policies.

Finally, the morality and religion frames and references to religious claimsmakers were used in articles that expressed support for abortion, as well as conservative perspectives. Bolivia and Peru had the highest proportion (80%) of articles discussing abortion in the context of morality or other moral issues. The *Bolivian Express*, for example, reported on the

---

claimsmakers. More democratic nations had an average of 1.30 claimsmakers, and less-democratic ones had an average of .71.

118 FETAL POSITIONS

artist Ejti Stih, who had an exhibit focused on women's experiences with abortion. As the article explained, one of her inspirations was the morally outrageous case of an eleven-year-old girl who was raped by her stepfather and forced to carry the pregnancy forward because abortion is illegal in Bolivia. The baby died a year later. Two strongly Catholic countries—Italy and the Philippines—had the highest proportion of religious claimsmakers. Perhaps not surprising, the pope was the most referenced claimsmaker. In Italy, other claimsmakers included the minister of families and disabilities, a local mayor, and a Democratic Party senator.

In addition to the extent of civil liberties and rights within a country, I examined several other country-level predictors (i.e., GDP, abortion attitudes and laws, religious importance, and the dominant religion). What other country-level forces shaped the odds that articles would include specific themes and claimsmakers? Not many. The measure of civil liberties and rights was the only country-level variable statistically significant across a wide range of outcomes. Overall levels of religious importance and abortion disapproval within a country, GDP, and the dominant language being English were rarely statistically significant. The English-language press in countries where English is not the dominant language is likely to be read by foreigners. Because of their English-language abilities, these individuals are likely more educated and richer, which may also lead them to have more liberal views. Yet, there were almost no statistically significant differences in the themes and claimsmakers presented in papers based on English being the country's official language.

As shown in Appendix B, abortion laws matter for explaining the odds that social movement activities or government claimsmaker are mentioned in discussions about abortion. In countries where abortion is legal, there is less mention of social movement activities and government claimsmakers, likely because these issues may be perceived as more settled. While the United States and Poland have recently passed more conservative laws, legislation across the world has largely moved in a more liberal direction since the 1970s when things began to change (see Figure C.1 in the Conclusion). In some countries, like Sweden and France, abortion laws and policies are not actively being challenged, and hence there is less organizing and fewer government officials mentioning abortion.

For some frames and claimsmakers, the dominant religion (e.g., majority Muslim or Catholic)[66] also mattered. For example, compared to newspapers

---

[66] I coded countries according to their dominant religion (see Appendix B for more information).

DEMOCRACY, LAWS, AND POLICY IN SHAPING ABORTION VIEWS   119

from Islamic- and Buddhist-majority nations, those from Catholic-majority countries were less likely to mention a social movement claimsmaker. Likewise, Catholic societies were more likely to have religious claimsmakers than nations dominated by Islam or a combination of Protestant and Catholic faiths, which is largely found in Africa and the United States. With Catholicism's hierarchical structure, strong history, and dominance, the Catholic pope is the most famous religious claimsmaker in the world. In Catholic-majority societies, he was often mentioned when abortion was discussed.

The media can play an important role in shaping the information that residents receive regarding abortion. At the same time, the media often reflects people's views at a particular moment in history. As shown here, democracy has an important role in shaping the diversity of frames and claimsmakers that are presented in newspaper articles when abortion is discussed. The next section examines how abortion and the public press differ in the United States and China.

Democracy and Media in the United States and China

While the United States has one of the oldest democracies and is often seen as a model for other countries, China has regularly been criticized for its lack of democratic structures and transparency. Interviewees from China and the United States both mentioned the relationship between public opinion about abortion and the diversity of views that could be found in the media. As I explain below, respondents from both countries took issue with how information was disseminated, with the government playing a pivotal role in China and media-related algorithms limiting exposure to different views in the United States.

In China, interviewees often mentioned the role of the government in restricting public discussions about abortion, as well as discourse more generally. One Chinese-based researcher put it bluntly: "In China, there is no free public discourse." He went on to say that in other countries people learn how to debate and have free exchange of ideas from very young ages, "but, even in [Chinese] universities, we all know there are many topics I'm not allowed to discuss." A Buddhist monk told me that "the government wouldn't allow any kind of public opinion. So maybe people do have certain views against abortion, or they might have some discussions, but you can't see them." Another professor added, "So, specifically, there's just

120 FETAL POSITIONS

no such room for public discussion, no such environment." Most Chinese respondents agreed that there was little freedom to publicly express views on controversial issue.

Indeed, as I was researching this book, I found minimal mention of abortion in the Chinese public press (and very little even in the academic literature). The lack of discourse may be related to the fact that abortion is simply not of great concern in China, where Buddhism, Taoism, and other belief systems, including Confucianism, do not tend to generate high levels of religious beliefs, as typically measured, and may not prompt the same level of religion-inspired social movement activity that is found for other countries and religions. Likewise, the leaders of these religions have not pressed the abortion issue in the same way that Christian officials have. Nevertheless, most Chinese respondents believed that the government was the main culprit in limiting discourse.

While many of the people interviewed in China talked about how the government prevented open discussion, some mentioned how much more information they got compared to previous generations, though the door may be closing again. For example, one professor said that today many Chinese have a better idea of what people think because "we have internet, we have Twitter and Facebook, Google, which is different from our parents' generations, when they didn't know what's happening in other countries. The TV only had government news." A journalist told me how the Chinese middle class today are providing a different education for their children by, for example, providing them textbooks from the United States, even though their parents "don't have political rights." And another academic explained that although firewalls restrict information, she believed that the Hollywood entertainment industry was introducing Chinese society to a more diverse range of perspectives. Hence, at least some respondents thought people today were accessing new sources of information.

Other interviewees were more critical of China's progress. A Buddhist monk said that previous generations "lived in darkness," but then the door began to open. However, around 2010, the Chinese government began to impose more regulations on the internet, which led "to the same strict orders, blocking out all the information coming from the western world, and having stricter control over the news and what's going on within China itself." Focusing on social media, a professor explained that regardless of its popularity, "I still think that public opinion is quite constrained. You don't hear a lot of different voices, even though the voices may not all come

DEMOCRACY, LAWS, AND POLICY IN SHAPING ABORTION VIEWS   121

from the state. The voices are quite monotonous. That's how successful our government is."

While many Chinese respondents believed that the government had a strong role in restricting access to information, Americans thought that a wide diversity of views were available. However, they were concerned that this plethora of information was being filtered through algorithms that either fed people false information or simply reinforced what they already knew. As one professor explained:

> We, at least in theory have a democratic republic and we have people trying to mobilize and influence public opinion. . . . [But] we are seeing anybody that uses social media on a regular basis and has a smartphone as being manipulated by algorithms that we're not even aware of. . . which means you're very, very unlikely to encounter views that are not your own.

While there may be a plethora of information available in more democratic nations, people often focus on viewpoints and information that support their own perspectives, which is aided by media algorithms. An American professor who does research on public opinion about abortion explained that just prior to one of her data collections there was a Facebook story about a woman who was nine months pregnant and chose to get an abortion. Even before the law changed, American women could not get an abortion after 24 weeks, unless there was a serious medical reason (e.g., life in danger). As she explained about the research interview, "So a really inflammatory, completely fabricated story, but as we know, these things circulate on social media. But I heard people in the interviews kind of having [trouble recalling] and they couldn't tell me where it came from, it was too diffuse." In this case social media provided a story that was false. But it nevertheless had an important role in shaping her subjects' views about abortion, even though they could not remember the source.

While many of the academics I interviewed had fairly liberal views about abortion rights, an organizer from a pro-life group expressed a similar sentiment despite her much more conservative stance. As she explained, "People feel like [other] people are constantly trying to manipulate them, and I think it has a lot to do with social media. It has a lot to do [with] how we're getting our information. . . . And so we only trust what we know." This particular activist was not trying to eliminate abortion access. Rather, she was trying to convince the public that there are better options for women. As a result of her more nuanced position, she regularly found herself debating people

122 FETAL POSITIONS

from both sides of the spectrum. She believed that many people were especially unwilling to consider alternative perspectives and that social media was at least partially responsible.

Consistent with the findings from the newspaper analysis, my US-based interviewees thought that there was plenty of information about abortion and that the government was not limiting debate or suppressing a diversity of views. Rather, they thought social media, or algorithms filtering the massive amount of information that was now available, were either sharing false information or limiting exposure to diverse perspectives. Whereas in China, many believed that the government works as a filter of information, in the United States respondents thought that algorithms had taken over, narrowing the otherwise-diverse range of views that democracies typically present.

Conclusion

This chapter focused on how democracy affects abortion attitudes and related policies. Democracy can influence public opinion in several ways, such as encouraging people to be fair and impartial, standing up for the rights of others, and introducing them to a diverse array of perspectives through the media. The United States and China offer important points of contrast for understanding how democracy shapes abortion attitudes and related laws and policies.

A couple of influences that democracy encourages were not discussed in this chapter, but they are useful for understanding how residents around the world are likely to view abortion. The next chapter examines how social movement activity and gender equality inform people's views about and understanding of abortion and related laws and policies.

Chapter 4
Gender Equality, Social Movement Activity, and Race for Understanding Views about Abortion

> Your lack of religion does not absolve you from perpetuating the ideals of patriarchy.
> —US-based medical doctor who performs abortion

Women's ability to control their fertility through abortion and birth control is understood as fundamental to improving their economic standing relative to men. No country in the world has women earning the same as men on average for doing the same job.[1] While in some societies young women start with similar incomes as men, the gender pay gap increases as they marry and have children.[2] At the same time, many people feel that women's primary role should be having and raising children, with academic and career aspirations being secondary pursuits. These diverse views of women and their societal contributions are directly connected to the public's feelings about abortion. They have fueled some of the abortion-related social movements that have influenced abortion laws across the world.

This chapter begins with a discussion about gender equality, which in many countries has led to more liberal abortion attitudes and legislation. Drawing on interviews from China and the United States, I explore how gender inequality shapes attitudes about abortion in these nations. Next, I discuss the forces that gave rise to the overturning of *Roe v. Wade*, which removed American women's constitutional right to an abortion. A significant contributor was social movement activity that helped perpetuate abortion

---

[1] Kottasova, "U.S. Is 65th in World on Gender Pay Gap."
[2] Ortiz-Ospina and Roser, "Economic Inequality by Gender."

124 FETAL POSITIONS

as a critical issue for many conservative Americans who supported Donald Trump's successful 2016 presidential campaign. The chapter ends with a discussion about the role of race in shaping public opinion about abortion.

Gender Equality and Abortion Attitudes

In studies of abortion attitudes, researchers often discuss the important role of gender, views about women, and inequality in shaping abortion approval.[3] Gender equality is influenced by democracy and contributes to it. People living in more democratic nations are exposed to diverse views regarding gender roles by witnessing women working outside of the home and having leadership and high-status positions and living with partners who share household and childrearing responsibilities. In this section, I explain the factors shaping gender differences in views about abortion and the role of gender inequality in influencing residents' cross-national attitudes. I then use World Values Survey (WVS) data to test for a relationship between gender inequality and abortion disapproval.

In deciding whether to get an abortion, women shoulder a much heavier burden than men because the ramifications of obtaining an abortion or carrying a pregnancy to term fall disproportionately on them. They will have to physically undergo the abortion or give birth, both of which have health implications.[4] Women are also more likely than men to shoulder psychological stress because they are directly involved in decision-making. Some men may not even know about the pregnancy. And if the woman chooses not to include the potential father or he decides not to contribute, the financial burden of raising a child or paying for an abortion will also likely fall on her.

In addition to shouldering higher abortion-related costs, women are generally more supportive than men of females' participation in economic, political, and cultural institutions beyond the domestic sphere.[5] Women directly benefit from having access to the same opportunities as men. Some

---

[3] See the following for excellent research in this area in Europe: Fernández, Valiente, and Jaime-Castillo, "Gender Balance in the Workforce and Abortion Attitudes."

[4] Carrying a pregnancy to term tends to have more significant health-related complications. Pittman, "Abortion Safer than Giving Birth."

[5] Greenwood, "Worldwide Optimism about Future of Gender Equality, Even as Many See Advantages for Men."

males may feel that allowing women more access limits their own options. Women also tend to have more liberal attitudes regarding issues such as same-sex relationships.[6] As such, they may generally be more empathetic about inequality issues. Thus, they may be more supportive of abortion because they are more likely to empathize with the burden an unanticipated pregnancy can bring.

Drawing on the WVS data for the last three waves, which includes eighty-eight societies and represents the vast majority of the world's population, I use t-tests to assess differences between genders. This analysis shows whether women, on average, are more supportive of abortion than men when examining attitudes across the globe. Before considering other factors, such as personal religious beliefs, I find that women have an abortion disapproval score of 7.68 on a scale ranging from 0 to 10, with higher numbers indicating justification for abortion. With a score of 7.74, men, on average, are less supportive.

Differences in attitudes between men and women are statistically significant, which other cross-national studies have also found.[7] But given the much higher burden women must shoulder in deciding whether to obtain an abortion, why isn't the gender gap in disapproval larger? The difference in the score between men and women is only 0.06 points. Although it is small, the gender gap is statistically significant here. It is also statistically significant in Model 4 of Table A.4 in Appendix A when only gender is included and appropriate adjustments are made for the multilevel nature of the WVS data (i.e., individuals nested within countries). However, within specific societies and over time, gender gaps vary considerably.[8] For example, in nations such as Uruguay, Slovenia, Burkina Faso, and Ukraine, WVS data show no statistically significant differences between men and women in their level of abortion disapproval. Conversely, in countries such as Thailand, Spain, and Trinidad and Tobago, men are *more* supportive of abortion than women— a difference that t-tests show is statistically significant. In countries such as Yemen, the gender gap widens substantially. Women are approximately

---

[6] Adamczyk, *Cross-National Public Opinion about Homosexuality.*
[7] Loll and Hall, "Differences in Abortion Attitudes by Policy Context and between Men and Women in the World Values Survey"; Adamczyk, "Religion as a Micro and Macro Property."
[8] Crotti et al., "Global Gender Gap Report."

126 FETAL POSITIONS

1.5 points more supportive than men (i.e., 7.84 for women vs. 9.32 for men, where 10 = abortion is never justified).

Religion may help explain why women in some countries are not statistically more opposed to abortion than men. When there is a slight gender gap in abortion disapproval, researchers typically find that it widens (with women being more supportive of abortion than men) after personal religious beliefs and affiliation are considered. In many countries, women report higher levels of religious belief and engagement than men, especially in Christian countries where most research on abortion attitudes has been conducted.[9] Drawing on a rational choice framework,[10] Landon Schnable argues that religion offers social compensation to people, such as women, racial minorities, and poor individuals in structurally disadvantaged positions.[11] These people tend to be more religious. Their religion-inspired values shape their political attitudes more than their disadvantaged societal position. Hence, in some countries, men and women have similar disapproval levels because women are more religious. Once researchers account for the strength of people's religious beliefs and engagement, the gender gap in abortion approval widens, with women becoming more supportive than men. Schnable makes the case that these differences are particularly pronounced in Christianity-majority countries and for Christian religions, which he argues are especially appealing to women, further boosting their religious engagement and belief.[12]

As noted above, if we do not consider the role of personal religious beliefs, we see relatively small but statistically significant differences in abortion disapproval across genders using WVS data. But once religious importance is considered, the gap doubles with women reporting even more support than men. Hence, the findings here provide support for Schnabel's hypothesis that personal religious beliefs moderate the link between gender and abortion disapproval.

Regardless of their own gender, researchers have also found that people who think a clear division of labor is essential tend to be more opposed to abortion. These individuals may feel that men should engage in tasks

---

[9] Stark, "Physiology and Faith"; Miller and Hoffmann, "Risk and Religion"; Pew Research Center, "The Gender Gap in Religion around the World."
[10] Stark and Finke, *Acts of Faith*.
[11] Schnabel, "Opiate of the Masses?"
[12] Schnabel, "Does Religion Suppress Gender Differences in Values?"

considered more "masculine" and that women should do those seen as more "feminine" by societal standards. People less supportive of gender equality, particularly men, tend to be more attracted to a conventional lifestyle that includes marriage and children.[13] Their religious views may have guided them to a more traditional life.[14] However, irrespective of whether they are married, have children, are religious, or even identify as female or male,[15] previous research has found that people who are less supportive of gender equality are more opposed to abortion on average.

Many individuals who are unsupportive of gender equality may feel that it is more important for women to carry all pregnancies to term, even if this action causes significant disruptions to their educational and career aspirations or presents major mental or health-related challenges. As one of my American respondents noted, "I think there's a kind of idealization of motherhood." Having and raising children is deemed more important. Researchers have examined the influence of hostile and benevolent sexism on abortion disapproval.[16] Whereas hostile sexism punishes norm-violating women, benevolent sexism idealizes women who conform to traditional gender roles while devaluing those who do not.[17] Benevolent sexism, but not hostile sexism, is associated with opposition to abortion for elective and health-related reasons. Moreover, the relationship between benevolent sexism and abortion opposition is fully explained by attitudes that idealize motherhood. Hence, this work finds that personal views about women can directly influence abortion disapproval. Below, I assess the role of gender inequality at the societal level.

Gender Inequality as a Societal Characteristic

When many residents feel strongly that men and women should have different roles in life, with women taking more responsibility for domestic tasks, their collective feeling can lead to a culture of gender inequality. As one of the medical doctors I interviewed explained about American culture, "I think

---

[13] Marks, Lam, and McHale, "Family Patterns of Gender Role Attitudes"; Bolzendahl and Myers, "Feminist Attitudes and Support for Gender Equality."

[14] Poushter and Fetterolf, "A Changing World."

[15] Strickler and Danigelis, "Changing Frameworks in Attitudes toward Abortion."

[16] Huang et al., "Benevolent Sexism, Attitudes toward Motherhood, and Reproductive Rights."

[17] Glick et al., "The Two Faces of Adam."

128 FETAL POSITIONS

that there is a lot of unrecognized patriarchy and not trusting that women are capable of making their own decisions." In this section, I explain and then test how gender inequality as a country characteristic can shape disapproval.

There are several processes through which societal gender inequality can shape abortion views. In less-equal countries, all residents may be less likely to see women holding prominent government or business leadership positions. They may also be less likely to know of or see females in higher-status jobs such as doctors, professors, and lawyers. Instead, in societies with greater gender inequality, residents may primarily witness women raising children, cleaning and cooking, and shopping for their families. People may see this division of labor in their own families. Likewise, newspapers, magazines, television, and social media may support these views, associating females with more traditional tasks.[18] Moreover, dominant religious or cultural traditions may explicitly favor men over women. As one Chinese respondent noted, "In general, it's Chinese traditional culture that values boys much more than girls." Hence, traditional, cultural, and religious beliefs may reinforce existing gender inequality.

In societies with more gender inequality, women may be discouraged from obtaining higher education and encouraged to have large families and marry at younger ages. Indeed, only about half of the countries in the world have achieved gender parity in primary education.[19] Furthermore, some governments directly contribute to this inequality by limiting women's legal access to education. Afghanistan offers an extreme example. Shortly after the United States pulled out its military in 2022, the Taliban-supported government forbid girls to attend secondary school (i.e., sixth to twelfth grades).[20] Informal interactions with family and friends, exposure to the media, educational, cultural, and religious institutions, and laws limiting women's educational and career aspirations may reinforce traditional values and gender inequality.

For all of these reasons, residents living in nations with higher levels of gender inequality may be more opposed to abortion, regardless of their gender. How big is the effect of a country's level of gender inequality in shaping abortion disapproval? WVS data show that the correlation between the two measures is quite strong (over 0.5, where 1 is a perfect correlation). However,

---

[18] Rao and Taboada, "Gender Bias in the News."
[19] UNICEF, "Girls' Education."
[20] Farr, "Female Education in Afghanistan after the Return of the Taliban."

GENDER EQUALITY, SOCIAL MOVEMENT ACTIVITY   129

gender inequality is related to many other factors that shape abortion disapproval, including economic development, overall levels of education, and democracy, complicating the relationship, especially in a multivariate model that accounts for several covariates.

Indeed, one of the most popular ways of empirically assessing gender inequality is the Gender Inequality Index, which is a composite of different measures reflecting differences between men and women. The Gender Inequality Index, which is used by the United Nations (UN), has three dimensions: (1) health (i.e., maternal mortality ratio and adolescent fertility rate), (2) empowerment (i.e., the share of parliamentary seats held by each gender and by secondary and higher education attainment levels), and (3) labor (i.e., women's participation in the workplace). The factors included in the Index, such as female labor force participation and educational attainment, are either closely associated with or are measures of economic development and democracy.

To further complicate matters, the UN's Gender Inequality Index[21] correlates exceptionally well with abortion legality (correlation = 0.65). Indeed, across the eighty-eight societies in Appendix A, which include the vast majority of the world's population, there are only five countries where abortion is illegal and gender equality is above the sample mean (Andorra, Chile, Kuwait, Libya, and Malaysia). Part of the reason for the strong relationship between gender inequality and abortion being illegal is that the Gender Inequality Index includes measures of maternal mortality and adolescent fertility rates. In most countries, even highly developed ones, carrying a pregnancy forward has more significant health consequences than an abortion.[22] In places where abortion is illegal or difficult to access, like Tanzania, women tend to have especially poor maternal health outcomes.[23] Of course, if they choose to obtain an illegal abortion, their health will suffer more than

---

[21] In a separate analysis, I also examined two other measures of gender inequality. One measure provides an assessment of political inequality—the percentage of seats in parliament held by women, 2008. A second measure assesses economic inequality, which is the gender gap in labor force participation rate for females (15+) minus the labor force participation rate for males (15+), 2012. Research by Fernández, Valiente, and Jaime-Castillo, "Gender Balance in the Workforce and Abortion Attitudes," found that this economic gender inequality measure was statistically associated with abortion disapproval across nations, even after accounting for other factors. However, more recent research using Ipsos data did not find that this measure had a statistically significant effect on abortion disapproval (see Adamczyk and Fernandez 2024). In the analysis presented in this book, the only gender inequality measure that was statistically significant ($p < 0.05$) in the multilevel multivariate context and before abortion laws were considered was the UN's Gender Inequality Index.

[22] Adesomo, "Pregnancy Is Far More Dangerous than Abortion."

[23] Goldberg, "Open Secret."

130   FETAL POSITIONS

if they could legally get one. Likewise, when abortion is allowed, adolescent fertility rates tend to decrease.[24] The correlation between the Gender Inequality Index and the abortion legality measure is so high that both cannot be included simultaneously; otherwise, the model becomes unstable.[25] Nevertheless, we can still see how gender inequality shapes residents' views about abortion.

Model 4 in Table 4 of Appendix A includes the effect of gender inequality in shaping disapproval, excluding the abortion legality measure. The model provides insight into whether or not overall country levels of gender inequality offer additional explanation for abortion support, even after accounting for gender differences, personal religious beliefs, and a host of other individual and country characteristics. The model shows that residents living in countries with more gender inequality are more likely to disapprove of abortion, even after accounting for other factors. As illustrated in Figure 4.1, marginal values indicate that in nations with high levels of inequality,[26] such as Haiti, Mali, Nigeria, Burkina Faso, and Yen, the mean level of abortion disapproval is 8.16 after accounting for a host of individual and country-level factors. Conversely, for people living in nations with much higher levels of gender equality,[27] like Taiwan, the Netherlands, Norway, Sweden, and Switzerland, residents' level of abortion disapproval decreases to an average score of 7.24.

The results presented here show that gender inequality matters in explaining abortion disapproval, even after accounting for factors like religion. One of the medical doctors I interviewed illustrated this point: "I think there are many people out there that would identify as non-religious or atheist yet are still deeply misogynistic." Because gender inequality is so highly correlated with abortion being legal, I am unable to disentangle their separate effects in shaping disapproval. The two measures are so closely connected that abortion access could almost serve as a proxy for gender inequality. In countries where gender inequality is high, abortion is unlikely to be legal. In the following section, I discuss the differences between China and the United States in how these societies saw the relationship between gender

[24] Ravi, "Limiting Abortion Access Contributes to Poor Maternal Health Outcomes."
[25] When either the Gender Inequality Index or the legality of abortion measures are included in Models 2 and 4 of Table A.4 in Appendix A, the measures are statistically significant. But if both are included in the model (i.e., Model 3), their statistical significance is reduced, as they are both measuring so much of the same variation.
[26] Two standard deviations above the mean.
[27] Two standard deviations below the mean.

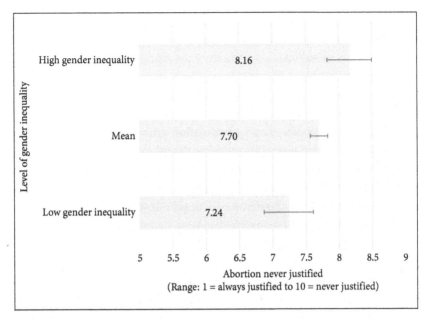

Figure 4.1 Marginal Values for Abortion Disapproval by Three Levels of Country-Level Gender Inequality (Society N = 88; Individual N = 211,317)

Notes: Marginal values are taken from Appendix A, Table A.4, Model 4. The low and high levels of gender inequality are based on the sample values. Because two standard deviations below the mean would have fallen outside of the sample range, I chose the lowest value possible within the sample and use the same difference between the lowest and the mean to select the high value of gender inequality.

Source: WVS, waves 5, 6, and 7

inequality and abortion, providing insight into how inequality in other countries may materialize and influence views.

Gender Inequality and Sex-Selective Abortions

Throughout the Chinese and American interviews, gender inequality was often mentioned in the context of abortion and other fertility-related restrictions, like the one-child policy. These countries have different levels of democracy, economic development, and religious contexts. But relative to other societies with similar levels of development, neither one is an outlier regarding gender inequality.[28] A key topic discussed repeatedly in the

---

[28] World Population Review, "Gender Equality by Country 2023."

132 FETAL POSITIONS

Chinese interviews was the issue of sex-selective abortions. Below, I talk about sex-selective abortions in China, which was minimally mentioned by the American respondents. I then analyze the many other ways that gender inequality was discussed amongst respondents from both countries.

As discussed previously, Chinese birth rates were especially high in the 1950s and 1960s, averaging five to six births per woman.[29] Chairman Mao encouraged large families, hoping population growth would increase economic and political power. But after his death, the Chinese government recognized the major economic and health-related burdens of a vast population. To address this concern, officials implemented the one-child legislation, which had some unintended consequences. In 2010, the global sex ratio at birth was 105 males for every 100 females.[30] While more males are born, they tend to be a bit weaker, ultimately leading to slightly more females than males. In China, the sex ratio at birth in 2010 was 118 males for every 100 females, indicating a major imbalance.[31] Researchers have attributed China's higher proportion of males to the abortion of female fetuses and infanticide, which are extreme forms of gender inequality,[32] as well as the delayed registration of daughters with the government.[33]

When Chinese respondents spoke about the relationship between gender inequality and abortion, they often focused on the abortion of female fetuses. Indeed, every single Chinese interviewee discussed sex-selective abortions. For Chinese interviewees, it was an important lens through which they approached public opinion about abortion more generally. One Chinese professor explained, "I think that a big part of the public discussion on abortion is the female fetus." Another talked about the value of boys being so strong that one couple she knew gave their daughter a name that means "younger brother." By naming their daughter "younger brother," these parents indicated their determination to keep trying for a son. She further clarified that some women are praying to have a boy: "Some people say that all these women are really bad. They're enforcing this kind of discrimination. But then again, they are also victims because they are shaped, or they're pressured by their family and husbands to have boys. And that's why they're so desperate." A culture that values boys over girls may lead both genders

[29] MacroTrends, "China Fertility Rate 1950–2023."
[30] Shi and Kennedy, "Delayed Registration and Identifying the 'Missing Girls' in China."
[31] Shi and Kennedy.
[32] Nie, "Limits of State Intervention in Sex-Selective Abortion"; Bongaarts and Guilmoto, "How Many More Missing Women?"
[33] Shi and Kennedy, "Delayed Registration and Identifying the 'Missing Girls' in China."

to value sons more than daughters. Furthermore, she felt that it was unfair to criticize these women when they acted in ways consistent with China's culture of gender inequality.

Like many other countries, China has strong structural and cultural forces that foster the belief that boys are more important than girls.[34] Historically, rural China deeply valued men's physical strength for manual labor. As one respondent explained, "For poor people in the rural areas, having boys is very important for them because they want to have enough manpower to do the farming and improve their living conditions in general." Son preference has been reinforced by the lack of social security in rural places,[35] meaning that aging parents often rely on adult sons for support. Many of the respondents I spoke to emphasized that the preference for male children was much stronger in rural areas and may have even disappeared in major cities. As one interviewee explained, "Sometimes the [rural] women themselves would think that it's just not worth keeping [the pregnancy], especially if she's already had a daughter."

Along with the importance placed on male labor in rural places, bloodlines run through the man's side of the family when couples marry in China. Further reinforcing the value of boys over girls, one Christian minister explained, "Sons carry on the father's last name and the privileges associated with it." Likewise, once they marry, women typically join their husband's household, leaving their own families behind. As one interviewee noted, in China there is a saying that "the guy is going to bring back one woman into his household. But if you have a daughter getting married, she is basically moving into another household." Hence, you lose out on household contributions if you have a daughter. Respondents thought these beliefs were reinforced or emerged from Confucianism or traditional Chinese culture. A Buddhist monk emphasized that "in terms of Confucianism, boys would be better than girls." The Chinese interviews made clear that historically boys were seen as much more valuable than girls. Some Chinese likely still feel this way.

Given the economic and cultural reasons for valuing boys over girls, the communist government encountered strong counterwinds when it implemented the one-child policy, which forced many couples to carry just one pregnancy to term. Gender equality tends to lead to more liberal views and

[34] Kaufman, "The Global Women's Movement and Chinese Women's Rights."
[35] China Labour Bulletin, "China's Social Security System."

134 FETAL POSITIONS

support for abortion.[36] But in the case of China, the centralized communist government encouraged abortion not for gender equality reasons but to limit population growth, which they saw as out-of-control and problematic for the country's future economic and political aspirations. While it may not have been their intention, by making abortion legal and highly accessible and forcing some women to limit their fertility, the Chinese government may have inadvertently encouraged women to make societal contributions beyond having and raising children since this was a limited option. At the same time, the one-child policy exacerbated the pressure on many women to produce a male heir.

Because of the differential valuing of males over females, once the one-child policy was implemented the ratio of male Chinese children to females was especially high.[37] To address this concern, the government instituted a mass campaign to change people's views.[38] In some areas, the "care for girls" campaign provided subsidies to families with only girls, and the government tried to increase their value in other ways.[39] One respondent noted that in rural areas especially "you could see slogans everywhere, 'boys and girls are both good.'" To further discourage the disproportionate aborting of female fetuses over male ones, the Chinese government outlawed ultrasounds to detect a fetus's gender.[40] However, as mentioned in previous chapters, many respondents felt that the Chinese could get around this restriction by traveling to another country or to Hong Kong. They could also have someone smuggle a blood sample to an establishment where the fetus's gender could be detected.[41]

After three and a half decades of the one-child policy that resulted in an only-child generation, the government ended the restriction in 2015. In part because of its shrinking population and young people's preferences for no children, the government is now encouraging couples to have multiple children.[42] Given these policy changes, are Chinese views about the value of girls relative to boys the same? Many respondents felt the same way as this Buddhist monk: "The dilemma has remained the same. . . . So even if they

---

[36] Bearak et al., "Unintended Pregnancy and Abortion by Income, Region, and the Legal Status of Abortion."

[37] Cameron, Dan-Dan, and Meng, "China's One-Child Policy."

[38] Li, "China's Propaganda Journey from 'Only One Child Is Good' to the Three-Child Policy."

[39] Xinhua News Agency, "More Care for Girls to Address Gender Imbalance."

[40] Shi and Kennedy, "Delayed Registration and Identifying the 'Missing Girls' in China"; Lai, "Boy or Girl?"

[41] Zaugg, "Blood Smuggling in China."

[42] Master, "Factbox."

have lifted the regulation of the number of children people can have, parents still want to have at least one boy." However, other respondents, such as this Chinese Catholic sister, felt differently: "There might be some people feeling that they want boys much more than girls. But in general, most people in my province prefer girls." Another respondent added that people today might want girls "so the parents will worry less about her financial situation." This interviewee assumes that the daughter's husband will have a higher income. Her statement speaks to a different indicator of gender inequality—China's economic and educational gender gaps, whereby women lag behind their male counterparts.[43]

In sharp contrast to the interviews done with Chinese respondents, in the United States the topic of sex-selective abortion arose only if I directly asked about it. Not surprisingly, when it emerged, respondents always thought that they were problematic. In talking with a doctor who conducts abortions in the United States, I asked if she could think of major differences in abortion discussions across countries. She explained, "I have had a few patients here in the US who have come to me for sex-selective abortion, but that's pretty rare. And it's usually patients where I need a translator, not those who are born and raised here." In the United States, several states have outlawed sex-selective abortions.[44] But as this doctor indicated, abortion service providers would not necessarily know if the fetus's gender were the reason for the abortion. Even if doctors ask and could deny an abortion based on sex selection, the patient is unlikely to be truthful, especially if she knows it is illegal.

American abortion advocates have argued that laws outlawing sex-selective abortions unduly target immigrant women, especially those from East Asian countries such as China.[45] Actually, researchers here found that foreign-born Chinese, Indian, and Korean women have proportionally *more* girls than white Americans.[46] Additionally, abortion supporters claim that laws that make sex-selective abortions illegal are really just a ploy to limit abortion access more generally.[47]

The interviews in China and the United States highlight some of the gender-inequality frames through which each country views the

---

[43] Li, "China's Propaganda Journey from 'Only One Child Is Good' to the Three-Child Policy."

[44] Guttmacher Institute, "Abortion Bans in Cases of Sex or Race Selection or Genetic Anomaly."

[45] Citro et al., "Replacing Myths with Facts"; Guttmacher Institute, "Abortion Bans in Cases of Sex or Race Selection or Genetic Anomaly."

[46] Citro et al.

[47] Guttmacher Institute, "Abortion Bans in Cases of Sex or Race Selection or Genetic Anomaly."

136   FETAL POSITIONS

abortion issue. At one point in the recent past, many Chinese thought that having a son was better than having a daughter. Hence, whether to abort a female fetus was a real issue when most women could only carry one pregnancy to term. But even in countries such as India and South Korea, which did not have the one-child policy, son preference has been strong.[48] In India, daughters often require dowries, which can be expensive, and South Korea shares China's Confucian values and paternal lineage.[49] Conversely, sex-selective abortions seem rare in the United States. The following section delves into another important point of contrast regarding gender inequality: the higher prevalence of unwed motherhood in the United States compared to China.

Shame, Financial, and Health Problems Fall on Women

When a woman has an unanticipated pregnancy, she will encounter challenges that her male counterpart is unlikely to face. As one professor in the United States noted, "We think about abortion as an issue only pertaining to the pregnant person. Not to her partner, not her family, not to society." A Chinese professor concurred, "The burden is much less on her male partner, because they don't have to go see a doctor at all." Throughout the American and Chinese interviews, respondents regularly discussed financial and medical challenges as additional hurdles women had to endure in an unequal society. Likewise, in both countries, interviewees felt that the shame associated with an unanticipated pregnancy fell disproportionately on women, especially those who were unmarried.

When respondents spoke about the challenges of managing an unanticipated pregnancy, they almost always thought about young unmarried women. As one American professor aptly explained, views about abortion have much to do with "who the person is envisioned to be having the abortion. Is she responsible? Young women are considered irresponsible." In Chapter 6, I discuss the situation most likely to lead to an abortion, abortion rates, and other factors, including an out-of-wedlock pregnancy, in elevating abortion risk. Understanding the role of gender inequality and how people think about the various costs associated with obtaining an abortion

[48] Hesketh, Lu, and Xing, "The Consequences of Son Preference and Sex-Selective Abortion in China and Other Asian Countries."

[49] Das Gupta et al., "Why Is Son Preference so Persistent in East and South Asia?"

or carrying a pregnancy to term, especially for young unmarried women, offers critical insight into public opinion, which I discuss below.

In China, some of the concerns for young unmarried people centered on the financial cost of obtaining an abortion—a burden women were much more likely to shoulder. One professor explained, "If you are going to abort a healthy baby, then it is not covered, and the surgery costs a lot." Hence, finances were a concern in China and the United States.[50]

Along with the financial costs, Chinese respondents regularly mentioned health-related concerns about obtaining an abortion. One respondent explained that parents would be irritated to hear that their daughter is pregnant because they do not want to think about her having premarital sex. "But I think they're more annoyed because having an abortion is a huge damage to your reproductive health."[51] Another respondent added, "So abortion, at least in the public perception, reduces the chances for future reproductive possibilities." A Chinese journalist added that a woman getting an abortion might wonder, "Does that mean I cannot have another baby ever because I have had abortions? So maybe I was damaged here?" Health concerns regularly emerged in discussions in China. Indeed, some studies have suggested that the abortion procedure itself may be linked to infertility in China.[52]

In contrast to the Chinese respondents, very few American interviewees mentioned the health-related costs of obtaining an abortion. Indeed, one of the few who noted it was a pro-life activist who commented, "And only in extreme cases does the woman [worry] that her uterus is perforated, there is an infection, and she has to get a hysterectomy. But I don't hear people outside of the pro-life movement ever really talking about that." Researchers have examined the potentially adverse health-related effects of abortion in the United States.[53] The findings show very few complications.[54] The pro-choice movement has used this information to advocate for the legality of abortion.

---

[50] Jerman et al., "Barriers to Abortion Care and Their Consequences for Patients Traveling for Services"; Parry, "Chinese Migrant Workers Are Vulnerable to Abortion Risks, Expert Says."

[51] Like many respondents, this interviewee thought that the girl's parents would want her to obtain an abortion, which would not necessarily be an assumption in the United States.

[52] Zhou, "'Shared Ignorance about Sex' in China Won't Change Any Time Soon"; Huang, "Infertility Anxiety, Middle Class Illusion and Reproductive Governmentality: Experience of Unmarried Rural-Urban Migrant Women Who Induced Abortion in Mainland China."

[53] Raymond and Grimes, "The Comparative Safety of Legal Induced Abortion and Childbirth in the United States."

[54] Raymond and Grimes.

138   FETAL POSITIONS

Along with financial and health-related challenges, in both the United States and China, respondents spoke negatively about how other people might view a woman who had an unanticipated pregnancy, abortion, or child outside of marriage. Respondents minimally mentioned the stigma and shame that potential fathers would endure. One of the Chinese journalists I interviewed said that a woman who gets an abortion might be viewed as "used shoes or her uterus is not as good as a girl who has not gotten an abortion." Another respondent mentioned that people would think that an unmarried woman who obtains an abortion is either very young or does not know how to protect herself. Furthermore, she could be seen as a woman who "takes sex lightly" or "might engage in sexual activities very often."

Especially in China, inadequate sex education was mentioned as an important reason why women, especially teenagers and college students, would need an abortion. One Chinese interviewee, for example, explained that if a young girl needs an abortion, "We feel pity that our sexual education was so lacking that she didn't know how to protect herself." In fact, Chinese schools offer minimal sex education. However, the demand for sex education programs is on the rise, and in 2020 China passed an "age-appropriate sex education" bill that hints at including sex education programs in high school.[55]

In the United States, respondents also spoke about the shame associated with obtaining an abortion, especially as illustrated by the silence surrounding it. As one interviewee explained, "One-third to 40% of women have abortions. We need to be talking about it and it shouldn't be silenced. It shouldn't be shameful, but it just is. I mean, it has to do with sexuality." An American doctor who performs abortions expressed a similar sentiment: "In terms of public opinion, I wish people could be more open about it, just because it is so common. It's just part of normal medical care and it doesn't need to be this weird thing that we put to the side and don't talk about." Given the frequency of abortions in America, both of these respondents thought that there should be more discussion about abortion, which could mitigate against the shame many women experience obtaining an abortion.

As in China, abortion in the United States was viewed as very private, partly because it was associated with sexuality. Additionally, in the United States and many other countries, there are more limited discussions because of high levels of religious belief. As one professor noted, the stigma attached

---

[55] Zhou, "'Shared Ignorance about Sex' in China Won't Change Any Time Soon."

to abortion "has to do with the kind of community, and certainly church community being an important part of that." While all religions have proscriptions related to abortion, Catholic and conservative Protestant faith leaders and communities have been especially vocal in condemning abortion. Hence, these religious women may be especially likely to feel shameful about an abortion. If people hear about a woman obtaining an abortion, they may not know who the potential father is or if he contributed to her decision. Hence, the woman is much more likely to be seen as responsible for the pregnancy resolution.[56] She will therefore have to endure most or all of the associated stigma and shame.

Single Mothers

People in both countries discussed abortion-related shame as something that women, much more so than men, would have to endure. However, Chinese and American respondents differed substantially in the extent to which they felt it was socially acceptable for a single woman to have a child. As I discuss in greater detail in this section, compared to Americans, Chinese respondents thought that abortion was much more acceptable than the shame and other costs that would accompany an out-of-wedlock birth. However, in both cases, women would have to shoulder substantially more burden than men.

When asked about the potential disgrace of having a child outside of marriage, Chinese respondents thought it would be especially problematic. As a Chinese Christian minister explained, "If a Chinese woman has a baby out of wedlock, then it will bring shame upon her. This is a very strong opinion in China. . . . It is a social stigma." Another respondent added, "I think this traditional opinion is very prevalent among Chinese people; they do not welcome pregnancy before marriage." One Chinese researcher who had also lived in the United States mentioned her shock at learning about America's relatively high proportion of teenage mothers: "It's rare and unacceptable for unmarried women to have children [in China]. So, I guess abortion is an option." The majority of Chinese respondents thought that having a child while unmarried was more shameful than obtaining an abortion.

---

[56] Chapter 6 discusses the role of religion, both as a personal characteristic and as a contextual factor, in shaping unmarried women's abortion decisions.

140 FETAL POSITIONS

American respondents also talked about the shame female residents would experience in having a child outside marriage, but not nearly to the same extent as the Chinese. As one interviewee from an American pro-life nonprofit organization explained, "And so then there's this loneliness and the shame of being a single mom and what is that going to look like to you?" Nevertheless, the comments in China were especially extreme. The strong Christian religious culture in the United States forbids sex outside of marriage. However, people often do not listen. Indeed, approximately 90% of ever-married Americans report premarital sex.[57] For all the country's focus on conservative religious beliefs, which elevates abortion disapproval, the vast majority of Americans have premarital sex. Even highly religious people are likely to have sex before marriage.[58]

While not as high as in the United States or other rich countries, the proportion of Chinese who report premarital sex is relatively high (over 70%).[59] As one of the Chinese journalists I interviewed explained, for the younger generation "it is totally okay to have sex before marriage. So, the chance to get pregnant before marriage is normal and we think that it is pretty understandable to get an abortion." Thus, differences in the premarital pregnancy rates in China and the United States offer limited insight into the high levels of shame associated with unmarried motherhood in China.

What might be the reason for the greater stigma in carrying an out-of-wedlock pregnancy forward in China? Part of the explanation concerns the rarity at which out-of-wedlock births occur in China, creating a culture whereby obtaining an abortion (rather than having a child outside of marriage) is much more common. In the United States, 40% of pregnancies today occur among unmarried women.[60] The rates of out-of-wedlock births are even higher in other rich countries such as Norway and Sweden.[61] In sharp contrast, in China, less than 5% of births occur to single women. Other countries with Confucian histories have similarly low rates, at approximately 7% for Japan and 4% for Vietnam.[62]

The one-child policy contributed to and reflected a culture where births outside of marriage were uncommon and even deviant. The policy meant

---

[57] "NSFG—Listing P—Key Statistics from the National Survey of Family Growth."
[58] Diamant, "Half of U.S. Christians Say Casual Sex between Consenting Adults Is Sometimes or Always Acceptable"; Warner, "Premarital Sex the Norm in America."
[59] Icenhower, "What China's Sexual Revolution Means for Women"; Perlez, "Women Who Have Premarital Sex Are 'Degenerates.'"
[60] World Population Review. "Out of Wedlock Births by Country 2024."
[61] World Population Review.
[62] Kramer, "U.S. Has World's Highest Rate of Children Living in Single-Parent Households."

that most women could not have a child outside of marriage and then have a second one with a different man. Hence, single motherhood severely limited women's future marriage and mating prospects. As one Chinese professor explained, "If they're unmarried, almost every single woman will be advised to abort because having a child outside of wedlock is going to be a big problem in the sense that nobody will want to marry you." Furthermore, the Chinese government can deny benefits to single mothers, although this has been changing.[63]

The one-child policy certainly made marital pregnancy even more desirable. However, Confucian countries without this policy also have relatively few single parents. As one respondent explained, this negative view of single mothers is linked to a "Confucian ideal about women's morality." A strong emphasis on traditional Chinese values that idealize a certain type of woman and family have likely contributed to extramarital births being seen as problematic, with the responsibility falling disproportionally on women.

Patriarchy and Feminist Perspectives in China and the United States

The United States and China are not particularly unequal societies in terms of gender compared to other countries worldwide. However, as noted previously, neither nation has economic parity between the genders. In fact, there is no country in the world where men and women, on average, earn the same amount for doing the same job.[64] Because abortion has long been legal in China with minimal public opposition, Chinese interviewees talked about gender inequality more abstractly than Americans, who saw gender inequality as related to abortion access. Additionally, many Chinese interviewees thought that younger generations were especially opposed to gender inequality, at least partially because of their access to social media and the internet and the high number of Chinese college students who study abroad and return with Western values and progressive ideas, which I discuss below.

As noted, abortion has long been legal in China, with minimal public opposition. Even if people were opposed, the communist government would likely suppress any protest. Historically, the state has closely involved itself in women's fertility-related decisions. In some Chinese provinces and

---

[63] Wang, "For China's Single Mothers, a Road to Recognition Paved with False Starts."
[64] Kottasova, "U.S. Is 65th in World on Gender Pay Gap."

142   FETAL POSITIONS

workplaces, the government would monitor women's menstruation cycles to assess whether anyone was pregnant.[65] Additionally, there have been widely discussed cases of women being firmly persuaded by Chinese government officials to abort their pregnancies when they were unmarried or already had a child.[66] There are also reports of Chinese women being physically forced to have abortions and undergo sterilization once they gave birth to one child.[67]

At the time of my interviews, China's family policies were changing, and the government was now allowing couples to have multiple children. Chinese officials were increasingly concerned that birth rates were too low to sustain the large aging population. Chinese respondents knew the government was attempting to control their fertility through various policies. One interviewee expressed her frustration, explaining, "Chinese women's bodies never belong to themselves. They belong to their fathers, their husbands, and then the state, because the state tells you, you have one child, now you have to have two." At the same time, many felt that the Chinese were increasingly aware of gender inequality. As one journalist explained, people consider abortion "the right of a female to control her fate; to control her life." An academic added, "At least among young urban females in the past few years, there is a pretty huge, I would say, rise in gender awareness, awareness of gender dynamics." And another professor thought that "the division of labor within the household is actually changing as well." Several respondents felt that fertility decisions were increasingly viewed as a woman's right.

Survey data show that the Chinese have become more liberal about gender-equality issues over time.[68] As is often the case, younger people are more likely than older ones to have liberal perspectives. Many interviewees thought that more progressive views among young individuals were aided by Western influences, which they were exposed to through travel, the internet, and social media. With over one million students attending college abroad, China sends a vast number of young people to other countries for education.[69] One respondent believed that these students were "changed by Western society, by the sex stuff, the feminist stuff, talking about abortion, talking about our bodies, the power relationship between men and women." She went on to say that "a lot of people bring new ideas from the

---

[65] Tyler, "Birth Control in China."

[66] Fong, "How China's One-Child Policy Led to Forced Abortions, 30 Million Bachelors"; Associated Press, "China Cuts Uighur Births with IUDs, Abortion, Sterilization."

[67] Associated Press.

[68] Ash, "China's New Youth."

[69] Educationfair.nl, "Study Abroad Market Report on China."

US and Europe." Another respondent thought that the MeToo movement, which originated in the United States and encouraged women to publicize their experiences of sexual abuse and harassment, may have also contributed to more liberal views. Others noted the important role of social media, with one respondent feeling that it was especially supportive of feminist views.

Notions about gender equality also arose in the US interviews. However, compared to the Chinese, American respondents were more likely to couple gender equality with abortion access. One interviewee explained that antiabortion advocates were opposed to abortion in part because of "respectability politics, which sort of demonized women who want abortions. And even the idea that women should have a justification, that they need a good reason [is problematic]." A medical doctor I interviewed felt that Americans held highly gendered views of men and women: "It's not just one place, it's our whole media.... And [society feels that] a good woman cannot have an abortion." Because America has such high levels of religious belief, I asked another medical doctor if she thought religion had a role in shaping views. She agreed, "But at the same time, I think it's just fundamentally the belief that women are not valuable. And you don't have to be religious to believe that.... Your lack of religion does not absolve you from perpetuating the ideals of patriarchy." Although it may be easy to blame religion for gender inequality in America, she thought that religion was not needed to motivate sexism.

A final distinction about gender inequality emerged in the US-based interviews in discussions about the pro-choice (supports legal abortion) and pro-life movements (opposes legal abortion), which I devote more attention to in the next section. Like the abortion supporters I interviewed in the United States, most of the pro-life advocates I corresponded with saw themselves as feminists, which many struggled to resolve with their antiabortion stance. One pro-life activist explained that the abortion debate "comes down to obviously the bodily autonomy argument, which as a feminist, I very much support." She felt that women should have the right to decide what happens to their bodies. However, with a pregnancy, "the issue is we now have two bodies, and we have one body [i.e., the fetus] that's more vulnerable." She explained that it was not then acceptable to use violence to end the fetus's life. An editor at a pro-life magazine talked about how she supported the views of a feminist-for-life organization; she explained, "We should make abortion unthinkable, not illegal, we should be more helpful to women, and women should not think that their fertility is something that they have to squash in order to compete with men." From her perspective,

144   FETAL POSITIONS

gender inequality made many women feel they can better compete with men when they abort an unanticipated pregnancy.

Abortion has been legal in China since 1956. At the time of my interviews, the US Supreme Court was about to decide *Dobbs*, creating a path for several states to make abortion illegal. American respondents would not have known that women were about to lose their constitutional right to an abortion. However, individual states had long differed in their level of abortion access (e.g., distance to a clinic, government-funded abortions, parental consent laws). Related in part to contrasting legal structures and cultural contexts, US respondents were more likely to couple gender inequality with abortion access. In the next section, I switch gears to focus on US-based social movements, which are closely connected to views about gender.

Social Movement Activity in Shaping Abortion Attitudes

Social movements across the world have drawn on gendered images of women to make their arguments. America offers a good case study in how gender can permeate protest activities. America's unique combination of relatively high levels of religious belief and democracy has contributed to active debates about abortion and social movement engagement, which have fought to portray women a certain way. Related to its much lower level of democracy and religious belief, as conventionally measured, I did not interview a single Chinese respondent who mentioned abortion-related social movement activity. This section focuses on abortion-related social movement activities and portrayals of women in the United States, which is relevant for understanding the abortion debate in other democracies.

Social movements, which are loosely organized efforts by a large group of people to achieve specific social goals, can influence public opinion in several different ways. To begin, they can offer residents information shortcuts that can influence their understanding of an issue.[70] In this way, organized activism plays a similar role as elites (e.g., government and media officials), helping to frame a given topic from a particular perspective. Whether abortion should be allowed and under which circumstances is a complicated topic. But, in the United States the pro-life (i.e., opposed to legalized abortion) and pro-choice (i.e., supportive of legalized abortion) movements

[70] Amenta and Polletta, "The Cultural Impacts of Social Movements."

GENDER EQUALITY, SOCIAL MOVEMENT ACTIVITY   145

have simplified the issue. As one of my pro-life interviewees explained, despite all the complexity of abortion, "people want to boil it down to this really simplistic black and white [thing] because it's so politicized." Another respondent noted that Americans' feelings about the issue are so clear that depending on whether you are pro-life or pro-choice, people will tell you "if you're bad or good based on their own feelings about it." In America, residents typically take one side or the other in the abortion debate.

In the United States, "pro-life" generally means that abortion should be illegal, unless there are unique circumstances, such as the mother's life is endangered. Conversely, "pro-choice" usually indicates support for abortion during the first trimester without any restrictions, and possibly later before fetal viability. In America, abortion is a highly polarized topic in part because of social movement framing. One of the researchers I interviewed explained that because of the issue's complexity, "you may not be able to get one hundred people in a room to agree on the definitions of pro-life and pro-choice, but they can all say which one they are." Many Americans draw on the pro-life and pro-choice social movement frames to describe their views.

Social movements can also influence attitudes by getting specific frames or messages to resonate with the public.[71] In the United States, the pro-life framing of abortion has shifted over time as it has searched for the most appealing message that could also counteract the pro-choice movement's focus on women's rights. In the 1970s, when *Roe v. Wade* was initially passed, the antiabortion movement tried to communicate that abortion was problematic because the fetus has a right to life. Hence, the movement focused on protecting the unborn. This narrative still resonates with many pro-life supporters. As one American activist explained, "Ultimately, being pro-life is a philosophical belief; if you don't accept the innate personhood of the unborn child, you don't have a reason to be pro-life." However, over time the pro-life movement has tried to shift the rationale for why people should oppose abortion from the rights of the fetus to helping women physically, mentally, and monetarily. One way they did this was by discussing the problems that abortion created for women (and others), using the term "abortion syndrome."[72] Although it received minimal scientific support,[73] the idea was that abortion harmed women mentally and physically. As one of my interviewees explained, "Post-traumatic abortion syndrome" was both invented

---

[71] Amenta and Polletta.
[72] Kelly, "The Spread of 'Post Abortion Syndrome' as Social Diagnosis."
[73] Dadlez and Andrews, "Post-Abortion Syndrome."

146 FETAL POSITIONS

and has been capitalized on so effectively by the pro-life movement—that women have bad abortion outcomes. And of course, that's been disproven again and again and again." Her point was that the pro-life movement was trying to promote the view that making abortion illegal helps women avoid new health problems.

A final way that social movements can shape public opinion is by raising the issue's profile, importance, or salience.[74] The pro-life and pro-choice movements have tried to move the abortion issue to the forefront of importance in the United States. In terms of making the abortion issue resonate with the public, one of my subjects who supported abortion spoke about how the pro-life movement had a more straightforward message that could more easily resonate with the public. He explained, "I think the antiabortion movement is just really good and very effective. It's also an easier argument. . . . Protect the unborn, protect the babies is a really easy statement." Conversely, telling people why abortion should be legal "takes a lot more explanation, and the soundbite isn't as good." He believed that the pro-choice message was more nuanced and less precise than the pro-life message that equated abortion to "killing babies."

Both sides of the abortion debate present a certain view of women, which men do not have to endure to the same extent. While the pro-choice movement has tried to portray women that obtain abortions as taking control over their lives, the pro-life movement has stressed women's responsibility in protecting the fetus. The pro-choice advocate quoted above felt that the pro-life movement had a clearer message. But some of the pro-life supporters felt differently. One spoke enviously of the cool image she throught the pro-choice movement put forth about women who got abortions: "[They] are all super hip, cute, tatted up like adorable, shouting their abortions, like they try to make it look like this is the ideal woman you want to be. She's really cool and drinks coffee with her hipster friends." The same respondent felt that "the pro-life movement wants to see her as this downtrodden woman that they can save." Especially some of the younger pro-life women I interviewed struggled with this view of females. As one noted, if you are pro-life, then society feels that "you hate women, you want to oppress women, you're part of the patriarchy." She was frustrated that the pro-life message seemed so antifeminist.

America's pro-life and pro-choice movements are trying to create an image of women that can garner support for their cause. Abortion-related social

[74] Amenta and Polletta, "The Cultural Impacts of Social Movements."

movements in other countries are likewise working to persuade the public to see abortion a certain way. In Poland, for example, abortion is only legal for reasons related to rape, incest, or the mother's health. The law does not criminalize the women themselves, but rather anyone who helps. In 2023, Human Rights Watch, which has strong liberal leanings, published an article discussing the invasion of privacy that women who have gotten legal abortions have endured.[75] The article argued that "laws criminalizing or restricting abortion access do not eliminate it, but rather drive people to seek abortion through means that may put their mental and physical health at risk and diminish their autonomy and dignity."[76] The international report is trying to portray abortion as an issue related to healthcare, autonomy, dignity, and human rights.

In addition to public opinion, social movements want to influence laws and policies that support their interests. Beginning in 2022, America's pro-life movement successfully made abortion illegal in several states during a period when many European countries (excluding Poland) have been passing more liberal legislation. In the next section, I explain how abortion rights were overturned in the United States.

Overturning American Women's Constitutional Right to an Abortion

On June 24, 2022, the Supreme Court ruled in *Dobbs v. Jackson Women's Health Organization* that women no longer had a constitutional right to an abortion.[77] The decision overturned almost fifty years of precedence (i.e., *Roe v. Wade*) conferring the right to abortion with relatively few restrictions during the first trimester. As a result, individual states now decide whether abortion is legal. Some states had a trigger ban in place, so when the *Dobbs* case was decided abortion immediately became outlawed, except for the narrow circumstances that were allowed (e.g., save the mother's life).[78] Other states quickly passed antiabortion legislation, and some strengthened their support for abortion access. Six months after the *Dobbs* ruling, almost half (i.e., 24) of the states either banned or were in the process of trying to ban

---

[75] Human Rights Watch. "Poland: Abortion Witch Hunt Targets Women, Doctors."
[76] Human Rights Watch.
[77] About six weeks before the official decision, Justice Thomas' decision was leaked to *Politico*, which then published it. Hence, the American public had a good sense of what was about to happen.
[78] "13 States Have Abortion Trigger Bans—Here's What Happens When Roe Is Overturned."

148 FETAL POSITIONS

abortion.[79] Below I explain how a host of factors, including the election of Donald Trump and his appointment of three conservative Supreme Court justices, ultimately led to the overturning of *Roe v. Wade* in June 2022. The United States is somewhat unique in being a rich country with high levels of religious belief and democracy and limiting legal abortion access. However, it shares some similarities with other countries both now (e.g., Poland) and in the past (Czech Republic) in using nationalism to justify outlawing abortion.

The *Dobbs* ruling (and the advanced notice that the public got when the media initially leaked the decision) was somewhat surprising because most Americans (roughly 60%) at the time believed that abortion should be legal in all or most cases.[80] If most Americans were opposed to the change, how did this happen? The simple answer is that in 2016 Donald Trump was elected president. He had an opportunity to nominate three Supreme Court justices (Amy Coney Barrett, Brett Kavanaugh, and Neil Gorsuch), whom the Senate confirmed. US Supreme Court justices are appointed for life. All three had conservative leanings. Together they disrupted the conservative versus liberal balance of the court, allowing for the overturning of *Roe v. Wade*.

The more complicated reason for the legal change relates to how Trump was initially elected and the forces, including the pro-life movement, that put him into office. The majority of America's white citizens voted for Trump in 2016.[81] Furthermore, 52% percent of his voters were white women, and 61% of white women without college degrees voted for him. Donald Trump has repeatedly made disparaging comments about women.[82] He publicly called one woman a "crazed, crying lowlife." He called another woman a "dog" and said another one had the "face of a pig."[83] He has regularly criticized the intelligence and appearance of females, including his Democratic opponent, Hillary Clinton. Hence, it may seem surprising that so many women voted for him.

Several media reports and researchers have suggested that his opposition to legal abortion helped him win office.[84] As discussed at the beginning of this chapter, on average women around the world are more supportive of

[79] "Six Months Post-Roe, 24 US States Have Banned Abortion or Are Likely to Do So."
[80] Hartig, "About Six-in-Ten Americans Say Abortion Should Be Legal in All or Most Cases."
[81] Jones, "An Examination of the 2016 Electorate, Based on Validated Voters."
[82] Davis and Rogers, "At Trump Rallies, Women See a Hero Protecting a Way of Life."
[83] Shear and Sullivan, "'Horseface,' 'Lowlife,' 'Fat, Ugly.'"
[84] Khazan, "Why Christians Overwhelmingly Backed Trump"; Schmalz, "Why Donald Trump Won the Catholic Vote"; Stewart, "Eighty-One Percent of White Evangelicals Voted for Donald Trump. Why?"

GENDER EQUALITY, SOCIAL MOVEMENT ACTIVITY   149

abortion than men. But the gap is small until personal religious beliefs are considered. Then the difference widens, resulting in women appearing more liberal on average than men, especially in countries with high levels of religious belief.[85] Religion helps explain why women are not more supportive. In addition to opposing abortion, religious women are also more likely to marry, have children, and leave the labor market to raise them, if they have the financial resources.[86]

Over the past fifty years, the United States and many other countries have undergone radical changes concerning birth control, women's rights, and the sexual division of labor. White women in particular have drastically increased their participation in the paid labor force. American academics often draw distinctions across racial groups, especially for people who are white versus black. The enduring legacy of slavery, systematic denial of civil rights and liberties, and continuing racial discrimination and prejudice have created stark income and wealth differences across racial and ethnic groups. As a result, white Americans have historically had much higher incomes and more wealth than African Americans. Many African American women and other racial and ethnic minorities have always had to work outside the home because their families needed the money.[87] Hence, the changes the feminist and sexual revolutions ushered in significantly impacted white women in particular, many of whom had traditionally been stay-at-home mothers.[88]

In the 1970s, women's college attendance substantially increased. As a result, many women, especially white women, had more desirable options to work outside of the home. Economic and social changes (e.g., divorce) also meant that their families increasingly relied on their wages. Birth control pills, which became popular in the 1960s, also gave women more power and control over when they had children.

Mothers who did not attend college and chose to stay home to raise children may have felt devaluated and excluded by these educational and economic advancements and the feminist movement more generally.[89] Additionally, many religions support a traditional division of labor. Women who choose traditional family roles may do so partly because their religious communities support and value them. Indeed, research has found that more religious women in the United States[90,91] and other countries are more likely

[85] See also Schnabel's research.
[86] Sandler and Szembrot, "New Mothers Experience Temporary Drop in Earnings."
[87] Goldin, "Female Labor Force Participation."
[88] Goldin.
[89] Luker, *Abortion and the Politics of Motherhood*.
[90] Chadwick and Garrett, "Women's Religiosity and Employment: The LDS Experience."
[91] Pew Research Center, "The Gender Gap in Religion around the World."

150   FETAL POSITIONS

to remain outside the traditional labor market.[92] When *Roe v. Wade* made abortion legal in 1974, many religiously conservative women were shocked because many did not know anyone who had gotten an abortion or would need one.[93] Their social circles primarily included other Christian white women who stayed home to raise families.

Once abortion was legalized, the pro-life movement pushed back against abortion access, slowly chipping away at legislation that made it increasingly difficult for women to access abortion. In 1992, for example, the Supreme Court ruled in *Planned Parenthood v. Casey* that state legislatures could restrict abortion as long as the law did not place an "undue burden" on women's access.[94] As a result, several states mandated various policies, including waiting periods. Waiting period laws required women to wait a certain number of hours between officially initiating their intent for abortion and obtaining it. Pro-life advocates hoped that the delay would make women change their minds.

During the early 1970s, the Catholic Church was the primary religious group opposing abortion in the United States. Indeed, at that time, many Evangelicals supported abortion access, and there was no difference between Republicans and Democrats in their level of support.[95] But this began to change as conservative Americans pushed back against the liberal values of the 1960s and early 1970s. The emerging Christian Right, consisting primarily of Evangelicals and conservative Protestants, began mobilizing against forces threatening American values and the traditional family.[96] In 1979, Reverend Jerry Falwell founded the Moral Majority, which was a conservative Christian political lobbying group and antiabortion profamily movement.[97] It coincided with the popularity of President Ronald Regan, who promoted a conservative political agenda. The coupling of religion with politics and the antiabortion movement was powerful. As one of my pro-life activists noted, "The pro-life movement would not have the juice it does if we were a more secular country."

During this time, the antiabortion movement began promoting the idea that eliminating abortion protects women and family values more

---

[92] Akyol and Ökten, "The Role of Religion in Female Labor Supply"; Alam, Amin, and McCormick, "The Effect of Religion on Women's Labor Force Participation Rates in Indonesia."
[93] Luker, *Abortion and the Politics of Motherhood.*
[94] Baker, "The History of Abortion Law in the United States."
[95] Griffith, *Moral Combat.*
[96] Lindgren, "Trump's Angry White Women: Motherhood, Nationalism, and Abortion."
[97] Wilcox, "Evangelicals and the Moral Majority."

GENDER EQUALITY, SOCIAL MOVEMENT ACTIVITY   151

generally. Movement leaders like Phyllis Schlafly brought together activists who opposed abortion and the Equal Rights Amendment, which wanted to guarantee protection against sexual discrimination. Together, conservative religious and political forces, along with the antiabortion movement, sought to defend the idealized American family against the moral threats of feminism, abortion, and gay rights.[98] The combination of forces contributed to a focus on the traditional homemaker-breadwinner family that idealized American life from a previous era in which abortion was portrayed as threatening.[99] Antiabortion rhetoric increasingly took on tones of nationalism[100] and sought to defend the traditional family and white female homemakers.[101]

When Donald Trump entered office in 2017, he was building on decades-long messaging that coupled the pro-life movement with conservative religious beliefs and nationalistic rhetoric about protecting the traditional American family. He used the "Make America Great Again" slogan, created legislation to build a border wall with Mexico,[102] and signed an executive order limiting travel to the United States from seven predominately Muslim countries, making an exception for Christian refugees.[103,104] His message spoke to many working-class people and stay-at-home moms. Many of these Americans may have felt left behind by a country that increasingly valued a college education and liberal values and witnessed minority groups economically advancing.

In 2016, Donald Trump was running for president against Hillary Clinton, the first female to be the Democratic party's nominee for president. Likewise, his election was coming on the heels of Barak Obama, the country's first black president. Hence, Trump had the white male demographic characteristics of a traditional candidate and was running for office during relatively progressive times. The *New York Times* captured the essence of supporters' feelings during the midterm election: "It is [white women's] visceral fear of immigrants and raw anger about changes in cultural mores . . . that appear to be driving the intensity of their support for the president." Trump was elected president to a large extent because he had the support

[98] Self, *All in the Family.*
[99] Spruill, *Divided We Stand.*
[100] The Reagan and Bush campaign was the first to coin the slogan "Make American Great Again."
[101] Lindgren, "Trump's Angry White Women: Motherhood, Nationalism, and Abortion."
[102] Wilkie, "Trump Declares National Emergency to Build Border Wall, Setting up Massive Legal Fight."
[103] Holpuch, "Trump Re-Ups Controversial Muslim Ban and Mexico Wall in First Campaign Ad."
[104] Stephenson and Rosenberg, "Trump Signs Order to Keep Out Some Refugees, Prioritize Syrian Christians."

152 FETAL POSITIONS

of white people from traditional backgrounds who had increasingly felt left behind.

Since Supreme Court Justices are elected for life, they leave the court only when they choose or pass away. During his time in office, Trump was lucky to have the opportunity to fill three vacancies. Given his voting base, all the justices he appointed were conservative and opposed abortion. Hence, after the three new justices were confirmed, they decided to hear the *Dobbs* case and took the opportunity to overturn women's constitutional right to an abortion.

Trump's message mixed nationalism with shared traditional values and antiabortion rhetoric, which is not unique to the United States. Other countries have made similar linkages.[105] For example, following the fall of the Soviet Union, democracy made possible the public coupling of Catholicism and Polish national identity. Poland has always had a strong Catholic identity, but Soviet-imposed communism splintered it. As Poland became more democratic, the Catholic Church regained power, coupling religion with national identity.[106] After several years of conservative and religious influence on government,[107] Poland's Constitutional Tribunal instituted an almost total ban on abortions in October 2020.[108]

The pro-life and pro-choice movements have different views of whether and under what circumstances abortion can be justified. They also have contrasting perspectives on women and their responsibilities. The people most likely to benefit from legal abortion are unlikely to be married religious stay-at-home mothers who did not attend college. Because of the low incomes of many racial and ethnic minority families, these women often need abortions more than traditional white women. One of the themes that repeatedly emerged in the US-based interviews was race, who people thought about in discussing abortion, and who abortion was supposed to protect. In the next and final section, I discuss the intersectionality of gender and race in shaping America's abortion debate.

---

[105] Albanese, "Abortion & Reproductive Rights under Nationalist Regimes in Twentieth Century Europe."

[106] Kozlowska, Béland, and Lecours, "Nationalism, Religion, and Abortion Policy in Four Catholic Societies."

[107] Mishtal, *The Politics of Morality.*

[108] "Poland's Constitutional Tribunal Rolls Back Reproductive Rights."

Race in the American Abortion Debate

Every American I interviewed mentioned the importance of race in shaping the nation's abortion debate. As noted above, US-based researchers often talk about differences between racial and ethnic groups. The legacy of slavery and historical differences in immigration patterns mean that some groups have garnered more privilege, wealth, and resources than others, substantially shaping the trajectories of their own lives and subsequent generations. The role of race in America's public discussions about abortion is further complicated by the influence of eugenics, the women's movement, conservative Protestant religious beliefs, and gender inequality, which I discuss in this section.

None of the respondents I spoke with felt that the movement they supported (i.e., pro-life vs. pro-choice) was overtly racist. However, they talked about what they saw as racist elements underlying the opposing side. For example, one pro-life woman said abortion supporters targeted minorities by putting abortion clinics in their neighborhoods, making "these women feel like they have no choice [but to get an abortion]." Conversely, a pro-choice supporter noted that "there are deeply racist structures in our society and people in the South and religious people have latched onto abortion as a way of feeling morally righteous." Another respondent concurred, "[Abortion] gives racist white people a way to say, 'I care about Black people more than you do. I might have all these other racist views, but I don't want Black babies being aborted, and you do. So, who's actually racist?'" He felt that by opposing abortion, white people could feel superior and less racist.

One reason that the relationship between race and abortion in the United States is especially complicated is that Planned Parenthood's founder, Margaret Sanger, aligned herself with the eugenics movement (i.e., certain people are unfit to have children), which remains associated with white supremacy.[109] While American women can get abortions at a range of different establishments (e.g., hospitals and clinics), over 90% are conducted at abortion clinics,[110] many of which are associated with Planned Parenthood. This nonprofit organization provides reproductive and sexual healthcare and education across the globe. The organization is closely associated with

[109] Lombardo, "Miscegenation, Eugenics, and Racism."
[110] Ranji, Diep, and Salganicoff, "Key Facts on Abortion in the United States."

154 FETAL POSITIONS

the pro-choice and feminist movements. Its clinics are often the cheapest places available to get an abortion. Planned Parenthood itself has long denounced its racist origins.[111] However, abortion opponents have repeatedly attacked the organization for its early association with eugenics.[112]

In the United States, African American women disproportionately get abortions compared to white women.[113,114] Several studies have shown that their higher rates are linked to less-reliable birth control use.[115] However, the pro-life movement has tried to capitalize on black women's higher abortion rates and Planned Parenthood's historical connection to eugenics by making the case that pro-choice supporters are encouraging the abortion of non-white babies. One of my pro-life supporters explained correctly that "[abortion clinics] are not in the rich, white areas." Instead, many are located in poorer places, which she attributed to the targeting of minority women for abortions.

One major effort to mobilize the prolife movement and reduce black women's high abortion rates was the 2010 Atlanta billboard campaign. The confusion over who sponsored the initiative offers insight into how both sides understand and have tried to frame the debate. During the weekend of the 2010 Super Bowl, which is one of the most popular American sporting events of the year, the pro-life organization Radiance paid for eighty billboards to be erected across Atlanta.[116] The billboards displayed a picture of a black baby and stated, "Black Children Are an Endangered Species," implying that abortion is a means of reducing the size of America's black population. At the time, Radiance, which was led by African Americans (Ryan Bomberger and Catharine Davis), paid for the billboards.[117] The signs were provocative and specifically targeted black women. Since then, other pro-life organizations, including a pro-life Latino group,[118] have erected similar billboards in other parts of the country.

Some of my respondents mentioned this high-profile campaign, arguing that it was an unfair, racist way to target black women who needed abortions.

[111] Planned Parenthood, "The History & Impact of Planned Parenthood."
[112] CNA, "Pro-Life Advocates."
[113] In 2020, only twenty-nine states and Washington DC reported racial and ethnic data on abortion to the Centers for Disease Control (CDC). The data indicate that "39% of all women who had abortions were non-Hispanic Black, while 33% were non-Hispanic White, 21% were Hispanic, and 7% were of other races or ethnicities." For more information, see: Diamant and Mohamed, "What the Data Says about Abortion in the U.S."
[114] Hill, Ndugga, and Artiga, "Key Data on Health and Health Care by Race and Ethnicity."
[115] Dehlendorf et al., "Disparities in Family Planning."
[116] Dewan, "Anti-Abortion Ads Split Atlanta."
[117] Luna, "'Black Children Are an Endangered Species.'"
[118] Llorente, "Controversial Billboard Targets Abortions by Latinas."

As one interviewee explained about similar billboards in Wisconsin, "It was white people trying to mobilize racist ideas to stigmatize women who were getting abortion[s] within those communities of color." She also thought that the billboards were funded by white evangelical pro-lifers. White religious people may have funded the Wisconsin billboards. But they were likely following the lead of the pro-life African American women who first erected them in Atlanta.

An important critique of the pro-choice and feminist movements is that they mainly fought for women's rights to obtain abortions. The movements may have unintentionally left behind many poor and minority females who did not have the economic resources to decide whether to carry their pregnancies to term and make desirable choices about raising children.[119] As one of my respondents noted, "All of these social problems fall more heavily on Black women because we live in a racist society." Rather than simply fighting for abortion rights, some social movement leaders (e.g., Loretta Ross) argue that the pro-choice movement's primary concern should be reproductive justice, which entails placing reproductive health issues in the larger context of the well-being and health of women, families, and communities.[120]

SisterSong Women of Color Reproductive Justice Collective was one of the pro-choice organizations that responded to Atlanta's Endangered Species billboard campaign. They fought back with an empowerment message, "Trust Black Women," which advocated for trusting women, especially the black females who were targeted in the billboards, to make the best decision given their circumstances.[121] Furthermore, they tried to contextualize black women's high abortion rates. They argued that a lack of human rights protection for black women has contributed to increases in sexual violence within their community and limited access to contraceptives, health services, comprehensive sex education, and pregnancy-prevention programs.[122] As a result, black women have higher rates of abortion because they have to contend with more unanticipated pregnancies.

If a lack of resources has increased the need for abortions in the African American community, restrictions on abortion access may further exacerbate the challenges many of these women encounter. One of the medical doctors I interviewed thought that abortion policies were also race based. She correctly pointed out that most people on Medicaid, which provides

[119] Almeling, "Reproduction," 343.
[120] Almeling.
[121] Luna, "'Black Children Are an Endangered Species.'"
[122] Thompson et al., "Racism Runs through It."

156 FETAL POSITIONS

federal health insurance for low-income people in America, are black or minorities.[123] As a result, her abortion patients at hospitals "are mostly well-off, educated, and white. And then the patients I see in the abortion clinic are almost all Black." Many of these patients "will forego anesthesia because they can't afford it, which is tragic." From her perspective, racism and economic inequality extended to the physical abortion experience.

Several studies have examined African Americans' attitudes about abortion, which are also complicated because of the group's high levels of conservative Protestant religious belief and engagement. As discussed previously, women, on average, are more religious than men,[124] and religiosity and conservative Protestant affiliation is associated with more abortion disapproval.[125] The traditional Black Church in America has many of the same guiding religious principles as other conservative Protestant faiths.[126] Likewise, the civil rights movement is closely connected to the traditional Black Church, an essential organizing force for racial equality.[127]

Indeed, surveys show that black Americans tend to be more opposed to abortion. However, once their higher levels of religiosity are considered, few differences emerge between them and other Americans in their level of abortion disapproval.[128] Indeed, some studies show that African Americans appear more liberal after accounting for religion.[129] I asked one black minister how religious African Americans might reconcile conservative biblical perspectives about abortion and black women's higher abortion rates. From his perspective, racial inequality was the primary concern for African Americans. Black women were making the best choices they could among the challenging circumstances produced by the legacy of slavery and ongoing racial inequality. In contrast to the prominence given racial inequality in the black community, polling data following the *Dobbs* decision showed that Americans generally felt abortion was a greater concern than racial inequality.[130] The majority of white Americans are likely more concerned about abortion than racial inequality.

---

[123] Guth and Artigua, "Medicaid and Racial Health Equity."
[124] Schnabel, "Does Religion Suppress Gender Differences in Values?"
[125] Adamczyk and Valdimarsdóttir, "Understanding Americans' Abortion Attitudes."
[126] Steensland et al., "The Measure of American Religion."
[127] Lincoln and Mamiya, *The Black Church in the African American Experience.*
[128] Wilcox, "Race, Religion, Region and Abortion Attitudes"; Adamczyk and Valdimarsdóttir, "Understanding Americans' Abortion Attitudes."
[129] Gay and Lynxwiler, "The Impact of Religiosity on Race Variations in Abortion Attitudes."
[130] Newport, "Abortion Moves Up on 'Most Important Problem' List."

When asked who the public thinks gets abortions, some of my respondents said that race entered the stereotype. As one person explained, "[The public] pictures minority women getting the abortions, but then all the stuff they do about saving lives on the pro-life side, they're talking about white babies." She felt that the pro-life movement was focused on saving white babies, but they tended to think of black women getting abortions. Another respondent clarified, "People think about who is responsible. Young women are considered irresponsible. Black women are considered irresponsible." From her perspective, the public would have racialized stereotypes of black women needing abortions because they are more likely to be seen as sexually active outside of marriage and irresponsible with birth control.

In the United States, race clearly complicates the abortion debate. Other ethnically and racially diverse countries may contend with similar complexity. In more monoethnic countries, discussions about disparities across diverse racial and ethnic groups may not be a major topic, or largely focus on small fringe groups such as gypsies or native populations. Even then, public understanding of abortion may not be affected. As noted in Chapter 2, although there were several news reports about ethnic Uyghurs in China being forced to get abortions at the time I was conducting interviews,[131] Chinese respondents minimally mentioned them.

Conclusion

This chapter examined the roles of gender inequality, social movement activity, and racism in understanding public opinion about abortion. Across the world, higher levels of gender inequality are linked to more abortion disapproval, even after accounting for a host of individual and country-level factors. In places where gender inequality is high, everyone is likely to be affected by cultural and societal forces that lead to more disapproval. In the United States and China, we can see how these influences play out with women shouldering high physical, emotional, and societal costs for having an abortion or becoming single mothers. In countries with high levels of economic inequality, such as the United States, some racial and ethnic groups may obtain abortions not because it is the choice they want but because they must for economic reasons. A mixture of high religiosity, democracy,

---

[131] Associated Press, "Uyghur Exiles Describe Forced Abortions, Torture in Xinjiang."

158 FETAL POSITIONS

and economic development has contributed to US abortion-related social movement activity. While this relatively prosperous and democratic country is unique in making abortion illegal, it is not alone in linking abortion opposition to white nationalism.

I turn now to Chapter 5, which considers the role of other cultural and personal values associated with disapproval. Throughout the world, communism has had an important historical impact on people's views about abortion, restricting abortion access in countries such as Romania and limiting the number of pregnancies women can have in China. Likewise, several nations in East Asia with Confucian histories are more opposed to abortion than their levels of religious belief, economic development, and democracy might otherwise suggest. In addition to examining these differences, I assess the various dimensions of abortion attitudes. I show how residents' views about the morality of abortion differ from their feelings about its legality and how asking about the circumstances for obtaining an abortion (e.g., a form of birth control vs. genetic defects) changes people's level of support. These findings add a layer of complexity to our understanding of public opinion about abortion.

Chapter 5

Communism, Confucianism, Cultural Values, and Survey Challenges for Understanding Abortion Attitudes

So far, this book has focused on the macro-level factors vital for understanding cross-national abortion attitudes. Some additional societal-level characteristics are needed to develop a fuller understanding of the measurable forces shaping individuals' abortion views across the globe. This chapter examines those remaining factors, including communism and differences between countries that have Confucian histories. Even though the Soviet Union collapsed in the early 1990s, the political system left an indelible mark on abortion attitudes and behaviors. Likewise, residents from societies with Confucian histories (e.g., China, South Korea, Japan, Taiwan) have different views about abortion than people living elsewhere. I discuss and test some of the factors that may be shaping disapproval.

In this chapter, I also show that personal values related to the family, sexual morality, and ending life are essential for understanding individual differences. However, they do not contribute to cultural effects that influence most residents' abortion views over and above their personal values. I then discuss the many other factors that I considered but were not statistically related to cross-national abortion disapproval once other measures were considered. Finally, I talk about the different dimensions of abortion public opinion and how changing the attitudinal questions administrators ask can shape survey findings. To assess the reliability of the World Values Survey (WVS), the chapter ends with a comparison of disapproval of abortion across three different international surveys.

Communism

In Chapter 3, I examined democracy's role in encouraging more liberal abortion attitudes across the globe. Whether a county has a communist

160   FETAL POSITIONS

history is also important for understanding cross-national views. Communist governments typically have low levels of democracy. But even after
accounting for government representation, survey respondents from countries with communist histories, especially those that were part of the former
Soviet Union, are unique from others in their attitudes.

The Soviet Union (i.e., the Union of Soviet Socialist Republics) was a
large socialist country that spanned Europe and Asia, lasting from 1922
until 1991. After Tsar Nicholas II lost power in 1917, Russia initiated
the building of a communist republic. The Soviet Union eventually grew
to include fifteen nations (Armenia, Azerbaijan, Belarus, Estonia, Georgia, Kazakhstan, Kyrgyzstan, Latvia, Lithuania, Moldova, Russia, Tajikistan,
Turkmenistan, Ukraine, and Uzbekistan) and several satellite states (Poland,
Romania, Czechoslovakia, Hungary, Bulgaria, East Germany, Yugoslavia,[1]
and Albania[2]). While some countries became part of the Soviet Union in
the 1920s, others joined later (e.g., after World War II). Throughout the
twentieth century, Russia had outsized influence on the other Soviet Union
countries. The Soviet government owned most business, set prices, and
decided what to produce. Its unofficial religion policy was state atheism, and
it tried to limit religion's influence.

In 1991, the Soviet Union internally dissolved. All the original republics
became independent and remain so today. With the disintegration, Moscow
lost most of its power over the other countries. Even though the Soviet Union
ended more than thirty years ago, it left a strong legacy with implications for
abortion attitudes and behaviors. In this section, I explain how early abortion legalization within Russia, efforts to minimize religion's influence, the
centralized government, and nation building shape how many former Soviet
Union residents likely see abortion today.

As part of communist-related efforts to support gender equality, Russia,
which was the largest and most influential Soviet Union country, legalized abortion in 1920. At the time, it was the first modern nation to do so.
Because of concerns about low fertility rates, Russia reversed its abortion
policy in 1936, banning and criminalizing abortion. Officials then made it
legal again in 1955. Because abortion was initially introduced long before
effective means of birth control, like the pill or intrauterine devices (IUDs),

---

[1] Yugoslavia was a satellite state until it broke away in 1948.
[2] Albania was a satellite state until it broke off from the Soviet Union in 1960.

COMMUNISM, CONFUCIANISM, CULTURAL VALUES 161

there is a history in former Soviet Union countries of using abortion to control fertility. Furthermore, because the Soviet Union was officially atheistic, there was little objection to abortion based on religious or moral grounds.[3]

For understanding the role of communism in shaping attitudes, residents' abortion behaviors are important. Before the Soviet Union legalized abortion in the 1920s, approximately 20% of Russian pregnancies ended in abortions.[4] Once it was legal, Soviet clinics provided abortions free of charge, leading to widespread abortion use, mainly because there were few reliable sources of birth control.[5] In the 1960s, after the Stalin-era ban was lifted, abortion rates again soared. While the Soviet Union constituted only about 5% to 6% of the globe's population, the Russians may have accounted for 25% of the world's abortions.[6] After the Soviet Union collapsed in the early 1990s, these countries reported some of the highest abortion rates in the world.[7]

Abortion rates are challenging to compare across nations because medical (i.e., mifepristone and misoprostol) and illegal abortions are difficult to track. Nevertheless, relative to countries where abortion is legal and thus data are likely more accurate, former Soviet Union countries continue to report some of the highest abortion rates in the world.[8] Additionally, in many Soviet Union countries, abortion was never stigmatized to the same extent as elsewhere because it had long been legal and normative.[9] Thus, women and medical establishments in this region may be more likely to provide accurate data on the number of abortions.

As other forms of birth control, like IUDs and hormone-based birth control pills became popular during the latter part of the twentieth century, they remained more difficult to obtain in the Soviet Union. Even if people could get them, some of these other forms of birth control had bad reputations, further increasing reliance on abortion. For example, the pills introduced into the Soviet Union had especially high hormone levels, causing major side

---

[3] Karpov and Kääriäinen, "'Abortion Culture' in Russia"; Mason, "Opposing Abortion to Protect Women."
[4] Popov and David, "Russian Federation and USSR Successor States."
[5] Westoff, *Recent Trends in Abortion and Contraception in 12 Countries.*
[6] Popov and David, "Russian Federation and USSR Successor States."
[7] Popov and David.
[8] Bearak et al., "Country-Specific Estimates of Unintended Pregnancy and Abortion Incidence."
[9] Jilozian and Agadjanian, "Is Induced Abortion Really Declining in Armenia?"

162   FETAL POSITIONS

effects for female consumers.[10] Likewise, even if people could obtain condoms, there were challenges. Soviet-era condoms consisted of rubber instead of latex, making them especially thick.[11] Moreover, they were unlubricated and therefore particularly uncomfortable.

Communist countries outside the Soviet Union have encountered some of the same quality-related challenges linked to the planned economy.[12] Reports from communist Cuba, for example, indicate that some of the early IUDs were poorly made, causing infections and other side effects.[13] Likewise, Cuba's medical establishment provided only minimal medical follow-up for IUDs, exacerbating health problems stemming from problematic devices and their placement.[14] Furthermore, in the Soviet Union abortions may have inadvertently been encouraged because they were free but typically required a hospital stay.[15] Hence, the Soviet Union medical establishment had a financial incentive to provide abortions rather than sterilization or medically prescribed birth control.[16]

In all former Soviet Union countries, abortion is legal through the first trimester. However, today abortion on demand is typically not free. Although several of these nations routinely report very high abortion rates, they have decreased over time.[17] Nevertheless, certain types of birth control are still challenging to obtain.[18] Likewise, the medications needed for medical or chemical abortions are cheap and widely available without a doctor's oversight. Although abortions without medical supervision are discouraged, there are reports that they may be common in some former Soviet Union countries.[19]

Based on the history of abortion in the Soviet Union, we might think these residents would strongly support abortion. However, there are several reasons for them to disapprove as well. Since the collapse of the Soviet Union, officials have tried to reduce high abortion rates partially because a meaningful minority of abortions caused women major health problems and

[10] Cooper, "Women Fault Soviet System for Abortion."
[11] Popov and David, "Russian Federation and USSR Successor States."
[12] Gammeltoft, *Women's Bodies, Women's Worries.*
[13] Bélanger and Flynn, "The Persistence of Induced Abortion in Cuba."
[14] Bélanger and Flynn.
[15] DaVanzo and Grammich, *Dire Demographics.*
[16] Popov and David, "Russian Federation and USSR Successor States."
[17] Westoff et al. *Replacement of Abortion by Contraception in Three Central Asian Republics* Agadjanian, "Is 'Abortion Culture' Fading in the Former Soviet Union?"; Jargin, "High Abortion Rate in Russia: On the Role of Condom Use and Alcohol Misuse."
[18] Jilozian and Agadjanian, "Is Induced Abortion Really Declining in Armenia?"
[19] Jilozian and Agadjanian.

infertility.[20] Additionally, as these countries have opened to Western products and improved birth control manufacturing, access to higher-quality options have increased, limiting the need for abortions. These nations have also launched major mass media campaigns encouraging women to use other types of contraception to control fertility.[21]

Gender inequality may also shape views about abortion in these countries. Like others, some former Soviet Union countries (e.g., Azerbaijan and Armenia)[22] have cultural histories where boys have historically been viewed as more valuable than girls, leading to sex-selective abortions and gender imbalances.[23] Today, sex-selective abortions are increasingly stigmatized.[24]

Finally, following the collapse of the Soviet Union, many residents developed a renewed interest in national identity related to their newfound independence. As I explain below, part of their strategy to rally support and forge a collective identity has focused on the importance of mothers in producing the next generation of citizens.

In 1991, the Soviet Union officially dissolved. Several of its states became independent, sometimes peacefully or after periods of war. Ultimately, the Soviet Union broke into 15 nations, with Russia being the largest (144 million), followed by Ukraine (36 million) and Uzbekistan (35 million).[25] Many of the satellite states (i.e., Poland, Romania, Czechoslovakia, Hungary, Bulgaria, East Germany, Yugoslavia,[26] and Albania[27]) joined the European Union in 2007. No longer underneath the yoke of the centralized government, countries closer to Europe became more European, and those in Central Asia developed stronger ties with the East.[28]

In an effort to forge a national identity and rally citizen support, several former Soviet Union countries have drawn on nationalist rhetoric. In Russia, for example, political and economic changes following the collapse of the Soviet Union were accompanied by a "celebration of masculinity" and women's loss of status.[29] In most of the former Soviet Union countries, birth rates were especially low in the 1990s, related to a chaotic

---

[20] DaVanzo and Grammich, *Dire Demographics*.
[21] Perlman and McKee, "Trends in Family Planning in Russia, 1994–2003."
[22] Guilmoto, *Sex Imbalances at Birth in Armenia: Demographic Evidence and Analysis*.
[23] Jilozian and Agadjanian, "Is Induced Abortion Really Declining in Armenia?"
[24] Jilozian and Agadjanian.
[25] "Total Population by Country 2023."
[26] Yugoslavia was a satellite state until it broke away in 1948.
[27] Albania was a satellite state until it broke off from the Soviet Union in 1960.
[28] Shleifer and Treisman, "The East 25 Years after Communism."
[29] Attwood, "The Post-Soviet Woman in the Move to the Market."

164   FETAL POSITIONS

and unpredictable social, economic, and political transition.[30] To increase fertility and reduce abortions, the Russian government removed abortion coverage from state-sponsored medical insurance in 1994.[31] At the same time, a pro-life movement aided by conservative Christians began to emerge within Russia and other former Soviet Union states.[32] Unencumbered by official atheist ideology, religious belief increased in many of these newly created nations.[33] With their newfound power, religious officials and organizations have tried to shape residents' attitudes and values, including those related to abortion. Similar to the United States, countries like Russia have developed rhetoric around preserving the dominant "white" population.[34]

What is the effect of living in a former communist country in shaping abortion disapproval? We have good reason to think that people from these countries would be more opposed. Residents in many former Soviet countries may be aware of their high abortion rates and officials have tried to discourage them. Additionally, a minority of women have had medical complications related to abortion. Sex-selective abortions are increasingly stigmatized. Likewise, political leaders have tried to fuse a sense of national identity with religion and the glorification of motherhood. Nevertheless, the former Soviet Union countries have mostly had very liberal abortion-related policies. Likewise, during communism, these countries lacked a moral or religious imperative to oppose abortion.

To assess the role of living in a country with a communist past in shaping abortion disapproval, I divided the eighty-eight available countries from the last three waves in the WVS into four groups: (1) currently communist (i.e., China, Macau, and Vietnam); (2) former Soviet satellite countries, but not a part of the Soviet Union; (3) the Soviet Union; and (4) no communist history. I then included them in a multivariate mixed model, which accounts for other personal and country characteristics. This analysis tells us whether there are statistical differences in disapproval across the countries based on communist history, after accounting for other important factors. Model 5 of Table A.3 in Appendix A shows that residents from former Soviet Union

[30] DaVanzo and Grammich, *Dire Demographics*; Westoff et al., "Replacement of Abortion by Contraception in Three Central Asian Republics."
[31] Sargent, "The 'Woman Question' and Problems of Maternity in Post-Communist Russia."
[32] Albanese, "Abortion & Reproductive Rights under Nationalist Regimes in Twentieth Century Europe"; Mason, "Opposing Abortion to Protect Women."
[33] Sarkissian, "Religion and Civic Engagement in Muslim Countries."
[34] Mason, "Opposing Abortion to Protect Women."

countries are *less* likely to approve of abortion than people from societies without a communist history.

Figure 5.1 provides the marginal values for each set of countries based on their communist past so that we can see how the four groups differ from each other. With an average disapproval score of 8.69 (on a scale ranging from 1 to 10, with higher numbers indicating more disapproval), people from the former Soviet Socialist Republic are the most opposed. Confidence intervals indicate statistically significant differences between the groups. There are no significant differences between the former Soviet Union countries (i.e., 8.69) and current communist societies (i.e., China, Macau, and Vietnam). However, residents from the former Soviet Republic are more opposed than those from the Soviet satellite states (i.e., 7.45) and nations without communist pasts (i.e., 7.61). These differences appear even after accounting for the countries' religious context, educational and economic development, democracy, and other individual and country-level factors (see Appendix A).

In a separate analysis, I examined attitudinal differences among residents from the former Soviet Union countries to isolate the nations that are most opposed. The last three waves of the WVS provide information on twelve of the fifteen former Soviet Union countries. The mean disapproval score across all eighty-eight countries in the sample is 7.71 (where 10 = never justified). Estonia (6.07) and Russia (6.64) are the former Soviet Union countries housing the most liberal populations. The most conservative ones predominantly reside in Central Asia, specifically Azerbaijan (8.07), Armenia (8.57), Uzbekistan (8.46), Tajikistan (8.67), Georgia (8.77), and Kyrgyzstan (8.88).[35]

Given the Soviet Union's legal history and high abortion rates, more conservative attitudes seem inconsistent. However, residents likely responded to the WVS question by drawing on the national, cultural, and historical context surrounding abortion in their society. The WVS question asks, "Please tell me for each of the following statements whether you think [abortion] can always be justified, never be justified, or something in between, using this card." Many residents may have interpreted the question as, "Is abortion always justified, including as a form of birth control or for sex selection?" These residents may generally want legal abortion access through

---

[35] While four of the six countries have Islam as a dominant religion, as shown in Chapter 1 there are few major differences between Muslims and other religious adherents. Kazakhstan is also largely dominated by Islam, but residents' average disapproval score is only 7.50, which is more liberal than the sample mean of 7.71, where high numbers indicate greater disapproval.

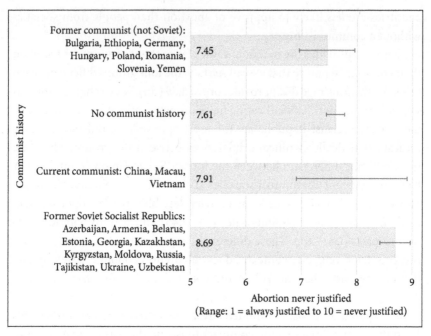

Figure 5.1 Marginal Values for Abortion Disapproval by Country's Communist History (Society N = 88; Individual N = 211,317)

Notes: Marginal values are drawn from Appendix A, Table A.3, Model 8. All other variables in the model are held constant. Statistically significant differences are found between countries that were a part of the former Soviet Union and two groups: (1) countries without a community history and (2) former community or Soviet satellite states but not officially part of the Soviet Union. There are no statistically significant differences between current communist countries and other groups. The countries without a communist history are Algeria, Andorra, Argentina, Australia, Bangladesh, Bolivia, Brazil, Burkina Faso, Canada, Chile, Colombia, Cyprus, Ecuador, Egypt, Finland, France, Ghana, Greece, Guatemala, Haiti, Hong Kong SAR, India, Indonesia, Iran, Iraq, Italy, Japan, Jordan, Kuwait, Lebanon, Libya, Malaysia, Mali, Mexico, Morocco, Myanmar, Netherlands, New Zealand, Nicaragua, Nigeria, Norway, Pakistan, Palestine, Peru, Philippines, Puerto Rico, Qatar, Rwanda, Serbia, Singapore, South Africa, South Korea, Spain, Sweden, Switzerland, Taiwan ROC, Thailand, Trinidad and Tobago, Tunisia, Turkey, United Kingdom, United States, Uruguay, Zambia, and Zimbabwe.

Source: WVS, waves 5, 6, and 7

the first trimester.[36] However, they may believe that it is less acceptable for sex-selective abortions and as a form of birth control, which is how some women used abortion in the past. This perspective would be consistent with the messaging residents have received since the collapse of the Soviet Union from government, health, and religious organizations. Likewise, many women may have first-hand or second-hand experience with

---

[36] Center for Reproductive Rights, "The World's Abortion Laws," 2023.

abortion-related medical problems, prompting them to respond that it is not always justifiable.[37]

Research also suggests that many survey respondents from former Soviet Union countries may still have a "Soviet habit" of telling outsiders, including researchers, officially sanctioned views regarding topics such as abortion, divorce, and premarital sex.[38] Many residents may distrust strangers conducting studies, even when survey administrators assure respondents that their answers are confidential. During Soviet times, many residents learned to intentionally report attitudes consistent with official views.

Many citizens may also express strong outward national pride. They may feel that their survey responses are a way to indicate support for their "new" country in forging a national identity based on "family values" that discourage divorce, premarital sex, and abortion. Citizens may reserve their personal feelings for private conversations and get abortions as needed.[39] After all, abortion was legal for decades. Many women got them and continue to do so today. Moreover, the Soviet Union promoted gender equality, and traditional religious beliefs that encouraged a patriarchal family system were largely obsolete. As the researchers of one study trying to make sense of similarly inconsistent findings concluded, seven decades of Soviet rule left an imprint that does not easily disappear, even if survey data show strong disapproval of abortion, premarital sex, and divorce.[40] In the next section, I discuss the potential influence of an "abortion culture" in these countries.

Abortion Culture

Given the lack of high-quality birth control, easy access to abortion, and few moral or religious restraints, many Soviet Union residents may have become accustomed to using abortion to manage unanticipated pregnancies. This may have led to the prevalence of abortion, establishing and reinforcing the abortion industry. Some researchers have suggested that within this "culture," abortion may have been viewed as a necessary, if painful, "medical procedure comparable to the removal of a tooth."[41] While abortion rates were

---

[37] Stewart, "Curbing Reliance on Abortion in Russia."
[38] Lopatina, Kostenko, and Ponarin, "Pro-Life vs. Pro-Choice in a Resurgent Nation."
[39] Lopatina, Kostenko, and Ponarin.
[40] Lopatina, Kostenko, and Ponarin.
[41] Remennick, "Epidemology and Determinants of Induced Abortion in the U.S.S.R.," 844.

168   FETAL POSITIONS

especially high following the collapse of the Soviet Union in the 1990s, they have fallen substantially since then. Nevertheless, available data suggest that they remain some of the highest in the world.

Is there evidence of an "abortion culture" in the former Soviet Union countries? Indeed, the public opinion data presented here suggest that there is not. On average, residents from the former Soviet Union are more opposed to abortion than others. But as discussed above, the survey data may not be very reliable.

Another way that scholars have tested for the existence of an "abortion culture" is to see whether personal characteristics related to abortion disapproval in societies with greater objection also has an effect in the former Soviet Union countries.[42] Using this logic, women from countries with "abortion cultures" should not differ substantially in their attitudes based on individual characteristics, such as gender, age, and educational attainment, because presumably everyone views abortion through the same cultural lens of acceptance.

To assess whether there is an abortion culture shaping attitudes in the former Soviet Union, I examined the influence of six personal characteristics[43] (gender, age, marital status, income, education, the strength of religious belief) from the models found in Appendix A, Table A.3 within each nation. I focused on these characteristics because in the cross-national sample they are associated with attitudes and other studies have confirmed their link.[44]

For every former Soviet Union country, there were at least two statistically significant characteristics. On average, I found that 3.3 out of 6 personal characteristics were significant. With a total of five, Russian survey respondents had the most factors (gender, age, marital status, income, and strength of religious importance) that were significant ($p < 0.05$). Conversely, Kyrgyzstan, Azerbaijan, and Uzbekistan had the fewest at two. As a comparison, the United States had five factors related to abortion disapproval, and China had three (marital status, education, and religious belief).

---

[42] Karpov and Kääriäinen, "'Abortion Culture' in Russia"; Lopatina, Kostenko, and Ponarin, "Pro-Life vs. Pro-Choice in a Resurgent Nation."

[43] For this analysis, I did not include religious affiliation because the number of different religions varied across nations and in some places all respondents identified with only two religious categories. There were four marital status categories where "married" was the reference.

[44] Adamczyk, "Religion as a Micro and Macro Property"; Scheepers, Te Grotenhuis, and Van Der Slik, "Education, Religiosity and Moral Attitudes"; Finke and Adamczyk, "Cross-National Moral Beliefs: The Influence of National Religious Context."

This analysis suggests that these countries do not have an easily measured "abortion culture." The following section shifts from an analysis of communism to the potential role of personal and cultural values in shaping disapproval.

Personal and Cultural Values in Shaping Disapproval

People may disapprove of abortion for a wide array of reasons, ranging from seeing it as a sexually immoral activity to feeling that women should follow traditional norms that discourage it. When a substantial portion of a nation feels strongly about a given value, norm, or belief, their combined feeling could create a contextual effect that in turn may shape the views of most residents in the country.

In Chapter 2, I showed how religious importance has a contextual effect. Regardless of their personal religious beliefs, residents in countries with higher overall religious importance are more likely to disapprove of abortion. This section considers other potential cultural contextual influences. I focus on views about sexual morality and euthanasia and the importance of obedience and the family. I dissect the relationships between these values and abortion disapproval. As I explain below, these values are meaningful for understanding differences between people in their personal feelings about abortion. However, none have a cultural influence that can explain cross-national differences.

Sexual Morality

Previous studies have suggested a range of values and views that may shape abortion disapproval. Chief among them are feelings about sexual deviance.[45] Sexual morality or deviance issues include sex-related behaviors that might be considered wrong or problematic as opposed to right or good, such as same-sex relations, prostitution, sex before marriage, and casual sex. People who think these behaviors are more acceptable may also be more supportive of abortion and vice versa. They may disapprove of all of these

---

[45] Finke and Adamczyk, "Cross-National Moral Beliefs: The Influence of National Religious Context"; Scheepers, Te Grotenhuis, and Van Der Slik, "Education, Religiosity and Moral Attitudes."

170   FETAL POSITIONS

issues because of an underlying factor, such as conservative values. Alternatively, they may value certain things, such as a traditional family structure, making them less supportive of at least some sexual deviance behaviors.

Most research on abortion disapproval has been conducted within individual countries. As a result, we do not know whether a "cultural" effect is related to views about sexual morality. However, the cross-national data from the last three waves of the WVS, which has information on over eighty nations, can provide insight.

The WVS asked respondents about the acceptability of prostitution and homosexuality,[46] which are two important sexual morality issues.[47] Table 5.1 provides information on the relationship between these values as individual and country-level attributes. People who are more likely to report that homosexuality and prostitution are not justified are also more likely to say that abortion is problematic. However, I do not find a cultural effect where people living in countries that are on average more opposed to these sexual morality issues are also more personally opposed to abortion. In other words, personal feelings about these topics are related to abortion disapproval, but there is no societal effect that extends further and could help explain cross-national differences.

Table 5.1 notes that there is an individual-level relationship between abortion disapproval and opposition to prostitution and homosexuality, showing the micro connections among these issues. However, this analysis is somewhat limited because it cannot tell us whether disapproval of prostitution and homosexuality "predict" abortion attitudes or views about abortion "explain" feelings about homosexuality and prostitution. In other words, we cannot establish the correct causal order among these factors. Additionally, while prostitution, homosexuality, and abortion are distinct behaviors, they could be part of a larger underlying concept of "sexual morality." Because they may be seen as similar, researchers sometimes combine them into a sexual morality scale.[48] In this case, the public opinion topic being examined is

---

[46] "Homosexuality" is the term used in the WVS. In many countries, this term is seen as antiquated, but it is still often used in many countries. Survey administrators have likely continued to use the same term so that they can assess changes over time using the same question wording.

[47] Some countries also asked questions about premarital, casual, and underage sex, but this included only a subset of nations.

[48] Finke and Adamczyk, "Cross-National Moral Beliefs: The Influence of National Religious Context"; Scheepers, Te Grotenhuis, and Van Der Slik, "Education, Religiosity and Moral Attitudes."

Table 5.1 Individual and Country-Level Values for Understanding Abortion Disapproval

		Level of Analysis for Examining Individuals' Abortion Disapproval	
		Individual	*Country/Cultural*
Values & Measures examined	Disapproval of sexual morality issues—homosexuality	Yes, significant effect	No significant effect
	Disapproval of sexual morality issues—prostitution		
	Obedience/ conforming are important—conforming is important trait in children		
	Disapproval of marital dissolution—divorce	More disapproval of abortion	
	Family values—family very important		
	Disapproval of ending life—euthanasia		

Notes: The individual and country values' measures were examined with all the other variables indicated in Model 7 of Table A.3 in Appendix A. In every model but the one for euthanasia the country values' effect did not reach statistical significance ($p < 0.05$). When all the individual-level values were included in the same model the country-level measure for euthanasia was no longer statistically significant either. When included together, all the individual-level values, as well as personal religious importance, were statistically significant, indicating that they each have an independent relationship with abortion disapproval.

not abortion or same-sex relations per se, but rather disapproval of sexual morality.

As I was conducting research for this book, I considered whether the WVS question about abortion was part of a larger dimension of sexual morality. In this case, much of my research source material would address sexual morality more generally. However, there are several reasons to feel confident that the findings speak to abortion specifically. To begin, the correlations among disapproval of homosexuality, abortion, and prostitution are relatively high. But they are not so high that quantitative social scientists would necessarily combine them into a single scale.[49] Additionally, some forces

---

[49] Mukaka, "Statistics Corner."

172 FETAL POSITIONS

that explain abortion disapproval, such as gender inequality, do not likewise explain views about homosexuality and prostitution, further suggesting that abortion is distinct.[50]

Moreover, in some countries, public opinion about issues such as abortion and homosexuality has evolved in dissimilar ways, suggesting that these topics are distinct. For example, in the United States, views about same-sex relations have become radically more liberal over the past forty years.[51] Specifically, in 1977, 43% of Americans thought that gay or lesbian relations between consenting adults should be legal. But by 2019, acceptance had climbed 40 points to 83%.[52] Conversely, Gallup data suggest that views about abortion changed fairly minimally between the 1970s—when the *Roe v. Wade* decision recognized women's constitutional right to abortion— and 2022. In 1977, 21% of Americans thought that abortion should be legal under any circumstance. By 2019, a similar percentage (25%) still felt this way.[53] In 2022, the proportion of Americans who said that it should be legal under any circumstance rose to 35%. Because of state trigger laws, the 2022 *Dobbs* decision resulted in abortion becoming illegal in several states, which likely energized abortion supporters.[54] Like the proportion feeling that it should be legal under *any* circumstances, the percentage reporting that abortion should be legal under *certain* circumstances has hovered between 50% and 60% for the past forty-five years.

In my interviews, I asked Americans why they thought abortion attitudes had not become more liberal over the past few decades as they have for issues related to lesbian, gay, bisexual, transgender, and queer (LGBTQ) individuals. Some of them noted that Americans have developed friendlier attitudes toward LGBTQ people partially because of the "coming out" movement, whereby people tell others how they sexually identify. By revealing their identities, many individuals may realize that they know someone from this community. Familiarity and humanization make it harder to dislike the entire group. But as one of my antiabortion respondents explained, "With abortion, it's not like every woman who's hiding it thinks that it was a great choice. So, in that sense, it's different." In other words, the LGBTQ community has supported people "coming out" so that they can live more authentic

[50] Adamczyk, *Cross-National Public Opinion about Homosexuality*; Cao and Stack, "Exploring Terra Incognita."
[51] Adamczyk, *Cross-National Public Opinion about Homosexuality*.
[52] Gallup Inc., "Gallup First Polled on Gay Issues in '77. What Has Changed?"
[53] Gallup Inc., "Abortion."
[54] Gallup Inc.

lives, and it helps the overall movement. But many women who get abortions may feel that it was a highly personal decision that they do not want to advertise.

Respondents also explained that the LGBTQ movement has a better message and that opposition is weaker. One pro-life supporter explained that the LGBTQ movement's focus on justice was fairly straightforward. But "with abortion, it's much more complicated. We have claims about justice from women or from men about women, and then you have claims about prenatal justice for the child." Relatedly, a professor noted that antiabortion advocates are much better organized than LGBTQ opponents. Likewise, one respondent explained that LGBTQ individuals can claim "this is how I was born." Conversely, "abortion is a choice." In other words, abortion advocates have a weaker message than LGBTQ supporters.

Finally, both pro-life and pro-choice supporters noted that ultrasounds help to humanize the fetus, contributing to abortion opposition. Conversely, the LGBTQ movement never had to contend with such sensitive images, though early supporters were careful to present a family-friendly perspective of gay and lesbian individuals.[55] For multiple reasons, many people are likely to see abortion and LGBTQ-related issues as distinct.

Obedience Orientation

In addition to more disapproving views about sexual morality issues in general, residents who share attributes of an authoritarian personality may also be less supportive. Some of the characteristics of an authoritarian personality include a strong desire for power, status, security, order, structured authority, and obedience. Because individuals with these traits have a stronger attachment to the status quo, they are more likely to oppose behaviors inconsistent with dominant norms and values. Abortion may be seen as challenging establishments like the traditional family.[56] Likewise, people with a stronger interest in abiding by dominant norms may be less supportive of sex outside of marriage, which could be seen as disrupting the world's natural order. Therefore, a potential unplanned pregnancy may be viewed as

[55] Schiappa, Gregg, and Hewes, "Can One TV Show Make a Difference?"; Bonds-Raacke et al., "Remembering Gay/Lesbian Media Characters"; Adamczyk and Liao, "Examining Public Opinion about LGBTQ-Related Issues in the United States and across Multiple Nations."

[56] Haddock and Zanna, "Authoritarianism, Values, and the Favorability and Structure of Antigay Attitudes."

174 FETAL POSITIONS

a deterrent against extramarital sex, which abortion could then undermine. Research has also found that people with authoritarian personality characteristics are more likely to respond punitively toward individuals whose behaviors are viewed as unconventional,[57] which may include women who get abortions.

The WVS allows us to assess the relationship between obedience,[58] which is one aspect of an authoritarian personality, and abortion disapproval. Are people with a stronger obedience orientation more opposed to abortion? As noted in Table 5.1, after accounting for all other attributes (e.g., age, religious importance, gender), respondents who are more likely to say that obedience is important are less supportive.

If a substantial number of people have a stronger obedience orientation, a cultural influence could emerge. Some researchers have argued that Confucianism, for example, emphasizes interdependence among individuals and others.[59] As a result, residents from countries with Confucian histories and cultures may be more likely to feel that success depends on the harmony and strength of the group. In those places, abortion could be viewed as disrupting the natural order of things.

I examined whether there is a societal effect of valuing obedience in shaping residents' views about abortion. As indicated in Table 5.1, I did not find a country-level obedience association. Instead, I found that the value of obedience is only related to abortion disapproval as an individual attribute.

Family Values

In many countries where abortion is contentious, the debate is often framed as a family values issue. In these places, the family might be viewed as laying the basis for people's expectations for their roles in public life, giving rise to a community of trust modeled on the family.[60] If the family is considered especially important, individuals may feel that all pregnancies should be brought to term since they extend the family. Likewise, people who value the family unit may also believe that divorce is problematic. Rather than dissolving the

---

[57] Abrams and Della Fave, "Authoritarianism, Religiosity, and the Legalization of Victimless Crimes."

[58] Specifically, the survey asks respondents what characteristics they think is important for a child and obedience is one option.

[59] Bond, "Beyond the Chinese Face"; Hsu, *Americans and Chinese.*

[60] Tu, "A Confucian Perspective on the Rise of Industrial East Asia."

COMMUNISM, CONFUCIANISM, CULTURAL VALUES   175

marriage, they may argue that spouses should remain together regardless of difficult circumstances.

Does family importance and feelings about divorce influence abortion attitudes? The findings presented in Table A.3 of Appendix A show that married individuals are more likely than single, divorced, and cohabitating people to disapprove of abortion. Widowed people are the only ones that are more conservative than married individuals. Beyond marital status, the WVS also includes questions about the importance of family and justification for divorce. These data provide additional insight into how family views shape abortion attitudes.

Across the world, most people feel that family is important. Indeed, 91% of respondents surveyed during the last three waves of the WVS report that family is "very important," which is the highest level of approval they can indicate. As noted in Table 5.1, people who specify that family is "very important" or feel that divorce is less justifiable are more opposed to abortion.

While individuals who emphasize family importance are less supportive of abortion, is there a cultural effect of family values in shaping abortion disapproval? Researchers have suggested that countries with Chinese histories or Confucian cultures are particularly family-oriented,[61] which may shape their views about abortion. For example, crude divorce rates worldwide have risen over the last thirty years. However, they have remained relatively low in East Asia, where several countries with Confucian cultures are located.[62] Likewise, in my previous research, I found that views about marriage had a powerful role in shaping disapproval of same-sex relations in Confucian countries.[63] Indeed, attitudes about the family, especially the importance of bloodlines, ancestral worship, and low fertility rates, helped me explain why many Confucian residents were so opposed to same-sex relations, despite their countries being relatively affluent and having low levels of religious importance, as conventionally measured, which often leads to more liberal views.[64]

Table 5.1 uses WVS data to examine the potential cultural influence of family values. After accounting for these values at the individual level, there

---

[61] Gao et al., "How Does Traditional Confucian Culture Influence Adolescents' Sexual Behavior in Three Asian Cities?"; Adamczyk, *Cross-National Public Opinion about Homosexuality*.

[62] Yang and Yen, "A Comparative Study of Marital Dissolution in East Asian Societies."

[63] Adamczyk and Cheng, "Explaining Attitudes about Homosexuality in Confucian and Non-Confucian Nations."

[64] Adamczyk, *Cross-National Public Opinion about Homosexuality*.

176 FETAL POSITIONS

is no cultural effect on abortion disapproval. Instead, people who personally feel that family is very important or are more opposed to divorce are more likely to report that abortion is problematic. In other words, individuals' family values have not gelled into a societal effect that shapes most residents' views about abortion.

Part of the reason that there is no societal effect may be related to the family situation of people who want abortions. In many countries, a substantial number of women who need them already have children.[65] Often, the rationale for why they desire an abortion is linked to concerns about having the emotional, physical, and financial resources to support existing children.[66] In other words, some people may feel that putting family first necessitates getting an abortion, complicating societal views about family importance in shaping disapproval. Furthermore, while some individuals may feel that abortion is a family values' issue, others may not see it this way. Instead, it might be viewed as a form of birth control. Likewise, in some countries, having a son may be seen as a family issue, which may necessitate aborting female fetuses. Hence, as a societal issue, the power of family values to shape abortion disapproval is not straightforward.

Views about Life

Finally, feelings about the sanctity of life could shape abortion disapproval. The Catholic Church has drawn on the idea that all life is sacred; hence, people should reject abortion as well as euthanasia and capital punishment.[67] But beyond personal religious beliefs, people who feel strongly that all life should be valued may oppose abortion, viewing it as the destruction of life.[68] The only life-related question that the WVS asks focuses on euthanasia, which is the painless killing of someone because of a dire medical condition and to prevent further suffering. Euthanasia is illegal in most countries.[69] People who think euthanasia is not right may also be more inclined to believe that abortion is problematic, viewing it as the premature ending of life.

How are views about ending life related to abortion disapproval? Survey respondents who were more likely to report that euthanasia is never justified

---

[65] Wind, "Concern for Current and Future Children a Key Reason Women Have Abortions."
[66] "Turnaway Study."
[67] USCCB Committee on Pro-Life Activities, "Respect for Unborn Human Life."
[68] Jelen, "The Subjective Bases of Abortion Attitudes."
[69] Linares, "These People Want to Die. Will Their Countries Allow Euthanasia?"

COMMUNISM, CONFUCIANISM, CULTURAL VALUES   177

were also more likely to say that abortion is problematic. However, like other values mentioned above, we cannot unravel the correct causal relationship among them. Hence, we do not know if attitudes about abortion are shaping feelings about euthanasia or vice versa. Rather, we know that they are correlated, and the relationship remains even after accounting for a host of other personal characteristics, including personal religious beliefs and affiliation (e.g., Catholicism).

Table 5.1 also notes that there is no societal effect of feelings about life and abortion attitudes over and above the individual influence. In other words, people who are more opposed to prematurely ending life, even if humanly, are more personally opposed to abortion. But there is no societal effect related to life views, which then shape personal feelings about abortion.

Other Personal Attributes

In addition to the characteristics discussed above, I examined associations with several other individual attributes, which previous studies have found important in shaping abortion disapproval.[70] These include gender, age, marital status, income, and educational attainment for shaping abortion disapproval (see Appendix A). Some of these have been discussed in previous chapters. I find that women, on average, tend to be more disapproving than men. Likewise, older people are more opposed than younger individuals. Wealthier people and those with higher levels of education tend to be more supportive of abortion than others. Finally, as noted in this chapter, married persons tend to have more conservative views about abortion than single, divorced, and cohabiting individuals. Within specific countries or groups of nations, characteristics like race and ethnicity or immigrant and migrant status may also be linked to public opinion. But they are omitted here because we do not have WVS questions that could be used to assess these influences consistently across countries. Moreover, these factors may only be relevant within some countries rather than across the world.

The way that researchers often present the role of personal characteristics, like an obedience orientation or disapproval of homosexuality, for shaping

---

[70] Adamczyk, "Religion as a Micro and Macro Property"; Loll and Hall, "Differences in Abortion Attitudes by Policy Context and between Men and Women in the World Values Survey"; Carol and Milewski, "Attitudes toward Abortion among the Muslim Minority and Non-Muslim Majority in Cross-National Perspective."

178   FETAL POSITIONS

abortion opposition makes it seem like these attributes are operating in isolation. Indeed, all the previously discussed characteristics have independent associations with abortion disapproval. Hence, regardless of marital status, people who value obedience more strongly oppose abortion. Likewise, while better-educated people tend to make more money, income and education uniquely affect abortion disapproval. Nevertheless, many of these personal characteristics overlap and have reciprocal relationships. Hence, someone who values obedience is also more likely to enter the conventional institution of marriage. Once married, husbands and wives are more likely to encounter other married people with more conservative views. This may reinforce abortion disapproval and reduce the likelihood that they will meet others who openly discuss abortion-related experiences. Fewer interactions with people discussing their abortion experiences will further limit more liberal perspectives and so on.

While each personal characteristic discussed above is uniquely associated with abortion disapproval, their collective influence is powerful. Hence, an unmarried twenty-five-year-old woman with a college degree, high income, and low level of religious importance has an abortion disapproval score of 6.03 (where 10 = never justified). Conversely, a sixty-year-old married man with less than a high school education, low income, and a high level of religious importance has a score of 8.76. He is substantially less supportive, with a 45% increase in disapproval. In this comparison, I did not include values related to obedience, sexual morality, family importance, or views about life, which would further exacerbate differences in disapproval. While each characteristic matters in shaping views, the overall effect is dramatic. The next section considers the role of Confucian values for understanding abortion support.

Confucian Nations

Some writers have suggested that residents from Confucian countries are influenced by the unique cultural values in these nations.[71] In Chapter 1, I investigated the role of religion for shaping abortion views. I discussed the potential influences of polytheistic religions, folk and ancestral beliefs, and Confucian values. This section extends that previous discussion to focus

[71] Hill, "'Asian Values' as Reverse Orientalism"; Adamczyk and Cheng, "Explaining Attitudes about Homosexuality in Confucian and Non-Confucian Nations."

more specifically on differences in abortion attitudes for people living in countries with substantial Chinese or Confucian histories.

For thousands of years, China was the leading civilization in East Asia, having a powerful effect on the culture, language, and perspectives of residents in surrounding countries. With over a billion people, a rapidly growing economy, and a one-party communist dictatorship, China continues to have an important role in the surrounding area and the world more generally. The societies with strong Chinese or Confucian history include China, Macau, Hong Kong, Taiwan, North and South Korea, Japan, Singapore, and Vietnam. Together, they constitute nearly a fifth of the global population.[72]

At first glance, people living in Confucian societies do not seem especially opposed to abortion. The last three waves of the WVS include all of the Confucian countries except North Korea. The average disapproval level across these nations is 7.50 (10 = abortion is never justified). For the eighty-eight countries included in the WVS, the average score is 7.71. Hence, they seem slightly more opposed than the average world survey respondent. However, Confucian societies appear especially disapproving after overall levels of religious importance are considered.

As noted in Chapter 1, few differences exist among people or across countries based on religious affiliation or the dominant organized religious traditions within nations. However, overall levels of religious importance within a society can shape abortion disapproval, even for people who are not religious. As previously discussed, there are some challenges to measuring religious belief across the world, especially for residents from countries with polytheistic religions and folk beliefs, which includes the Confucian countries. Hence, we find that religious belief, as conventionally measured, is very low in Confucian nations. Indeed, all Confucian societies have levels of religious importance below the sample mean for the eighty-eight societies in the WVS. China is the least religious, followed by Japan, Hong Kong, Vietnam, South Korea, Taiwan, and Macau. In this group, Singapore has the highest overall level of religious importance, but it is still only at the WVS sample mean.

Because overall levels of religious belief play a decisive role in shaping abortion disapproval across many countries, they mask the otherwise higher levels of abortion disapproval that Confucian residents have. Figure 5.2 illustrates the effect. Before mean levels of religious importance are included in

---

[72] China alone contributes 18%.

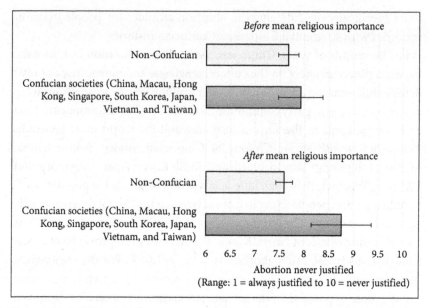

Figure 5.2 Marginal Differences in Attitudes between Residents Living in Societies with and without Confucian Histories before and after Mean Levels of Religious Importance Are Included

Notes: Values are taken from the final model in Appendix A, Table A.3. All other variables are included in creating estimates, except for abortion legality and mean levels of religious importance. "Before mean religious importance" indicates that mean religious importance has not yet been included in the model but personal religious importance and all other country-level variables have. "After mean religious importance" indicates that mean religious importance has now been added to the model.

Source: WVS, waves 5, 6, and 7

the model, the average abortion disapproval score for Confucian residents is 7.92. For people from other parts of the world, it is 7.67. At this point, there is no statistically significant difference between these groups of countries. But in the second set of estimates, overall levels of religious importance are included. The disapproval score for residents from Confucian societies shoots up to 8.75. But for people living in other parts of the world, the score changes (7.59), but not nearly as much as for Confucian residents. After overall levels of religious importance are included, people from Confucian societies appear statistically *more* likely to disapprove of abortion than those from other nations (i.e., confidence intervals no longer overlap). Only when we pull apart these various factors do we see how very low levels of religious importance in this region masks otherwise higher levels of abortion disapproval.

What might explain why the Confucian nations appear more opposed to abortion? As noted previously, in 1971 China took its first steps toward the one-child policy, and in 1982, it was added to the constitution. At the time, the nation had a vast population and major concerns about how it could sustain itself if residents continued to have large families. Many Chinese likely believed that abortion and even the one-child policy were acceptable at that time. But as noted in Chapter 3 (on democracy), the Chinese may have increasingly thought that the policy was no longer necessary as time passed. Indeed, the WVS data show that over time disapproval of abortion increased in China (see Figure 3.2). There is no other country in the WVS where attitudes have become so rapidly opposed.

Are high levels of opposition to abortion in China weighing down disapproval across Confucian countries? In other words, is China an outlier? I removed China from the analysis and found that Confucian residents continued to be more opposed to abortion than those from other nations. Hence, China is not an outlier that is making the entire set of Confucian countries appear more opposed. Put differently, the Confucian countries, on average, are more opposed once we account for overall levels of religious belief, even after China is removed as a potential anomaly.

Another explanation could relate to Buddhism, which is the majority world religion across Confucian countries. However, in Chapter 1 (on religion), my analysis revealed relatively few differences across major religions. WVS data showed that the world's Buddhists are significantly different from Catholics. However, on average, they are more supportive of abortion than Catholics, not less. Hence, Buddhist religious beliefs are unlikely to explain why Confucian nations are, on average, more opposed to abortion once the overall strength of religious belief is included. In the next section, I consider the role of Confucian values.

The Potential Influence of Confucian-Inspired Values

Some scholars, academics, and government officials have argued that nations with Confucian histories and influence have cultural values that differ distinctly from those found elsewhere.[73] People who abide by Confucian values would not necessarily describe themselves as "Confucian" in the same

---

[73] Hill, "'Asian Values' as Reverse Orientalism," 200.

182   FETAL POSITIONS

way that people who identify as Christian or Muslim would. Rather than a set of explicit beliefs and directives that often accompany major religions, Confucianism is a set of interrelated values and morals that may influence how people interact and justify their actions. Social scientists who study Confucian values typically explain how the traits they define fit within the more extensive system of Confucianism. For example, some scholars have described Confucian values as including "a sense of community and nation-hood, a disciplined and hardworking people, strong moral values, and family ties."[74] Others have identified collective well-being and respect for order and hierarchy as essential elements of a Confucian value system.[75]

Several values could be described as "Confucian" and may be associated with abortion disapproval and can be measured with WVS data. All the values discussed above (e.g., obedience and the importance of behaving properly, sexual morality, views about maintaining life, and family connectedness) could fit within a Confucian framework. For example, some researchers have found that Chinese residents vehemently oppose prostitution, which could destabilize the family.[76] Likewise, researchers have also suggested that because Confucianism emphasizes interdependence and, thus, conformity, these residents have a strong obedience orientation.[77]

Is there evidence that people from Confucian countries are more likely to value obedience and the family and disapprove of sexual immorality and humanly ending life, making them more opposed to abortion? In the above section, I examined the societal influence of these values. I did not find any "cultural" effects. Instead, people who personally feel strongly about these things are more disapproving. However, these societal-level values do not mediate or explain away the distinction between Confucian and other countries. Thus, the reason why people from Confucian nations are more opposed to abortion (after accounting for overall levels of religious importance) appears unrelated to cultural values regarding obedience, sexual morality, the family, and views about ending life.

If Confucian cultures contribute to values related to obedience, family importance, views about life, and sexual morality, their residents should be more likely to affirm these values than others. To further understand the relationship between values and abortion disapproval in Confucian

---

[74] Tong, "Social Values, Singapore Style."
[75] Shin and Dalton, *Citizens, Democracy, and Markets around the Pacific Rim.*
[76] Cao and Stack, "Exploring Terra Incognita."
[77] Bond, "Beyond the Chinese Face"; Hsu, *Americans and Chinese.*

countries, I examined mean differences in values related to the family, obedience, sexual morality, and humanely ending life (i.e., euthanasia) using a simple statistical technique called a t-test, which tests for a significant difference between the means of two groups before any other individual or country-level factors are considered.

Figure 5.3 presents the mean differences. For all of these values, I found the opposite of what we might expect. Rather than valuing obedience in children, people from Confucian countries are *less* likely to report that it is an important characteristic. Specifically, 13% of respondents from Confucian nations say obedience is an important attribute in children (see Figure 5.3). Conversely, 43% of people living elsewhere feel this way. They are also more supportive of homosexuality, euthanasia, and prostitution than residents from other parts of the world. Over 90% of residents across the globe say that they value the family. However, 87% of WVS respondents from Confucian countries feel this way. Despite their relatively low divorce rates, respondents from Confucian countries are *less* likely to say that divorce is never justified (22%) compared to people from other countries (29%).

Finally, I examined whether people from Confucian societies differ in the extent that they value boys over girls. As discussed in Chapter 4, people who think that men and women should have distinct social roles and responsibilities are, on average, more opposed to abortion. Some research has argued that Confucian societies emphasize distinct roles for men and women.[78] Even if women participate in the labor force, they may still be seen as responsible for most housework and childcare. Likewise, in societies with a strong gender division of labor, men may be more likely viewed as leaders and the primary breadwinner.[79]

Based on these ideas, we might think that views about gender equality would lead to more abortion disapproval. However, the history of the one-child policy complicates the relationship, at least in China. Historically, the Chinese have preferred sons over daughters partially because daughters tend to live with their husband's families, depriving their own parents of labor and income.[80] With China's one-child-policy, most parents could only have one child. Therefore, a minority of Chinese chose to abort female fetuses, which

---

[78] Yang and Yen, "A Comparative Study of Marital Dissolution in East Asian Societies."

[79] Raymo and Ono, "Coresidence with Parents, Women's Economic Resources, and the Transition to Marriage in Japan"; Xu and Lai, "Gender Ideologies, Marital Roles, and Marital Quality in Taiwan."

[80] Das Gupta et al., "Why Is Son Preference so Persistent in East and South Asia?"

184 FETAL POSITIONS

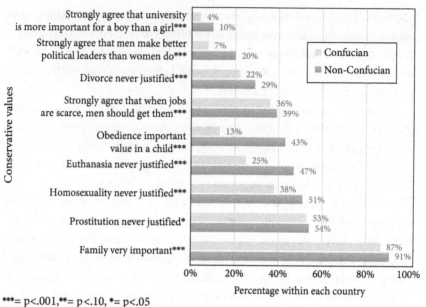

***= p<.001, **= p<.10, *= p<.05

Figure 5.3 Differences between Confucian and Non-confucian Nations in Conservative Values

Note: T-tests were used to determine statistically significant differences between people living in Confucian and non-Confucian nations. ***= p < .001, **= p < .10, *= p < .05

Source: WVS, waves 5, 6, and 7

some scholars argue can explain China's gender imbalance.[81] These ideas suggest that in societies where males are more valued, respondents may be *more* supportive of abortion.

The WVS includes several questions that can be used to assess the relative value that people place on females versus males. These questions ask: (1) do men make better political leaders than women; (2) when jobs are scarce, should men get them; and (3) is university more important for a boy than for a girl? I examined whether people from Confucian societies differed from others in their gender-related values. Using a t-test, I found that Confucian residents were *less* likely to indicate support for boys over girls (see Figure 5.3). In other words, Confucian residents have more gender-equal attitudes for all three questions. Despite these differences, this scale is not statistically significant across the eighty-eight countries for explaining abortion disapproval once other variables are considered. Likewise, as a societal value, it is not associated with attitudes.

[81] Chan et al., "Gender Selection in China: Its Meanings and Implications."

Many values described as "Confucian" are not necessarily more prevalent among Confucian residents. Other studies have also found that Confucian residents are not substantially more likely than others to value these things.[82] However, the stereotype has been difficult to shake because many prominent writers, officials, and researchers have maintained that such differences exist.[83] Indeed, politicians, including the Singaporean patriarch Lee Kuan Yew, popularized the idea that "Asian values" derived from Confucian cultural traditions are inconsistent with democracy in East Asia.[84] The findings presented here make clear that at least some of the differences thought to be prevalent in Confucian countries are not empirically supported.

Alternative Explanations for Understanding Abortion Disapproval in Confucian Societies

The Confucian values discussed above cannot explain why people from Confucian nations are more opposed to abortion after accounting for overall low levels of religious importance. In this section, I provide insight into some other explanations.

To begin, the questions offered by WVS administrators may not adequately capture "Confucian" values. As noted above, some researchers have maintained that countries with Chinese histories have distinctly different values than others.[85] But these studies typically do not use the appropriate mixed-modeling techniques to distinguish between individual-level preferences and societal-level values that might explain cross-national differences. Moreover, as mentioned above, I could not find even simple (i.e., t-tests) differences between people from Confucian countries and others. If there are clear differences in values, more empirical work is needed to show them.

Rather than the values mentioned above, an important explanation may relate to the adverse health-related effects that abortion might be perceived as causing to a woman's body. In my Chinese interviews, respondents regularly discussed health-related concerns. As one professor explained, "The public perception is that if you have an abortion, you are hugely damaging

---

[82] Dalton and Ong, "Authority Orientations and Democratic Attitudes"; Kim, "Do Asian Values Exist?"

[83] Hofstede and Bond, "Confucius and Economic Growth"; Jung, "Is Culture Destiny?"; Zakaria and Yew, "Culture Is Destiny."

[84] Zakaria and Yew, "Culture Is Destiny."

[85] Robertson and Hoffman, "How Different Are We?"; Hofstede and Bond, "Confucius and Economic Growth"; Dalton and Ong, "Authority Orientations and Democratic Attitudes."

186 FETAL POSITIONS

your future fertility and also not just that, you're damaging your health, like you will become weak." A Catholic sister from China conferred, "Abortions damage their physical health, and that's why it's harder for them to get pregnant again or give birth." A Chinese academic thought that more education would increase residents' understanding "that abortion is probably damaging their own health." Concerns about health and fertility arose in almost every Chinese interview.

Just as worries about abortions' adverse physical effects are prevalent in China, other residents in the region may have similar concerns. Conversely, respondents from the United States were much less likely to mention abortion-related health problems as a major issue. When it arose, people spoke about antiabortion activists using health concerns as a weapon to publicly discourage abortion. One respondent explained that abortion opponents "would overemphasize the ill effects, and the sort of 'Post-Traumatic Abortion Syndrome' was both invented and has been capitalized on so effectively by the pro-life movement. . . . And, of course, that's been disproven again and again and again." Likewise, one of the medical doctors I interviewed explained that "[health concerns] are not as common, but I do hear it every once in a while because this myth is out there, perpetuated by people who are against abortion." Even an American antiabortion advocate noted that women typically have few health concerns about getting an abortion "and only in extreme cases." Hence, American respondents were much less likely than the Chinese to indicate health worries.

Because Chinese respondents often mentioned health-related concerns, I asked American experts about it. When I raised it, US-based respondents were more likely to note that health might be an issue. However, as one academic explained

> My guess would be that a lot of people probably don't think about it or
> don't necessarily know one way or the other. But if you made them choose,
> "Do you think abortion is bad or good for a woman's health?" I think more
> people would say it is bad, rather than good.

His key point is that most Americans do not think about health-related concerns and abortion. But if they did, they would be more inclined to think that abortion could produce adverse effects.

Differences in health concerns may be related to how the procedure is conducted and its success in various countries. For example, in China, there are reports of abortion being linked to higher infertility rates.[86] Indeed, infertility affects about 18% of Chinese couples, but the global average is only around 15%.[87] But even if abortion is unrelated to infertility in China and East Asia, the perception that there could be a link may affect abortion disapproval. Likewise, Confucian values related to maintaining a healthy body may extend across countries with Chinese histories.[88]

Finally, China's one-child policy has no doubt had a powerful influence on Chinese abortion attitudes. The policy may have inadvertently affected abortion views in other Confucian countries as well. As discussed in previous chapters, the one-child policy dominated my interviews with Chinese experts. Additionally, Figure 3.2 in Chapter 3 shows that across the decades Chinese respondents have grown more opposed to abortion since the early 1990s. When the Chinese government first enacted the policy, many Chinese were likely supportive, as they understood the rationale. Because it was so large, the country's population was difficult to support, and the nation would have challenges developing. However, over time many countries that became richer, including all the surrounding Confucian societies, saw their birth rates naturally decline.[89] Although fertility decreased across the region as economic development rose, the Chinese government continued to subject residents to the one-child policy through 2015.

In Chapter 3, Figure 3.2 shows abortion disapproval over time in other countries with Chinese histories. Residents from Japan and Vietnam have steadily become more liberal over time. However, people from South Korea, Hong Kong, and Taiwan have not become more accepting. Some of the disapproval we see in the Confucian countries (after accounting for overall levels of religious beliefs) may be related to a diffusion of opposition related to China's one-child policy. The policy was well publicized and lasted over three decades. With over a billion people, the third largest land mass in the world, and powerful economic and political policies, China has a big influence in East Asia, where all other Confucian countries are located. When the WVS administrators asked about abortion justification, respondents were not instructed to limit their outlook to only their society. Instead, they were generally asked about their views. The one-child policy may have loomed

---

[86] Cong et al., "Prevalence and Risk Factors of Infertility at a Rural Site of Northern China."
[87] Stevenson and Wang, "China Needs Couples to Have More Babies."
[88] Badanta et al., "How Does Confucianism Influence Health Behaviors, Health Outcomes and Medical Decisions?"
[89] World Bank, "Fertility Rate, Total (Births per Woman)—East Asia & Pacific Data."

188 FETAL POSITIONS

large in their minds. Thus, many residents from Confucian societies may have interpreted the question about whether abortions, even those coerced by the state, are justified. Given the long history of the policy, many may have felt that abortion is not entirely justified.

Because the policy is so unique to China, which is culturally distinct, people living outside East Asia may not contextualize their abortion views the same way. At least in the United States, the idea of the local government forcing abortions or enacting policies that limit fertility rarely emerged in my interviews. Instead, all American respondents mentioned concerns about their government limiting abortion access.

Additional Cross-National Influences

This chapter has considered a range of country-level forces that may shape abortion views. These include the role of Soviet and Chinese histories and societal values related to sexual morality, family importance, the sanctity of life, and obedience orientations. What other factors might explain cross-national attitudes about abortion?

Several other country-level characteristics could theoretically be related to public opinion about abortion. These include other economic measures, such as the proportion below the poverty level or the unemployment rate, and population and fertility-related factors. When the adolescent fertility rate is high, for example, respondents may express more abortion support, feeling that having children at such a young age is problematic. Likewise, public expenditures on education could lead to less opposition. Chapter 2 showed that overall education and economic development levels increase societal acceptance. Hence, when the government is dedicated to increasing people's education, as indicated by its educational expenditures, residents may generally be more supportive of abortion. Additionally, country-level health indicators, such as life expectancy, maternal mortality, and the number of infant or child deaths, may increase support. Suppose residents witness high levels of child morbidity, for example. In that case, they may believe that abortion is acceptable because it gives parents more resources to devote to a smaller number of children, which could increase healthier lives.

I examined close to thirty additional characteristics that could hypothetically shape abortion support, including different dimensions related to religion, economics, population, fertility, education, and health (see Appendix C). These measures were taken from the United Nations, Central Intelligence Agency World Factbook, and US State Department's International Religious Freedom Reports.

None of these factors are statistically significant in explaining abortion disapproval after other influences (i.e., education and economic development, democracy, religion, gender inequality) that have already been discussed were considered (see Table A.2 in Appendix A). While several of the factors seem promising for shaping views, any effects disappear when other country-level influences are considered. Part of the reason for this is that several factors, such as fertility rates, educational expenditures, and child morbidity, are highly correlated with measures, such as GDP and overall levels of education. Factors like GDP, overall levels of religious beliefs, and democracy have greater explanatory power. Some of these other measures may be especially important within individual countries. However, for an analysis focused on understanding differences across dozens of nations, they do not offer any additional explanation in the context of the influences already considered.

Surveys about Abortion: Differences in Question Wording

The first part of this chapter focused on the various factors that can shape abortion disapproval. I now discuss the challenges in assessing public opinion. In this section, I dissect how survey responses may change depending on the different elements of abortion being investigated (e.g., moral and legal aspects, circumstances surrounding the pregnancy, gestational age, and developmental markers). I also explain how historical, cultural, and legal contexts may shift respondents' feelings. Much of what we know comes from research done is wealthy countries with strong research infrastructures that have fielded hundreds of surveys. Unfortunately, attitudinal information on abortion from across the globe is largely limited to a few surveys. In the following section, I also explain why we can still have confidence in them.

One of the most popular ways abortion is discussed in the public press and academic literature is as a legal issue. My previous analysis of Americans' abortion attitudes found that of the ninety-four articles published in English language peer-reviewed journals between 2001 and 2016, 54% of them focused on legal aspects.[90] The next most popular category related

---

[90] Adamczyk, Kim, and Dillon, "Examining Public Opinion about Abortion."

190 FETAL POSITIONS

to women's partner and relationship status (35%) and then women's physical health (33%). Likewise, Chapter 3 presented an analysis of newspapers across forty-one countries and found that the most popular way that abortion was discussed was as a legal issue. Researchers and newspaper writers often talk about abortion laws and policies and related attitudes because abortion can be controversial and laws may be in flux. Moreover, abortion access can impact women, families, fertility rates, the economy, democratic elections, and so forth. Since public opinion can shape laws and policies, understanding the extent to which the public feels that abortion should be legal provides insight into where legislation may be headed.

Because there are so few cross-national surveys that examine abortion attitudes across dozens of different countries, much of the analyses presented in this book have focused on a single WVS question. The question asks if abortion can ever be justified, never be justified, or something in-between using a 10-point scale. The survey item captures a moral judgment about abortion. People's views about the legal and moral dimensions of abortion are correlated.[91] However, the relationship is not so strong that one can serve as a proxy for the other.[92]

When asked about their moral judgments, survey respondents provide opinions about what they think is right and wrong. Many people do not necessarily want their moral views to become law.[93] For example, some survey respondents may feel that they would not personally obtain an abortion and that perhaps others should not either. Nevertheless, they may feel that the pregnant woman should ultimately decide whether to get an abortion, not the government. Likewise, some people may think they do not have enough information about the circumstances and situations that would lead some females to want an abortion. Hence, they may want to allow some leeway, which making abortion illegal would preclude.

Consistent with these ideas, research done in the United States has found that roughly half of Americans surveyed say there are situations where abortion is morally wrong, but it should nevertheless still be legal.[94] Likewise,

---

[91] Buyuker et al., "A Mixed Methods Approach to Understanding the Disconnection between Perceptions of Abortion Acceptability and Support for *Roe v. Wade* Among US Adults."

[92] Buyuker et al. found that the correlation ranged from 0.40 to 0.43 for survey questions that asked about abortion unacceptability and preference for overturning *Roe v. Wade*.

[93] Buyuker et al., "A Mixed Methods Approach to Understanding the Disconnection between Perceptions of Abortion Acceptability and Support for *Roe v. Wade* Among US Adults"; Singh and Williams, "Attitudes and Behavioral Intentions about Abortion."

[94] Pew Research Center, "America's Abortion Quandry."

COMMUNISM, CONFUCIANISM, CULTURAL VALUES   191

many Latin American residents strongly disapprove of abortion, but a much smaller proportion think it should be illegal. Specifically, while an average of 81% of people from nineteen Latin American countries report that abortion is morally wrong, only 48% of residents say it should be illegal in all cases.[95]

Cross-national survey administrators may focus on moral views about abortion because they may be easier to study than legal preferences.[96] In less-democratic nations, the government may not want researchers assessing people's attitudes about potentially controversial laws. Public opinion may not match official policy, which could undermine the government's authority. Hence, surveyors may instead ask about morality.

Many different factors shape abortion decisions. Likewise, public opinion is influenced by the many reasons women may want or need an abortion. Survey questions that ask whether abortion should be legal or acceptable may not capture this complexity. To further dissect attitudes, some researchers distinguish between hard and soft reasons for getting an abortion.[97] Hard reasons generally refer to physical elements, such as whether the pregnancy resulted from rape or incest, the female's health is in danger, or congenital disabilities are likely. Soft reasons include the woman no longer wanting children, the family having a low income and hence cannot afford them, or the potential parents not being in a relationship. While many people may support abortion to save the mother's life, which is a "hard" reason, they may be less supportive for "softer" reasons.

To a certain extent, the "hard" and "soft" reasons for obtaining an abortion coincide with the circumstances under which abortion is legally allowed. While abortion is entirely illegal in only a few countries (e.g., Egypt, Iraq, Madagascar), a larger proportion of nations only permit it to save the mother's life (e.g., Brazil, Iran, and Indonesia).[98] Several countries that

---

[95] Pew Research Center and Bell, "Religion in Latin America: Widespread Change in a Historically Catholic Region."

[96] In a 2014 study that examined both dimensions, Pew researchers asked residents in nineteen Latin American countries whether abortion should be legal or illegal under most circumstances. For all but one country (Uruguay) the majority felt that it should be illegal under most circumstances, though less than 50% felt is should be illegal for all circumstances. In Paraguay and Guatemala, over 90% of residents felt that abortion should be illegal for some or all reasons. Strong disapproval is consistent with Paraguay's and Guatemala's national laws, which only permit abortion to save the woman's life. In fact, most Latin American countries do not permit abortion on demand. An important reason why many Latin American residents disapprove of abortion is related to the Catholic Church's strong regional influence (see Chapter 2). While a correlation exists between legal and moral stances on abortion, they focus on distinct aspects, including personal versus public preferences.

[97] Benin, "Determinants of Opposition to Abortion: An Analysis of the Hard and Soft Scales."

[98] Center for Reproductive Rights, "The World's Abortion Laws." 2024.

192 FETAL POSITIONS

are moving in a more liberal direction allow abortion for broad health-related reasons (e.g., Morocco, Algeria, Peru, Bolivia), which may include the woman's mental well-being. In a handful of societies, abortion is legal for various social or economic reasons (e.g., India), although patients need to specify them. Finally, as of 2024, seventy-seven countries across the globe had legalized abortion,[99] which typically means that women do not need a reason for getting one during the first trimester. Differences in cross-national abortion policies support the idea that people and their governments often think about the circumstances under which abortion should be permitted.

The fetus's gestational age may also shape people's views.[100] Even when abortion is legal, doctors and their patients often need a specific reason to get an abortion in later trimesters. The pregnancy stage is also likely to shape public opinion. Most abortions occur during the first trimester.[101] Likewise, researchers have found that Americans, for example, typically assume that survey questions about abortion acceptability are referring to the first trimester, even when surveyors do not specifically mention the pregnancy stage.[102] When social scientists include fetal development markers (e.g., fetal heartbeat or ability to experience pain) in public opinion surveys, respondents tend to be more opposed than when no time period is indicated. Terms such as "heartbeat" and "pain" are likely to personify the fetus, leading to more abortion disapproval.[103]

As the technology available to support very early births improves and becomes widely available, people may become increasingly concerned about acceptable abortion timing. When America made abortion legal in 1974, for example, the earliest a fetus could survive outside of the womb was twenty-four to twenty-eight weeks.[104] Today, there are cases of fetuses surviving at twenty-two weeks after birth, albeit with major medical intervention and ongoing health challenges.[105] Even strong abortion supporters are more opposed to it when the fetus can survive outside the womb.[106]

---

[99] Center for Reproductive Rights.

[100] Hans and Kimberly, "Abortion Attitudes in Context."

[101] In the United States, 93% occur during the first trimester. Diamant and Mohamed, "What the Data Says about Abortion in the U.S."

[102] Crawford, LaRoche, and Jozkowski, "Examining Abortion Attitudes in the Context of Gestational Age."

[103] Bueno et al., "Do Fetal Development Markers Influence Attitudes toward Abortion Legality?"

[104] D, "The Limit of Viability."

[105] D.

[106] Bueno et al., "Do Fetal Development Markers Influence Attitudes toward Abortion Legality?"

At the other end of the spectrum, assisted reproductive technology (ART), including in vitro fertilization, have become increasingly popular, accessible, and affordable. These techniques often require creating multiple embryos, only some of which will be used. In the United States alone, researchers estimate that over one million embryos are discarded each year.[107] Only a minority of these could have become viable fetuses. But as people increasingly use ART, public debates are likely to highlight concerns about when life begins and how unused embryos should be managed.

The Catholic Church and conservative Protestant denominations argue that life begins at conception, which includes fertilized eggs.[108] In my prior research,[109] I examined the role of personal and overall country levels of religious belief in shaping attitudes about ART versus abortion across thirty-five European countries where these survey questions were asked.[110] Personal and country levels of religious beliefs affected disapproval of both abortion and ART. But the religious effects were stronger for abortion disapproval than ART. While most people know about abortion, reproductive techniques, such as in vitro fertilization, are still relatively new, costly, and largely confined to richer people and countries. Likewise, religious officials have not advocated against ART to the same extent as abortion. In contrast to abortion, many religions and denominations are likely to view ART as family-friendly technology.

A nation's abortion politics may also shape responses to survey questions. When abortion rights are threatened, people's feelings about its moral and legal dimensions may solidify. Indeed, for the thirty years before *Roe v. Wade* was overturned in the United States, approximately 25% of Americans reported that abortion should be legal under any circumstances. As noted above, support increased to 35% in 2022.[111] In other words, over a one-year period, there was a 30% increase in support. Conversely, across the previous three decades Americans did not appear to meaningfully change their views. Increases in support were likely a response to the legal change.

Finally, the region of the country where respondents live can also shape attitudes. The research presented in this book has focused on country-level

---

[107] Pflum, "'We Were Not Prepared for Any of This.'"

[108] USCCB Committee on Pro-Life Activities, "Respect for Unborn Human Life."

[109] Adamczyk, Suh, and Lerner, "Analysis of the Relationship Between Religion, Abortion, and Assisted Reproductive Technology: Insights into Cross-National Public Opinion."

[110] See also Silber Mohamed, "Embryonic Politics"; Bartolomé-Peral and Coromina, "Attitudes towards Life and Death in Europe."

[111] Gallup Inc., "Abortion."

194 FETAL POSITIONS

influences. But within nations, the regional economic, cultural, and educational context may vary, shaping residents' views in some of the same ways that these factors produce differences across countries.[112] For example, rural Chinese may be less supportive of abortion than urban residents because large families can be especially helpful for farming, but may be a financial burden in cities. Indeed, I found geographical differences in China using survey data (see Chapter 3). In other countries, such as the United States, researchers have also found that residential location matters.[113]

Many factors can influence survey responses regarding abortion.[114] We know about these differences because of studies done within countries that have well-developed research infrastructures. In rich nations such as the United States, an army of social scientists have administered dozens of studies examining question wording and conducting complex statistical analyses so that we can see how small survey changes affect responses. This prior work suggests that the public may be more or less accepting depending on the legal and moral dimensions and hard and soft reasons for getting an abortion. Likewise, the fetus's development stage, where people live (e.g., Bible Belt), and recent events related to abortion legislation can affect attitudes. ART and other technological developments (e.g., early survival outside of the womb) add further complexity.

In contrast to research done within nations, cross-national studies on public opinion about abortion are largely limited to the questions included in pre-existing surveys. In the following section, I explain why we can still have confidence in those survey findings.

Cross-national Surveys about Abortion Attitudes

As discussed previously, social scientists only have a few cross-national surveys that include a question that asks about abortion across a wide range of different nations. Part of the problem is that cross-national survey data can be extremely difficult to collect. The surveys require translation

---

[112] Adamczyk and Valdimarsdóttir, "Understanding Americans' Abortion Attitudes."

[113] Adamczyk and Valdimarsdóttir.

[114] Jozkowski, Crawford, and Hunt, "Complexity in Attitudes toward Abortion Access"; Crawford et al., "Examining the Relationship Between *Roe v. Wade* Knowledge and Sentiment Across Political Party and Abortion Identity"; Crawford et al., "An Exploratory Examination of Attitudes toward Illegal Abortion in the U.S. through Endorsement of Various Punishments"; Buyuker et al., "A Mixed Methods Approach to Understanding the Disconnection between Perceptions of Abortion Acceptability and Support for *Roe v. Wade* Among US Adults."

into multiple languages. Some governments may not approve of the questions, and respondents may not want to respond truthfully to sensitive ones. Likewise, researchers face logistical challenges in gathering these data, especially in less-developed countries. Weaker infrastructures can make estimating a representative sample or traveling to interview people especially challenging.

Given all of these complications, how do we know that cross-national estimates of abortion disapproval are reliable? Likewise, how do we know that small differences in question wording only minimally affect responses? Below I explain why we can have confidence in the cross-national survey findings presented in this book.

Survey reliability refers to a measure's consistency. When a question is reliable, then other researchers should obtain similar estimates using an equivalent research technique. One way to assess consistency is to see if other surveys have similar estimates of abortion support for the same countries. Likewise, we can see how survey questions that are worded differently affect abortion disapproval levels. In addition to the WVS, the International Social Survey Program (ISSP) and Pew's international surveys ask questions about abortion disapproval. The three surveys do not share the exact same set of nations. But there is enough country overlap to assess correlations among them. The last three waves of the WVS include eighty-eight countries. Only twenty-four WVS countries overlap with nations from recent ISSP surveys. Likewise, the WVS and Pew surveys only share thirty-two societies.

Each of these data sources include an abortion-related question focused on morality, which I analyze below. As previously noted, the WVS asked whether abortion is always justified, never justified, or something in-between, on a scale ranging from 0 to 10 (with 10 = never justified). For the country-level estimate, I calculated the mean value for each society.

Pew survey researchers asked, "Do you personally believe that having an abortion is morally acceptable?" Respondents had three options: (1) morally acceptable, (2) morally unacceptable, and (3) not a moral issue.[115] Only a minority (16%) felt that abortion was not a moral issue. I calculated the proportion of people who felt that abortion was morally unacceptable based on the number that thought it was a moral issue.

---

[115] Respondents could also volunteer the response "depends on the situation," which consisted about 10% of responses.

196   FETAL POSITIONS

Finally, the ISSP asked a question about moral acceptance for getting an abortion based on a "soft" reason. Specifically, the survey asked, "Do you personally think it is wrong or not wrong for a woman to have an abortion if the family has a very low income and cannot afford any more children?" Responses ranged from 1 to 4, where higher numbers indicate that abortion is "always wrong." I produced a mean measure for each available country.

The two scatter plots in Figure 5.4 present the correlations among the mean values for abortion disapproval using the WVS and Pew data and WVS mean values and ISSP proportion who disapprove. The correlations for both figures are over 0.8, which is high and statistically significant. These correlations are so high that estimates from one survey could serve as a proxy for the other. Despite different question wording and survey administrations, these findings show that there is a high level of reliability or consistency across these surveys and countries for examining moral disapproval of abortion.

These findings suggest that despite challenges to studying cross-national abortion views, different questions, surveys, and data collection teams produce valid results. Indeed, other cross-national studies have found some similar relationships to those presented here using different databases, time periods, sets of nations, model specification, and control variables.[116] At least for understanding the moral dimension of abortion attitudes, the WVS is likely to yield similar results as other cross-national surveys. Nevertheless, cross-national research about abortion attitudes has a long way to go in providing a comprehensive understanding of abortion views. All three major cross-national surveys focus on the moral dimension of abortion. But researchers, government officials, journalists, social movement leaders, nonprofit organizations, and the general public may be even more interested in feelings about the legality of abortion, which is only moderately related to moral perspectives. Of course, as mentioned above, in less-democratic nations, this information may be more difficult to collect as the government may not value such a clear understanding of residents' legal preferences, which may conflict with official policy.

Cross-national research would also benefit from a better understanding of the role of hard and soft reasons for shaping disapproval. Likewise, most

---

[116] Adamczyk, "Religion as a Micro and Macro Property"; Adamczyk, Suh, and Lerner, "Analysis of the Relationship between Religion, Abortion, and Assisted Reproductive Technology: Insights into Cross-National Public Opinion"; Loll and Hall, "Differences in Abortion Attitudes by Policy Context and between Men and Women in the World Values Survey"; Fernández, Valiente, and Jaime-Castillo, "Gender Balance in the Workforce and Abortion Attitudes."

COMMUNISM, CONFUCIANISM, CULTURAL VALUES 197

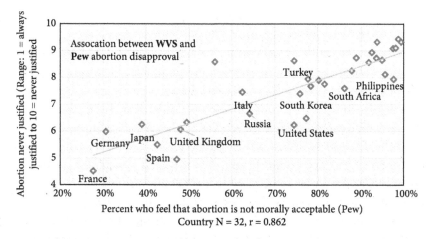

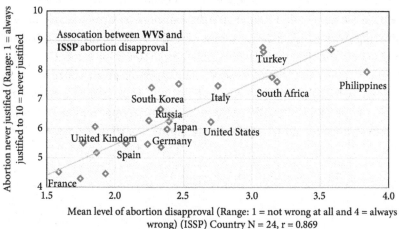

Figure 5.4 Scatterplots of Abortion Disapproval for Three Different Cross-National Data Collections
Note: Only some country names are indicated to make the figure readable.
Sources: WVS, ISSP, and Pew

abortions occur during the first trimester. But even supporters may disapprove of later-term abortions. Future studies should also consider how changes to the wording of questions, including the timing (e.g., gestational time period), affect disapproval. Finally, in countries where abortion is illegal, or disapproval is high, future research should investigate who respondents think should be punished and what the penalty should be for getting an abortion.

Conclusion

This chapter began by examining the role of different cultural contexts in shaping abortion attitudes. I examined the complicated abortion views in the former Soviet Union countries, which have a long history of legal abortion, distrust of surveyors, and high levels of nationalism. I also showed that after accounting for overall levels of religious belief in Confucian societies, these residents are more opposed. The interviews suggest that health-related concerns, which may be linked to traditional beliefs, could shape disapproval. Likewise, China's one-child policy left an indelible mark and may have led residents in nearby societies to moderate their views.

Next, I examined over two dozen other country-level factors that hypothetically could shape abortion attitudes. Finally, I discussed various ways question-wording could influence survey responses. Despite challenges in gathering cross-national data, I showed that the WVS survey question about abortion is valid. However, there is much room for improvement in understanding the various dimensions of public opinion about abortion. More research is badly needed to comprehensively understand cross-national views. I hope this book will inspire more cross-national studies. Chapter 6 switches from a focus on attitudes to examining abortion behaviors.

Chapter 6

Investigating Cross-National Abortion Behavior and Its Relationship with Attitudes

> I think it would depend on who you talk to. For someone who identifies as pro-life, [she might be] sexually irresponsible and wants to cover up a mistake. . . . But [from the pro-choice person] it's almost always something about desperation and difficulty and social circumstances that's involved.
>
> —American researcher

Until now, this book has focused on assessing the factors shaping differences in public opinion about abortion in countries across the globe. One reason people are often interested in abortion views is that they can influence laws, access, and stigma, which, in turn, can shape the lives of women who need or want an abortion. This final substantive chapter investigates the relationship between abortion public opinion and behavior.

I begin by examining the factors shaping cross-national abortion rates. Readers will be surprised to learn that neither legislation, abortion disapproval, nor overall levels of religious importance are significantly associated with abortion rates. Rather, the critical country-level factors are development and gender equality, which largely influence abortion rates by decreasing unintended pregnancies. Throughout this chapter, I highlight the importance of "unintended pregnancies" because they are the ones most likely to be aborted. If female residents can avoid them, abortion rates substantially decrease. Hence, when thinking about the factors associated with abortion risk, we need to consider not only the decision to abort but also whether the pregnancy was planned.

From there, this chapter assesses the key characteristics associated with women's abortion decisions in a set of economically, politically, and religiously diverse countries. These first two sections—covering abortion rates

200 FETAL POSITIONS

across the world and abortion risk within nations—rely heavily on statistics. But even for readers who are not well versed in quantitative analysis techniques, the findings are digestible.

Because strength of religious belief (as conventionally measured with religious importance) is key for understanding abortion attitudes, I next conduct an analysis where I give religion special attention for understanding abortion risk in the United States. Using longitudinal data from young American women, I trace the pathways through which personal religious beliefs influence abortion risk. Readers are likely to find this section on young American women especially fascinating because the results challenge intuition about how personal religious beliefs relate to pregnancy resolution.

The final two sections return to the interview data. I unpack how stigma and shame are related to abortion behaviors in these countries. I also analyze differences between the United States and China in who the public thinks get abortions, the circumstances surrounding a woman's decision, and how this discrepancy may shape attitudes.

Understanding the Factors Shaping Abortion Rates around the World

Cross-national public opinion data on abortion disapproval is challenging to obtain partially because questions must be translated into multiple languages, and the government may not approve the survey questions. Furthermore, residents may not respond truthfully, and surveyors may encounter logistical challenges in creating a sampling frame and administering surveys. Thankfully, international efforts such as the World Values Survey (WVS) provide some information on cross-national views. Compared to public opinion data, researchers encounter even more challenges in collecting information about abortion behavior because getting one is such a private and often stigmatized decision and is often illegal. Below I explain the available data and how they can provide insight into our understanding of abortion behaviors and their relationship to public opinion. I then analyze the factors shaping abortion rates around the world.

Unlike the cross-national public opinion data analyzed in this book, researchers do not have access to similar data for understanding abortion decisions. The best information we have comes from a diverse set of six countries where demographic and health survey administrators asked women whether they had gotten an abortion in the past five years. These data are used in the next section to examine the personal characteristics associated with abortion risk. While we do not have cross-national individual-level data on abortion behaviors, researchers have generated country-level estimates of abortion incidences around the world.[1] These data[2] can be merged with the same country-level information used to examine public opinion, including overall religiosity, disapproval levels, and abortion laws. Combined, this dataset provides insight into the societal characteristics associated with abortion rates.

When analyzing cross-national rates, we need to be especially mindful about whether the pregnancy was intended. As mentioned above, the majority of the world's women get abortions for unanticipated pregnancies. Only a minority of pregnancies are ended because the mother's health is in danger or because the fetus has major developmental problems. Relatedly, women in different societies vary in their fertility preferences. In poorer countries, for example, women often desire larger families. In richer nations, though, parents are more inclined to devote resources to just a few or no children. When comparing abortion rates around the world, we need to consider whether the pregnancy is intended because this is a major factor in determining if it will prematurely end.

In previous chapters, I showed that country-level variables related to education, economics, religion, abortion laws, gender inequality, and communist history were associated with abortion disapproval. Are similar factors associated with abortion rates across nations? Some of the same forces that shaped attitudes (e.g., gender inequality and economic and educational development) are strongly associated with abortion rates. However, as I explain further, other country attributes, such as abortion laws, are surprisingly unrelated. In the following section, I discuss the roles of gender inequality and educational and economic development in shaping abortion rates before addressing other factors.

---

[1] Bearak et al., "Country-Specific Estimates of Unintended Pregnancy and Abortion Incidence."
[2] They gathered information from official statistics, country-based surveys (including the DHS), and one-time studies. The availability of reliable abortion data varied substantially by region, ranging from 12% of countries in western Asia and northern Africa to 73% of countries in Europe and Northern America.

202 FETAL POSITIONS

Gender Equality and Development

In Chapter 2, I showed that nations with lower levels of economic and educational development had more approving residents. Chapter 4 also revealed that people living in countries with higher levels of gender equality are more supportive of abortion. Cultural and structural norms related to economics and gender inequality seem to shape views about women's societal roles and norms related to liberal attitudes. We have good reason to think that these same forces are also related to abortion rates.

As noted above, because women are much more likely to abort an unintended pregnancy, knowing the factors influencing unanticipated pregnancy risk are likely key for understanding abortion behavior. There are several reasons why women in poorer and less equal countries are more likely to have unintended pregnancies, which, in turn, increases their abortion risk. Female residents from these countries typically have less access to reliable birth control, especially long-lasting types such as intrauterine devices (IUDs), which are more expensive, discrete, and easier to use than other types (e.g., condoms).[3] Likewise, they may not know that reliable birth control is available, understand how to properly use it, or be able afford to get a prescription or purchase it.[4]

Additionally, in less-equal societies a woman's sexual partner may not allow her to use contraception, and she may not feel empowered to insist on it. Her husband may prefer that she keep having children. Likewise, he may believe that birth control (e.g., condoms) decreases his sexual pleasure. Researchers have found that in poorer and less-equal societies (e.g., Congo, Malawi, Cameroon, Zambia) women are more likely to report that intimate partner violence (e.g., husband beating his wife for burning dinner) is acceptable.[5] If a woman feels that there are circumstances where it is okay for her partner to assault her, she is unlikely to feel that she can insist on birth control (e.g., condoms), especially if it impinges on his sexual pleasure or preferences (e.g., family size).

Drawing on the same country-level measures used to analyze abortion disapproval, I examine the roles of gender equality and education and economic development for shaping abortion and unintended pregnancy

---

[3] Ali, Folz, and Farron, "Expanding Choice and Access in Contraception."

[4] Gahungu, Vahdaninia, and Regmi, "The Unmet Needs for Modern Family Planning Methods among Postpartum Women in Sub-Saharan Africa."

[5] Ahinkorah, Dickson, and Seidu, "Women Decision-Making Capacity and Intimate Partner Violence among Women in Sub-Saharans Africa."

rates. Figure 6.1 presents the marginal values for abortion rates for unintended pregnancies per 1,000 women of reproductive age. The regression analysis underlying these estimates and the other factors that I considered can be found in Appendix D. Consistent with my analysis of attitudes, Table D.1 in Appendix D shows that in countries with greater gender inequality, the number of abortions from unintended pregnancies is higher. As shown in Figure 6.1, when gender inequality is high, the average abortion rate for unintended pregnancies is approximately 40 per 1,000 women of reproductive age. In the most gender-equal countries, the rate plummets to about fourteen abortions. Likewise, in nations with lower levels of economic development and mean levels of education (i.e., the same measure used in Appendix A's models), abortion rates are higher (see Model 6 of Table D.1 in Appendix D).

Does gender inequality or economic/educational development have a bigger impact on cross-national abortion rates? When researchers only use country-level measures from a relatively small group of nations to examine relationships, correlations among some variables can be exceptionally high. Therefore, it is difficult to untangle the influence of the two factors in the same model. Indeed, gender inequality and economic and educational development are highly correlated (over 0.78), leading to multicollinearity concerns. Nations with higher levels of education and economic development also have more gender equality.[6] Likewise, both measures capture similar concepts, such as labor force participation and educational levels. Hence, it is challenging to unravel the "real" effect.

An alternative way to assess these two factors' impact is to examine how much variation in abortion rates they explain. The findings presented in Models 6 and 7 of Appendix D show that the gender inequality index ($R^2 = 0.54$, where 1.00 indicates 100% of the variation is explained) accounts for more variation in abortion rates than the combined measure of gross domestic product (GDP) and education ($R^2 = 0.39$). Likewise, the effect sizes of the two measures are similar (see Figure 6.2). This information suggests that gender inequality's effect size may be somewhat larger than the combined education and economic development measures. Nevertheless, there is a great deal of overlap.

---

[6] Gender inequality is a composite measure, reflecting inequality between men and women in (1) reproductive health (i.e., maternal mortality and adolescent fertility rate), (2) the share of parliamentary seats held by each gender and educational attainment), and (3) women's labor force participation.

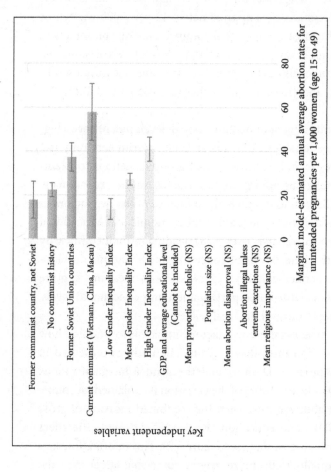

Figure 6.1 Marginal Values of Statistically Significant Variables for Examining the Model-Estimated Annual Average Abortion Rates for Unintended Pregnancies per 1,000 Women, 2015–2019 (age 15 to 49) (N = 71 countries) ("NS" indicating that the variable was tested but not statistically significant)

Notes: Estimates are taken from Appendix D, Table D.1, Model 8. The combined measure of gross domestic product (GDP) and education are not included because they are so highly correlated with gender inequality that the sign is flipping in an unanticipated direction, suggesting multicollinearity concerns. The estimates for the combined GDP and educational level measure can be found in Appendix D, Table D.1, Model 6. In that model, all the same variables are statistically significant and in the same direction as those presented here. All the variables are coded in the same way as they are for the main analysis of abortion attitudes (see Appendix A). The sample sizes differ because fewer countries had abortion rate data than had public opinion information.

Source: Bearak et al., "Country-Specific Estimates of Unintended Pregnancy and Abortion Incidence," 2015–2019

As noted above, gender inequality and lower economic development are associated with higher abortion rates through the pathway of unintended pregnancies. Between 2015 and 2019, roughly 121 million unintended pregnancies occurred worldwide. Approximately 61% of them ended in abortion.[7] In poorer and less-gender-equal nations, women are much more likely to have unintended pregnancies,[8] even though they desire more children on average than females from wealthier societies.[9] Figure 6.2 illustrates the mediating influence of unintended pregnancy rates in explaining the relationship between gender inequality and abortion rates. The first set of bars shows the effect of gender inequality before and after the unintended pregnancy rate is included. Based on the level of gender inequality within a nation, differences in the abortion rate range from forty in the most gender unequal countries to fourteen in the most equal ones. However, once the unintended pregnancy rate is considered (i.e., second set of bars), there are no longer any differences based on gender inequality. Note that in the second set of bars, the confidence intervals, which are the black lines, overlap, typically indicating a lack of statistical difference (see also Appendix D). Gender inequality appears to increase unintended pregnancy rates, which, in turn, lead to higher abortion rates.

The third set of bars in Figure 6.2 shows a similar relationship for economic and educational development and abortion rates. Before the unintended pregnancy rate is considered, nations with lower education and economic development levels have significantly higher abortion rates. But once the unintended pregnancy rate is considered (i.e., final set of bars in Figure 6.2), there are no significant differences based on education and economic levels. Other studies have found a similar relationship between unintended pregnancy and abortion rates and economic development measures.[10]

The unintended pregnancy rate can explain why abortion rates are higher in less-developed and gender-equal societies. Reasons related to gender inequality, economics, and education provide insight into why these women find themselves with pregnancies that they did not intend, making abortions desirable. The next section focuses on Soviet histories in shaping abortion use.

---

[7] Guttmacher Institute, "Unintended Pregnancy and Abortion Worldwide."
[8] Bearak et al., "Country-Specific Estimates of Unintended Pregnancy and Abortion Incidence."
[9] World Bank, "World Development Indicators, 2.14 Reproductive Health," 2017.
[10] Bearak et al., "Unintended Pregnancy and Abortion by Income, Region, and the Legal Status of Abortion"; Bearak et al., "Alignment between Desires and Outcomes among Women Wanting to Avoid Pregnancy."

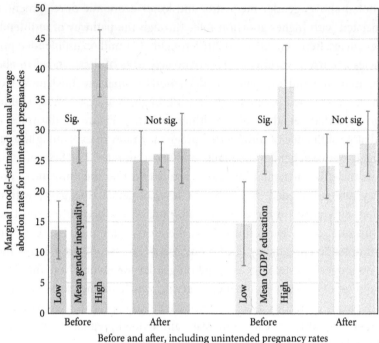

Figure 6.2 Marginal Values for Country Abortion Rates at Three Different Country Levels of Gender Inequality and GDP/education before and after Including the Unintended Pregnancy Rate (Country N = 71)

Notes: The values for gender inequality are the minimum and maximum that could be obtained while still remaining within the range for countries included in the analysis. The estimates for low and high mean GDP/education are two standard deviations above and below the mean. "Sig." indicates that there are statistically significant differences across the measure, and "Not sig." indicates that there are not. The estimates for gender inequality are taken from Appendix D, Table D.1, Model 8 (before) and Model 9 (after). The estimates for mean GDP/education are taken from Model 6 (before) and Model 7 (after) from the same table.

Source: Bearak et al., "Country-Specific Estimates of Unintended Pregnancy and Abortion Incidence", 2015–2019

Soviet Past

In Chapter 5, I discussed the complicated relationship between living in a former Soviet Union country (USSR[11]) and abortion disapproval. WVS data show that former Soviet Union residents are more opposed to abortion than people from countries without a communist past or from former USSR

---

[11] Officially known as the Union of Soviet Socialist Republics (USSR).

satellite nations (e.g., Romania and Hungary). In this section, I investigate differences in abortion rates based on Soviet history.

As discussed in Chapter 5, there are some good reasons to expect especially high abortion rates in former Soviet Union countries. Russia was the first modern nation to legalize abortion. It did so in 1920 and long before other forms of birth control (e.g., pills, IUDs) were available. But once other types became accessible, the Soviet Union incentivized their medical system to provide abortions rather than long-lasting forms of birth control such as sterilization.[12] Additionally, the Soviet Union was officially atheistic. Hence, many residents did not object to abortion based on religious or moral grounds.[13]

Much has changed since the Soviet Union collapsed (1989–1991). Abortion rates have fallen from previous highs. In the 1960s and 1970s, the average Russian woman, for example, would have four to five abortions during her reproductive years. By 1991, the number had dropped to 3.39, and by 2015 it had plummeted to 0.78.[14] But many former Soviet women still rely on abortions, which are legal in all former Soviet Union nations during the first trimester.[15]

Figure 6.1 presents differences in annual abortion rates for countries with Soviet pasts while also accounting for gender inequality. The findings show that former Soviet Union countries have substantially higher abortion rates than nations without communist histories or former Soviet satellite states (e.g., Poland, Romania, and Hungary). Indeed, Georgia (80 abortions for unintended pregnancies per 1,000 women of reproductive age) and Azerbaijan (71 abortions) have the two highest abortion rates among countries included in Figure 6.1. Two other former Soviet countries, Kazakhstan (47 abortions) and Russia (46), also make the top ten list of highest abortion rates per 1,000 women of reproductive age who had an unintentional pregnancy. China (49 abortions) has the fourth-highest abortion rate, and India (47 abortions) is ranked seventh.

In trying to make sense of the especially high abortion rates in this region, some have suggested that women in the former Soviet Union countries did

---

[12] Popov and David, "Russian Federation and USSR Successor States."

[13] Karpov and Kääriäinen, "'Abortion Culture' in Russia"; Mason, "Opposing Abortion to Protect Women."

[14] PONARS Eurasia, "Abortion in Russia: How Has the Situation Changed Since the Soviet Era?"

[15] Denisov, Sakevich, and Jasilioniene, "Divergent Trends in Abortion and Birth Control Practices in Belarus, Russia and Ukraine."

208 FETAL POSITIONS

not have high-quality, long-lasting birth control.[16] Hence, they were bur-
dened with more pregnancies than they desired. Women would therefore
use abortion to resolve the high unintentional pregnancy rates. Is this still an
issue? In Models 7 and 9 of Table D.1 in Appendix D, I include unintended
pregnancy rates in the model. The findings show that even after accounting
for unintended pregnancies, women from the former Soviet Union countries still have significantly higher abortion rates than women from countries
without communist histories or those from the former USSR's satellite states.

These findings suggest that many women from the former Soviet Union
may be using abortions to manage pregnancies more often than females
from other countries with similar unintended pregnancy rates. Moreover,
Chapter 5 showed that people from Soviet Union countries reported high
abortion disapproval in the WVS. Hence, residents may feel that they
"should" disapprove of abortion and therefore tell survey researchers that
they are highly opposed. However, the abortion rate data make clear that
public opinion survey responses are misaligned with behavior. Although
abortion rates in the former Soviet Union countries have decreased substantially since it dissolved, many women still use abortion to control fertility. In
the next section, I discuss factors that are not associated with abortion rates
but seem like they should be.

Religion, Abortion Disapproval, and Laws

To unpack the forces shaping abortion rates, I considered all the measures
(e.g., mean religious importance, abortion laws, population size) that were
important for understanding abortion attitudes. I also examined the relationship between abortion disapproval and rates. As indicated in Figure 6.1,
none of these country characteristics help explain rates. In this section, I
elaborate on why so few factors seem to matter.

Religious importance is the most important force shaping abortion support. People who say they have strong religious beliefs, regardless of the
specific religion, are more likely to disapprove. Likewise, living in a country where residents, on average, report that religion is important are less
supportive. However, Figure 6.1 indicates that overall religious importance
is not meaningful for explaining abortion rates worldwide.

---

[16] Cooper and Times, "Women Fault Soviet System for Abortion"; Popov, "Family Planning in
the USSR. Sky-High Abortion Rates Reflect Dire Lack of Choice."

Why isn't there a relationship? The findings presented in Table D.1 of Appendix D test for the effect of multiple factors (e.g., religious belief, communism, gender inequality, development) simultaneously. However, a simple correlation reveals that higher levels of religious importance are associated with higher abortion rates. This relationship is the opposite of what we might expect. Shouldn't religion work to limit abortions, not increase them? The strength of religious belief is also correlated with gender inequality and economic and educational development. More prosperous, educated, and gender-equal nations, on average, have residents with lower levels of religious belief.[17] They also have lower abortion rates, largely because they are having fewer unanticipated pregnancies. Hence, once we account for gender inequality and economic/educational development, the spurious relationship between the strength of religious beliefs and abortion rates disappears.[18]

Because these analyses examine aggregate measures across nations, we cannot unravel whether more religious women are just as likely to get abortions as others, a segment of irreligious females are obtaining a disproportionate number of abortions, or personal religious beliefs are unrelated to abortion decisions. Later in this chapter, I use survey data from young American women to trace the pathways through which religion shapes their abortion risk. The country-level data presented here generally show that more religious societies are as likely to have high abortion rates as more secular ones.

Like the relationship between average religious importance and abortion rates, neither the proportion Catholic nor overall abortion disapproval are associated with abortion rates. Before considering any other variables, greater abortion disapproval is associated with higher abortion rates, just as we saw with stronger religious beliefs and rates. But gender inequality and economic/educational development are also associated with attitudes. Hence, once we control for development, the relationship between abortion disapproval and rates disappears. Finally, while the proportion Catholic within a nation is associated with more substantial abortion disapproval,

---

[17] Halman and van Ingen, "Secularization and Changing Moral Views"; Inglehart, *Modernization and Postmodernization*.

[18] Compared to abortion attitudes, there may be greater uncertainty in the behavior measure. More precise abortion rate data may find associations with a greater range of variables, albeit the current abortion rate data are reliable enough to detect statistically significant associations with communist history and gender inequality and education and economic measures.

it is unrelated to abortion rates. Likewise, studies within individual countries have also found that Catholic women are as likely as others to obtain abortions.[19]

While readers may be surprised to learn that overall religious importance is unrelated to abortion rates, they may be shocked to find that abortion laws do not influence them. Many people advocate for abortion restrictions with the hope that they will limit abortions. But the findings in Figure 6.1 make clear that laws are not associated with abortion rates.[20] Indeed, abortion being legal during the first trimester is unrelated to abortion rates, even before additional factors are considered. Other studies find the same nonsignificant relationship.[21]

Why would abortion laws be unrelated to rates? In some countries where abortion is illegal, government officials may not be incentivized to punish women who obtain abortions or their doctors. As a result, women may be able to easily obtain illegal abortions. Likewise, in some societies, such as the United States, abortion pills or medical abortions (i.e., mifepristone and misoprostol) have become more popular than surgical abortions.[22] Pills are more convenient than surgical abortions and can be mailed or easily obtained on the black market. When abortion pills are readily available, authorities may find it challenging to enforce antiabortion laws.

Finally, women who want abortions, but live in countries where they are technically illegal, may travel to places where they are allowed. Google search data show that when a nation's government restricts abortion, residents are more likely to search for abortion-related information, suggesting they are trying to seek services elsewhere.[23] In other words, abortion laws do not necessarily decrease demand. Indeed, after the US state of Texas, for example, eliminated abortion access, border cities in Mexico, where it had been recently legalized, experienced a surge in demand for abortion pills.[24]

---

[19] Jerman, Jones, and Onda, "Characteristics of U.S. Abortion Patients in 2014 and Changes Since 2008"; Adamczyk, "Understanding the Effects of Personal and School Religiosity on the Decision to Abort a Premarital Pregnancy."

[20] For an examination of the relationship between abortion laws and fertility rates, see also Fernández and Juif, "Does Abortion Liberalisation Accelerate Fertility Decline?" Consistent with the findings presented here, they do not find that country-level abortion reforms are associated with fertility declines.

[21] Bearak et al., "Unintended Pregnancy and Abortion by Income, Region, and the Legal Status of Abortion."

[22] Jones et al., "Medication Abortion Now Accounts for More than Half of All US Abortions."

[23] Reis and Brownstein, "Measuring the Impact of Health Policies Using Internet Search Patterns."

[24] Burnett, "Texas' Abortion Law Led Some to Get Abortion Pills in Mexico, with Grim Consequences."

This analysis of rates shows that communist history and gender inequality, which is closely linked to economic and educational development, are associated with abortion rates through their influence on unintended pregnancies. In richer and more educated and gender-equal countries, women have fewer unintended pregnancies and hence are less likely to need or want an abortion. The next section focuses on key personal characteristics for explaining abortion decisions.

Individual Characteristics for Shaping Personal Abortion Decisions in Six Diverse Nations

So far, this chapter has examined the country-level factors associated with abortion rates worldwide. One of the challenges with assessing country-level relationships is that we do not know how macro-level factors, such as economic development, shape a woman's decision to obtain an abortion over and above her own income level. Likewise, the vast majority of research examining abortion decisions are conducted within a single country.[25] Hence, we do not have a clear sense of the characteristics of women who have gotten abortions across different nations, especially those from different world regions where culture, history, and economic structures vary substantially. Are personal characteristics associated with abortion behaviors country specific, or are there general trends across the globe in what shapes abortion risk?

To answer these questions, we would ideally have cross-national data on women who got abortions. Unfortunately, there is no equivalent of the WVS, which includes respondents from dozens of different societies, for examining abortion behavior. However, the Demographic and Health Surveys (DHS) program offers insight into the individual-level factors associated with women's abortion decisions in six diverse nations (India, Albania, Cambodia, Cameroon, Cote d-Ivoire, and Indonesia). In this section, I explain why higher levels of urbanicity, wealth, education, already having a child, and Christian affiliation would increase abortion risk. I then test these relationships. This analysis provides insight into which personal factors are

---

[25] See, for example, Murray et al., "Factors Related to Induced Abortion among Young Women in Edo State, Nigeria"; Nyarko and Potter, "Effect of Socioeconomic Inequalities and Contextual Factors on Induced Abortion in Ghana"; Adamczyk, "Understanding the Effects of Personal and School Religiosity on the Decision to Abort a Premarital Pregnancy."

212   FETAL POSITIONS

meaningful across a diverse array of countries for explaining abortion decisions. If we find that some characteristics are consistently associated with elevated abortion risk across this assorted set of nations, then these factors may be especially important for understanding abortion risk more generally across the world.

As noted above, the majority of abortions occur as a result of unanticipated pregnancies. Likewise, many women who get abortions already have children, who likely have a major role in their decision-making process. Mothers who have an unintended pregnancy may want an abortion because they do not have the financial or emotional resources to support more children and because they may have met their fertility preference.[26] They likely have strong ties to their current children. They may feel that having another child would limit resources (e.g., financial, emotional, time) for everyone.

Previous research also suggests that money likely matters for abortion decisions.[27] Wealthier women are better positioned to pay for abortions. Likewise, when abortions are difficult to find, richer women are more likely to have the resources to locate a provider. Even in countries where abortion is illegal, richer women should be more likely to get them because financial resources should make locating medication or a provider easier. Finally, women with more money may also have more ambition and access to opportunities that could lead them to pursue a higher standard of living for their families, making fewer children and abortion more appealing. Hence, there is good reason to think that across nations wealthier women will be more likely to report having gotten an abortion.

The DHS includes information on women's educational level, which may also matter for abortion risk, even after accounting for wealth. Women with more education may have higher career and educational ambitions. When they have an unexpected pregnancy, an abortion may be desirable to help pursue other goals. They may also value smaller families. Likewise, as noted above, an abortion can be financially costly and challenging to find, especially in a country where it is illegal. Hence, women with no schooling or only a primary education may not have the wherewithal to locate an abortion provider or obtain the necessary medications, increasing the likelihood that they will instead carry an unexpected pregnancy to term. Finally,

---

[26] "Turnaway Study."
[27] Ng and Diener, "What Matters to the Rich and the Poor?"

less-educated women may have more conservative leanings, leading them to feel that wives should have large families.

Along with education, wealth, and motherhood status, in the following analysis I also examine urbanicity for understanding abortion risk. Access to abortion providers or medications may be more prevalent in urban areas. Additionally, people living in denser places may be exposed to more diverse and less-traditional values.[28] As a result, urban women may feel more comfortable getting an abortion, and their partners may also be drawn to or influenced by the more liberal environment, increasing abortion support. Women in urban areas may also have smaller support networks to raise another child. Likewise, their economic standards for raising children may be higher, including more and better schooling and enrichment opportunities. As a result, they may be less inclined to feel they can afford a bigger family.

Finally, religious affiliation may also matter for understanding abortion behavior. DHS survey administrators did not consistently ask about strength of religious belief or engagement. But they inquired about religious adherence. As a result, I can examine religious affiliation differences in shaping abortion odds. The sample of countries included in this analysis is religiously diverse, including nations with different dominant religions. Hinduism is the majority religion in India, Islam dominates in Indonesia and Albania, Christianity is prevalent in Cameroon, and Cambodia has a majority Buddhist population. Finally, Cote d'Ivoire has equal parts Muslims and Christians.

All the major religions have some opposition to abortion. Hence, personal religiosity is typically more important for understanding views about abortion than religious affiliation. Nevertheless, without data on religious importance or engagement, we might expect Muslim women to have lower abortion risk compared to Christians. As discussed in Chapter 1, religious affiliates of the major world religions do not differ substantially from each other in their abortion disapproval. Hence, Muslims would not necessarily have a lower abortion risk because they are more religiously opposed than other religious followers. Rather, they may be less likely to be in the predicament where an abortion is desirable, decreasing their risk of wanting one.

---

[28] Parker et al., "1. Demographic and Economic Trends in Urban, Suburban and Rural Communities."

214 FETAL POSITIONS

In the next section, I discuss how religious beliefs and engagement shape American women's abortion decisions. I draw on longitudinal data to explain that strong religious beliefs can decrease abortion odds, at least for first pregnancies. More religious women may be on a trajectory where they do not have premarital sex. And if they do, they may be less likely to have an extramarital pregnancy where abortion becomes an appealing option. Many Muslim women may follow a similar trajectory. My previous coauthored work on women from the developing world showed that Muslims are less likely than Jews and Christians to have premarital sex.[29] They also get married at an earlier age, limiting the risk of pregnancy outside of marriage. Moreover, married Muslim women are less likely than married Christian females to have sex outside of marriage.[30]

Women may be especially interested in obtaining abortions for pregnancies resulting from extramarital relationships. Rather than Muslim women having lower abortion risk because they disapprove of abortion, they may have lower risk because they are less likely to follow a pathway that leads to a predicament where abortion is a necessary or very appealing option to manage a premarital or extramarital pregnancy. The next section tests the links between these personal attributes and abortion behavior in six diverse countries.

Testing the Personal Characteristics Shaping Abortion Risk

To assess the personal factors shaping abortion behavior, I use data from the DHS. The DHS are nationally representative household surveys that provide population, health, and nutrition information.[31] The data are collected in poorer nations where information about population health is not prevalent and health concerns are greater than in wealthier societies. Because they focus on health, some DHS country surveys ask women about sex behaviors, pregnancies, and abortions. They also collect basic information about age, marital status, educational level, and income. However, they do not survey women about their abortion attitudes or strength of religious belief; though, as noted above, they ask about religious affiliation (i.e., Muslim, Christian, Buddhist).

[29] Adamczyk and Hayes, "Religion and Sexual Behaviors Understanding the Influence of Islamic Cultures and Religious Affiliation for Explaining Sex Outside of Marriage."
[30] Adamczyk and Hayes.
[31] "The DHS Program—Demographic and Health Survey (DHS)."

My research team combed through dozens of DHS surveys from 2006 to 2021 to isolate the latest handful of them that asked about women's abortion behavior.[32] Ultimately, only six countries (India, Albania, Cambodia, Cameroon, Cote d'Ivoire, and Indonesia) included this abortion question. We merged information on age, marital status, having one or more children, wealth, education, and religious affiliation from all available women who were surveyed. Within each country, the data were then analyzed using multivariate regression techniques that account for the proper survey design and weights.[33] By examining the influence of the same personal characteristics for abortion risk within each country, we can see which ones are meaningful across a diverse set of societies for understanding abortion behavior more generally.

Table 6.1 presents the results. Arrows that point upward (↑⇧) indicate that the factor is associated with an increased risk of reporting abortion. Downward pointing arrows (↓⇩) suggest that there is a decreased risk. When the arrow is shaded black (↑), the relationship is statistically significant ($p < 0.05$ two-tailed test). White arrows (⇧) indicate that the coefficient did not reach statistical significance. The highlighted cells suggest a pattern is emerging.

In almost every model, whether a woman had at least one child was significant in explaining abortion risk. In a separate analysis, I also examined whether each additional child increased a woman's abortion risk. In some countries, such as India, it did. But the most consistent finding was having at least one child versus none. In some countries, such as Albania, where women on average have relatively few children (i.e., less than two), the coefficient for having had at least one child was massive—clearly the biggest predictor for getting an abortion among the factors examined in Table 6.1. As discussed previously, abortion is more common in some countries that have ties to the Soviet Union (e.g., Albania).[34] While Albania had a strict pronatalist stance, abortion was legalized in 1995. At that time, Albania had an abortion rate that was higher than the European average.[35] Additionally, it has largely been viewed as a secular or atheistic country.[36]

---

[32] All six of the countries included in this analysis had women reporting abortions for the previous five years.

[33] I also considered including all the countries in the same analysis, but India comprised 85% of the sample. I considered modeling differences between countries, but interactions between a set of country dummy variables and the key predictors were often statistically significant, partially because the sample size was so big, producing enough power to detect even very small effects.

[34] Krisafi, "Albania and the Soviet Union, a Complicated Relationship . . . a Short Review."

[35] "WHO European Health Information at Your Fingertips."

[36] Bezati, "How Albania Became the World's First Atheist Country."

Table 6.1 Logistic Regression Analysis of the Factors Increasing Abortion Risk for Women[a] (age 15–49) across Individual Countries Using Data from the Demographic and Health Surveys[b] (highlighted cells suggest trends across countries)

Country Abortion law	(1) India Partially legal	(2) Albania[c] Legal	(3) Cambodia Legal	(4) Cameroon Illegal[d]	(5) Cote d'Ivoire Illegal	(6) Indonesia Illegal
Survey year standardized[e]	↑	⇑			↓	
Married vs. all others	↑	⇑	↑	↓	↓	⇑
Age	↓	↓	↓	↓	↑	↑
One or more children	↑	↑	↑	↑	↑	⇑
Higher family wealth	↑	⇓	↑	↑	↑	⇑
Primary education vs. none	↑	⇓	⇑	↑	↑	⇑
Secondary education vs. none	↑	↓	⇓	↑	↑	↑
More than secondary vs. none	↑	⇓	↓	⇑	↑	↑
Urban vs. rural	↑	⇑	↑	⇓	⇑	⇑
Christian vs. Muslim[f]	⇓	⇓	↑	↑	↑	
No religion vs. Muslim	↑			↑	↑	
Other religion vs. Muslim	⇑		⇑	↑	↑	
Buddhist vs. Muslim	⇑		↑			
Hindu vs. Muslim	↑					
Prob > F	***	***	***	***	***	***
Number of Strata	72	24	38	21	21	67
Number of PSUs	30,106	712	611	426	351	1,970
Respondent N	672,582	10,152	17,575	12,401	9,957	47,612

Two-tailed significance test p < .05. ↑ = positive and significant; ↓ = negative and significant; ⇑ = positive, but not statistically significant; ⇓ = negative, but not statistically significant. When no arrow is indicated, data were not collected.

[a] All the countries included in this analysis had women reporting abortions for the previous five years.

[b] All models include weights and were run with the proper survey techniques.

[c] Albania is the only communist country and has especially high abortion rates. The findings for this country work in the opposite direction of trends in the other countries, suggesting that the wide use of abortion is not being driven by the same forces as it is in other low- and medium-income countries.

[d] "Illegal" indicates that it is not legal on demand within gestational limits.

[e] Some country surveys were all completed in the same year. Hence, survey year for these countries is missing because there is no variation.

[f] The nations vary substantially in terms of their dominant religion. Hence, in some countries they did not ask about certain religious groups. The findings include all the categories that were included in the survey for each country. When coefficients are missing, it indicates that surveys did not ask about that religious group.

As anticipated, urbanicity, money, and education also matter for understanding abortion risk.[37] The DHS administrators categorized households into five standardized income groups based on their finances. Women from wealthier families have greater odds of reporting an abortion. Table 6.1 also shows that education is important for shaping a woman's abortion decision, even after accounting for family wealth.[38] Across the countries examined, education was mostly associated with higher abortion risk. The six countries examined in Table 6.1 include some very poor and more middle-income countries. As a result, some of these nations have a substantial number of women without any education (e.g., Cote d'Ivoire), and others have higher proportions of college graduates (e.g., Albania). In general women of reproductive age with higher levels of educational attainment are more likely to report having gotten an abortion than less-educated females, which is consistent with findings from richer nations.[39] Later in this chapter, I use data from the United States to examine abortion risk, finding a similar link with education.

The results presented in Table D.1 in Appendix D examine abortion odds. Could the relationship between education and abortion odds work in the opposite direction? Some female respondents, for example, could have been in school when they got pregnant. If they did not get an abortion, then having a child could have disrupted their educational plans as they cared for a child instead. In this scenario, the causal relationship between abortion risk and educational attainment would run in the opposite direction with getting an abortion increasing educational attainment.

In a separate analysis, I unraveled the causal relationship by running an analysis for women who were thirty years old or older. By age thirty, most women in this sample would have completed their education, especially because only a minority of them (12%) report any college attendance. In the sample of women age thirty to forty-nine, the positive relationship

---

[37] Ng and Diener, "What Matters to the Rich and the Poor?"

[38] Psaki et al., "Causal Effects of Education on Sexual and Reproductive Health in Low and Middle-Income Countries."

[39] Plotnick, "The Effects of Attitudes on Teenage Premarital Pregnancy and Its Resolution"; Finer et al., "Reasons U.S. Women Have Abortions."

218   FETAL POSITIONS

between educational attainment and increased abortion risk over the previous five years is the same as it was when the younger women are also included in the sample. Hence, educational attainment likely increases abortion risk, rather than the other way around (i.e., getting an abortion increases educational attainment).

In the previous section, I showed that across the world, nations with higher levels of education and GDP have *lower* abortion rates than countries with poorer and less-educated residents. But within the countries examined in Table 6.1, more educated and richer women have *higher* abortion risk. Is there a discrepancy?

The individual-level analysis presented in Table 6.1 does not include information on whether women had an unintended pregnancy, which the macro analysis illustrates is vital. As shown in Figure 6.2, after the unintended pregnancy rate is included, we no longer see a difference in abortion rates by economics and education. Women living in richer and more educated nations more successfully avoid unintended pregnancies, leading to lower abortion rates. Table 6.1 does not consider unintended pregnancies because DHS administrators did not ask about them. But if we had these data, we would likely see that just as women in richer and more educated countries are better at avoiding unintended pregnancies, so are more educated and richer women in general. But if they do get pregnant, these more educated and richer women are more successful at obtaining abortions as part of their family planning. In other words, they are better at getting and using birth control and locating an abortion for unintended pregnancies.[40]

Finally, Table 6.1 includes an analysis of religious affiliation for understanding abortion risk. Muslim women are the reference group, so the other religious affiliates are compared to them. Arrows that point upward indicate that abortion odds are higher for the comparison group (i.e., Christians, Hindus, Buddhists, non-affiliates) than they are for Muslim women. The arrows indicate that Christians have higher odds of obtaining an abortion than Muslims in India, Cambodia, Cameroon, and Cote d'Ivoire. We do not find this relationship in Albania. But as noted above, Albania has a strong atheistic past and ties to the former Soviet Union, which may help explain why few characteristics that are statistically significant in other countries

---

[40] A similar relationship can be found in richer nations as well. For example, see Reeves and Venator, "Sex, Contraception, or Abortion? Explaining Class Gaps in Unintended Childbearing."

matter here. Also, the Indonesia's DHS country survey did not ask about religious affiliation, possibly because the vast majority of Indonesians are Muslim. Hence, administrators may not have felt that religious affiliation distinctions are important.

The religion-related results presented in Table 6.1 find that Muslim women in several societies are less likely than others to get an abortion. Unfortunately, the DHS does not include a measure of abortion disapproval. But Chapter 1 showed that there are few major differences in abortion disapproval based on religious affiliation. These findings suggest that Muslim women do not necessarily have a lower abortion risk because they are more ideologically or religiously opposed to abortion than others. A more logical explanation may relate to the pathways that would make abortion desirable.

As discussed previously, a key component for understanding abortion risk is whether a woman has an unintended pregnancy. Compared to other religious affiliates, Muslim women may be less likely to have premarital and extramarital sex, they may be sexually active for a shorter time period outside of marriage, and they may have fewer sex partners. As a result, they may have lower odds of an unanticipated pregnancy and thus risk of an abortion. The next section discusses how religious beliefs and engagement shape women's abortion decisions in the United States. Muslim women may journey down some of the same behavioral pathways that lower abortion risk for more religious American women.

Using data from a set of six countries located across the world, we see that prior motherhood, wealth, education, and urbanity matter in shaping abortion decisions. Likewise, Muslim women have lower abortion risk than Christians. If we had more survey information, we would likely find other personal and country characteristics are also meaningful for understanding abortion decisions. The next section takes a closer look at the role of religious belief and engagement in shaping abortion risk in the United States.

Additional Pathways for Religion's Influence on Abortion Decisions

As noted above, the DHS did not collect information on religion measures other than affiliation (i.e., Islam, Hindu, and Christianity) across multiple country surveys. Hence, we cannot use those data to examine the other pathways through which religious belief and engagement, as

220 FETAL POSITIONS

conventionally measured, may shape abortion decisions. However, the high-quality National Longitudinal Study of Adolescent Health (Add Health) can provide insight into religion's role for understanding young American women's decisions[41] to abort their first pregnancies.

How might religious beliefs and participation influence abortion decisions? Surveys of American women who are about to get an abortion show that roughly 27% of them do not claim a religion.[42] A slightly smaller proportion of Americans (22%) report not having a religion.[43] Women who obtain abortions may be somewhat less religious than the US general population. But they may also feel less religious on the day they get an abortion. Indeed, in countries with high overall levels of religious belief, such as the United States, many residents disapprove of abortion, elevating its stigma.[44] Women who are about to undergo an abortion may experience some cognitive dissonance (i.e., holding conflicting beliefs) related to religion. Our understanding of the correct causal relationship between religion and abortion decisions becomes murky when researchers collect survey data about a woman's religious beliefs and engagement on the day she is getting an abortion.

Furthermore, the link between religion and abortion decisions is complicated because women are much more likely to abort unintended pregnancies.[45] Religion may shape the pathways that lead to an unintended or unexpected pregnancy and the circumstances surrounding it. These factors may then influence her abortion risk.

To understand the causal direction and pathways adequately, we need to measure the strength of women's religious beliefs and participation *before* they get pregnant. My research team has conducted some of the only studies

[41] Because abortion is taboo for many Americans, there is a high level of underreporting in any US-based abortion study using self-reported data. The findings presented in this section come from three studies that I conducted using Add Health data. These studies are: Adamczyk and Felson, "Fetal Positions"; Adamczyk, "The Effects of Religious Contextual Norms, Structural Constraints, and Personal Religiosity on Abortion Decisions"; Adamczyk, "Understanding the Effects of Personal and School Religiosity on the Decision to Abort a Premarital Pregnancy." The findings from these studies may be less susceptible to social desirability bias because the data were collected using audio-CASI and controls were included to account for social desirability bias. Additionally, in a separate analysis, I found that more religious women were *not* more likely to report miscarriages, which might otherwise suggest that they are underreporting abortions and framing them as miscarriages instead.

[42] Jones, Finer, and Singh, "Characteristics of US Abortion Patients, 2008."

[43] Mitchell, "About Three-in-Ten U.S. Adults Are Now Religiously Unaffiliated."

[44] Cockrill et al., "The Stigma of Having an Abortion"; Cockrill and Nack, "'I'm Not That Type of Person'"; Hanschmidt et al., "Abortion Stigma."

[45] Bearak et al., "Country-Specific Estimates of Unintended Pregnancy and Abortion Incidence."

examining the processes linking religion and abortion decisions in the United States.[46] These findings offer insight into how religion may shape cross-national abortion behaviors.

To better understand how religion influences abortion decisions, we used Add Health longitudinal data (not cross-sectional) from the same young women over a six-year period, beginning when they were still in high school and before any pregnancy.[47] We were, therefore, able to measure the strength of religious belief and engagement *before* a potential abortion or unintended pregnancy could shape their religious beliefs. We focused only on females and first pregnancies for those who had one. We had minimal information on second pregnancies because the respondents were still relatively young during subsequent surveys. Different forces likely influence later pregnancy resolutions, especially if she already has children.[48]

We found that women's higher personal religiosity (i.e., a combination of religious importance and engagement) largely shaped abortion decisions through the sex-related behaviors that decreased the likelihood of an extramarital pregnancy.[49] Specifically, more religious women had more conservative sex-related behaviors, which lowered their odds of having a pregnancy outside of a relationship. Furthermore, more religious women who got pregnant before marriage were more likely to have done so with a romantic partner they were willing to marry before birth (i.e., "shotgun wedding").[50]

Figure 6.3 illustrates the processes through which personal religiosity shaped abortion decisions. Religious beliefs and engagement affect abortion risk through pathway A. More religious women were more likely to have first sex after marriage.[51] Almost all the married women who got pregnant gave birth. If they had premarital sex, more religious women had a smaller

---

[46] Adamczyk, "The Effects of Religious Contextual Norms, Structural Constraints, and Personal Religiosity on Abortion Decisions"; Adamczyk and Felson, "Fetal Positions"; Adamczyk, "Understanding the Effects of Personal and School Religiosity on the Decision to Abort a Premarital Pregnancy."

[47] We excluded women who got pregnant in high school and before the first survey was administered. There were very few high school students who already had a pregnancy. We focused on within person changes. See the three individual studies published by Adamczyk and colleagues noted above for specific information on how the analyses were conducted.

[48] "Turnaway Study."

[49] Unfortunately, we could not unravel the correct causal relationship between birth control use and abortion behavior. The causal order could work in either direction.

[50] Among more religious females, out-of-wedlock pregnancies are likely to occur within long-term serious relationships. If marriage is on the horizon, an unplanned pregnancy may simply hasten the inevitable rather than cause major disruptions in planned life trajectories.

[51] See also Adamczyk and Felson, "Friends' Religiosity and First Sex"; Adamczyk, "Socialization and Selection in the Link between Friends' Religiosity and the Transition to Sexual Intercourse."

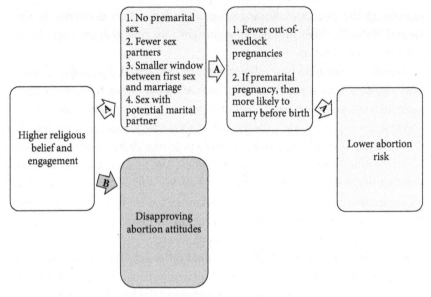

Figure 6.3 Processes That Explain the Influence of Religion on American Women's Risk of Aborting First Pregnancies

window between their sexual debut and first marriage, decreasing their risk of an out-of-wedlock pregnancy. They also had fewer sex partners, further limiting the odds of an unintended pregnancy. Finally, unmarried religious women had higher odds of getting married before giving birth, suggesting they may have already been in a relationship with the potential father. Hence, an unexpected pregnancy simply sped up an anticipated wedding.

Are more religious women who conceive and choose not to marry the father less likely to get an abortion? No. Once young women are in the predicament of being pregnant without a marital partner, person religious beliefs offer no protection against abortion risk. They are just as likely as women who lack religious interest to get an abortion. Moreover, religious beliefs and engagement do not affect her level of abortion disapproval to shape odds of an abortion once she is pregnant without a marriage mate (see pathway B in Figure 6.3).[52] Instead of shaping abortion attitudes, personal religiosity influences the pathways that lead to an extramarital pregnancy with someone they are willing to quickly marry (i.e., "shotgun wedding").

One reason for religion's limited direct effect on abortion decisions may relate to shame and embarrassment. All the major religions proscribe sex outside of marriage. In the United States, which is dominated by Catholic and Protestant religious beliefs, most religious leaders discourage premarital

---

[52] Adamczyk and Felson, "Fetal Positions."

sex. Some US Christian organizations even encourage teenagers to publicly proclaim their intention to remain virgins until marriage (i.e., virginity pledges).[53] The disapproving climate created by these religious congregations may exacerbate the embarrassment religiously engaged young women likely feel when they have a premarital birth. By being visibly pregnant, they announce their transgression of premarital sex. If they get an abortion, they avoid the embarrassment of everyone knowing that they had premarital sex. However, more religious females may then feel internal shame for violating religious proscriptions regarding abortion.[54]

Likewise, religion may minimally influence abortion decisions once women are pregnant without a viable marriage partner because more practical concerns become pertinent.[55] She may have to consider whether to raise a child independently and disrupt life plans. Indeed, in our analysis, two of the most important predictors of out-of-wedlock pregnancy and abortion risk were parents' education and high school grades.[56] Good grades and better-educated parents, who likely have higher academic expectations for their daughters, lower the odds that she would have an out-of-wedlock pregnancy. These women either delayed premarital sex or were very careful with birth control and their number of sex partners because of their high academic and career aspirations. However, if these women had a premarital pregnancy, they were more likely to get an abortion. Academic achievement and parents' educational expectations are related to the opportunity costs women endure by unexpectedly having a child that disrupts their education and paid labor potential. Table 6.1 above shows a similar increase in abortion risk for more educated and richer women from middle and low-income nations.

Young, academically ambitious American women who want to protect their future economic and career prospects are more successful at avoiding unanticipated pregnancies and more likely to get abortions when needed. Partially because the United States is a prosperous and more gender-egalitarian country, access to quality birth control and males who support their partners' wishes and want to avoid an anticipated pregnancy themselves are more prevalent. Thus, high-achieving women are less likely to get pregnant before marriage. These findings are also consistent with other surveys, showing that academic aspiration is an essential reason young women

---

[53] Teens who sign "virginity pledges" typically have premarital sex but lose their virginity at older ages than others. See Bearman and Brückner, "Promising the Future"; Rostosky et al., "The Impact of Religiosity on Adolescent Sexual Behavior."

[54] Cockrill et al., "The Stigma of Having an Abortion"; Cockrill and Nack, "'I'm Not That Type of Person.'"

[55] Lie, Robson, and May, "Experiences of Abortion."

[56] Adamczyk and Felson, "Fetal Positions."

224 FETAL POSITIONS

get abortions.[57] Conversely, females who perceive fewer opportunity costs to having an out-of-wedlock child may be less likely to get an abortion. Indeed, we found that if their parents received public assistance, which suggests that their household income is around the poverty level, these young women were more likely to give birth than obtain an abortion.[58] For some women, becoming a parent may be a more straightforward and rewarding goal than obtaining a college degree.

Are the religion-related findings presented here likely found in other societies? For countries with high levels of religious beliefs, gender equality, and development, the pathways through which it affects abortion decisions for first pregnancies may be similar. But the picture gets murkier when we consider the factors shaping abortion decisions for later pregnancies. While this analysis focused only on first pregnancies, most abortions are performed on women with children. For example, US-based data collected in 2019, before abortion on demand became illegal in many states, 58% of women who got abortions were already mothers.[59] More than half of them had two or more children. In China, the proportion of women who got abortions and already have a child was over 90%.[60] Hence, existing children radically complicate how women resolve unintended pregnancies.

At the beginning of this chapter, I showed that cross-national levels of religious importance are unrelated to abortion rates. If that analysis had only focused on abortion rates for first pregnancies, we might find a correlation between religious importance and rates. At least in the United States, the most religious women are likely to wait until their wedding night to have sex for the first time. Then, when they get pregnant for the first time in their marriages, they almost always carry the pregnancy to term.[61] But in many countries, including the United States, the typical abortion patient already has at least one child.[62]

In contrast to first pregnancies, women who get pregnant again will have new considerations.[63] They may have to contemplate the financial consequences of another child for current ones. Likewise, some will have to ponder the challenges of raising another child after a divorce or in a

---

[57] Plotnick, "The Effects of Attitudes on Teenage Premarital Pregnancy and Its Resolution"; Finer et al., "Reasons U.S. Women Have Abortions."

[58] Adamczyk and Felson, "Fetal Positions."

[59] Kortsmit, "Abortion Surveillance—United States, 2019."

[60] These data were gathered between 2013 and 2016.

[61] Adamczyk and Felson, "Fetal Positions."

[62] Jerman, Jones, and Onda, "Characteristics of U.S. Abortion Patients in 2014 and Changes Since 2008."

[63] "Turnaway Study."

problematic relationship. In other societies, male children may be more valuable than females.[64] While couples might have one daughter, a second or third girl when they still do not have a son may be highly undesirable. When the abortions for first and later pregnancies are combined, as they were for the analysis of rates (i.e., Figure 6.1), we no longer see an effect of religion in shaping abortion decisions at the macro level.

In this sample of young American women, stronger religious beliefs and engagement do not affect abortion decisions through more disapproving attitudes. Instead, the strength of personal religious beliefs and engagement decrease the odds that females will abort their first pregnancy by limiting the risk of an out-of-wedlock pregnancy within a less-committed relationship. While this analysis focused only on the United States, many of the processes found here for explaining the link between religion and abortion risk may be similar in other countries.

Abortion-Related Stigma and Shame in China

Personal religious beliefs can make women feel worse about their abortions.[65] But even in countries where abortion rates are high and the patient or fellow residents are not particularly religious, getting an abortion can still be stigmatizing. Stigma is an "attribute that is deeply discrediting" and can "taint" a person's identity.[66] People affected by stigma typically hold the same beliefs as society about what is considered "normal." Hence, they know when something is stigmatized. As a result, they often correctly perceive that society will not fully accept them when they possess the stigmatized trait. In Chapter 4, I discussed the role of shame in relation to gender inequality for shaping abortion disapproval. Focusing specifically on women who get abortions, here I talk about the similarities and differences in stigma across China and the United States.

In China, there was an estimated 40.2 million pregnancies annually between 2015 and 2019. Of these, 17.7 million (61%) of the 23.3 million (78%) unintended pregnancies ended in abortion.[67] The one-child policy

[64] Hesketh, Lu, and Xing, "The Consequences of Son Preference and Sex-Selective Abortion in China and Other Asian Countries"; Nie, "Limits of State Intervention in Sex-Selective Abortion"; Guilmoto, *Sex Imbalances at Birth in Armenia: Demographic Evidence and Analysis*.

[65] Frohwirth, Coleman, and Moore, "Managing Religion and Morality within the Abortion Experience."

[66] Goffman, *Stigma*.

[67] Tsui, "China Set to Discourage Abortion amid Concern over Birthrates."

226 FETAL POSITIONS

has historically limited the number of births any woman could have, leading many to obtain abortions. Likewise, as noted previously, the nation does not have high levels of religious belief that elsewhere can exacerbate abortion disapproval. Nevertheless, about half of my Chinese interviewees thought obtaining an abortion was associated with stigma and shame. As one professor explained, "Chinese society is mostly collective oriented. Most people would just follow the mainstream values. So, if you have an abortion, it means that you are sort of being different from the rest of the people." Other Chinese residents spoke about abortion in moral terms, as one journalist explained: "There's also shame if you must lose a child, just this human feeling. I think every girl in every country will have this feeling that it is not morally okay to get an abortion." The same respondent told me that her ex-husband felt abortion was so problematic that they quickly married before giving birth. "Because [abortion] is for him immoral, because he wants to be a good man. . . . He wants to play the role of a very traditional Chinese man." Like some American women, some Chinese have a "shotgun" wedding if the pregnancy resulted from relations with a potential marriage partner. Finally, a researcher who does reproductive-related work said he was surprised to find that the "Chinese people have serious reservations about abortion for moral reasons" (as well as other concerns such as health). Religion, as conventionally understood, has little influence on the everyday lives of most Chinese. Nevertheless, Chinese survey data show that abortion disapproval was exceptionally high in China during the late 2010s (see Figure 4.2 in Chapter 4). The interviews also reveal that many Chinese residents see abortion as problematic and view it through the lens of morality and shame.

The respondents I interviewed often referred to the circumstances surrounding the aborted pregnancy to assess the level of stigma and shame that would be associated. The most acceptable and least shameful reason for getting an abortion was because the fetus had abnormalities (e.g., genetic defect) that increased the likelihood of an unhealthy or abnormal baby or because the mother's health was in danger. As one academic explained, "If it is for some medical reasons, nobody will feel shame; though, of course, they will be sad." A different expert explained that he and his wife were distraught to find that there were medical problems with their fetus. As they waited for confirmation, his in-laws insisted they quickly move forward with pregnancy termination. Many Chinese respondents felt that abortion for health-related reasons was acceptable, especially because the government limited the number of children couples could have, making a healthy baby especially desirable. Conversely, in the United States, getting an abortion, even when there are congenital disabilities, may still be shameful (in addition to sad or disappointing), with 46% of Americans saying it is unacceptable for any reason.[68] However, when asked more specifically if they feel "abortion is okay when there is a strong chance of serious defect," 77% of Americans report that it is acceptable.[69] Hence, Americans moderate their disapproval when specifically told that there is a serious health or developmental concern. In this regard, the American and Chinese are similar.

On the other end of the spectrum, the most shameful situation for getting an abortion in China is being an unmarried pregnant woman. As noted in Chapter 4, which addressed the role of gender inequality, less than 5% of births occur to single Chinese women. Conversely, 40% of pregnancies in the United States are to unmarried women.[70] Moreover, in highly developed and liberal countries such as Norway and Sweden, over 50% of pregnancies are among unmarried women.[71] Hence, the rarity of being an unmarried mother in China, combined with the economic challenges of raising a child alone and a history of government policies limiting the number of allowable children, makes getting pregnant before marriage especially problematic. One respondent explained, "If it's teenage pregnancy, it's usually very shameful in China. So probably for teenage girls, they do not tell anyone but their own parents, because they need their help." The interviewees also described the Chinese as highly practical. They thought that few would see the value of forfeiting future economic and romantic prospects to give birth, especially since religious leaders have not publicly objected to abortion. As one respondent explained, "For teenage pregnancy, especially for those who are not married or those who got pregnant because of being raped, it's extremely shameful. And that's a very different situation, particularly in the rural areas. Those girls are usually forced to do abortion by their parents." In China, the legacy of the family-planning policy and economic concerns have contributed to the shame unmarried mothers may experience.

Because the Chinese were so adamant about the stigma surrounding premarital pregnancy, I had to ask, "Is the problem with abortion or premarital sex?" As one Chinese Christian official explained, "Getting an abortion is definitely much more shameful and much less acceptable. Because having premarital sex nowadays is becoming much more common unless you go to

[68] GSS Data Explorer, "GSS Data Explorer, NORC at the University of Chicago."
[69] GSS Data Explorer.
[70] World Population Review.
[71] World Population Review.

228 FETAL POSITIONS

church." Another respondent added that premarital sex might not be acceptable, but in getting an abortion, more people know that you had sex outside of marriage. A third person put it this way, "Having sex before marriage is normal behavior; but getting pregnant should take place within marriages, because if you go for abortion, then it might affect your physical health, and it might also damage your future fertility. So that's probably why people feel more shameful about it." Respondents tended to think that many people have premarital sex in China. Indeed, survey data show that about 70% of them do.[72] But getting pregnant announces your indiscretion and suggests you are irresponsible because now you have to get an abortion, which many Chinese thought could lead to adverse health outcomes and be consequential for you and your potential husband's offspring.

Several respondents felt that the collectivist nature of Chinese society could also result in shame transferring from the mother to the child if she gave birth. As a Buddhist master explained, "So if a woman got pregnant before getting married, then she would bring a lot of shame and guilt to her own family." Furthermore, an unmarried woman could bring shame to her offspring. As a Christian minister added, "A woman may feel that she does not want her future child to live in a state of perpetual shame, you know, being discriminated against . . . then in those cases, maybe even the pastors will say that, yes, sister, go get an abortion." Both getting an abortion and having an out-of-wedlock child were shameful. But a mother could inadvertently make life very hard for a child born outside of marriage because it is so deviant. The blame would fall on her.

I also interviewed several respondents who did not think abortion was especially problematic. But their logic often related to the commonality of abortion. Indeed, China has higher abortion rates than most other countries.[73] Likewise, because abortions had been regularly advertised, some respondents had the impression that abortion was not especially problematic. As one professor explained, "There's a lot of TV commercials or newspaper advertisements about painless abortions posted by all those hospitals. It is very common. And you can see them everywhere. . . . So, abortion is not an ethical issue at all." Another academic felt that the ease at which his coworkers talked about abortion and underdeveloped fetuses meant it was not shameful. But as noted above, Chinese respondents were clear that abortion for fetal abnormalities was acceptable. Getting an abortion because one is unmarried is more shameful, though necessary.

---

[72] Icenhower, "What China's Sexual Revolution Means for Women"; Perlez, "Women Who Have Premarital Sex Are 'Degenerates.'"

[73] Bearak et al., "Country-Specific Estimates of Unintended Pregnancy and Abortion Incidence."

While Chinese respondents focused on the challenges of premarital pregnancies, only about 30% of abortions are done for unmarried patients.[74] A much higher proportion of Chinese women abort unintended pregnancies within a marital relationship.[75] However, the experts I interviewed did not talk much about these situations, suggesting that they were not nearly as shameful or problematic, though they may still be emotionally upsetting. As one respondent noted, "Getting pregnant accidentally is very common." An abortion within marriage would be much easier to manage since, presumably, a wife would have more money for an abortion. Likewise, she would be less likely to encounter the abortion provider's disapproval, which respondents felt was much more common for young unmarried females. Moreover, for decades the Chinese government has limited the number of children many women could have. As a result, abortion was often necessary for married women who were likely more sexually active and at significant risk of an unintended pregnancy. Even if they did not want the abortion, the government sometimes felt differently and could pressure or force women to get them.[76] In the next section, I discuss some of the key themes related to stigma and shame that ran through the US-based interviews and the extent to which similar ones were found in the Chinese ones.

Abortion-Related Stigma and Shame in the United States

The American interviews included many of the same discussions about embarrassment and shame as those found in the Chinese discussions. The American experts thought that abortion was shameful partially because it had to do with sex, which they thought was not openly discussed. As one researcher explained, "But we still have a sort of Puritan history, where there's a lot of shame around sexuality.... We don't teach our kids how to talk about sexuality in a comfortable way." An American journalist added, "Leaving activists and Hollywood aside, I would think the majority of women would not want to talk about [their abortions]. Because there is a lot of shame. It's also very private." The lack of comfort in talking about sex was a common theme that ran throughout the Chinese and US-based interviews.

---

[74] Tang et al., "Repeat Induced Abortion among Chinese Women Seeking Abortion."
[75] Tang et al.
[76] Fong, "How China's One-Child Policy Led to Forced Abortions, 30 Million Bachelors"; Associated Press, "Uyghur Exiles Describe Forced Abortions, Torture in Xinjiang."

230 FETAL POSITIONS

While the Chinese and American experts spoke about shame and stigma in many similar ways, one unsurprising difference was the role of religion in exacerbating negative feelings in the US context. Because many American religious leaders have taken such a strong pro-life stance, female residents have to be especially careful about hiding their abortions to religious adherents who might negatively judge them. As one academic explained, "I think [the stigma] very much has to do with the kind of community, and certainly church community being an important part of that [because] both neighborhood community and church community overlap to some extent." Another professor noted that "religious communities love to talk about [abortion], but only in a political context, as 'This is something I'd never do.'" She also thought that religious organizations gave the impression that "none of us has ever had abortions, which is, I'm sure, not true." The Chinese interviews make clear that even in a country where religious belief, as conventionally measured, is some of the lowest in the world,[77] abortion can still be seen as shameful. However, the religion-related stigma and shame in the United States adds an extra layer and could further limit women from sharing their abortion experiences.

One of the advocacy tools that America's pro-choice movement has tried to use to make abortions more acceptable is the "Shout Your Abortion" campaign.[78] Women who have had abortions let others know, normalizing the behavior, which close to 25% of Americans will experience during their reproductive years.[79] But given the high levels of shame and stigma surrounding abortion, even the pro-choice supporters I interviewed thought that the campaign was unsuccessful. As one academic explained, "In the overwhelming majority of cases, there's still a sense of stigma and loss and difficulty. You know, the #ShoutYourAbortion thing has not taken off more broadly at all in the culture."

Finally, some American interviewees spoke about the challenges the pro-choice movement faced when women who got abortions continued to support pro-life perspectives. As one professor explained, "The pro-choice movement should be more robust than it is. But I think there's so many women who've had abortions and were still antiabortion. So that's not a segment of the population you can count on to speak to the [pro-choice]

---

[77] Albert, "Religion in China."

[78] "Shout Your Abortion—Normalizing Abortion and Elevating Safe Paths to Access, Regardless of Legality."

[79] Guttmacher Institute, "Abortion Is a Common Experience for U.S. Women, Despite Dramatic Declines in Rates."

issue." Indeed, she went on to say that the pro-life movement had capitalized on the ambivalence that many women feel about abortions that they obtained when they were younger. She lamented, "They forget what it was like" to be young with an unanticipated pregnancy. Indeed, one of my interviewees was a pro-life organizer who told me she had an abortion. As she explained, "I didn't talk about mine because I was ashamed. . . . I can't be proud of something that I'm not proud of." One of the doctors I interviewed thought that many of the women for whom she provides abortions do not necessarily think it is acceptable. However, in their minds, "the reason why they're there in that office with you that day is the right reason, even if they don't necessarily support or believe in abortion themselves." Given the high levels of religious belief and stigma and shame surrounding abortion in America, the pro-choice movement has not always been able to count on women who had abortions to support their cause. In the following section, I assess the alignment between abortion behavior and public opinion in the United States and China.

Who the Public Thinks Get Abortions Versus Who Is Most Likely to Get Them

This chapter has focused on the factors shaping abortion behavior around the world, the role of religion, and the degree to which stigma and shame are associated with abortion behaviors. In this final section, I examine the extent of overlap between who the public thinks are likely to get an abortion and who actually gets one.

As noted above, information on cross-national views about abortion is limited to a handful of cross-national surveys that mostly ask whether or not abortion is acceptable. Hence, we do not have information across a large number of countries in how the public views women who get abortions and the circumstances surrounding them, which may shape their support or disapproval. When I was developing my interview questions, I knew I wanted to understand more about who the public thought was getting abortions. I therefore asked all of my respondents who their fellow residents thought of as getting abortions. Chinese and American researchers have also compiled demographic, social, and financial information about the women who have gotten abortions and their reasons. Hence, we can assess the extent to which information about abortion patients coincides with public perceptions in these countries.

232   FETAL POSITIONS

When I asked experts in China who they thought most residents felt were getting abortions, many were quick to say that the woman must have had an unanticipated pregnancy.[80] As one professor explained, "If they have to come to the abortion clinic, then usually it's [because of an] unwanted pregnancy." Another academic added, "So, they got pregnant accidentally, and that's why they are getting abortions." A third researcher confirmed, "So the first situation would be those who got pregnant accidentally, those who do not follow their family planning. This is against the law." The Chinese interviewees responded very matter-of-factly. Moreover, their perspectives are consistent with data showing that women across the world, including the Chinese, largely obtain abortions when they have an unanticipated pregnancy, as opposed to one that is planned.[81]

Like the Chinese, many of the Americans I interviewed were experts on women's health, society, or medicine. Hence, they knew that most abortions occurred to women who had an unanticipated pregnancy. Likewise, I was asking about the perspectives of the general public. Nevertheless, while an unexpected pregnancy may have been an obvious reason for getting an abortion, it was not regularly mentioned as something the public would note. One reason the Chinese were so quick to link abortion with an unintended pregnancy is likely related to the history of the one-child policy under which people had to carefully avoid an unwanted pregnancy. If they did not, the government could intervene. For example, in some regions women's menstruation cycles were carefully monitored, and there were reports of women being forced to have abortions if they already had children.[82] Likewise, some employees could be fired for having an unplanned birth. One of the Chinese civil servants I interviewed explained that her "coworkers had abortions because they got pregnant. And they were not supposed to have more than two children." The Chinese were quicker to link unplanned pregnancy to abortion, which is likely related to the government's family planning policy.

In both the United States and China, interviewees believed that the public would feel that women who want abortions do not have the financial resources to raise this child. Across the globe when abortion patients are asked why they are getting abortions, financial concerns are the most popular reason.[83] Respondents in China and the United States were acutely

---

[80] Bearak et al., "Alignment between Desires and Outcomes among Women Wanting to Avoid Pregnancy."

[81] Bearak et al.

[82] NPR interview, "How China's One-Child Policy Led to Forced Abortions, 30 Million Bachelors."

[83] Chae et al., "Reasons Why Women Have Induced Abortions."

aware of the role of finances in shaping abortion decisions, and they thought the public knew that as well. For example, one Chinese expert explained, "She cannot afford this kid. It's quite simple." An American pro-life advocate added, "It is absolutely a monetary decision." A third Chinese respondent added that the legacy of the one-child policy meant that many couples have to take care of four parents because they are only children. As a result, women may not have the resources—time and finances—to care for a child.

Finances were a major concern in the United States and China for raising children, especially for pregnancies that were unanticipated. But the legacy of the one-child policy may have further eroded the likelihood that an unintended pregnancy would result in a live birth. Of the 23,200,000 pregnancies that were unintended annually between 2015 and 2019 when the government was ending its one-child policy, abortion was used to resolve 78% of them.[84] Conversely, during the same time period, 34% of American's women's unintended pregnancies ended in abortion.[85] A much higher proportion of American women (66%) carry unintended pregnancies to term than Chinese women (22%). Many other factors likely contribute to the differences between the two nations in abortion use, but the legacy of the one-child policy certainly has a role. Many Chinese grew up anticipating that they would only have one child. Now, regardless of the number of children the government allows, most Chinese women only have one.[86]

Related to financial concerns, another key distinction between the United States and China was the rarity of having a child on one's own. In China, about 30% of women who get abortions are unmarried.[87] Conversely, in the United States, nearly 46% are single and have never been married.[88] It is much more common to have a child outside of marriage in the United States. Many respondents spoke about young unmarried women getting abortions. The Chinese experts largely felt that many women who want abortions must have had an unintended pregnancy outside of marriage. As one professor explained, "Chinese people always think the children should be raised up in a family." Another academic added, "If they're unmarried, almost every single woman will be advised to abort . . . because having a child outside of wedlock is going to be a big problem." Hence, if she is a young female getting an abortion, then the public might assume that she does not have a husband.

---

[84] Guttmacher Institute, "Unintended Pregnancy and Abortion" (China).
[85] Guttmacher Institute, "Unintended Pregnancy and Abortion" (United States).
[86] De Guzman, "Why China Needs to Learn to Live With Its Low Fertility Rate."
[87] Tang et al., "Repeat Induced Abortion among Chinese Women Seeking Abortion."
[88] Sanger-Katz, Miller, and Bui, "Who Gets Abortions in America?"

234   FETAL POSITIONS

Few American respondents mentioned that the public would feel that a woman is getting an abortion because she lacks a spouse or partner, though this was sometimes implied when respondents mentioned financial concerns. Moreover, given the prevalence of single parents and religious proscriptions regarding abortion, few religiously conservative Americans would feel that being unmarried is acceptable grounds for an abortion. Nevertheless, in the United States, nearly 50% of patients report relationship concerns as a reason why they are getting an abortion.[89] Hence, the American public may not put as much weight on a woman's connection to the potential father as pregnant women themselves do in deciding to get an abortion.

People from both countries thought that the public might think that some women who need abortions are irresponsible. As one Chinese journalist explained, "But for my parents, if they think young women who are not married get an abortion, they may think they are too easy . . . and maybe very slutty." A Chinese professor added that these women might "take sex lightly." The American experts felt that many residents would feel similarly and tie her behavior to religion and the abortion political debate. As one pro-life advocate who works for a nonprofit organization explained, "I think there's a lot of stereotypes about who she is: she's usually young and irresponsible and probably promiscuous. That's the idea that people have." In both countries, the public might think these women are immoral or irresponsible. However, the Chinese public seemed more inclined to think that an abortion is likely best for the woman and her potential child because of the stigma and shame that would follow them. Conversely, religiously conservative Americans would think that she should give birth.

A final distinction between the two countries relates to gender-selective abortions. As discussed in previous chapters, China has a history of sexselective abortions, which has contributed to a gender imbalance with more males than females.[90] The government has tried to change norms, which seems to be working to some extent, especially in urban areas. Also, in the 1990s, the Chinese made it illegal to detect a fetus's gender. Nevertheless, there are reports of parents circumventing the law to discover the gender.[91] Several Chinese respondents noted that when a woman gets an abortion,

[89] Finer et al., "Reasons U.S. Women Have Abortions."
[90] Chan et al., "Gender Selection in China: Its Meanings and Implications"; Hesketh, Lu, and Xing, "The Consequences of Son Preference and Sex-Selective Abortion in China and Other Asian Countries."
[91] Lai, "Boy or Girl?"

people may wonder if she is intentionally aborting a female fetus, especially if she already has a daughter. As one professor explained, "So in earlier times, some women who really wanted boys rather than girls would get an abortion once they learned that the baby was a girl." A Buddhist monk added that in northern China "women choose to get an abortion because they want a son instead." A final Chinese academic added, "If for some reason people find out that the unborn child is a daughter, it's very likely that she will get an abortion, especially if you live in a rural area." None of the American respondents mentioned sex selection as a possible reason why a woman would get an abortion. A pro-choice academic stated succinctly that in the United States the public largely feels that it is "culturally unacceptable" for "people to use abortion for sex selection." That said, some American women may get sex-selective abortions. However, the country's relatively even rate of baby girls versus boys suggests that sex-selective abortions are not popular.

A final similarity that residents from both countries mentioned for getting abortions was because something is wrong with the fetus. As a Chinese Catholic sister explained, "Some women realize that their babies have medical deficiencies, genetic deficiencies, and that would be the reason for them to get an abortion." A professor added that getting abortion for medical reasons would be "for her own good, her child's good or even for the benefit of her own family." An American academic noted that "the easiest things [for the public] to justify are things like fetal anomalies." Compared to the Chinese, Americans were less likely to mention health or genetic-related reasons as regularly acceptable for justifying an abortion. Because many Chinese could only have one child, avoiding genetic abnormalities was especially important. Across the world, only a minority of abortions occur for health or developmental reasons.[92] In the United States, for example, only about 5% of women report getting an abortion because of concerns about the fetus's health.[93] While the public in both countries may wonder if an abortion is motivated by health or development, this reason accounts for a tiny minority of abortions.

In China and the United States, respondents provided a range of scenarios that the public might consider for why a woman would want an abortion (e.g., she doesn't have a husband or enough money). Some themes across

[92] Bearak et al., "Unintended Pregnancy and Abortion by Income, Region, and the Legal Status of Abortion"; Bearak et al., "Alignment between Desires and Outcomes among Women Wanting to Avoid Pregnancy."
[93] Biggs, Gould, and Foster, "Understanding Why Women Seek Abortions in the US."

236 FETAL POSITIONS

the two countries are quite similar. For example, people in both societies felt that residents would label some women who get abortions as irresponsible, financial considerations are a primary concern, and some might suspect that something is wrong with the fetus. But because of different policy, legal, and social movement histories, there are also key differences. The Chinese public is more likely to think that women who want abortions may do it for sex-selective reasons. Likewise, if the abortion patient is young, the Chinese public may assume she is unmarried and hence an abortion is a reasonable resolution. Finally, because of its family planning history, the Chinese may be especially aware of the strong link between unanticipated pregnancies and abortion desire.[94] They may also be more focused on avoiding genetic abnormalities because for close to thirty years most residents could only have one, making a healthy child especially desirable.

Conclusion

This chapter has focused on the factors associated with abortion risk, which can be insightful for understanding public opinion. Some of the most important findings presented in this chapter relate to the lack of a relationship between abortion rates and overall religious importance, disapproval, and laws. Especially in democracies, residents often hope that their attitudes matter for shaping abortion behaviors. At the macro level, the data do not show a link. At the micro level, the strength of religious belief at least in the United States seems to matter more for shaping the sex-behavior pathways that influences the risk of aborting one's first pregnancy, rather than increasing abortion disapproval to reduce abortion odds.

Many women around the world who get abortions are already mothers. We do not have much evidence that religion is involved in aborting later pregnancies, possibly because the personal decision to have an unexpected birth is so consequential. Finally, across nations residents share some consistent views about the reasons why women get abortions (e.g., fetal abnormality, irresponsible). The Chinese and American public may also feel that potential abortion patients will experience stigma and shame. But there are also some key contrasts related to differences in culture (e.g., sex selection, religion) and the nation's legal history of abortion.

---

[94] The American interviewees felt that the public would not necessarily know that many women who get abortions already have children. In China, the family-planning policy resulted in most families only having one child. Hence, there was not any discussion about the public being aware of other children like there was in the US-based interviews.

Conclusion

Drawing on a wealth of data from surveys, interviews, and newspapers, the research presented in this book provides major insight into why and how abortion attitudes vary across the world. A substantial minority of the world's women will have an abortion during their lifetime. There are major social, health, and economic consequences to their abortion-related decisions. Public opinion about abortion matters for shaping how residents view these women, the likelihood that they will disclose their decisions, and whether they have safe access to the procedure. By understanding the processes shaping cross-national views, we have clearer insight into how major cultural, economic, and political institutions within nations function to shape people's attitudes more generally. In this Conclusion, I provide a summary of key findings and offer insight into where abortion-related attitudes and laws may be headed in the future.

Country-Level Factors Shaping Abortion Disapproval

Within individual countries, a range of individual characteristics, including age, gender, education, and marital status, are associated with abortion support. Differences in attitudes based on personal characteristics such as age are relatively constant across countries. Hence, they provide limited insight into major cross-national differences. For understanding why abortion disapproval varies so substantially around the world, we need to focus on country characteristics, such as economics, politics, and religion. Country-level factors are powerful and intriguing because they can shape individuals' attitudes over and above personal attributes (e.g., religious affiliation, educational attainment).

This book has isolated the major country-level factors shaping public disapproval of abortion across the world and described many of the processes through which they have an effect. These forces include religion, economic and educational development, democracy, gender inequality, and communist history. Within this group of country characteristics, religion, specifically religious importance, as conventionally assessed, appears

238 FETAL POSITIONS

to be the most powerful measurable factor for explaining cross-national support around the globe.[1] In the following section, I discuss the major religion-related findings before moving onto the others.

Religion's Role in Shaping Abortion Disapproval

Across the world, levels of religious importance within countries vary substantially. In nations such as Indonesia, Pakistan and Uganda, the proportion of people who say that religion is important rises above 85%.[2] Conversely, in countries such as Germany, Sweden, and the United Kingdom, the percentage plummets to about 10%.[3] In places such as China the proportion who says religion is very important is tiny, although there are major challenges to assessing religious belief in countries such as China. The extent to which someone feels that religion is personally important shapes their abortion disapproval. However, for understanding cross-national differences, overall levels of religious importance are especially important. Even if someone is not personally religious, living in a country where other residents say that religion is very important can shape personal abortion disapproval. Moreover, the effect sizes for personal religious beliefs and country religiosity for explaining abortion disapproval are similar (see Figure 1.2). In other words, strength of personal religious beliefs has a similarly strong influence on abortion attitudes as living in a country where a high proportion of people say religion is important, regardless of your personal religious beliefs. This is powerful!

In Chapter 1, I examined the many processes through which higher overall levels of religious importance can lead religious and secular residents to disapprove of abortion. In more religious Christian nations, such as the United States, a high proportion of Americans will wake up on Sunday morning, get dressed up, and drive to church for Sunday morning services. On their way, they may pass billboards that say things like "Abortion Breaks God's Heart," "Abortion: One Dead, One Hurting . . . A Life of Regret & Sorrow," and "Two Hearts, Two Souls, Two Lives." At church, many congregants will get the impression that abortion is wrong. They may even hear that

---

[1] Appendix A presents a discussion about how effect sizes are compared. Note too that figures with standardized marginal effects for every country-level variable, aside from population size, are presented throughout the book.
[2] Pew, "How Religious Commitment Varies by Country among People of All Ages."
[3] Pew.

CONCLUSION 239

abortion is akin to murder. In some religious organizations, adherents may be encouraged to attend antiabortion rallies and support elected officials who oppose abortion. Many religious leaders will encourage their congregants to support conservative values, including a gender division of labor whereby women are encouraged to marry, have children, and stay home to raise them.

In Muslim-majority nations, many residents may have similar experiences. Rather than regularly attending Sunday morning religious services, they may stop what they are doing to pray five times a day. Likewise, women may cover their hair or wear a hijab to show their religious devotion. During important religious holidays, like Ramadan, the majority of people may fast during daylight hours. They may then break the fast with friends and family, many of whom feel strongly about their religious beliefs. In these societies, women will be encouraged to remain virgins until marriage[4] and stay home to raise children while their husbands go out to work. Many Muslims do not drink alcohol, and it may be more difficult to purchase, just as it is in some Christian counties on Sundays.

In nations where more people feel that religion is important, religious rituals, such as prayer and religious service attendance, are going to reinforce religious proscriptions, including those related to abortion. Not only are religious adherents susceptible to religion-inspired norms but so are nonreligious people. Across a given country, levels of religious importance may vary, but most resident will not be isolated from religious influences. In nations with higher levels of religious importance, many family members and friends will be more opposed to abortion for religious reasons. Their religiously inspired perspectives may transfer to more secular people through social learning and control processes.

Religious norms may also seep into attitudes through government institutions and announcements, public services, and by limiting abortion disclosure. When abortion is discussed by government officials, religious perspectives may be mentioned, further enforcing conservative views. In more religious nations, religious organizations may provide many public services (e.g., healthcare, social services). When people get married or have a child, for example, they may register this information with a religious institution, reinforcing religion's societal importance. Because of the religiously

---

[4] Adamczyk and Hayes, "Religion and Sexual Behaviors Understanding the Influence of Islamic Cultures and Religious Affiliation for Explaining Sex outside of Marriage."

240   FETAL POSITIONS

infused climate, women may be especially unlikely to discuss their abortions because they may rightly feel that their friends, family, and community disapprove. As a result, more religious people may be less likely to hear about their experiences and develop empathy for why women get them.

The interviews in China and the United States made clear that most people are likely to view abortion as a private matter. Chapter 6 also showed that overall levels of religious importance are unrelated to abortion rates. Strength of personal religious beliefs and overall levels of religious importance are meaningful for understanding abortion disapproval. However, religion appears to have a minor role for explaining abortion behavior. For first pregnancies, my analysis of young American women showed that religion influences their abortion risk through prior sex-related behaviors, such as delaying sexual debut, reducing the number of sex partners and length of time between first sex and marriage, and having sex with a potential marital spouse.[5] Religious beliefs do not seem to affect abortion risk through religious women's higher abortion disapproval. Additionally, in many countries, females are more likely to abort pregnancies after they already have children, rather than their first one. Abortion decisions may be less susceptible to religious norms and values than attitudes because carrying an unintended pregnancy to term will have a profound impact on one's life. The personal stakes for either getting an abortion or having a live birth are steep!

In contrast to religious importance, I found minor differences in abortion attitudes based on affiliation with a major religion. Unfortunately, the few available cross-national surveys for examining abortion disapproval do not include finer-grained religious affiliation distinctions. However, we know from data within nations that congregants from more conservative religious brands (e.g., Evangelical Christians) hold more traditional views on a range of issues.[6]

As discussed at length in the first few chapters, traditional measures of religious belief, such as asking people how important religion is in their lives, may not adequately assess religion's influence for followers of polytheistic faiths, Confucianism, or folk beliefs. Furthermore, examining religious salience in countries where religion is heavily restricted further complicates

---

[5] See also Adamczyk and Felson, "Fetal Positions."
[6] Bartkowski et al., "Faith, Race-Ethnicity, and Public Policy Preferences"; Ellison, Echevarria, and Smith, "Religion and Abortion Attitudes among US Hispanics"; Adamczyk and Valdimarsdóttir, "Understanding Americans' Abortion Attitudes"; Adamczyk, Boyd, and Hayes, "Place Matters: Contextualizing the Roles of Religion and Race for Understanding Americans' Attitudes about Homosexuality."

CONCLUSION 241

measurement. As noted, the Chinese government strongly discourages and regulates religious belief. Hence, residents from some countries may not feel comfortable disclosing their level of religious importance on government-supported surveys, such as the World Values Survey (WVS).

When conventionally measured, a tiny portion of Chinese say that religion is very important. Researchers[7] have found that asking other types of questions, such as belief in Buddha/bodhisattva or frequency of burning incense, registers higher levels of religious interest.[8] However, these estimates are typically not as high as traditional religion measures (e.g., importance, frequency of prayer) that are gathered in majority-Christian or majority-Muslim nations. Polytheistic religions and folk beliefs may not generate especially high levels of religious commitment and engagement, we may not have the right survey measures, or the government in places such as China may successfully suppress reports of religious interest.

For understanding the role of religious belief, practice, and perspectives in China, the interviews were therefore especially helpful. They provided insight into how some Chinese may use religion (e.g., cope with abortion) and the ways that it may shape attitudes (e.g., sex-selective abortions, health concerns). Although China may be classified as an atheist country, rituals, beliefs, and values are important for understanding how the Chinese think about abortion attitudes and behaviors, which is consistent with previous work as well.[9]

Most nations are dominated by a single faith tradition and have a historical relationship with a specific religion. For the most part, I found few attitudinal differences across societies based on the dominant religion. However, the proportion Catholic had a small and meaningful influence on abortion disapproval partially because the religion has a well-organized hierarchical structure, major cultural and political presence in many countries, and church officials have vocally advocated against abortion. That said, Catholics themselves do not appear substantially different from other religious affiliates in their level of abortion disapproval (see Figure 1.3).

This book has provided insight into how people living in a relatively religious nation (i.e., the United States) view abortion and how residents from a highly secular country (i.e., China), as traditionally measured, see it. My interviews confirm the survey findings, unpack the processes explaining

---

[7] Pew Research Center, "Measuring Religion in China."
[8] Pew Research Center; Hackett, "Is China a Religious Country or Not?"
[9] Nie, *Behind the Silence.*

242 FETAL POSITIONS

relationships, and offer insight that goes beyond the broad macro analysis. In the United States, all the experts I interviewed thought that Americans experienced a religious contextual effect, which shaped how its residents then viewed abortion.

Chinese experts also highlighted their relatively secular culture (as conventionally measured for organized religion) for explaining cross-national differences in approval. Nevertheless, religion (i.e., Buddhism, Confucianism, and folk beliefs) still seeped into how the Chinese saw abortion. Religion was linked to gender-selective abortions in a way that was almost never discussed in the United States. Moreover, almost all the Chinese interviewees felt that abortion attitudes were shaped by the high economic cost of living and the legacy of the one-child policy. Many thought that at least some women used religion to justify or cope with abortion-related loss, especially for those who did not feel like they had much decision-making power for economic or political reasons (i.e., during the one-child policy era). Additionally, Chapter 5 showed that the Chinese were especially concerned about the health-related consequences of abortion, which may be linked to Confucianism, other beliefs, and concerns about the procedure itself.

The survey and interview data made clear that religion has an important role in shaping attitudes around the globe. Religious contexts are especially intriguing because residents may not be fully aware of their influence. Likewise, even in places that are typically described as secular (e.g., China), I showed that ritual, faith, and folk beliefs were still important for how residents saw abortion.

Money, Political Power, Gender Inequality, and Culture

In addition to religion, several other country-level influences were important for understanding cross-national abortion disapproval. These include economic and educational development, democracy, communist history, Confucian culture, and gender inequality. In this section, I highlight some key findings.

Concerns about the high financial cost of having an unanticipated child rang throughout the interviews in China and the United States. Americans and Chinese lamented the way that worries about a potentially expensive childhood could lead women to abort an unintended pregnancy. Pro-life

CONCLUSION 243

Americans especially wanted more options for women who did not have the financial resources to raise another child but wanted to keep the pregnancy.

Fertility researchers have noted a demographic paradox whereby rich nations, which can most afford children, have some of the world's lowest fertility rates. In these wealthy countries, residents are especially interested in providing a high-quality life for their children. Their fertility rates are low not because they are having more abortions.[10] Rather, reliable birth control and more gender-equal relationships help females avoid unintended pregnancies, reducing abortion reliance.

The findings presented here also show that residents from richer and more educated countries also have more liberal abortion attitudes. More economic and educational development seems to affect everyone within society, regardless of personal income and academic achievement. Economic development increases security and comfort. Higher overall levels of education further contribute to progressive values and strengthen a medical culture that is likely to value autonomy in making medical decisions. As a result, residents from richer and more educated nations appear more open to alternative perspectives and are willing to support the rights and freedom of others, leading to more abortion support.

Many religious people from nations with high economic and educational levels are especially opposed to abortion, even though residents may generally be more liberal. For example, the United States is one of the richest countries in the world. Many Christian Americans with strong religious beliefs do not support abortion rights.[11] In Chapter 3, I showed that religious followers are more likely to use their beliefs as a guide for attitudes in richer nations when secular norms and values are ambiguous. Many religious Americans cannot rely on secular sources, such as the government or dominant norms, to guide their attitudes about controversial subjects because the government may not have taken a clear stance by making it illegal. But many religious leaders, especially Catholics and conservative Protestants, have publicly opposed abortion. As a result, more religious Americans are more likely to use religion to guide their views, especially when secular norms are ambiguous. Hence, even though the United States is a rich nation with high levels of education, personal religious beliefs have a stronger relationship

---

[10] Bearak et al., "Country-Specific Estimates of Unintended Pregnancy and Abortion Incidence."
[11] Adamczyk, "Religion as a Micro and Macro Property."

with abortion disapproval there than they do in less-developed countries where residents on average are more opposed.

The findings in this book also make clear that democracy and communist history are meaningful for shaping abortion disapproval. In more democratic societies, residents are on average more supportive. The ideas that democracy engenders, including equality, freedom, and representation, contribute to more liberal abortion views. Likewise in more democratic societies, abortion-related laws and policies are more likely to reflect the public's attitudes, as politicians take seriously their constituents' preferences.

The United States is one of the oldest modern democracies. Yet, in 2022 the Supreme Court overturned nearly fifty years of precedence by removing women's constitutional right to abortion. The survey findings presented in this book offer a broad overview of the major macro factors shaping abortion disapproval around the globe. But the survey analysis presents only averages. In general, democratic societies are more likely than others to have residents with more supportive abortion views. In Chapter 4, I unpacked the processes that changed US abortion law. An important factor was social movement activity that helped perpetuate abortion as a critical issue for many Americans. In 2016, politically and religiously conservative Americans elected Donald Trump as president. During his term, he fulfilled his promise to help make abortion illegal by appointing three conservative Supreme Court justices. The new justices tilted the court's ideological balance, ultimately returning the power to make abortion illegal back to states.

Along with democracy, the Soviet Union left an indelible imprint on residents' abortion attitudes and behaviors that remains to this day. In Chapter 5, I revealed that people living in the former Soviet Union countries on average have more conservative views about abortion than residents from former Soviet Union satellite states or those without communist histories. Chapter 6 showed that despite their higher levels of abortion disapproval, women from these nations have some of the highest abortion rates in the world. The link between former Soviet Union countries and abortion disapproval is complicated by their history with abortion, a strong desire to forge a national identity based on family values, and an inclination for residents to present their nations in a positive light, especially to survey administrators.

The cross-national survey analysis also showed that people living in Confucian nations are more disapproving of abortion once we account for lower overall levels of religious belief, as traditionally measured. What processes might explain this "Confucian" cultural effect? I considered a range

CONCLUSION 245

of macro-level factors. For example, I examined whether residents from Confucian countries are more family friendly and hence more opposed to abortion. They are not. I looked at whether they are more likely to value obedience and therefore disapprove of abortion because it violates norms. Nope. I examined whether they are more opposed to sexual morality issues in general, such as prostitution and homosexuality, and hence they are more disapproving of abortion as well. There was no effect. In Chapter 5, I mined the survey data for everything I could to explain the "Confucian" influence. I did not find that people from countries with Chinese history are more likely to exhibit typical Confucian views. Rather, as shown in Figure 5.3, people from Confucian societies are *less* likely to exhibit values that might be called "Confucian."

The survey data showed that people from Confucian countries are more disapproving once religious importance is considered. Unfortunately, these data could not provide the rationale, although they could eliminate some hypotheses. The interviews, in turn, offered valuable insight. In China, many respondents thought that abortion was linked to negative health outcomes and infertility, which only rarely emerged in the US-based interviews. Confucian values related to maintaining a healthy body may extend to other countries with Chinese histories.[12]

Likewise, the one-child policy may have affected abortion views in Confucian countries outside of China. Hence, when asked on a survey whether abortion is ever justified, people across the Confucian world may have considered China's one-child policy and thus been less likely to report that it is "always" justified. While neighboring Confucian countries have not become radically more disapproving, China has (see Figure 3.2). From the early 1990s to the late 2000s, the Chinese increasingly reported that abortion is not always justified, which may have been related to growing frustration with the policy. If Chinese attitudes in general are more disapproving because of the policy, then the public's perspective on the "justifiability" of abortion in nearby countries may have also been affected.

Gender inequality also loomed large in the interviews and shaped survey respondents' attitudes. When people feel that men and women have distinctive roles within society, with women taking on most childcare responsibilities, they tend to oppose abortion. Individual views about gender inequality

[12] Badanta et al., "How Does Confucianism Influence Health Behaviors, Health Outcomes and Medical Decisions?"

246 FETAL POSITIONS

contribute to a cultural effect. When gender inequality is high across the nation, residents may be less likely to envision women in nontraditional roles outside of the home. As a result, people may have more difficulty understanding why women want abortions, especially if they are seen as primarily responsible for family and home. Not only was a societal measure of gender inequality associated with more abortion disapproval, but the correlation between gender inequality and abortion legality was so high in my analysis that both measures could not be included in the same model (see Table A.4 in Appendix A). Abortion legality could almost serve as a proxy for gender equality. The connection between legal abortion access and gender equality is strong!

When I was conducting my interviews, abortion was still legal in China and the United States, which have moderate levels of gender equality. Nevertheless, the Chinese and American respondents spoke at length about gender inequality underlying residents' views. Indeed, while progress is being made in many nations, no single country in the entire world has full gender equality. The Chinese interviews also revealed another deeply embedded notion of gender inequality. Several respondents noted that there was strong son preference, especially in more rural parts of China. While not prevalent in the United States, a preference for boys can be found in many other nations around the world.

The book's findings have isolated the major forces associated with abortion disapproval across the globe. I also considered close to thirty other factors that might hypothetically be related to more abortion disapproval (see Appendix C). Within a single country, some of these forces might be meaningful for shaping residents' attitudes. But across the eighty-eight nations included in this study and representing the majority of the world's population, the most important cross-national factors are religion, economic and educational development, democracy, communism, Chinese history, and gender inequality.

Are there any factors for which we do not have quantitative measures that might affect cross-national abortion disapproval? The mixed-modeling techniques provide an estimate of the proportion of variation occurring at individual and country levels before and after measures are added. Before any factors were included, I found that country-level differences were responsible for 25% of the variation in attitudes across the globe. Once all of the statistically significant forces were added in Model 8 of Table A.3 in Appendix A, only 6% of the variation remained at the country level. Hence, the factors discussed above account for 75%—the majority—of the macro variation in cross-national abortion attitudes. Hence, the findings presented here have likely captured the major forces driving disapproval across the world.

This book is interested in understanding the factors shaping cross-national public opinion about abortion. Cross-national attitudinal and abortion rate data were used to unpack the major characteristics shaping cross-national views. Examples from several countries, interviews with experts from the United States and China, and a large newspaper analysis provided insight into the processes that shape views and helped to isolate influences that the quantitative data could not capture. The interviews especially offer unique insight. On the one hand, China and the United States offer meaningful points of contrast in terms of religion, government, and economic development. On the other hand, they also share many similarities. Religion, for example, was discussed throughout both sets of interviews for understanding various aspects of abortion. Likewise, the government and education and economic development played key roles in the United States and China in intentionally and unintentionally influencing views. Finally, both countries have moderate levels of gender inequality, which shaped how their residents saw abortion.

The findings presented in this book offer only a snapshot at a particular time point for understanding attitudes across the globe. Within individual nations, factors that may be unique to them are also important. The interviews in China and the United States revealed some of these forces, such as the one-child policy in China and the strong antiabortion movement in the United States. The vast majority of studies on abortion disapproval have been conducted in the Global North. More work needs to be done outside of this region to better understand the factors driving disapproval and the processes involved. My hope is that the insights presented here will serve as a starting point for additional research—historical, cross-national, and within individual or sets of countries.

Attitudes and Laws into the Future

The large macro survey findings have focused on attitudes from the past ten to fifteen years. Data limitations make it challenging for researchers to examine attitudinal changes over longer time periods across many nations.

However, we can examine the history of legal changes to abortion laws and how attitudes have changed within individual countries where the data are available to better understand what the future holds.

Where might laws be headed? Figure C.1 presents legislative changes from 1994 to 2023 for 196 nations, almost every country across the world. The most restrictive countries prohibit abortion altogether. Over the almost thirty-year period between 1994 and 2023, the number of countries that prohibit abortion decreased from thirty-six to nineteen. Close to half the number of countries that outlawed abortion for any reason in 1994 now allow it under certain circumstances. For example, in the early 1990s the Democratic Republic of the Congo, Eswatini, Lesotho, Mauritius, and Niger prohibited abortion altogether. But over the past thirty years, they have changed their legislation to permit abortion to preserve the mother's health.

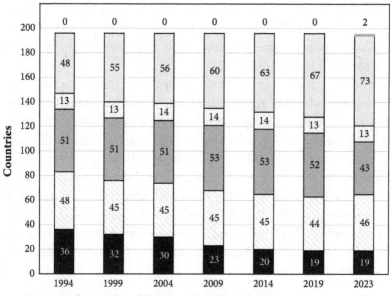

Figure C.1 Legal Changes to Abortion Legislation between 1994 and 2022 (Country N = 196)
Source: Center for Reproductive Rights

CONCLUSION   249

Likewise, in 1994, forty-eight countries allowed abortion on request during the first trimester. By 2024, the number had increased to seventy-three. Approximately one-third more countries legalized abortion on demand (within gestational limits) in 2024 than in 1994. Societies in Europe and North America were initially some of the first to allow abortion on demand. But over the past thirty years, nations across the world have increased legal abortion access. For example, over the past thirty years Chad and Kenya have moved from only allowing abortion to save the mother's life to preserving health as well. Likewise, since the early 1990s, Nepal and Sao Tome and Principe shifted from prohibiting abortion altogether to making it legal on demand within gestational limits.

Based on the findings presented in Figure C.1, abortion legislation appears to be moving in a more liberal direction, which other studies have noted as well.[13] The increase in more liberal abortion policy is a sharp contrast to high-profile legislative changes that have occurred in Poland and the United States. In October 2020, the Poland Constitutional Tribunal ruled that abortion on grounds of "severe and irreversible fetal defect or incurable illness that threatens the fetus' life" was unconstitutional. The ruling essentially removed the most popular exemption for obtaining an abortion.[14] As of 2023, Poland allowed abortion only when there were risks to the life or health of the pregnant woman, or if the pregnancy resulted from rape or incest. Conversely, almost every other European country allows for abortion on demand within gestational limits or for broad social and economic reasons. Countries that have moved in a more conservative direction, such as the United States and Poland, are a reminder that policy changes across the world are complicated and not always becoming more supportive.

Attitudes also seem to be moving in a more liberal direction, but the relationship is more challenging to assess because researchers have less information about public opinion than laws. WVS data from eighty-eight societies show that people who answered surveys during later years were on average more supportive than those who responded earlier. Specifically, in 2004, the average WVS respondent had a disapproval score of 7.9 (where 10 = never justified), controlling for all other factors (see Model 8 in Table

[13] The vast majority of data were taken from the Center for Reproductive Rights, "The World's Abortion Laws." When information for a given country or years was unavailable, the internet was scoured for open access information.

[14] Levels, Sluiter, and Need, "A Review of Abortion Laws in Western-European Countries. A Cross-National Comparison of Legal Developments between 1960 and 2010."

A.3 of Appendix A). By 2020, the average score dropped to 7.58, suggesting that attitudes were liberalizing.

Figure C.2 uses WVS data from the ten most populous countries in the world, presenting changes in abortion disapproval over the past thirty years. These ten countries represent approximately 57% of the global population. The names of countries that have more liberal abortion legislation are in bold. The nations with the least-restrictive legislation are China, Russia, Mexico, the United States, and India. The countries with the most conservative legislation and attitudes are Brazil, Nigeria, Indonesia, Pakistan, and Bangladesh.

In some countries, such as the United States, Brazil, Indonesia, and Pakistan, attitudes appear to have liberalized over the last thirty years. But attitudinal changes in other countries make clear that the world is not uniformly marching in a more liberal direction. As discussed at length in

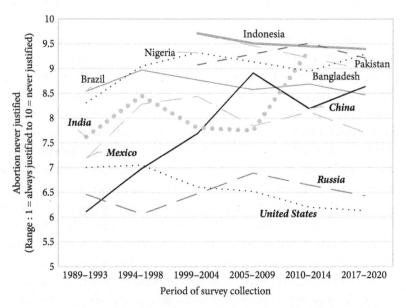

Figure C.2 Changes in Abortion Disapproval over Time for the World's Ten Most Populous Countries

Notes: **Bolded** country names indicate that abortion is either available on demand (China, Russia), legal in parts of the country (Mexico and the United States), or available based on a woman's social or economic situation (India). In the five remaining countries (Indonesia, Pakistan, Bangladesh, Nigeria, and Brazil), abortion access is legal only for health-related reasons.

Source: WVS

previous chapters, China has long allowed for abortion on demand, and Russia was one of the earliest modern societies to legalize abortion (in 1920). But as fertility rates have slowed and the one-child policy has impacted an entire generation of children, Chinese attitudes have become increasingly more conservative. Likewise, Russian views about abortion today are quite similar to what they were when the Soviet Union collapsed in the early 1990s, which was more than thirty years ago!

Abortion's legal status is associated with disapproval (see Figure 0.2 in the Introduction). But the relationship is far from a perfect correlation. Moreover, the question that the WVS asks focuses on the extent to which abortion is "justified." We cannot extrapolate from this moral question to legal preferences. People may feel that abortion is *not* "justified" under any circumstances. However, as discussed in Chapter 5, they may still believe that it should be legally available on request because they cannot anticipate all the valid reasons why a woman may want or need an abortion. Likewise, during China's one-child era, for example, many women had few reasonable alternatives other than abortion to resolve an unintended pregnancy. As a result, they may feel that abortion is not justified when the state requires it, which is how the one-child policy was sometimes enforced. To further complicate matters, other studies have shown that differences in question wording and the reason for an abortion can influence survey responses.

Finally, for many years, public support for abortion in the United States was not substantially different from earlier decades, albeit it fluctuated somewhat. But as mentioned above, when the Supreme Court overturned *Roe v. Wade* in 2022, we saw a liberal shift in support for the legality of abortion.[15] Hence, while public opinion can shape attitudes, policy and legal changes can also affect views.

Despite measurement challenges, Figure 5.4 shows a correlation between various measures of abortion support as assessed on different cross-national surveys. Hence, the findings presented in this book are likely valid. Nevertheless, more research is needed to better unpack respondents' perspectives. Variation across legal landscapes, for example, leads to new questions. In countries where abortion is illegal, who does the public want to punish when a woman gets an abortion (e.g., doctor, patient, people who helped)? Likewise, what is a reasonable reprimand (e.g., prison sentence,

---

[15] Norrander and Wilcox. "Public Opinion and Policymaking in the States: The Case of Post-Roe Abortion Policy."

252 FETAL POSITIONS

parole, fine)? Conversely, in countries where abortion has long been legal and is not especially contested, do people feel that it is an acceptable form of birth control? Or what should be the gestational limits for obtaining an abortion?

Some studies have framed abortion as one of several sexual morality topics, including same-sex relations, prostitution, and extramarital sex.[16] As discussed in Chapter 5, I considered whether the findings related to abortion disapproval are relevant to understanding sexual deviance or morality more generally. Topics such as same-sex relations, abortion, prostitution, and extramarital sex share some commonality. However, researchers do not always find high correlations among these attitudinal issues. Likewise, abortion views are distinct in some key ways. For example, within countries such as the United States, social scientists have found that some measures of abortion support remained relatively stagnant for decades[17]—until *Roe v. Wade* was overturned in 2022. Conversely, views about same-sex relations (i.e., described in the WVS as "homosexuality") have consistently and incrementally liberalized over the past twenty years.[18] Hence, the factors explaining and driving changes in abortion attitudes and other sexual morality issues and the processes through which they have an effect may not be closely aligned.

The ramifications of abortion attitudes and laws are profound for humans across the globe. For individuals or couples who need or want an abortion, lack of access can have major ramifications. While a direct link between laws and abortion decisions might not exist, when access is limited women have to work harder and spend more money to get abortions. Less-educated and poorer females will have fewer accessible abortion options. Some will turn to illegal medical practices and medications, which can have major health consequences. Public opinion often drives policies, laws, and availability, which in turn can affect attitudes. Understanding the forces influencing abortion disapproval sheds light on the legal landscape. Moreover, public opinion alone can have a substantial influence on how others view abortion. In turn, it can affect how women feel about abortion and motherhood and their physical and mental health after they make important fertility decisions.

---

[16] Scheepers, Te Grotenhuis, and Van Der Slik, "Education, Religiosity and Moral Attitudes"; Finke and Adamczyk, "Cross-National Moral Beliefs: The Influence of National Religious Context."

[17] Norrander and Wilcox. "Public Opinion and Policymaking in the States: The Case of Post-Roe Abortion Policy."

[18] Gallup Inc., "Abortion."

Public opinion about abortion also has consequences for nations. In many societies, people on both sides of this potentially contentuous issue may work to protest legal decisions they find problematic and elect preferred officials. Attitudes about abortion can shape who residents see in positions of power, the government and medical decisions that get made, whether they feel that their country is in grave moral danger, and the level of divisiveness within their society.

Across the globe, views about the rightness and wrongness of abortion vary considerably. This book has unpacked the many factors driving public opinion and the processes through which they shape cross-national public opinion. Attitudes and laws appear to be heading in a more liberal direction. However, this movement forward is neither uniform nor straightforward.

APPENDIX A

WVS Analysis

World Values Survey (WVS) data are used for many of the quantitative survey analyses presented in this book. The WVS was developed to enable cross-national comparisons on a range of attitudes, values, and behaviors and to monitor changes across countries and over time. Much of the analyses rely on data from wave 5 (2005–2009), 6 (2010–2014), and 7 (2017–2020), resulting in a sample size of 211,317 individuals clustered within 88 societies. The data are publicly available.[1] To maximize the sample size, all three waves were used for each country that had available data. Representing the majority of the world's population, Table A.1 lists the eighty-eight countries included in the analyses. Descriptive statistics for all variables are presented in Table A.2.

Table A.1 Societies Included in World Values Survey Analysis (N = 88)

Algeria	France	Malaysia	Singapore
Andorra	Georgia	Mali	Slovenia
Argentina	Germany	Mexico	South Africa
Armenia	Ghana	Moldova	South Korea
Australia	Greece	Morocco	Spain
Azerbaijan	Guatemala	Myanmar	Sweden
Bangladesh	Haiti	Netherlands	Switzerland
Belarus	Hong Kong SAR	New Zealand	Taiwan ROC
Bolivia	Hungary	Nicaragua	Tajikistan
Brazil	India	Nigeria	Thailand
Bulgaria	Indonesia	Norway	Trinidad and Tobago
Burkina Faso	Iran	Pakistan	Tunisia
Canada	Iraq	Palestine	Turkey
Chile	Italy	Peru	Ukraine
China	Japan	Philippines	United Kingdom
Colombia	Jordan	Poland	United States
Cyprus	Kazakhstan	Puerto Rico	Uruguay
Ecuador	Kuwait	Qatar	Uzbekistan
Egypt	Kyrgyzstan	Romania	Vietnam
Estonia	Lebanon	Russia	Yemen
Ethiopia	Libya	Rwanda	Zambia
Finland	Macau SAR	Serbia	Zimbabwe

[1] WVS, "World Values Survey Official Aggregate File: 1981-2022"

APPENDIX A 255

Table A.2 Descriptive Statistics of Variables Included in Models Using World Values
Survey Data (Individual N = 211,317; Country N = 88)

Individual-level	Mean/proportion	Std. dev.	Min	Max
Abortion not justified	7.730	2.815	1	10
Year	2012.235	4.917	2004	2020
Female	0.518	0.500	0	1
Age	41.832	16.293	15	103
Married (reference)	0.569	0.495	0	1
Living together	0.067	0.250	0	1
Divorced	0.057	0.233	0	1
Widowed	0.057	0.233	0	1
Single	0.249	0.432	0	1
Income	2.424	1.258	0	4
Educational level	2.096	0.934	1	4
Catholic (reference)	0.189	0.392	0	1
No religion	0.186	0.389	0	1
Protestant	0.097	0.296	0	1
Orthodox Christian	0.104	0.306	0	1
Jewish	0.002	0.044	0	1
Muslim	0.267	0.442	0	1
Hindu	0.026	0.160	0	1
Buddhist	0.049	0.216	0	1
Other Christian religion	0.037	0.188	0	1
Other religion	0.032	0.176	0	1
Religious affiliation missing	0.010	0.099	0	1
Religious importance	0.003	1.049	−2.101	0.899
Country-level				
Combination of logged GDP and average educational level	−0.004	0.884	−2.222	2.012
Mean amount of religious importance	0.006	0.333	−0.885	0.527
Democratic (yes/no)	0.836	0.370	0	1
No communist history (reference)	0.757	0.429	0	1
Communist history, not Soviet	0.084	0.278	0	1
Soviet history	0.116	0.320	0	1
Currently communist	0.042	0.201	0	1
Population size in millions	120.194	275.949	0.085	1336.718
Proportion Catholic	0.193	0.250	0	0.942
Confucian history[a]	0.120	0.324	0	1
Abortion is not legal on demand	0.398	0.490	0	1
Gender Inequality Index	0.336	0.172	0.048	0.803

[a]Confucian countries are China, Taiwan, Hong Kong, Japan, Singapore, South Korea, Macau, and
Vietnam.

256 FETAL POSITIONS

Dependent Variable

The key outcome variable is disapproval of abortion, which is measured using a single question that asks whether abortion can always be justified, never be justified, or something in between. The variable is reverse coded so that 1 = always justified and 10 = never justified. Higher numbers indicate less support.

Key Individual-Level Variables

Personal religious importance is the key religiosity indicator. Religious importance indicates how important religion is in the respondent's life and ranges from 1 = not at all important to 4 = very important, which was standardized.

In a separate analysis, I also considered a measure of relative religious importance. Respondents who report that religion is important may also be more likely to say that family and work are important. To account for an inclination to report that a variety of things in one's life are important, I created and tested a measure of relative religious importance by dividing religious importance by the sum of the importance of family and work. Relative religious importance functioned similarly (i.e., same p-value and direction) as the original religious importance measure, and the two measures have a statistically significant correlation of 0.9. Hence, the effect of religious importance does not appear to be driven by an inclination to report that a variety of things are important. I use the straightforward measure of religious importance.

Individual religious affiliation is measured with a set of dummy variables: Buddhist, Protestant, Hindu, Jewish, Christian Orthodox, Islam, other religion, other Christian religion, and no religious affiliation. Catholics are used as the reference category. Unfortunately, the WVS did not ask survey questions that would have make it possible to distinguish among religious subgroups, such as mainline and Evangelical Protestants or Shia and Sunni Muslims.

The remaining individual-level variables include gender, age, education, income, and marital status. Gender is assessed with a dichotomous variable where 1 = female and 0 = male. Age is a continuous variable that is measured in number of years. The level of education completed is measured with a variable that ranges from 1 = primary or less to 5 = completed university education. Marital status is measured with a set of dummy variables for living with partner, divorced or separated, widowed, and single, where married is the reference group.

To measure personal income, each respondent was given a card and told, "On this card is a scale of incomes on which 1 indicates the 'lowest income decile' and 10 the 'highest income decile' in your country. We would like to know in what group your household is. Please, specify the appropriate number, counting all wages, salaries, pensions and other incomes that come in." The variable was rescaled into roughly five categories, with each one including between 9% (i.e., the lowest category) and 30% (i.e., second to highest) of respondents. This rescaling had a stronger relationship with the outcome than the original ten-category measure, which included only about 2% of people at the highest steps, but not at the lowest ones. Survey year was also included to account for differences between waves.

APPENDIX A   257

Country-Level Variables

This study examines several country-level variables. The ones that are included in the main models for Appendix A are discussed here. But Appendix C includes close to thirty additional measures that were also considered.

Country religious importance is derived from individual-level responses to the question about religious importance. To take into consideration the number of people contributing to each country-level measure, Bayesian weighted averages are implemented to produce the mean level of religious importance within each country, which was then standardized.

I also considered a measure of relative country religious importance like I did for individuals. This measure was created by first aggregating the weighted individual measures for importance of religion, family, and work to the country level. I then divided country religious importance by the sum of family and work importance at the macro level. At the country level, relative religious importance works similarly (i.e., same p-value and direction) as the simpler country religious importance measure, suggesting that overall religiosity is not unduly affected by any national inclination to report that multiple things in life are important. I present results using the more straightforward measure that mirrors the individual-level variable.

The proportion Catholic is also taken from the individual measure, producing a proportion of the population within each country that is Catholic.

The measure of development is produced from a combined measure of logged gross domestic product (GDP) (US constant dollars for 2011) and the percentage of the population age twenty-five and older with at least a secondary education, which was obtained from the United Nations' (UN) database and distributed by the Association of Religion Data Archives (ARDA).[2] Both measures were first standardized. The Cronbach alpha for the combined measure is quite high at 0.706. The variable was then centered after it was created. Table A.5 presents the findings using separate measures for GDP and mean education.

The democracy measure is also taken from the UN database that was distributed by the ARDA.[3] The UN categorized nations into three categories: (1) non-democratic, (2) democratic with no alternation, and (3) democratic. These categories were recoded to assess non-democratic and democratic with or without alternation. Communist history is assessed with a set of dummy variables that include Soviet history, currently communist, and communist history, but not Soviet. The reference group is no communist history. Population size is measured in millions and taken from the 2011 Central Intelligence Agency (CIA) World Factbook, which was accessed through the ARDA.[4] Nations are also coded by whether they have Chinese or Confucian histories.

The Gender Inequality Index (GII) 2012 is a composite metric of gender inequality using three dimensions: reproductive health, empowerment, and the labor market. This measure is taken from the UN.[5] Nations that did not have a measure in 2012 are given one that is closest for when there was a measure.

---

[2] ARDA, "Cross-National Socio-Economic and Religion Data."
[3] ARDA.
[4] ARDA.
[5] Human Development Reports, "Gender Inequality Index."

258   FETAL POSITIONS

Finally, abortion policy information is taken from the Center for Reproductive Rights, which provides the legal grounds on which abortion is permitted for 196 nations. The abortion law measure used here indicates whether abortion is legal on demand (within gestational limits, which is typically twelve weeks) as of 2020, which is the last WVS survey year included in the sample. At that point, the United States had not yet given states the right to decide abortion's legality, and only some states in Mexico had legalized it. In the findings presented here, the United States is coded as having legal abortion, and Mexico is coded as abortion being illegal. In general, countries have moved in a more liberal legal direction (see the Conclusion). I also considered a seven-point measure indicating the legal grounds on which abortion is permitted, but the dichotomous measure had a stronger relationship with attitudes. In some nations, abortion may be viewed as a particularly deviant topic that is prone to social desirability bias. Unfortunately, the WVS does not have any measures that could account for this bias.

Analysis

The data are analyzed using generalized linear mixed models making it possible to discern the variance within nations (micro-level effects) from between them (macro-level effects).[6] Using information from the intraclass correlation, I found that 25% of the variation is occurring at the country level, which is substantial and warrants the use of multilevel modeling techniques that account for clustering.

To adequately assess the moderating influence of mean levels of religious importance and GDP and keep the structure of the models consistent throughout, making comparisons possible, the slope for individual religiosity is allowed to vary along with the country-level intercept across all the models presented in Appendix A. The analysis uses the recommended weights, which account for the unequal probability of selection of persons within nations.

Finally, missing data were listwise deleted across the sample because very little were missing (approximately 4%). The 88 nations that had the survey questions needed for this analysis included 220,238 respondents. Once the 8,921 respondents with missing data were eliminated at the individual level, the final sample size was 211,317. The question about income was the culprit. People were hesitant or unsure about how to respond. There were no missing data at the country level.

Results

The first set of models in Table A.3 present the effects of individual and country-level variables. Positive coefficients indicate that the variable is associated with more conservative views about abortion. Negative coefficients show that the predictor variables are associated with more liberal abortion views. The figures presented throughout the body of the book include marginal values for the predictors to aid in understanding effect sizes. All figures created from marginal values and WVS data are based on the findings presented in the following tables, and controlling for all other variables in the specified models.

Table A.4 focuses on the interactions between personal religious importance and the combined GDP and mean education measure and country religious importance, as well

---

[6] Breslow and Clayton, "Approximate Inference in Generalized Linear Mixed Models."

Table A.3 Mixed Models for Explaining Abortion Disapproval

	1	2	3	4	5	6	7	8
Year survey was completed	−0.020*	−0.020*	−0.020*	−0.020*	−0.020*	−0.020*	−0.020*	−0.020*
Female	−0.122***	−0.122***	−0.122***	−0.122***	−0.122***	−0.122***	−0.122***	−0.122***
Age	0.006***	0.006***	0.006***	0.006***	0.006***	0.006***	0.006***	0.006***
Living together (Ref.: married)	−0.148***	−0.148***	−0.147***	−0.147***	−0.147***	−0.147***	−0.147***	−0.147***
Divorced/separated	−0.269***	−0.269***	−0.269***	−0.269***	−0.269***	−0.269***	−0.268***	−0.269***
Widowed	0.092**	0.092**	0.093**	0.092**	0.092**	0.092**	0.092**	0.092**
Single/never married	−0.087***	−0.087***	−0.087***	−0.087***	−0.087***	−0.087***	−0.087***	−0.087***
Income	−0.080***	−0.080***	−0.080***	−0.080***	−0.080***	−0.080***	−0.080***	−0.080***
Educational level	−0.170***	−0.170***	−0.170***	−0.170***	−0.170***	−0.170***	−0.170***	−0.170***
No religion (Ref.: Catholic)	−0.365***	−0.365***	−0.366***	−0.367***	−0.367***	−0.365***	−0.365***	−0.365***
Protestant	0.057	0.056	0.056	0.055	0.055	0.057	0.057	0.057
Orthodox Christian	−0.177+	−0.180+	−0.180+	−0.185+	−0.185+	−0.181+	−0.180+	−0.180+
Jewish	−0.969**	−0.971**	−0.971**	−0.972**	−0.973**	−0.971**	−0.970**	−0.971**
Muslim	0.088	0.081	0.078	0.075	0.074	0.080	0.080	0.079
Hindu	0.058	0.055	0.054	0.053	0.047	0.051	0.050	0.050
Buddhist	−0.284***	−0.281***	−0.283***	−0.283***	−0.283***	−0.278***	−0.281***	−0.280***
Other Christian	0.123+	0.122+	0.122+	0.122+	0.122+	0.124+	0.124+	0.124+
Other religion	0.049	0.049	0.049	0.049	0.048	0.051	0.049	0.049
Religious affiliation missing	−0.401**	−0.401**	−0.402**	−0.403**	−0.404**	−0.401**	−0.401**	−0.401**
Religious importance (grand mean centered)[a]	0.494***	0.495***	0.496***	0.496***	0.496***	0.496***	0.498***	0.497***
Mean GDP per capita (logged) and education combined	−0.406***	−0.163	−0.189+	−0.228*	−0.188*	−0.168*	−0.225**	−0.177*

continued

Table A.3 Mixed Models for Explaining Abortion Disapproval *continued*

	1	2	3	4	5	6	7	8
Mean amount of religious importance[b] (grand mean centered)		1.724***	1.604***	1.810***	1.897***	1.971***	2.379***	2.249***
Democratic (yes/no)			−0.564**	−0.453**	−0.461**	−0.598***	−0.677***	−0.452*
Communist history, not Soviet (Ref.: No communist history)				−0.350	−0.305	−0.294	−0.254	−0.127
Soviet history				0.523***	0.550***	0.708***	0.989***	1.165***
Currently communist				0.690	0.358	0.351	−0.411	−0.162
Population size in millions					0.001*	0.001*	0.001*	0.001***
Proportion Catholic						0.706*	0.967**	0.747*
Confucian history (yes/no)							1.159**	1.279***
More conservative abortion policies (yes/no)								0.446**
Intraclass correlation coefficient (ICC)	.141	.114	.104	.0871	.084	.082	.067	.060
Constant	48.034**	47.920**	48.408**	48.257**	48.160**	48.065**	47.918**	47.599**
Observations	211,317	211,317	211,317	211,317	211,317	211,317	211,317	211,317
Number of groups	88	88	88	88	88	88	88	88

***p < 0.001, **p < 0.01, *p < 0.05, + p < 0.10 (two-tailed test)
[a]A measure of relative religious importance produced similar effects (i.e., same direction and significance level).
[b]A measure of relative country religious importance produced similar effects (i.e., same direction and significance level).

Note: The Intraclass Correlation Coefficient for the empty model with just the outcome included indicates that 25% of the variance is occurring across nations and 75% is occurring at the individual level.

Source: WVS, waves 5, 6, and 7

as the Gender Inequality Index. In addition to assessing the moderating influence of GDP and mean education for explaining the relationship between personal religious beliefs and abortion disapproval, I also examine the moral communities' effect. The idea behind this relationship is that when more religious people are around other religious individuals, they become especially opposed to behaviors that religion proscribes. Model 1 of Table A.4 shows that there is no moral communities' effect at least at the societal level for explaining abortion disapproval. Conversely, as the level of economic and educational development increases, more religious people are more opposed to abortion than less-religious residents (See Model 2 in Table A.4) In other words, there is a bigger gap between more religious and less religious people in their level of abortion disapproval in richer and more educated nations than there is in less-developed countries. Model 3 includes the GII. It initially appears statistically significant, but it is highly correlated with abortion legislation. Hence, once abortion legalization is excluded from the model, the GII is statistically significant (see Model 4).

Table A.5 examines the separate and joint effects of economic and educational development in shaping abortion disapproval. The first model focuses on GDP, which is marginally significant ($p < 0.05$ with a one-tailed test). The second model includes overall levels of education, which is also marginally significant ($p < 0.05$ with a one-tailed test). Model 3 includes both measures in the same model, showing that neither is statistically significant. The final model includes the combined measure, which is statistically significant at the 0.05 level using a two-tailed test.

Effect Sizes

Assessing relative effect sizes in mixed models can be challenging. Using a couple of different techniques, I find that the macro and micro measures of religious importance provide the greatest explanatory power. First, I produced beta coefficients for all variables in Model 8 of Table A.1. Country religiosity has the largest standardized coefficient (0.268), followed by personal religious importance (0.186).

Next, I focused on the individual-level variables found in Table A.3, entering them into an ordinary least square regression analysis and accounting for clustering at the country level. I examined how the variance explained (i.e., R^2) changed with the subtraction of each individual-level variable or set of dummy variables when categorical measures (i.e., marital status, religious affiliation) are used, while the other individual-level measures remain in the model. When all the individual-level variables from Table A.1 are included, the total amount of variance explained in abortion disapproval is 18%. As the percentage increases, more variance is explained. When religious importance is *excluded* from the model, the percentage explained drops to 11%. In other words, religious importance explains an additional 7% of unique variation in abortion disapproval. The next highest amount of variation explained is religious affiliation, at 16.9%, so only 1.1% more than what the other variables in the model are explaining once they are all included. When they are added one by one, no remaining individual-level measure has an R-squared over 17%, suggesting that personal religious importance is clearly the most powerful individual-level explanatory factor for understanding abortion disapproval. This finding coincides with two US-based meta studies showing that religion is the most powerful factor for understanding abortion disapproval.[7]

---

[7] Jelen and Wilcox, "Causes and Consequences of Public Attitudes toward Abortion"; Adamczyk, Freilich, and Kim, "Religion and Crime."

262 FETAL POSITIONS

Table A.4 Additional Analyses Examining the Interactions between Personal Religious Importance and GDP/Mean Education and Country Religious Importance and Gender Inequality for Understanding Abortion Disapproval

	1	2	3	4
Year survey was completed	−0.020*	−0.020*	−0.020*	−0.020*
Female	−0.122***	−0.122***	−0.122***	−0.122***
Age	0.006***	0.006***	0.006***	0.006***
Living together (Ref.: married)	−0.147***	−0.147***	−0.147***	−0.147***
Divorced/separated	−0.269***	−0.269***	−0.269***	−0.269***
Widowed	0.092**	0.092**	0.092**	0.092**
Single/never married	−0.087***	−0.087***	−0.087***	−0.087***
Income	−0.080***	−0.080***	−0.080***	−0.080***
Educational level	−0.170***	−0.170***	−0.170***	−0.170***
No religion (Ref.: Catholic)	−0.365***	−0.364***	−0.364***	−0.364***
Protestant	0.057	0.057	0.057	0.057
Orthodox Christian	−0.180+	−0.180+	−0.179+	−0.179+
Jewish	−0.971**	−0.972**	−0.972**	−0.972**
Muslim	0.079	0.079	0.079	0.080
Hindu	0.050	0.050	0.050	0.050
Buddhist	−0.281***	−0.280***	−0.280***	−0.280***
Other Christian	0.124+	0.124+	0.124+	0.124+
Other religion	0.049	0.049	0.049	0.048
Religious affiliation missing	−0.401**	−0.402**	−0.402**	−0.402**
Religious importance (grand mean centered)	0.496***	0.493***	0.492***	0.493***
Mean GDP per capita (logged) and education combined	−0.175*	−0.243**	−0.145+	−0.144+
Mean amount of religious importance (grand mean centered)	2.350***	2.250***	2.040***	2.030***
Democratic (yes/no)	−0.454*	−0.440*	−0.437*	−0.566**
Communist history, not soviet (Ref.: No communist history)	−0.125	−0.132	−0.180	−0.273
Soviet history	1.160***	1.182***	1.141***	1.024***
Currently communist	−0.160	−0.150	−0.160	−0.307
Population size in millions	0.001***	0.001***	0.001**	0.001*
Proportion Catholic	0.742*	0.735*	0.816*	0.976**
Confucian history (yes/no)	1.273***	1.311***	1.369***	1.324***
More conservative abortion policies (yes/no)	0.372*	0.377*	0.251	
Moral communities' hypothesis: Personal religious importance X Country religious importance	−0.258			

continued

APPENDIX A   263

Table A.4 *continued*

	1	2	3	4
Personal religious importance X Mean GDP per capita and education combined		0.153**	0.153**	0.152**
Gender Inequality Index			1.124+	1.586**
Constant	47.608**	47.550**	47.228**	47.277**
Intraclass correlation (ICC)	0.060	0.058	0.057	0.059
Observations	211,317	211,317	211,317	211,317
Number of groups	88	88	88	88

***p < 0.001, **p < 0.01, *p < 0.05, + p < 0.10 (two-tailed test)
Source: WVS, waves 5, 6, and 7

I then examined changes in the intraclass correlation coefficient (ICC) for the country-level variables when all the individual-level variables were included in the mixed-level models specified in Table A.3, Model 1. An empty model examining abortion disapproval shows that 25% of the variation is happening across countries. I entered each country-level variable separately with just the individual-level variables in the model. Among the country-level variables, country religious importance explains the most variation, with only 12% of the country-level variance remaining once it is included. The variable with the second largest explanatory power is the combined GDP and country education measure, which left 14% of the variation remaining after it is included. The Confucian country-level variable explains the least amount of variation with 18% remaining after it is included.

Like I did for the individual-level analysis, I also examined how much unique variation each of the country-level variables explain when all individual and country-level measures are included, except for the macro measure being examined. Again, I found that country religious importance is explaining more unique country-level variation than any of the other macro factors. Other studies have also found a robust effect of country religious importance for understanding abortion disapproval as a single-issue item,[8] or as part of an index of sexual morality.[9] Hence, these findings are consistent with other studies.

Having shown that personal and mean country religious importance have the greatest explanatory power among individual and country-level variables for understanding disapproval, I plot their effect sizes with one standard deviation above and below the mean in Figure 1.2 in Chapter 1. Consistent with the findings comparing the beta coefficients, country religiosity appears to have a slightly larger effect than personal religiosity, albeit they are quite similar. Throughout the book, marginal effect sizes are presented for all the country-level measures, except for population size, giving readers a sense of how they compare to country religiosity.

[8] Adamczyk, "Religion as a Micro and Macro Property"; Adamczyk, Suh, and Lerner, "Analysis of the Relationship Between Religion, Abortion, and Assisted Reproductive Technology: Insights into Cross-National Public Opinion."
[9] Scheepers, Te Grotenhuis, and Van Der Slik, "Education, Religiosity and Moral Attitudes"; Finke and Adamczyk, "Cross-National Moral Beliefs: The Influence of National Religious Context."

264   FETAL POSITIONS

Table A.5 Mixed Models Examining the Independent and Joint Influences of Country Levels of Education and GDP on Abortion Disapproval

	1	2	3	4
Year survey was completed	−0.020*	−0.020*	−0.020*	−0.020*
Female	−0.122***	−0.122***	−0.122***	−0.122***
Age	0.006***	0.006***	0.006***	0.006***
Living together (Ref.: married)	−0.147***	−0.147***	−0.147***	−0.147***
Divorced/separated	−0.269***	−0.269***	−0.269***	−0.269***
Widowed	0.093**	0.093**	0.092**	0.092**
Single/never married	−0.087***	−0.087***	−0.087***	−0.087***
Income	−0.080***	−0.080***	−0.080***	−0.080***
Educational level	−0.170***	−0.170***	−0.170***	−0.170***
No religion (Ref.: Catholic)	−0.365***	−0.365***	−0.365***	−0.365***
Protestant	0.057	0.058	0.057	0.057
Orthodox Christian	−0.180+	−0.180+	−0.180+	−0.180+
Jewish	−0.971**	−0.970**	−0.971**	−0.971**
Muslim	0.079	0.078	0.079	0.079
Hindu	0.050	0.050	0.050	0.050
Buddhist	−0.280***	−0.281***	−0.280***	−0.280***
Other Christian	0.124+	0.124+	0.124+	0.124+
Other religion	0.049	0.050	0.050	0.049
Religious affiliation missing	−0.401**	−0.401**	−0.401**	−0.401**
Religious importance (grand mean centered)	0.497***	0.497***	0.497***	0.497***
Mean amount of religious importance (grand mean centered)	2.297***	2.307***	2.255***	2.249***
Democratic (yes/no)	−0.412*	−0.439*	−0.455*	−0.452*
Communist history, not Soviet (Ref.: No communist history)	−0.101	−0.103	−0.125	−0.127
Soviet history	1.046***	1.291***	1.209***	1.165***
Currently communist	−0.063	−0.148	−0.172	−0.162
Population size in millions	0.001***	0.001***	0.001***	0.001***
Proportion Catholic	0.734*	0.747*	0.749*	0.747*
Confucian history (yes/no)	1.259***	1.246***	1.274***	1.279***
More conservative abortion policies (yes/no)	0.479**	0.460**	0.445**	0.446**
Country mean GDP per capita (logged)	−0.127+		−0.069	
Country mean level of education		−0.453+	−0.346	
Mean GDP per capita and education combined				−0.177*
Constant	48.772**	48.510**	48.971**	47.599**
Intraclass correlation (ICC)	0.062	0.061	0.061	0.061
Observations	211,317	211,317	211,317	211,317
Number of groups	88	88	88	88

***$p < 0.001$, **$p < 0.01$, *$p < 0.05$, + $p < 0.10$ (two-tailed test)
Source: WVS, waves 5, 6, and 7

APPENDIX B

Newspaper Analysis

To examine the themes and claimsmakers associated with abortion in the English-language press, my research team and I hand coded over 800 articles across 80 newspapers in 41 countries to produce the sample.[1] When we began the study at the end of 2019, the most recent one-year period for which we had access to newspaper articles was from January 1, 2018, to December 31, 2018. Articles that mention the term "abortion" over the year constitute the population of documents. I wanted a diverse set of countries with different religious histories and levels of economic development and democracy. Thus, the analysis includes eighty newspapers from forty-one countries with various economic levels and religious backgrounds. You can find a full list of the newspapers in Table B.1.

Ideally, we would have a random sample of countries for this study. However, not all nations have English-language newspaper articles with online access. Hence, the sample is constrained by available and accessible information. The countries and their dominant religions can be found in Table B.2, which also includes descriptive statistics.

The selection of newspaper articles was based on a few criteria. First, the newspaper had to be published in English since our research team did not speak all the possible languages in the countries examined, and the study was focused on the English-language press. This decision is in line with other published studies, which have focused on the English-language press when conducting cross-national research.[2] Second, articles had to be published at least five days a week. Third, the entire one-year period of papers needed to be accessible through the newspaper's website or Factiva. Factiva is a research tool that provides access to more than 30,000 media sources from 200 countries across the world in over 32 languages. In many nations, the government publishes newspapers. When we had a choice, we selected papers independent of the government. Additionally, whenever possible, we selected two to three newspapers from every country to limit bias that might appear when analyzing a single paper within the nation.

English is an unofficial global language, is one of the most commonly spoken languages worldwide, and most people who use it are not native speakers. While some studies have found reporting differences when English is used, rather than the native language, others have not found major alterations.[3] Hence, bias might be more limited than it is for other languages. On the surface, only twenty-two of our selected countries spoke English in some official or secondary capacity. However, several selected countries (including Turkey, Finland, Romania, Italy, France, Poland, and Germany) do not list English as an official or secondary language. Yet, citizens maintain high levels of English proficiency.[4] For example, in Finland, where Finnish and Swedish are the official languages, 66% of the population has some knowledge of English.[5]

Every model includes a control for whether English is the dominant language within the countries. The variable is statistically significant for only one outcome (religious themes). I also ran all analyses for countries where English is not the dominant language and did not find any differences in the direction or statistical significance

---

[1] Adamczyk and Lerner, "Synthesizing the Global English-Language Abortion Narrative."

[2] See Gupta et al., "Media Coverage of COVID-19 Health Information in India"; Adamczyk, Kim, and Schmuhl, "Newspaper Presentations of Homosexuality: Comparing Muslim and Protestant Countries."

[3] Abdul-Mageed, "Arabic And English News Coverage On Aljazeera.Net"; Alexandre and Rehbinder, "Separate but Equal."

[4] Clark, "English Proficiency in Europe 2019."

[5] Clark.

266 FETAL POSITIONS

Table B.1 Newspapers and Countries Included in the Analysis

Country	Newspaper 1	Newspaper 2	Newspaper 3
Argentina	*Argentina Reports*		
Bangladesh	*The Daily Star*	*The New Nation*	
Bolivia	*Bolivian Express*		
Botswana	*Mmegi*		
Brazil	*Valor Economico*	*Agencia Brasil*	*Folha de San Paulo*
Canada	*The Toronto Star*	*The Hamilton Spectator*	
China	*China Daily*	*Shanghai Daily*	
Colombia	*The Bogota Post*		
Egypt	*Al-Ahram Gate*	*Daily News Egypt*	
Finland	*Helsinki Times*	*Daily Finland*	
France	*The Local*	*AFP*	
Germany	*The Local*	*Deutsche Welle*	
Ghana	*The Herald*	*The Ghanaian Times*	*Daily Guide*
India	*The Times of India*	*The Hindu*	
Indonesia	*The Jakarta Post*		
Iran	*Tehran Times*	*Iran Daily*	*Iran News*
Ireland	*The Irish Time*	*Irish Independent*	
Italy	*The Local*	*ANSA*	
Japan	*The Mainichi*	*The Japan Times*	
Jordan	*Al Ghad*	*The Jordan Times*	*The Jordan News Agency*
Kenya	*Daily Nation*	*The Star*	
Mexico	*The News*	*El Universal*	
Morocco	*Agence Marocaine De Presse*	*Morocco World News*	
Namibia	*The Namibian Times*	*New Era*	
Pakistan	*Dawn*	*The Nation*	
Peru	*Peru Reports*		
Philippines	*Manila Bulletin*	*Philippine Daily Inquirer*	
Poland	*Polish News Bulletin*		
Romania	*Romania-Insider*	*Nine O'Clock*	*Romania Journal*
Saudi Arabia	*Arab News*	*Al Riyadh*	
South Africa	*The Star*	*Daily News*	
South Korea	*Korea Joongang Daily*	*The Korea Times*	
Taiwan	*Taiwan News*	*Taipei Times*	

continued

APPENDIX B   267

Table B.1 *continued*

Country	Newspaper 1	Newspaper 2	Newspaper 3
Thailand	*The Nation*	*The Bangkok Post*	
Tunisia	*Agency Tunis Afrique Press*	*African Manager*	
Turkey	*Turkish Daily News*	*Daily Sabah*	
Uganda	*New Vision*	*Daily Monitor*	
United Kingdom	*The Times*	*The Daily Telegraph*	
United States	*Wall Street Journal*	*USA Today*	
Vietnam	*Tuoi Tre Newspaper*	*Vietnam News Summary*	
Zimbabwe	*The Herald*	*The Zimbabwean*	

Table B.2 Descriptive Statistics for Variables Included in the Analysis

	Mean	SD	Min	Max
Laws/policies are part of the discussion.	0.77	0.42	0.00	1.00
Government claimsmaker is mentioned.	0.69	0.46	0.00	1.00
Social movement/protest activities are part of the discussion.	0.27	0.44	0.00	1.00
Social movement claimsmaker is mentioned.	0.23	0.42	0.00	1.00
Religion is mentioned in the discussion.	0.16	0.37	0.00	1.00
Religious claimsmaker is in news or opinion piece.	0.09	0.29	0.00	1.00
Morality/immorality or related issues are part of the discussion.	0.19	0.39	0.00	1.00
Global freedom score higher (0–100).	63.41	28.26	7.00	100.00
Abortion on demand is allowed.	0.28	0.45	0.00	1.00
Religion is very important (on average).	54.45	31.97	3.00	94.00
Logged GDP.	9.12	1.26	6.64	11.27
English is the dominant/official language.[a]	0.28	0.45	0.00	1.00
Newspaper published daily.	0.89	0.31	0.00	1.00
Online = 1 vs. Other = 0.	0.33	0.47	0.00	1.00

continued

268 FETAL POSITIONS

Table B.2 *continued*

	Mean	SD	Min	Max
Dominant historical/cultural religious tradition.				
Catholic (reference): Argentina, Bolivia, Brazil, Canada, Colombia, France, Ireland, Italy, Mexico, Peru, the Philippines, and Poland	0.30	0.46	0.00	1.00
Mainline Protestant: Finland, Germany, and the United Kingdom	0.08	0.28	0.00	1.00
Mixed and other Christian: Botswana, Ghana, Kenya, Namibia, Romania, South Africa, Zimbabwe, Uganda, and the United States	0.18	0.38	0.00	1.00
Islam: Bangladesh, Indonesia, Iran, Jordan, Morocco, Pakistan, Saudi Arabia, Tunisia, Turkey, and Egypt	0.26	0.44	0.00	1.00
Buddhism: China, Taiwan, Japan, South Korea, Vietnam, and Thailand	0.16	0.36	0.00	1.00
Hinduism: India	0.03	0.16	0.00	1.00

[a]In a separate analysis, control variables for whether English is a first or second language and the level of English comprehension were also considered, but these did not make any meaningful difference.

level for key variables. In separate analyses, I also examined the effect of English being a dominant first or second language in the country, and the English Proficiency Index, which ranks countries on a proficiency scale ranging from 0, which indicates very low, to 5, which indicates very high English proficiency. These variables were never statistically significant in any of the models, and neither did they change key findings. Nevertheless, because the study is focused on English-language newspapers, the findings are necessarily constrained to this population of articles.

After isolating the newspapers that met the above criteria, we searched for every article over the one-year period that used the term "abortion." We selected up to twenty-five articles from each paper. When a newspaper had fewer than twenty-five articles that mentioned abortion, we used all of them. When it had more than twenty-five articles, we randomly selected a subset, reducing the total number to twenty-five. The average paper had ten articles that mentioned abortion.

The dependent variables are abortion-related associations or claimsmakers. After reviewing several articles published previously and assessing research in this area, we created lists of themes and claimsmakers associated with the text surrounding the term "abortion." We then developed a protocol to systematically code each article for the presence of the following themes: (1) laws and policies, (2) social movements and protest, (3) religion, and (4) terms about morality or morality-related issues. We also coded the following claimsmakers: (1) government, (2) social movement leaders or activities, and (3) religious affiliates.

When needed, coders researched specific individuals and organizations to ensure they were categorized correctly. While multiple survey analyses have examined abortion disapproval, our study was interested in the themes and claimsmakers used when abortion was discussed. As such, themes and claimsmakers could either support or oppose abortion.[6] Our coding categories were not mutually exclusive, and each article could have up to four different associations and three different claimsmakers. Our coding instrument provided the criteria for coding articles into each category.

Our coding team consisted of five people, with two coding each article. Using articles from 2017, outside of our analysis period, all the coders underwent several weeks of training. First, we reviewed the instructions with them, and they coded articles. We then discussed inconsistencies and the logic for the decision-making process. Based on these meetings, the coding instrument was periodically updated during the training period. However, the codebook no longer changed once we started coding the articles included in this analysis. Each coder entered their information into a spreadsheet, which the head coder merged. When there were inconsistencies between the two coders, the head coder made the final determination, which is a similar process used in other studies.[7]

The key explanatory variables are the proportion who say religion is very important, a democracy freedom score, and whether abortion is allowed on demand. The proportion who say religion is very important is taken from the Pew Research Center. They asked respondents worldwide about the importance of religion in one's life.[8] Since religions differ in their emphasis on behaviors such as religious service attendance and prayer, religious importance is instrumental when examining views across nations with different dominant religions. Abortion on demand is taken from the Center for Reproductive Rights. We use data from their abortion law database, which provides the legal status of abortion in countries.[9] We considered using a measure with a greater range of legal and policy categories, but they were not sensitive enough to detect differences. Instead, the major distinction across the world seems to be a dichotomous measure of whether abortion is allowed on demand within gestational limits.

Finally, the measure of democracy is a 2020 Global Freedom measure produced by Freedom House, which annually rates people's access to political rights and civil liberties.[10] According to Freedom House, a country's freedom score is created from its aggregate Political Rights score on a scale of 0 to 40 and its aggregate Civil Liberties score ranging from 0 to 60. In the Global Freedom measure calculation, the Political Rights and Civil Liberties scores are equally weighted, ranging from 0 = least free to 100 = most free. We considered other measures of democracy, but this one was the most sensitive for detecting differences. A t-test revealed that the countries with government-owned English-language newspapers had lower freedom scores (42 vs. 67, where 100 indicates total freedom). As mentioned above, some newspapers are government owned. Hence, the two measures are moderately correlated and, to some extent, are both measuring dimensions of democracy.

Several different control variables are also considered. Because of the limited number of countries (N = 41), I carefully selected ones that made the most theoretical sense and were statistically significant in at least some of the analyses. These are logged gross

---

[6] In a separate analysis, we examined if the average level of abortion disapproval within a country was associated with the themes and claimsmakers and did not find meaningful associations. We used information on disapproval from the World Values Survey. Only thirty-six of the forty-one nations had public opinion information.

[7] Adamczyk, Kim, and Paradis, "Investigating Differences in How the News Media Views Homosexuality across Nations."

[8] Pew, "Modeling the Future of Religion in America."

[9] Center for Reproductive Rights, "The World's Abortion Laws."

[10] Freedom House, "Countries and Territories Global Freedom Index."

270 FETAL POSITIONS

domestic product (GDP), English being the dominant/official language, which was discussed above, the major historical/cultural, religious tradition, daily publication of the newspaper, and whether it is an online-only paper.

Based on information from the Association of Religion Data Archives and the Pew Research Center, countries are categorized into six dominant cultural/religious traditions: Catholic, mainline Protestant, mixed or other Christian, Muslim, Buddhist, and Hindu, which only included India. Several studies have found that conservative Protestants have been especially opposed to abortion and that mainline Protestants tend to be very liberal.[11] Therefore, these groups were coded separately with the mixed or other Christian group, including countries with a substantial proportion of more conservative Christian faiths. There would have been a separate category for Christian Orthodox nations, but there was only one (Romania). Romania was included in the mixed Christian category to maximize the degrees of freedom.

GDP is logged, and values were taken from the World Bank's 2018 measure[12] in current US dollars per capita. Countries where English is the dominant/official language are coded 1, and all others were coded 0. Newspapers are also coded 1 if they are published daily and 0 if they are not. Finally, papers only published online are coded as 1, and all others are coded 0.

Several other control variables were considered. However, they were either not statistically significant in the models or did not affect results meaningfully. These included fertility rates, population size, and being a former communist country or part of the former Soviet Union, where some researchers have suggested there was an "abortion culture."[13] In a separate analysis, I also examined circulation rates for the 77% of articles where this information was available (i.e., mostly larger papers that were in print a year after we coded the articles). The circulation rates were not statistically significant in any of the models.

Before beginning the analysis, I first assessed whether there was enough significant variation at the country and newspaper levels to warrant three-level multilevel models. The pretest concluded that there was not only significant variation but that the variation at the country level was over 20% for some outcomes. Across countries, the law and policy theme (21%), government claimsmakers (20%), and morality (18%) had the most societal variation to be explained. With just 11% of the variation occurring across countries, social movement claimsmakers had the least societal-level variation to be explained. Across newspapers, the morality theme (32%) and laws and policies (29%) had the most variation to be explained at the newspaper level. With 17% of variation occurring across papers, the social movement claimsmaker outcome had the slightest variation.

The analysis uses multilevel mixed-effects logistic regression. The findings are presented in Table B.3. Exponentiated odds are reported so numbers over 1 indicate a positive relationship and those below 1 indicate a negative relationship. Marginal differences for statistically significant variables are presented in Figure 3.4 in Chapter 3.

---

[11] Adamczyk and Valdimarsdóttir, "Understanding Americans' Abortion Attitudes"; Bartkowski et al., "Faith, Race-Ethnicity, and Public Policy Preferences."
[12] Iran's 2017 measure was used because 2018 was unavailable.
[13] Karpov and Kääriäinen, "'Abortion Culture' in Russia."

Table B.3 Multilevel Mixed-Effects Logistic Regression Models Examining the Country-Level Factors Shaping the Odds That Abortion Is Discussed in the Context of Key Themes and Claimsmakers (Exponentiated Odds Are Reported[a])

	1	2	3	4	6	7
	Laws/policies are part of the discussion.	Government claims-makers are part of the discussion.	Social move-ment/protest activities are part of the discussion.	Social movement claimsmaker is mentioned	Religious claims-maker is mentioned[b]	Morality and related issues are part of the discussion
Global freedom score	1.020*	1.020**	1.014*	1.018**	1.025+	1.032**
Abortion is legal within gestational limits	0.697	0.382*	0.401**	0.550	0.974	0.406
Religion is very important (on average)	0.992	0.982	0.989	1.000	0.999	1.010
Mainline Protestant (Ref. Catholic)	1.664	1.039	1.500	1.921	0.434	4.704*
Mixed and other Christian	0.367	0.816	1.610	1.219	0.227	0.447
Islam	2.371	2.999*	2.091	2.953*	0.257+	0.533
Buddhism	1.001	1.237	3.554**	3.495**	0.404	1.990
Hinduism	4.203	13.060*	0.361	0.724		0.466
Logged GDP	0.976	1.038	0.891	0.835	0.497+	0.620
English is the dominant/official language	1.051	0.847	0.476+	0.905	0.471	0.507
Newspaper published daily	0.426+	1.604	1.084	1.312	2.848+	1.772

continued

Table B.3 *continued*

	1	2	3	4	6	7
	Laws/policies are part of the discussion.	Government claims-makers are part of the discussion.	Social move-ment/protest activities are part of the discussion.	Social movement claimsmaker is mentioned	Religious claims-maker is mentioned[b]	Morality and related issues
Online = 1 vs. Other = 0	1.520	1.188	1.877*	2.370**	0.745	0.598
Constant	5.012	1.074	0.616	0.200	12.395	1.514
Observations	810	810	810	810	788	810
Country variance	0.016	0.116	0	0	0	0.377
Newspaper variance	0.502	0.258	0.132	0.174	0.576	0.557
Number of groups	41	41	41	41	40	41

***p < 0.001, **p < 0.01, *p < 0.05, + p < 0.10 (two-tailed test)
[a]Numbers above 1 indicate a positive relationship, and those below 0 indicate a negative relationship.
[b]Religious themes were also examined, but the Freedom Index was not associated with this outcome.

APPENDIX C

Additional Indicators

Table C.1 Additional Indicators Considered for Explaining Survey Respondent's Abortion Disapproval in Multivariate Mixed Models

Indicator	Significant in explaining disapproval?[b]
Religion	
Government regulation of religion index[c]	No
Government favoritism of religion index[d]	No
Modified social regulation of religion index[d]	No
Economic	
Percentage of population below the national poverty line[e]	No
Percent of total population that was undernourished[e]	No
Percentage of children ages 5 to 14 engaged in child labor[e]	No
Percentage of population without electricity[e]	No
Unemployment rate[f]	No
Population	
Projected percent average annual population growth[e]	No
Percentage of the total population living in urban areas[e]	No
Median age in years[e]	No
Percentage of population age 0 to 14[e]	No
Number of births per 1,000 population[f]	No
Net migration rate per 1,000 population[f]	No
Fertility	
Total fertility rate[e]	No
Projected total fertility rate[e]	No
Adolescent fertility rate[e]	No
Contraceptive prevalence rate (percent of married women ages 15 to 49)[e]	No

continued

274   FETAL POSITIONS

Table C.1 *continued*

Indicator	Significant in explaining disapproval?[b]
Education	
Public expenditure on education as a percentage of GDP[e]	No
Adult literacy rate (percentage of population age 15 or older)[e]	No
Percentage of the population ages 25 and older with at least secondary education[e]	No
Health	
Life expectancy at birth, total population[f]	No
Maternal mortality ratio[e]	No
Percentage of 1-year-olds lacking immunization against measles[e]	No
Number of infant deaths per 1,000 live births[e]	No
Number of deaths of children under 5 years of age per 1,000 live births[e]	No
Infant mortality rate: Number of deaths per 1,000 live births[f]	No
Gender inequality[c]	
Gender gap in labor force participation rate for females (15+) minus the labor force participation rate for males (15+), 2012 (i.e., economic dimension of inequality)[g]	No
Percentage of seats in parliament held by women, 2008 (i.e., political dimension of inequality)[e]	No

[a]Measured on a scale ranging from 1 to 10, where 10 = never justified.
[b]Measures were included in the mixed models found in Appendix A, Table A.3, Model 8. None of these variables were statistically significant at the .05 level (two-tailed test).
[c]These measures were included without abortion laws and the UN's Gender Inequality Index, which is discussed in Chapter 4 and included in the models presented in Appendix A.
[d]Measure was from the 2008 US State Department's International Religious Freedom Reports.
[e]Measure was from the 2010 United Nations Human Development Report (HDR).
[f]Measure was from the 2011 edition of the Central Intelligence Agency's (CIA) World Factbook.
[g]Measure is from 2012 and taken from the International Labour Organization and includes their modeled estimates, which provide a complete set (without missing observations) of internationally comparable labor statistics.

APPENDIX D

Abortion Rate Analysis

Table D.1 Ordinal Least Squares Regression Models Examining of the Cross-National Factors Shaping Rates of Unintended Pregnancy and Abortions of Unintended Pregnancies (per 1,000 women, ages 15–49)

	(1)	(2)	(3)	(4)	(5)	(6)	(7)	(8)	(9)
	Model-Estimated Annual Unintended Pregnancy Rates			Model-Estimated Annual Average Abortion Rates					
Mean religious importance	−18.633			5.379					
Abortion illegal unless rape, health, death, fetal problems	−12.234+			−0.219					
Mean abortion disapproval	1.414			1.917					
population size	−0.021+			0.005					
Mean proportion Catholic[b]	20.713*	15.814	16.303+	2.821					
combination of higher logged gdp and average educational level[c]	6.747	−14.943***		6.539*	6.335*	−5.772***	0.945		
Gender Inequality Index	171.812***		105.653***	58.845**	77.015***			47.011***	3.335
Communist country, not Soviet (Reference: Former Soviet Union countries[d]	−6.189	−20.846+	−11.264	−15.183*	−15.875**	−23.414***	−16.252***	−19.400***	−16.853***

No communist history	4.367	−4.567	−2.830	−12.766**	−13.395***	−15.326***	−15.334***	−14.899***	−15.673***
Current communist (Vietnam, China, Macau)	38.574**	15.333	29.242*	24.777**	25.625***	14.819+	7.698	20.532**	8.262
Model-Estimated Annual Unintended Pregnancy Rates per 1,000 Women (ages 15–49)							0.455***		0.417***
Constant	−15.386	53.504***	17.795**	2.001	11.783*	38.277***	13.826***	22.733***	15.068***
Country N	71	71	71	71	71	71	71	71	71
R²	0.645	0.391	0.594	0.605	0.578	0.392	0.741	0.540	0.739

***p < 0.001, **p < 0.01, *p < 0.05, + p < 0.10 (two-tailed test)

[a]Rates are taken from Bearak et al., "Country-Specific Estimates of Unintended Pregnancy and Abortion Incidence."

[b]Mean proportion Catholic was not sig correlated with either outcome at the bivariate level, suggesting that the relationship here, which indicates that abortion rates are higher in nations with a greater proportion of Catholics, may be related to multicollinearity concerns.

[c]The measure of higher logged GDP and average education are highly correlated with the Gender Inequality Index. When both variables are included in the same model, the sign for GDP and average education flips, likely because of multicollinearity.

[d]In a separate analysis I also examined the influence of democracy, which is the same dichotomous variable used in Table 3 of Appendix A. However, the overlap with other variables, especially communism, and the small number of countries in the analysis led to multicollinearity concerns. Rather than democracy, the key factor seems to be communist history status.

Bibliography

19-1392 Dobbs v. Jackson Women's Health Organization, 597 U.S. 215 (2022).

Abdul-Mageed, Muhammad M. "Arabic and English News Coverage on Aljazeera.Net," n.d.

Abrams, J. Keith, and L. Richard Della Fave. "Authoritarianism, Religiosity, and the Legalization of Victimless Crimes." *Sociology and Social Research* 61, no. 1 (1976): 68–82.

Adamczyk, Amy. *Cross-National Public Opinion about Homosexuality: Examining Attitudes across the Globe*. Oakland: University of California Press, 2017.

Adamczyk, Amy. "Religion as a Micro and Macro Property: Investigating the Multilevel Relationship between Religion and Abortion Attitudes across the Globe." *European Sociological Review* 38, no. 5 (2022): 816–31. https://doi.org/10.1093/esr/jcac017.

Adamczyk, Amy. "Socialization and Selection in the Link between Friends' Religiosity and the Transition to Sexual Intercourse." *Sociology of Religion* 70, no. 1 (2009): 5–27. https://doi.org/10.1093/socrel/srp010.

Adamczyk, Amy. "The Effects of Religious Contextual Norms, Structural Constraints, and Personal Religiosity on Abortion Decisions." *Social Science Research* 37, no. 2 (2008): 657–72.

Adamczyk, Amy. "Understanding Delinquency with Friendship Group Religious Context: Delinquency with Friendship Group Religious Context." *Social Science Quarterly* 93, no. 4 (2012): 482–505. https://doi.org/10.1111/j.1540-6237.2012.00839.x.

Adamczyk, Amy. "Understanding the Effects of Personal and School Religiosity on the Decision to Abort a Premarital Pregnancy." *Journal of Health and Social Behavior* 50, no. 2 (2009): 180–95.

Adamczyk, Amy, Katherine Boyd, and Brittany E Hayes. "Place Matters: Contextualizing the Roles of Religion and Race for Understanding Americans' Attitudes about Homosexuality." *Social Science Research* 57 (2016): 1–16.

Adamczyk, Amy, and Yen-hsin Alice Cheng. "Explaining Attitudes about Homosexuality in Confucian and Non-Confucian Nations: Is There a 'Cultural' Influence?" *Social Science Research* 51 (2015): 276–89.

Adamczyk, Amy, and Jacob Felson. "Fetal Positions: Unraveling the Influence of Religion on Premarital Pregnancy Resolution*." *Social Science Quarterly* 89, no. 1 (2008): 17–38.

Adamczyk, Amy, and Jacob Felson. "Friends' Religiosity and First Sex." *Social Science Research* 35, no. 4 (2006): 924–47. https://doi.org/10.1016/j.ssresearch.2005.04.003.

Adamczyk, Amy, Joshua D. Freilich, and Chunrye Kim. "Religion and Crime: A Systematic Review and Assessment of Next Steps." *Sociology of Religion* 78 (2017): 192–232.

BIBLIOGRAPHY 279

Adamczyk, Amy, and Brittany E Hayes. "Religion and Sexual Behaviors Understanding the Influence of Islamic Cultures and Religious Affiliation for Explaining Sex Outside of Marriage." *American Sociological Review* 77, no. 5 (2012): 723–46. https://doi.org/10.1177/0003122412458672.

Adamczyk, Amy, Chunrye Kim, and Leevia Dillon. "Examining Public Opinion about Abortion: A Mixed-Methods Systematic Review of Research over the Last 15 Years." *Sociological Inquiry* 90, no. 4 (November 2020): 920–54. https://doi.org/10.1111/soin.12351.

Adamczyk, Amy, Chunrye Kim, and Lauren Paradis. "Investigating Differences in How the News Media Views Homosexuality Across Nations: An Analysis of the United States, South Africa, and Uganda." *Sociological Forum* 30, no. 4 (2015): 1038–58.

Adamczyk, Amy, Chunrye Kim, and Maggie Schmuhl. "Newspaper Presentations of Homosexuality: Comparing Muslim and Protestant Countries." *Sociological Perspectives* 61 (2018): 399–425.

Adamczyk, Amy, and Lindsay J. Lerner. "Synthesizing the Global English-Language Abortion Narrative: A Comparative Analysis of Media Discourse." *Sociological Inquiry*, April 22, 2024. https://doi.org/10.1111/soin.12607.

Adamczyk, Amy, and Yen-Chiao Liao. "Examining Public Opinion about LGBTQ-Related Issues in the United States and across Multiple Nations." *Annual Review of Sociology* 45, no. 1 (July 30, 2019). https://doi.org/10.1146/annurev-soc-073018-022332.

Adamczyk, Amy, and Ian Palmer. "Religion and Initiation into Marijuana Use: The Deterring Role of Religious Friends." *Journal of Drug Issues* 38, no. 3 (2008): 717–41.

Adamczyk, Amy, and Cassady Pitt. "Shaping Attitudes about Homosexuality: The Role of Religion and Cultural Context." *Social Science Research* 38, no. 2 (June 2009): 338–51. https://doi.org/10.1016/j.ssresearch.2009.01.002.

Adamczyk, Amy, Brittany Suh, and Lindsay Lerner. "Analysis of the Relationship between Religion, Abortion, and Assisted Reproductive Technology: Insights into Cross-National Public Opinion." *Social Science Research* 120, (May 2024). https://doi.org/10.1016/j.ssresearch.2024.103012.

Adamczyk, Amy, and Margrét Valdimarsdóttir. "Understanding Americans' Abortion Attitudes: The Role of the Local Religious Context." *Social Science Research* 71 (March 2018): 129–44. https://doi.org/10.1016/j.ssresearch.2017.12.005.

Adesomo, Adebayo. "Pregnancy Is Far More Dangerous than Abortion." Scientific American, May 30, 2022. https://www.scientificamerican.com/article/pregnancy-is-far-more-dangerous-to-women-than-abortion/.

Agadjanian, Victor. "Is 'Abortion Culture' Fading in the Former Soviet Union? Views about Abortion and Contraception in Kazakhstan." *Studies in Family Planning* 33, no. 3 (2002): 237–48. https://doi.org/10.1111/j.1728-4465.2002.00237.x.

Ahinkorah, Bright Opoku, Kwamena Sekyi Dickson, and Abdul-Aziz Seidu. "Women Decision-Making Capacity and Intimate Partner Violence among Women in Sub-Saharan Africa." *Archives of Public Health* 76, no. 1 (December 2018): 5. https://doi.org/10.1186/s13690-018-0253-9.

280 BIBLIOGRAPHY

Akers, Ronald L. *Social Learning and Social Structure: A General Theory of Crime and Deviance*. New Brunswick, NJ: Transaction Books, 2009.

Akyol, Pelin, and Çağla Ökten. "The Role of Religion in Female Labor Supply: Evidence from Two Muslim Denominations." *Journal of Demographic Economics*, February 2, 2022, 1–38. https://doi.org/10.1017/dem.2022.3.

Alam, Imam M., Shahina Amin, and Ken McCormick. "The Effect of Religion on Women's Labor Force Participation Rates in Indonesia." *Journal of the Asia Pacific Economy* 23, no. 1 (January 2, 2018): 31–50. https://doi.org/10.1080/13547860.2017.1351791.

Albanese, Patrizia. "Abortion & Reproductive Rights under Nationalist Regimes in Twentieth Century Europe," 2004. https://tspace.library.utoronto.ca/handle/1807/1055.

Albert, Eleanor. "Religion in China." Journalism. Council on Foreign Relations, June 10, 2015. http://www.cfr.org/china/religion-china/p16272.

Alexandre, Laurien, and Henrik Rehbinder. "Separate but Equal." *Columbia Journalism Review* 41, no.4, (December 2002): 99–101.

Ali, Moazzam, Rachel Folz, and Madeline Farron. "Expanding Choice and Access in Contraception: An Assessment of Intrauterine Contraception Policies in Low and Middle-Income Countries." *BMC Public Health* 19, no. 1 (December 2019): 1707. https://doi.org/10.1186/s12889-019-8080-7.

Almeling, Rene. "Reproduction." *Annual Review of Sociology* 41, no. 1 (August 14, 2015): 423–42. https://doi.org/10.1146/annurev-soc-073014-112258.

Amenta, Edwin, and Francesca Polletta. "The Cultural Impacts of Social Movements." *Annual Review of Sociology* 45, no. 1 (July 30, 2019): 279–99. https://doi.org/10.1146/annurev-soc-073018-022342.

Amnesty International. "Poland: Regression on Abortion Access Harms Women," January 26, 2022. https://www.amnesty.org/en/latest/news/2022/01/poland-regression-on-abortion-access-harms-women/.

Andersen, Robert, and Tina Fetner. "Economic Inequality and Intolerance: Attitudes toward Homosexuality in 35 Democracies." *American Journal of Political Science* 52, no. 4 (2008): 942–58.

Arceneaux, Kevin. "Direct Democracy and the Link between Public Opinion and State Abortion Policy." *State Politics & Policy Quarterly* 2, no. 4 (2002): 372–87.

ARDA. "Cross-National Socio-Economic and Religion Data." Association of Religious Data Archives, 2011. http://www.thearda.com/Archive/Files/Descriptions/ECON11.asp.

Ash, Alec. "China's New Youth: The Diverse Post-Tiananmen Generation Shaping the Country." The China Project, April 8, 2021. https://thechinaproject.com/2021/04/08/chinas-new-youth-the-diverse-post-tiananmen-generation-shaping-the-country/.

Associated Press. "China Cuts Uighur Births with IUDs, Abortion, Sterilization." AP NEWS, April 20, 2021. https://apnews.com/article/ap-top-news-international-news-weekend-reads-china-health-269b3de1af34e17c1941a514f78d764c.

Associated Press. "Uyghur Exiles Describe Forced Abortions, Torture in Xinjiang." AP NEWS, June 3, 2021. https://apnews.com/article/only-on-ap-middle-east-europe-government-and-politics-76acafd6547fb7cc9ef03c0dd0156eab.

Attwood, L. "The Post-Soviet Woman in the Move to the Market." In *Women in Russia and Ukraine*, by Rosalind Marsh, 255–66. Cambridge, England: Cambridge University, 1997.

Badanta, Barbara, María González-Cano-Caballero, Paola Suárez-Reina, Giancarlo Lucchetti, and Rocío de Diego-cordero. "How Does Confucianism Influence Health Behaviors, Health Outcomes and Medical Decisions? A Scoping Review." *Journal of Religion and Health* 61, no. 4 (August 1, 2022): 2679–725. https://doi.org/10.1007/s10943-022-01506-8.

Baker, Carrie N. "The History of Abortion Law in the United States." *Our Bodies Ourselves Today*, 2022. [accessed 4 March 2023]. https://www.ourbodiesourselves.org/health-info/u-s-abortion-history/.

Barker, Gina G. "Cultural Influences on the News Portrayals of the Iraq War by Swedish and American Media." *International Communication Gazette* 74, no. 1 (2012): 3–22.

Bartkowski, John P., Aida I. Ramos-Wada, Chris G. Ellison, and Gabriel A. Acevedo. "Faith, Race-Ethnicity, and Public Policy Preferences: Religious Schemas and Abortion Attitudes Among US Latinos." *Journal for the Scientific Study of Religion* 51, no. 2 (2012): 343–58.

Bartolomé-Peral, Edurne, and Lluis Coromina. "Attitudes towards Life and Death in Europe: A Comparative Analysis." *Czech Sociological Review* 56, no. 6 (February 15, 2021): 835–62. https://doi.org/10.13060/csr.2020.052.

BBC. "China Allows Three Children in Major Policy Shift." *BBC News*, May 31, 2021, sec. China. https://www.bbc.com/news/world-asia-china-57303592.

Bearak, Jonathan Marc, Leontine Alkema, Vladimíra Kantorová, and John Casterline. "Alignment between Desires and Outcomes among Women Wanting to Avoid Pregnancy: A Global Comparative Study of 'Conditional' Unintended Pregnancy Rates." *Studies in Family Planning* 54, no. 1 (March 2023): 265–80. https://doi.org/10.1111/sifp.12234.

Bearak, Jonathan Marc, Anna Popinchalk, Cynthia Beavin, Bela Ganatra, Ann-Beth Moller, Özge Tunçalp, and Leontine Alkema. "Country-Specific Estimates of Unintended Pregnancy and Abortion Incidence: A Global Comparative Analysis of Levels in 2015–2019." *BMJ Global Health* 7, no. 3 (March 1, 2022): e007151. https://doi.org/10.1136/bmjgh-2021-007151.

Bearak, Jonathan, Anna Popinchalk, Bela Ganatra, Ann-Beth Moller, Özge Tunçalp, Cynthia Beavin, Lorraine Kwok, and Leontine Alkema. "Unintended Pregnancy and Abortion by Income, Region, and the Legal Status of Abortion: Estimates from a Comprehensive Model for 1990–2019." *The Lancet Global Health* 8, no. 9 (September 2020): e1152–61. https://doi.org/10.1016/S2214-109X(20)30315-6.

Bearman, Peter S., and Hannah Brückner. "Promising the Future: Virginity Pledges and First Intercourse." *American Journal of Sociology* 106, no. 4 (January 2001): 859–912. https://doi.org/10.1086/320295.

Béland, Daniel, and André Lecours. *Nationalism and Social Policy: The Politics of Territorial Solidarity*. OUP Oxford, 2008.

282 BIBLIOGRAPHY

Bélanger, Danièle, and Andrea Flynn. "The Persistence of Induced Abortion in Cuba: Exploring the Notion of an 'Abortion Culture." *Studies in Family Planning* 40, no. 1 (2009): 13–26. https://doi.org/10.1111/j.1728-4465.2009.00183.x.

Bengtson, Vern L. *Families and Faith: How Religion Is Passed down across Generations.* Oxford University Press, 2013.

Benin, Mary Holland. "Determinants of Opposition to Abortion: An Analysis of the Hard and Soft Scales." *Sociological Perspectives* 28, no. 2 (1985): 199–216.

Berer, Marge. "Abortion Law and Policy Around the World." *Health and Human Rights* 19, no. 1 (June 2017): 13–27.

Bezati, Valbona. "How Albania Became the World's First Atheist Country." *Balkan Insight*, August 28, 2019. https://balkaninsight.com/2019/08/28/how-albania-became-the-worlds-first-atheist-country/.

Biggs, M. Antonia, Heather Gould, and Diana Greene Foster. "Understanding Why Women Seek Abortions in the US." *BMC Women's Health* 13, no. 1 (2013): 1.

Blumberg, Antonia. "What You Need To Know About The 'Quiverfull' Movement." Huff-Post, May 26, 2015. https://www.huffpost.com/entry/quiverfull-movement-facts_n_7444604.

Blumler, Jay G., and Stephen Coleman. "Democracy and the Media—Revisited." *Javnost-The Public* 22, no. 2 (April 2015): 111–28. https://doi.org/10.1080/13183222.2015.1041226.

Bobo, Lawrence, and Frederick C. Licari. "Education and Political Tolerance Testing the Effects of Cognitive Sophistication and Target Group Affect." *Public Opinion Quarterly* 53, no. 3 (1989): 285–308.

Bogner, Alexander, and Wolfgang Menz. "The Theory-Generating Expert Interview: Epistemological Interest, Forms of Knowledge, Interaction." In: Bogner, A., Littig, B., Menz, W. (eds) *Interviewing Experts. Research Methods Series.* (2009): 43–80. Palgrave Macmillan, London. https://doi.org/10.1057/9780230244276_3.

Bogner, A., Menz, W. (2009). The Theory-Generating Expert Interview: Epistemological Interest, Forms of Knowledge, Interaction. In: Bogner, A., Littig, B., Menz, W. (eds) *Interviewing Experts. Research Methods Series.* Palgrave Macmillan, London. https://doi.org/10.1057/9780230244276_3.

Bolzendahl, C. I., and D. J. Myers. "Feminist Attitudes and Support for Gender Equality: Opinion Change in Women and Men, 1974-1998." *Social Forces* 83, no. 2 (December 1, 2004): 759–89. https://doi.org/10.1353/sof.2005.0005.

Bond, Michael Harris. "Beyond the Chinese Face," 1991. http://dspace.lib.cuhk.edu.hk/handle/2006/32003.

Bonds-Raacke, Jennifer M., Elizabeth T. Cady, Rebecca Schlegel, Richard J. Harris, and Lindsey Firebaugh. "Remembering Gay/Lesbian Media Characters: Can Ellen and Will Improve Attitudes toward Homosexuals?" *Journal of Homosexuality* 53, no. 3 (2007): 19–34.

Bongaarts, John, and Christophe Z. Guilmoto. "How Many More Missing Women? Excess Female Mortality and Prenatal Sex Selection, 1970-2050." *Population and Development Review* 41, no. 2 (2015): 241–69. https://doi.org/10.1111/j.1728-4457.2015.00046.x.

Brenan, Megan. "Record-High 47% in U.S. Think Abortion Is Morally Acceptable." Gallup, June 9, 2021. https://news.gallup.com/poll/350756/record-high-think-abortion-morally-acceptable.aspx.

Breslow, Norman E., and David G. Clayton. "Approximate Inference in Generalized Linear Mixed Models" *Journal of the American Statistical Association*, 88, no. 421 (1993): 9–25.

Brookman-Amissah, Eunice, and Josephine Banda Moyo. "Abortion Law Reform in Sub-Saharan Africa: No Turning Back." *Reproductive Health Matters* 12, no. sup24 (January 2004): 227–34. https://doi.org/10.1016/S0968-8080(04)24026-5.

Brooks, Clem, and Jeff Manza. "Social Policy Responsiveness in Developed Democracies." *American Sociological Review* 71, no. 3 (June 1, 2006): 474–94. https://doi.org/10.1177/000312240607100306.

Brooks, Joel E. "Abortion Policy in Western Democracies: A Cross-National Analysis." *Governance* 5, no. 3 (July 1992): 342–57. https://doi.org/10.1111/j.1468-0491.1992.tb00 043.x.

Bruce A. Chadwick, and H. Dean Garrett. "Women's Religiosity and Employment: The LDS Experience." In ed. James T. Duke, *In Latter-Day Saint Social Life Social Research on the LDS Church and Its Members*, 401–24. Provo, UT: Religious Studies Center, Brigham Young University, 1998, 1998. https://rsc.byu.edu/latter-day-saint-social-life/womens-religiosity-employment.

Bueno, Xiana, Kathryn J. LaRoche, Brandon L. Crawford, Ronna C. Turner, Wen-Juo Lo, and Kristen N. Jozkowski. "Do Fetal Development Markers Influence Attitudes toward Abortion Legality?" *Social Currents* 10, no. 2 (April 2023): 107–20. https://doi.org/10.1177/23294965221137830.

Burkett, Steven R., and Mervin White. "Hellfire and Delinquency: Another Look." *Journal for the Scientific Study of Religion* 13, no. 4 (1974): 455–62.

Burnett, John. "Texas' Abortion Law Led Some to Get Abortion Pills in Mexico, with Grim Consequences." *NPR*, May 6, 2022, sec. Law. https://www.npr.org/2022/05/06/1097261242/texas-abortion-law-led-some-to-get-abortion-pills-in-mexico-with-grim-consequenc.

Burstein, Paul. "Bringing the Public Back in: Should Sociologists Consider the Impact of Public Opinion on Public Policy?" *Social Forces* 77, no. 1 (1998): 27–62.

Busemeyer, Marius R. "Policy Feedback and Government Responsiveness in a Comparative Perspective." *Politische Vierteljahresschrift* 63, no. 2 (June 1, 2022): 315–35. https://doi.org/10.1007/s11615-022-00377-8.

Buyuker, Beyza E., Kathryn J. LaRoche, Xiana Bueno, Kristen N. Jozkowski, Brandon L. Crawford, Ronna C. Turner, and Wen-Juo Lo. "A Mixed Methods Approach to Understanding the Disconnection between Perceptions of Abortion Acceptability and Support for *Roe v. Wade* Among US Adults." *Journal of Health Politics, Policy and Law*, January 23, 2023, 10449896. https://doi.org/10.1215/03616878-10449896.

Cameron, L, Z Dan-Dan, and Meng. "China's One-Child Policy: Effects on the Sex Ratio and Crime." Text. GlobalDev | Supported by GDN and AFD, September 10, 2018. http://globaldev.blog/blog/china%E2%80%99s-one-child-policy-effects-sex-ratio-and- crime.

Cao, Liqun, and Steven Stack. "Exploring Terra Incognita: Family Values and Prostitution Acceptance in China." *Journal of Criminal Justice* 38, no. 4 (2010): 531–37.

Carol, Sarah, and Nadja Milewski. "Attitudes toward Abortion among the Muslim Minority and Non-Muslim Majority in Cross-National Perspective: Can Religiosity Explain the Differences?" *Sociology of Religion* 78, no. 4 (January 8, 2018): 456–91. https://doi.org/10.1093/socrel/srx015.

Center for Reproductive Rights. "Abortion Laws by State." Center for Reproductive Rights, 2022. https://reproductiverights.org/maps/abortion-laws-by-state/.

Center for Reproductive Rights. "Kenya's Abortion Provisions." Accessed June 3, 2022. https://reproductiverights.org/maps/provision/kenyas-abortion-provisions/.

Center for Reproductive Rights. "The World's Abortion Laws," 2019. https://reproductiverights.org/worldabortionlaws.

Center for Reproductive Rights. "The World's Abortion Laws." Center for Reproductive Rights, 2023. https://reproductiverights.org/maps/worlds-abortion-laws/.

Center for Reproductive Rights. "The World's Abortion Laws." Center for Reproductive Rights, 2023. https://reproductiverights.org/maps/worlds-abortion-laws/.

Center for Reproductive Rights. "The World's Abortion Laws." Center for Reproductive Rights, 2024. https://reproductiverights.org/maps/worlds-abortion-laws/.

Center for Reproductive Rights. "The World's Abortion Laws." Center for Reproductive Rights, Accessed May 15, 2020. https://reproductiverights.org/worldabortionlaws.

Central Statistics Office. "Religious Change." CSO. Accessed April 4, 2022. https://www.cso.ie/en/releasesandpublications/ep/p-cp8iter/p8iter/p8rrc/.

Chae, Sophia, Sheila Desai, Marjorie Crowell, and Gilda Sedgh. "Reasons Why Women Have Induced Abortions: A Synthesis of Findings from 14 Countries." *Contraception* 96, no. 4 (October 1, 2017): 233–41. https://doi.org/10.1016/j.contraception.2017.06.014.

Chan, Cecilia L W, Paul S F Yip, Ernest H Y Ng, P C Ho, Celia H Y Chan, and Jade S K Au. "Gender Selection in China: Its Meanings and Implications." *Journal of Assisted Reproduction and Genetics* 19, no. 9 (2002): 5.

China Labour Bulletin. "China's Social Security System," August 18, 2021. https://clb.org.hk/node/15436.

Chong, Dennis. "How People Think, Reason, and Feel about Rights and Liberties." *American Journal of Political Science* 37, no. 3 (1993): 867–99.

Chorley, Susan. "I'm a Minister and a Mother—and I Had an Abortion." The Daily Beast, April 13, 2017. https://www.thedailybeast.com/im-a-minister-and-a-motherand-i-had-an-abortion.

Chzhen, Yekaterina, Anna Gromada, and Gwyther Rees. "Are the World's Richest Countries Family Friendly?" Policy in the OECD and EU, June 2019. https://www.unicef-irc.org/publications/pdf/Family-Friendly-Policies-Research_UNICEF_%202019.pdf.

Cipolla, Carlo M., ed. *Economic History of World Population.* 7th edition. Sussex, England: New York: Trophy Pr, 1978.

Citro et al. "Replacing Myths with Facts: Sex-Selective Abortion Laws in the United States." *SSRN Electronic Journal*, 2014. https://doi.org/10.2139/ssrn.2476432.

Clark, V. "English Proficiency in Europe 2019." Statista, 2019. https://www.statista.com/statistics/990547/countries-in-europe-for-english/.

Clements, Ben. "Religion and the Sources of Public Opposition to Abortion in Britain: The Role of 'Belonging', 'Behaving'and 'Believing'." *Sociology* 48, no. 2 (2014): 369–86.

CNA. "Pro-Life Advocates: Planned Parenthood Can't Simply Wish Away Margaret Sanger's Racism, Eugenics." Catholic News Agency, April 20, 2021. https://www.catholicnewsagency.com/news/247330/pro-life-advocates-planned-parenthood-cant-just-wish-away-margaret-sangers-racism-eugenics.

Cockrill, Kate, and Adina Nack. "'I'm Not That Type of Person': Managing the Stigma of Having an Abortion." *Deviant Behavior* 34, no. 12 (December 2013): 973–90. https://doi.org/10.1080/01639625.2013.800423.

Cockrill, Kate, Ushma D. Upadhyay, Janet Turan, and Diana Greene Foster. "The Stigma of Having an Abortion: Development of a Scale and Characteristics of Women Experiencing Abortion Stigma." *Perspectives on Sexual and Reproductive Health* 45, no. 2 (June 2013): 79–88. https://doi.org/10.1363/4507913.

Coleman, James S. "Social Theory, Social Research, and a Theory of Action." *American Journal of Sociology* 91, no. 6 (1986): 1309–35.

Collins, Randall. "On the Microfoundations of Macrosociology." *American Journal of Sociology* 86, no. 5 (1981): 984–1014.

Cong, Jimei, Pingping Li, Liqiang Zheng, and Jichun Tan. "Prevalence and Risk Factors of Infertility at a Rural Site of Northern China." *PLOS ONE* 11, no. 5 (May 13, 2016): e0155563. https://doi.org/10.1371/journal.pone.0155563.

Cooper, Ann. "Women Fault Soviet System For Abortion". *New York Times*, February 28, 1989, sec.A, p.3. https://www.nytimes.com/1989/02/28/world/women-fault-soviet-system-for-abortion.html.

Coyne, Imelda T. "Sampling in Qualitative Research. Purposeful and Theoretical Sampling; Merging or Clear Boundaries?" *Journal of Advanced Nursing* 26, no. 3 (1997): 623–30.

Crawford, Brandon L., Kristen N. Jozkowski, Lucrecia Mena-Meléndez, and Ronna C. Turner. "An Exploratory Examination of Attitudes toward Illegal Abortion in the U.S. through Endorsement of Various Punishments." *Contraception*, January 2023, 109952. https://doi.org/10.1016/j.contraception.2023.109952.

Crawford, Brandon L., Kristen N. Jozkowski, Ronna C. Turner, and Wen-Juo Lo. "Examining the Relationship Between Roe v. Wade Knowledge and Sentiment across Political Party and Abortion Identity." *Sexuality Research and Social Policy* 19, no. 3 (September 2022): 837–48. https://doi.org/10.1007/s13178-021-00597-4.

Crawford, Brandon L., Kathryn J. LaRoche, and Kristen N. Jozkowski. "Examining Abortion Attitudes in the Context of Gestational Age." *Social Science Quarterly* 103, no. 4 (2022): 855–67. https://doi.org/10.1111/ssqu.13157.

Creswell, John. *Research Design: Qualitative, Quantitative and Mixed Methods Approaches*. USA: SAGE Publications, 2004.

Creswell, John W., Vicki L. Plano Clark, Michelle L. Gutmann, and William E. Hanson. In Ed. Abbas Tashakkori and Charles Teddlie. *Sage Handbook of Mixed Methods in Social and Behavioral Research*. SAGE Publications Inc. 2003: 209–40.

Crotti, Robert, Kali Pal Kusum, Vesselina Ratcheva, and Saadia Zahidi. "Global Gender Gap Report." Geneva, Switzerland: World Economic Forum, March 15, 2021. https://www.weforum.org/reports/global-gender-gap-report-2021/.

D, D. "The Limit of Viability." *The Economist*, May 2015. https://www.economist.com/the-economist-explains/2015/05/19/the-limit-of-viability.

Dadlez, E. M., and William L. Andrews. "Post-Abortion Syndrome: Creating an Affliction." *Bioethics* 24, no. 9 (November 2010): 445–52. https://doi.org/10.1111/j.1467-8519.2009.01739.x.

Dalton, Russell J., and Nhu-Ngoc T. Ong. "Authority Orientations and Democratic Attitudes: A Test of the 'Asian Values' Hypothesis." *Japanese Journal of Political Science* 6, no. 2 (2005): 211–31.

Damian, Constantin-Iulian. "Abortion from the Perspective of Eastern Religions: Hinduism and Buddhism." *Romanian Journal of Bioethics* 8, no. 1 (2010): 124–36.

D'Antonio, William V. *American Catholics Today: New Realities of Their Faith and Their Church*. Rowman & Littlefield, 2007.

D'Antonio, William V. "The American Catholic Family: Signs of Cohesion and Polarization." *Journal of Marriage and the Family* 47, no. 2 (1985): 395–405.

Das Gupta, Monica, Jiang Zhenghua, Li Bohua, Xie Zhenming, Woojin Chung, and Bae Hwa-Ok. "Why Is Son Preference so Persistent in East and South Asia? A Cross-Country Study of China, India and the Republic of Korea." *The Journal of Development Studies* 40, no. 2 (December 1, 2003): 153–87. https://doi.org/10.1080/00220380412331293807.

DaVanzo, Julie, and Clifford Grammich. *Dire Demographics: Population Trends in the Russian Federation*. RAND Corporation, 2001. https://doi.org/10.7249/MR1273.

Davis, Julie Hirschfeld, and Katie Rogers. "At Trump Rallies, Women See a Hero Protecting a Way of Life." *The New York Times*, November 3, 2018, sec. U.S. https://www.nytimes.com/2018/11/03/us/politics/trump-women.html.

De Graaf, Nan Dirk, Paul Nieuwbeerta, and Anthony Heath. "Class Mobility and Political Preferences: Individual and Contextual Effects." *American Journal of Sociology* 100, no. 4 (1995): 997–1027.

De Guzman, Chad. "Why China Needs to Learn to Live with Its Low Fertility Rate." Time, August 18, 2023. https://time.com/6306151/china-low-fertility-trap-birth-rate-policies/.

Dehlendorf, Christine, Maria Isabel Rodriguez, Kira Levy, Sonya Borrero, and Jody Steinauer. "Disparities in Family Planning." *American Journal of Obstetrics and Gynecology* 202, no. 3 (March 1, 2010): 214–20. https://doi.org/10.1016/j.ajog.2009.08.022.

Delaney, Nora. "Roe v. Wade Has Been Overturned. What Does That Mean for America?," June 28, 2022. https://www.hks.harvard.edu/faculty-research/policy-topics/fairness-justice/roe-v-wade-has-been-overturned-what-does-mean.

Denisov, Boris P., Victoria I. Sakevich, and Aiva Jasilioniene. "Divergent Trends in Abortion and Birth Control Practices in Belarus, Russia and Ukraine." Edited by Hamid Reza Baradaran. *PLoS ONE* 7, no. 11 (November 30, 2012): e49986. https://doi.org/10.1371/journal.pone.0049986.

Dewan, Shaila. "Anti-Abortion Ads Split Atlanta." *New York Times*, February 6, 2010, sec. U.S. https://www.nytimes.com/2010/02/06/us/06abortion.html.

Diamant, Jeff. "Half of U.S. Christians Say Casual Sex between Consenting Adults Is Sometimes or Always Acceptable." *Pew Research Center*, August 31, 2020. https://www.pewresearch.org/fact-tank/2020/08/31/half-of-u-s-christians-say-casual-sex-between-consenting-adults-is-sometimes-or-always-acceptable/.

Diamant, Jeff, and Besheer Mohamed. "What the Data Says about Abortion in the U.S." *Pew Research Center*, January 11, 2023. https://www.pewresearch.org/fact-tank/2023/01/11/what-the-data-says-about-abortion-in-the-u-s-2/.

Durkheim, Emile. *Suicide: A Study in Sociology*. Translated by J.A. Spaulding and G. Simpson. Glencoe, IL: Free Press, 1951. Originally published in 1897.

Durkheim, Emile. *The Division of Labor in Society*. New York: Simon and Schuster, 2014.

Durkheim, Emile. *The Elementary Forms of Religious Life*. New York: NY; The Free Press, [1912] 1995.

Durkheim, Emile, and G. Simpson. *Suicide: A Study in Sociology*. Translated by J.A. Spaulding. Glencoe, IL: Free Press, 1897.

Edelstein, Alex S. *Comparative Communication Research*. Beverly Hills, CA: Sage Publications, 1982.

educationfair.nl. "Study Abroad Market Report on China." *Educationfair.Nl*. Accessed March 3, 2023. https://www.educationfair.nl/market-reports/asia/china/.

Ellison, Christopher G., Samuel Echevarria, and Brad Smith. "Religion and Abortion Attitudes among US Hispanics: Findings from the 1990 Latino National Political Survey." *Social Science Quarterly* 86, no. 1 (2005): 192–208.

Evans, Jonathan, Kelsey Jo Starr, Manolo Corichi, and William Miner. "Buddhism, Islam and Religious Pluralism in South and Southeast Asia." *Pew Research Center*, September 12, 2023. https://www.pewresearch.org/religion/2023/09/12/religious-beliefs-3/.

Farr, Grant. "Female Education in Afghanistan after the Return of the Taliban." *E-International Relations*, April 23, 2022. https://www.e-ir.info/2022/04/23/female-education-in-afghanistan-after-the-return-of-the-taliban/.

Feng, Wang, Baochang Gu, and Yong Cai. "The End of China's One-Child Policy." *Studies in Family Planning* 47, no. 1 (2016): 83–86. https://doi.org/10.1111/j.1728-4465.2016.00052.x.

Fernández, Juan J., and Antonio M. Jaime-Castillo. "Positive or Negative Policy Feedbacks? Explaining Popular Attitudes towards Pragmatic Pension Policy Reforms." *European Sociological Review* 29, no. 4 (August 1, 2013): 803–15. https://doi.org/10.1093/esr/jcs059.

Fernández, Juan J., and Dácil Juif. "Does Abortion Liberalisation Accelerate Fertility Decline? A Worldwide Time-Series Analysis." *European Journal of Population* 39, no. 1 (December 5, 2023): 36. https://doi.org/10.1007/s10680-023-09687-y.

Fernández, Juan J., Celia Valiente, and Antonio M. Jaime-Castillo. "Gender Balance in the Workforce and Abortion Attitudes: A Cross-National Time-Series Analysis." *The British Journal of Sociology*, 2023, 1–23. https://doi.org/10.1111/1468-4446.13044.

288 BIBLIOGRAPHY

Ferrant, Gaëlle, Luca Maria Pesando, and Keiko Nowacka. "Unpaid Care Work: The Missing Link in the Analysis of Gender Gaps in Labour Outcomes." OECD Development Centre, 2014. https://www.oecd.org/dev/development-gender/Unpaid_care_work.pdf.

Ferris-Rotman, Amie. "Putin's Next Target Is Russia's Abortion Culture." *Foreign Policy*. Accessed July 29, 2022. https://foreignpolicy.com/2017/10/03/putins-next-target-is-russias-abortion-culture/.

Fidan, Ahmet, Rezzan Alagoz, and Nuray Karaman. "Liberal Sexual Morality, Religion, and Attitudes toward Abortion in Turkey." *Journal for the Scientific Study of Religion* 60, no. 4 (2021): 914–33. https://doi.org/10.1111/jssr.12755.

Finer, Lawrence B., Lori F. Frohwirth, Lindsay A. Dauphinee, Susheela Singh, and Ann M. Moore. "Reasons U.S. Women Have Abortions: Quantitative and Qualitative Perspectives." *Perspectives on Sexual and Reproductive Health* 37, no. 3 (September 2005): 110–18. https://doi.org/10.1363/psrh.37.110.05.

Finke, Roger, and Amy Adamczyk. "Cross-National Moral Beliefs: The Influence of National Religious Context." *Sociological Quarterly* 49, no. 4 (2008): 617–52. https://doi.org/10.1111/j.1533-8525.2008.00130.x.

Flordia, R. E. "Buddhist Approaches to Abortion." *Asian Philosophy* 1, no. 1 (1991): 39–50.

Fong, Mai. "How China's One-Child Policy Led To Forced Abortions, 30 Million Bachelors." *NPR*, February 1, 2016, sec. World. https://www.npr.org/2016/02/01/465124337/how-chinas-one-child-policy-led-to-forced-abortions-30-million- bachelors.

Fong, Mei. *One Child: The Story of China's Most Radical Experiment by Mei Fong; China's Hidden Children: Abandonment, Adoption and the Human Costs of the One-Child Experiment.* Houghton Mifflin Harcourt, 2016. https://dialnet.unirioja.es/servlet/articulo?codigo=5534865.

Forman-Rabinovici, Aliza, and Udi Sommer. "An Impediment to Gender Equality?: Religion's Influence on Development and Reproductive Policy." *World Development* 105 (May 2018): 48–58. https://doi.org/10.1016/j.worlddev.2017.12.024.

Freedom House. "Countries and Territories Global Freedom Index." Freedom House, 2022. https://freedomhouse.org/countries/freedom-world/scores.

Frohwirth, Lori, Michele Coleman, and Ann M. Moore. "Managing Religion and Morality within the Abortion Experience: Qualitative Interviews with Women Obtaining Abortions in the U.S." *World Medical & Health Policy* 10, no. 4 (December 2018): 381–400. https://doi.org/10.1002/wmh3.289.

Gahungu, Jumaine, Mariam Vahdaninia, and Pramod R. Regmi. "The Unmet Needs for Modern Family Planning Methods among Postpartum Women in Sub-Saharan Africa: A Systematic Review of the Literature." *Reproductive Health* 18, no. 1 (December 2021): 35. https://doi.org/10.1186/s12978-021-01089-9.

Gallup Inc. "Abortion." Gallup.com, 2022. https://news.gallup.com/poll/1576/Abortion.aspx.

BIBLIOGRAPHY   289

Gallup Inc. "Gallup First Polled on Gay Issues in '77. What Has Changed?" Gallup.com, June 6, 2019. https://news.gallup.com/poll/258065/gallup-first-polled-gay-issues-changed. aspx.

Gammeltoft, Tine. *Women's Bodies, Wommen's Worries: Health and Family Planning in a Vietnamese Rural Community.* Vietnam in Transition Series. Richmond, Surrey [England]: Curzon Press, 1999.

Gao, Ersheng, Xiayun Zuo, Li Wang, Chaohua Lou, Yan Cheng, and Laurie S. Zabin. "How Does Traditional Confucian Culture Influence Adolescents' Sexual Behavior in Three Asian Cities?" *Journal of Adolescent Health* 50, no. 3 (2012): S12–17.

Gay, David, and John Lynxwiler. "The Impact of Religiosity on Race Variations in Abortion Attitudes." *Sociological Spectrum* 19, no. 3 (1999): 359–77.

"GDP—per Capita (PPP)—Country Comparison," 2022. https://www.indexmundi. com/g/r.aspx?c=tw&v=67.

Gietel-Basten, Stuart, Xuehui Han, and Yuan Cheng. "Assessing the Impact of the 'One-Child Policy' in China: A Synthetic Control Approach." *PLOS ONE* 14, no. 11 (November 6, 2019): e0220170. https://doi.org/10.1371/journal.pone.0220170.

Glendon, Mary Ann. *Abortion and Divorce in Western Law.* Harvard University Press, 1987.

Glick, Peter, Jeffrey Diebold, Barbara Bailey-werner, and Zhu Lin. "The Two Faces of Adam: Ambivalent Sexism and Polarized Attitudes Toward Women." *Personality and Social Psychology Bulletin* 23 (December 1, 1997): 1323–34. https://doi.org/10.1177/01461672972312009.

"Global Agricultural Productivity Report: China's Agricultural Productivity Imperative," October 1, 2018. https://globalagriculturalproductivity.org/sustainable-food-and-agriculture-systems-are-built-on-productivity/regional-productivity-growth-progress-and-challenges/china/.

Goffman, Erving. *Stigma: Notes on the Management of Spoiled Identity.* Simon and Schuster, 2009.

Goldberg, Justin. "Open Secret: The Toll of Unsafe Abortion in Tanzania." Center for Reproductive Rights, November 3, 2020. https://reproductiverights.org/open-secret-the-toll-of-unsafe-abortion-in-tanzania-2/.

Goldin, Claudia. "Female Labor Force Participation: The Origin of Black and White Differences, 1870 and 1880." *The Journal of Economic History* 37, no. 1 (1977): 87–108.

Green, Donald P., Bradley Palmquist, and Eric Schickler. *Partisan Hearts and Minds: Political Parties and the Social Identities of Voters.* Yale University Press. 2004.

Greenwood, Shannon. "Worldwide Optimism about Future of Gender Equality, Even as Many See Advantages for Men." *Pew Research Center's Global Attitudes Project,* April 30, 2020. https://www.pewresearch.org/global/2020/04/30/worldwide-optimism-about-future-of-gender-equality-even-as-many-see-advantages-for-men/.

Griffith, R. Marie. *Moral Combat: How Sex Divided American Christians and Fractured American Politics.* Illustrated edition. New York: Basic Books, 2017.

Gromada, Anna, and Dominic Richardson. "Where Do Rich Countries Stand on Child-care?" Florence, Italy: UNICEF Office of Research, 2021. https://www.unicef-irc.org/publications/pdf/where-do-rich-countries-stand-on-childcare.pdf.

290 BIBLIOGRAPHY

GSS Data Explorer. "GSS Data Explorer | NORC at the University of Chicago," 2022. https://gssdataexplorer.norc.org/trends?category=Current%20Affairs&measure=abany.

Gu, Chien-Juh. "Bargaining with Confucian Patriarchy: Money, Culture, and Gender Division of Labor in Taiwanese Immigrant Families." *Qualitative Sociology* 42, no. 4 (December 1, 2019): 687–709. https://doi.org/10.1007/s11133-019-09427-x.

Guérin, Daniel, Francois Petry, and Jean Crête. "Tolerance, Protest and Democratic Transition: Survey Evidence from 13 Post-Communist Countries." *European Journal of Political Research* 43, no. 3 (2004): 371–95.

Guilmoto, Christophe. *Sex Imbalances at Birth in Armenia: Demographic Evidence and Analysis.* Yerevan, Armenia: UNFPA, 2013. https://eeca.unfpa.org/en/publications/sex-imbalances-birth-armenia.

Gupta, Medhavi, Vikash Ranjan Keshri, Pompy Konwar, Katherine L Cox, and Jagnoor And Jagnoor. "Media Coverage of COVID-19 Health Information in India: A Content Analysis." *Health Promotion International* 37, no. 2 (April 29, 2022): daab116. https://doi.org/10.1093/heapro/daab116.

Guth, Madeline, and Samantha Artigua. "Medicaid and Racial Health Equity." *KFF*, March 17, 2022. https://www.kff.org/medicaid/issue-brief/medicaid-and-racial-health-equity/.

Guttmacher Institute. "13 States Have Abortion Trigger Bans—Here's What Happens When Roe Is Overturned," June 6, 2022. https://doi.org/10.1363/2022.33571.

Guttmacher Institute. "Abortion Bans in Cases of Sex or Race Selection or Genetic Anomaly," January 1, 2023. https://www.guttmacher.org/state-policy/explore/abortion-bans-cases-sex-or-race-selection-or-genetic-anomaly.

Guttmacher Institute. "Abortion Is a Common Experience for U.S. Women, Despite Dramatic Declines in Rates." Guttmacher Institute, October 18, 2017. https://www.guttmacher.org/news-release/2017/abortion-common-experience-us-women-despite-dramatic-declines-rates.

Guttmacher Institute. "An Overview of Abortion Laws." New York, NY: Guttmacher Institute, October 1, 2019. https://www.guttmacher.org/print/state-policy/explore/overview-abortion-laws?gclid=CjwKCAjwusrtBRBmEiwAGBPgEwVEcfxn9cfP1kv7EltxldYmAs5gBUFIKfd6CwUR447pAaPpElvX6xoCbnAQAvD_BwE.

Guttmacher Institute. "Six Months Post-Roe, 24 US States Have Banned Abortion or Are Likely to Do So: A Roundup," January 9, 2023. https://doi.org/10.1363/2023.300254.

Hackett, Conrad. "Is China a Religious Country or Not? It's a Tricky Question to Answer." *Pew Research Center*, August 30, 2023. https://www.pewresearch.org/short-reads/2023/08/30/is-china-a-religious-country-or-not-its-a-tricky-question-to-answer/.

Hadaway, C. Kirk, Kirk W. Elifson, and David M. Petersen. "Religious Involvement and Drug Use among Urban Adolescents." *Journal for the Scientific Study of Religion* 23, no. 2 (1984): 109–28.

Haddock, Geoffrey, and Mark P. Zanna. "Authoritarianism, Values, and the Favorability and Structure of Antigay Attitudes.," 1998. http://psycnet.apa.org.ez.lib.jjay.cuny.edu/psycinfo/1998-07094-005.

BIBLIOGRAPHY 291

Hadler, Markus. "The Influence of World Societal Forces on Social Tolerance. A Time Comparative Study of Prejudices in 32 Countries." *The Sociological Quarterly* 53, no. 2 (2012): 211–37.

Halfmann, Drew. *Doctors and Demonstrators: How Political Institutions Shape Abortion Law in the United States, Britain, and Canada.* Chicago: University of Chicago Press, 2011.

Halman, Loek, and Erik van Ingen. "Secularization and Changing Moral Views: European Trends in Church Attendance and Views on Homosexuality, Divorce, Abortion, and Euthanasia." *European Sociological Review* 31, no. 5 (October 1, 2015): 616–27. https://doi.org/10.1093/esr/jcv064.

Hans, Jason D., and Claire Kimberly. "Abortion Attitudes in Context: A Multidimensional Vignette Approach." *Social Science Research* 48 (November 2014): 145–56. https://doi.org/10.1016/j.ssresearch.2014.06.001.

Hanschmidt, Franz, Katja Linde, Anja Hilbert, Steffi G. Riedel- Heller, and Anette Kersting. "Abortion Stigma: A Systematic Review." *Perspectives on Sexual and Reproductive Health* 48, no. 4 (December 2016): 169–77. https://doi.org/10.1363/48e8516.

Hartig, Hannah. "About Six-in-Ten Americans Say Abortion Should Be Legal in All or Most Cases." *Pew Research Center*, June 2022. https://www.pewresearch.org/fact-tank/2022/06/13/about-six-in-ten-americans-say-abortion-should-be-legal-in-all-or-most-cases-2/.

Haubert, Jeannie, and Elizabeth Fussell. "Explaining Pro-Immigrant Sentiment in the U.S.: Social Class, Cosmopolitanism, and Perceptions of Immigrants." *International Migration Review* 40, no. 3 (September 1, 2006): 489–507. https://doi.org/10.1111/j.1747-7379.2006.00033.x.

Hazelrigg, Lawrence. "The Problem of Micro-Macro Linkage: Rethinking Questions of the Individual, Social Structure, and Autonomy of Action." *Current Perspectives in Social Theory* 11 (1991): 229–54.

Heinen, Jacqueline, and Stéphane Portet. "Reproductive Rights in Poland: When Politicians Fear the Wrath of the Church." *Third World Quarterly* 31, no. 6 (2010): 1007–21.

Hesketh, T., L. Lu, and Z. W. Xing. "The Consequences of Son Preference and Sex-Selective Abortion in China and Other Asian Countries." *Canadian Medical Association Journal* 183, no. 12 (September 6, 2011): 1374–77. https://doi.org/10.1503/cmaj.101368.

Hildebrandt, Achim. "What Shapes Abortion Law?—A Global Perspective." *Global Policy* 6, no. 4 (2015): 418–28. https://doi.org/10.1111/1758-5899.12208.

Hill, Layola, Nambi Ndugga, and Samantha Artiga. "Key Data on Health and Health Care by Race and Ethnicity." *KFF*, March 15, 2023. https://www.kff.org/racial-equity-and-health-policy/report/key-data-on-health-and-health-care-by-race-and-ethnicity/.

Hill, Michael. "'Asian Values' as Reverse Orientalism: Singapore." *Asia Pacific Viewpoint* 41, no. 2 (2000): 177–90.

Hirschi, Travis. *Causes of Delinquency.* Piscataway, New Jersey: Transaction Publishers, 2002.

Hofstede, Geert, and Michael H. Bond. "Confucius and Economic Growth: New Trends in Culture's Consequences." *Organizational Dynamics* 16, no. 4 (1988): 4–21.

292 BIBLIOGRAPHY

Hofstede, Geert H. *Culture's Consequences: Comparing Values, Behaviors, Institutions and Organizations across Nations*. Thousand Oaks, CA: Sage Publications, 2001.

Holpuch, Amanda. "Trump Re-Ups Controversial Muslim Ban and Mexico Wall in First Campaign Ad." *The Guardian*, January 4, 2016, sec. US news. https://www.theguardian.com/us-news/2016/jan/04/donald-trump-great-again-first-campaign-ad-isis-mexico-wall-muslim-ban.

Hongladarom, Soraj. "Buddhism and Abortion." In *Abortion: Global Positions and Practices, Religious and Legal Perspectives*, edited by Alireza Bagheri, 179–89. Cham: Springer International Publishing, 2021. https://doi.org/10.1007/978-3-030-63023-2_15.

Hsu, Francis LK. *Americans and Chinese: Passages to Differences*. Honolulu: University of Hawaii Press, 1981.

Huang, Dan. "Infertility Anxiety, Middle Class Illusion and Reproductive Governmentality: Experience of Unmarried Rural-Urban Migrant Women Who Induced Abortion in Mainland China." ProQuest Dissertations & Theses Global, July 1, 2018. https://www.proquest.com/dissertations-theses/infertility-anxiety-middle-class-illusion/docview/2138730122/se-2.

Huang, Yanshu, Paul G. Davies, Chris G. Sibley, and Danny Osborne. "Benevolent Sexism, Attitudes toward Motherhood, and Reproductive Rights: A Multi-Study Longitudinal Examination of Abortion Attitudes." *Personality and Social Psychology Bulletin* 42, no. 7 (July 1, 2016): 970–84. https://doi.org/10.1177/0146167216649607.

Hui, Zhang. "S.China's Guangdong No Longer Uses Birth Registration to Restrict Births; Moves Closer to 'Scraping All Restrictions.'" Global Times, May 6, 2022. https://www.globaltimes.cn/page/202205/1264957.shtml.

Human Development Reports. "Gender Inequality Index." *Human Development Reports*. United Nations, 2023. https://hdr.undp.org/data-center/thematic-composite-indices/gender-inequality-index.

Human Rights Watch. "Women's Human Rights: Abortion in Brazil." Accessed October 6, 2022. https://www.hrw.org/legacy/women/abortion/brazil.html.

Human Rights Watch. "Poland: Abortion Witch Hunt Targets Women, Doctors," September 14, 2023. https://www.hrw.org/news/2023/09/14/poland-abortion-witch-hunt-targets-women-doctors.

Human Rights Watch. "Poland's Constitutional Tribunal Rolls Back Reproductive Rights," October 22, 2020. https://www.hrw.org/news/2020/10/22/polands-constitutional-tribunal-rolls-back-reproductive-rights.

Human Rights Watch. "Religious Repression in China." Accessed October 3, 2023. https://www.hrw.org/legacy/campaigns/china-98/religion.htm.

Icenhower, Alexandria. "What China's Sexual Revolution Means for Women." *Brookings*, April 9, 2015. https://www.brookings.edu/blog/brookings-now/2015/04/09/what-chinas-sexual-revolution-means-for-women/.

Index Mundi. 2015. "GDP - per Capita (PPP) - Country Comparison." *Index Mundi*. Retrieved September 15, 2015 (http://www.indexmundi.com/g/r.aspx?c=tw&v=67).

Inglehart, Ronald. *Culture Shift in Advanced Industrial Society*. Princeton, NJ: Princeton University Press, 1990.

BIBLIOGRAPHY   293

Inglehart, Ronald. "Mapping Global Values." *Comparative Sociology* 5, no. 2 (2006): 115–36.

Inglehart, Ronald. *Modernization and Postmodernization: Cultural, Economic, and Political Change in 43 Societies*. Vol. 19. Cambridge, UK: Cambridge University Press, 1997. http://journals.cambridge.org.ez.lib.jjay.cuny.edu/production/action/cjo GetFulltext?fulltextid=6296904.

Inglehart, Ronald, and Wayne E. Baker. "Modernization, Cultural Change, and the Persistence of Traditional Values." *American Sociological Review* 65, no. 1 (2000): 19–51.

Inglehart, Ronald, Pippa Norris, and Christian Welzel. "Gender Equality and Democracy." *Comparative Sociology* 1, no. 3 (2002): 321–45.

Inglehart, Ronald, and Daphna Oyserman. "Individualism, Autonomy, Self-Expression. The Human Development Syndrome." *International Studies in Sociology and Social Anthropology* 93 (2004): 74–96.

Inkeles, Alex. "Industrialization, Modernization and the Quality of Life." *International Journal of Comparative Sociology* 34, no. 1 (January 1, 1993): 1–23.

Jackman, Mary R., and Michael J. Muha. "Education and Intergroup Attitudes: Moral Enlightenment, Superficial Democratic Commitment, or Ideological Refinement?" *American Sociological Review* 49, no. 6 (1984): 751–69.

Jackson, Jesse. "How We Respect Life Is the Over-Riding Moral Issue." *Right to Life*, January 1977.

Jargin, ed. "High Abortion Rate in Russia: On the Role of Condom Use and Alcohol Misuse." *Journal of Addiction and Preventive Medicine* 2, no. 1 (June 11, 2019): 01–04. https://doi.org/10.31579/2688-7517/003.

Jelen, Ted G. "Respect for Life, Sexual Morality, and Opposition to Abortion." *Review of Religious Research* 25, no. 3 (March 1984): 220–31. https://doi.org/10.2307/3511120.

Jelen, Ted G. "The Subjective Bases of Abortion Attitudes: A Cross National Comparison of Religious Traditions." *Politics and Religion* 7, no. 03 (September 2014): 550–67. https://doi.org/10.1017/S1755048314000467.

Jelen, Ted G. "The Subjective Bases of Abortion Attitudes: A Cross National Comparison of Religious Traditions." *Politics and Religion* 7, no. 03 (September 2014): 550–67. https://doi.org/10.1017/S1755048314000467.

Jelen, Ted G., and Jonathan Doc Bradley. "Abortion Opinion in Emerging Democracies: Latin America and Central Europe." *Politics, Groups, and Identities* 2, no. 1 (January 2, 2014): 52–65. https://doi.org/10.1080/21565503.2013.876916.

Jelen, Ted G., and Jonathan Doc Bradley. "Abortion Opinion in Emerging Democracies: Latin America and Central Europe." *Politics, Groups, and Identities* 2, no. 1 (January 2, 2014): 52–65. https://doi.org/10.1080/21565503.2013.876916.

Jelen, Ted G., John O'Donnell, and Clyde Wilcox. "A Contextual Analysis of Catholicism and Abortion Attitudes in Western Europe." *Sociology of Religion* 54, no. 4 (1993): 375. https://doi.org/10.2307/3711780.

Jelen, Ted G., and Clyde Wilcox. "Causes and Consequences of Public Attitudes toward Abortion: A Review and Research Agenda." *Political Research Quarterly* 56, no. 4 (2003): 489–500.

BIBLIOGRAPHY

Jelen, Ted G., and Clyde Wilcox. "Continuity and Change in Attitudes toward Abortion: Poland and the United States." *Politics & Gender* 1, no. 02 (June 2005): 297–317. https://doi.org/10.1017/S1743923X05050099.

Jerman, Jenna, Lori F. Frohwirth, Megan L. Kavanaugh, and Nakeisha Blades. "Barriers to Abortion Care and Their Consequences for Patients Traveling for Services: Qualitative Findings from Two States." *Perspectives on Sexual and Reproductive Health* 49 (April 11, 2017): 95–102. https://doi.org/10.1363/2017.28266.

Jerman, Jenna, Rachel K. Jones, and Tsuyoshi Onda. "Characteristics of US Abortion Patients in 2014 and Changes since 2008." *New York: Guttmacher Institute*, May 10, 2016. https://www.guttmacher.org/report/characteristics-us-abortion-patients-2014.

Jiang, Min. "Authoritarian Informationalism: China's Approach to Internet Sovereignty." *SAIS Review of International Affairs* 30, no. 2 (2010): 71–89.

Jilozian, Ann, and Victor Agadjanian. "Is Induced Abortion Really Declining in Armenia?" *Studies in Family Planning* 47, no. 2 (2016): 163–78. https://doi.org/10.1111/j.1728-4465.2016.00053.x.

Johnson, Amber, and Kesha Morant Williams. "'The Most Dangerous Place for an African American Is in the Womb': Reproductive Health Disparities." *Journal of Contemporary Rhetoric* 5 (2015): 145–59.

Jones, Bradley. "An Examination of the 2016 Electorate, Based on Validated Voters." *Pew Research Center—U.S. Politics & Policy*, August 9, 2018. https://www.pewresearch.org/politics/2018/08/09/an-examination-of-the-2016-electorate-based-on-validated-voters/.

Jones, Jeffrey M. "U.S. Church Membership Falls Below Majority for First Time." Gallup.com, March 29, 2021. https://news.gallup.com/poll/341963/church-membership-falls-below-majority-first-time.aspx.

Jones, Rachel K., Lawrence B. Finer, and Susheela Singh. "Characteristics of US Abortion Patients, 2008." *New York: Guttmacher Institute*, 2010, 20101–08.

Jones, Rachel, Elizabeth Nash, Lauren Cross, Jesse Philbin, and Marielle Kirstein. "*Medication Abortion Now Accounts for More than Half of All US Abortions.*" Guttmacher Institute, February 22, 2022. https://www.guttmacher.org/article/2022/02/medication-abortion-now-accounts-more-half-all-us-abortions.

Jozkowski, Kristen N., Brandon L. Crawford, and Mary E. Hunt. "Complexity in Attitudes Toward Abortion Access: Results from Two Studies." *Sexuality Research and Social Policy* 15, no. 4 (December 1, 2018): 464–82. https://doi.org/10.1007/s13178-018-0322-4.

Jung, Kim Dae. "Is Culture Destiny? The Myth of Asia's Anti-Democratic Values." *Foreign Affairs*, 1994.

Kann, Sharon, and Julie Tulbert. "Right-Wing Media Are Filling a Void of Abortion-Related Coverage with Misinformation." *Mediamatters for America*, May 21, 2018. https://www.mediamatters.org/tucker-carlson/right-wing-media-are-filling-void-abortion-related-coverage-misinformation.

Karpov, Vyacheslav, and Kimmo Kääriäinen. "'Abortion Culture' in Russia: Its Origins, Scope, and Challenge to Social Development." *Journal of Applied Sociology* 22, no. 2 (2005): 13–33.

Kaufman, Joan. "The Global Women's Movement and Chinese Women's Rights." *Journal of Contemporary China* 21, no. 76 (July 2012): 585–602. https://doi.org/10.1080/10670564.2012.666830.

Kaur, Ravinder. "Mapping the Adverse Consequences of Sex Selection and Gender Imbalance in India and China." *Economic and Political Weekly* 48, no. 35 (2013): 37–44.

Kelly, Kimberly. "The Spread of 'Post Abortion Syndrome' as Social Diagnosis." *Social Science & Medicine* 102 (February 1, 2014): 18–25. https://doi.org/10.1016/j.socscimed.2013.11.030.

Kelman, Herbert C. "Interests, Relationships, Identities: Three Central Issues for Individuals and Groups in Negotiating Their Social Environment." *Annual Review of Psychology* 57 (2006): 1–26.

Khazan, Olga. "Why Christians Overwhelmingly Backed Trump." *The Atlantic*, November 9, 2016. https://www.theatlantic.com/health/archive/2016/11/why-women-and-christians-backed-trump/507176/.

Kim, So Young. "Do Asian Values Exist? Empirical Tests of the Four Dimensions of Asian Values." *Journal of East Asian Studies* 10, no. 2 (2010): 315–44.

Knill, Christoph, Caroline Preidel, and Kerstin Nebel. "Brake Rather than Barrier: The Impact of the Catholic Church on Morality Policies in Western Europe." *West European Politics* 37, no. 5 (September 3, 2014): 845–66. https://doi.org/10.1080/01402382.2014.909170.

Kortsmit, Katherine. "Abortion Surveillance—United States, 2019." *MMWR. Surveillance Summaries* 70 (2021). https://doi.org/10.15585/mmwr.ss7009a1.

Kottasova, Ivana. "U.S. Is 65th in World on Gender Pay Gap." CNNMoney, October 27, 2014. https://money.cnn.com/2014/10/27/news/economy/global-gender-pay-gap/index.html.

Kozlowska, Iga, Daniel Béland, and André Lecours. "Nationalism, Religion, and Abortion Policy in Four Catholic Societies: Nationalism, Religion, and Abortion Policy." *Nations and Nationalism* 22, no. 4 (October 2016): 824–44. https://doi.org/10.1111/nana.12157.

Kramer, Stephanie. "U.S. Has World's Highest Rate of Children Living in Single-Parent Households." *Pew Research Center.* Accessed February 23, 2023. https://www.pewresearch.org/fact-tank/2019/12/12/u-s-children-more-likely-than-children-in-other-countries-to-live-with-just-one-parent/.

Krisafi, Juljana. "Albania and the Soviet Union, a Complicated Relationship . . . a Short Review." *Proceedings of International Academic Conferences*, Proceedings of International Academic Conferences, July 2015. https://ideas.repec.org//p/sek/iacpro/0100833.html.

Kunovich, Robert M. "Social Structural Position and Prejudice: An Exploration of Cross-National Differences in Regression Slopes." *Social Science Research* 33, no. 1 (2004): 20–44.

Lai, C. "Boy or Girl? Hong Kong at Centre of Banned China Gender Test." Hong Kong Free Press, May 22, 2019. https://hongkongfp.com/2019/05/22/boy-girl-hong-kong-centre-banned-china-gender-test/.

BIBLIOGRAPHY

Lee, Yueh-Ting, Russ Kleinbach, Pei-Cheng Hu, Zu-Zhi Peng, and Xiang-Yang Chen. "Cross-Cultural Research on Euthanasia and Abortion." *Journal of Social Issues* 52, no. 2 (July 1996): 131–48. https://doi.org/10.1111/j.1540-4560.1996.tb01572.x.

Lesthaeghe, Ron. "The Unfolding Story of the Second Demographic Transition." *Population and Development Review* 36, no. 2 (2010): 211–51. https://doi.org/10.1111/j.1728-4457.2010.00328.x.

Levels, Mark, Roderick Sluiter, and Ariana Need. "A Review of Abortion Laws in Western-European Countries. A Cross-National Comparison of Legal Developments between 1960 and 2010." *Health Policy* 118, no. 1 (October 2014): 95–104. https://doi.org/10.1016/j.healthpol.2014.06.008.

Li, Jane. "China's Propaganda Journey from 'Only One Child Is Good' to the Three-Child Policy." Quartz, June 7, 2021. https://qz.com/2015205/chinas-propaganda-journey-from-one-child-to-three-child-policy/.

Liao, Pei-Ju. "The One-Child Policy: A Macroeconomic Analysis." *Journal of Development Economics* 101, no. C (2013): 49–62.

Lie, Mabel LS, Stephen C. Robson, and Carl R. May. "Experiences of Abortion: A Narrative Review of Qualitative Studies." *BMC Health Services Research* 8, no. 1 (July 17, 2008): 150. https://doi.org/10.1186/1472-6963-8-150.

Ligita, Titan, Nichole Harvey, Kristin Wicking, Intansari Nurjannah, and Karen Francis. "A Practical Example of Using Theoretical Sampling throughout a Grounded Theory Study: A Methodological Paper." *Qualitative Research Journal* 20, no. 1 (January 1, 2019): 116–26. https://doi.org/10.1108/QRJ-07-2019-0059.

Linares, Albinson. "These People Want to Die. Will Their Countries Allow Euthanasia?" NBC News, October 21, 2021. https://www.nbcnews.com/news/latino/people-want-die-will-countries-allow-euthanasia-rcna3307.

Lincoln, C. Eric, and Lawrence H. Mamiya. *The Black Church in the African American Experience.* Durham: Duke University Press, 1990.

Lindgren, Yvonne. "Trump's Angry White Women: Motherhood, Nationalism, and Abortion." *Hofstra Law Review* 48, no. 1 (2019): 1–46.

Lindh, Arvid, and Leslie McCall. "Class Position and Political Opinion in Rich Democracies." *Annual Review of Sociology* 46, no. 1 (2020): 419–41. https://doi.org/10.1146/annurev-soc-121919-054609.

Lipset, Seymour Martin. *Political Man; the Social Bases of Politics.* Garden City, NY: Doubleday, 1960.

Liska, Allen E. "The Significance of Aggregate Dependent Variables and Contextual Independent Variables for Linking Macro and Micro Theories." *Social Psychology Quarterly* 53, no. 4 (December 1990): 292. https://doi.org/10.2307/2786735.

Llorente, Elizabeth. "Controversial Billboard Targets Abortions by Latinas." Fox News, January 4, 2017. https://www.foxnews.com/politics/controversial-billboard-targets-abortions-by-latinas.

Loi, Rehnström Ulrika, Kristina Gemzell-Danielsson, Elisabeth Faxelid, and Marie Klingberg-Allvin. "Health Care Providers' Perceptions of and Attitudes towards Induced Abortions in Sub-Saharan Africa and Southeast Asia: A Systematic Literature Review of Qualitative and Quantitative Data." *BMC Public Health* 15, no. 1 (December 2015). https://doi.org/10.1186/s12889-015-1502-2.

Loll, Dana, and Kelli Stidham Hall. "Differences in Abortion Attitudes by Policy Context and between Men and Women in the World Values Survey." *Women & Health* 59, no. 5 (May 28, 2019): 465–80. https://doi.org/10.1080/03630242.2018.1508539.

Lombardo, Paul A. "Miscegenation, Eugenics, and Racism: Historical Footnotes to Loving v. Virginia Essay." *U.C. Davis Law Review* 21, no. 2 (1988 1987): 421–52.

Lopatina, Sofia, Veronica Kostenko, and Eduard Ponarin. "Pro-Life vs. pro-Choice in a Resurgent Nation: The Case of Post-Soviet Armenia." *Frontiers in Political Science* 4 (August 11, 2022): 932492. https://doi.org/10.3389/fpos.2022.932492.

Lopes, Marina. "A 10-Year-Old Rape Victim Sought an Abortion. A Judge Urged: Stay Pregnant." *Washington Post*, July 2, 2022. https://www.washingtonpost.com/world/2022/07/02/brazil-child-rape-abortion/.

Loseke, Donileen R. *Thinking about Social Problems: An Introduction to Constructionist Perspectives*. New Brunswick, NJ: Transaction Publishers, 2011.

Loveland, Matthew T. "Religious Switching: Preference Development, Maintenance, and Change." *Journal for the Scientific Study of Religion* 42, no. 1 (2003): 147–57. https://doi.org/10.1111/1468-5906.00168.

Lovenduski, Joni. "Feminism and Western European Politics." In *Politics Western Europe Today*, Eds. D. W. Urwin and W. E. Paterson. New York: Longman, 1990.

Lowery, Shearon A., and Melvin L. DeFleur. *Milestones in Mass Communication Research*. 3rd edition. White Plains, NY: Pearson, 1995.

Luker, Kristin. *Abortion and the Politics of Motherhood*. Berkeley: University of California Press, 1984.

Luna, Zakiya. "'Black Children Are an Endangered Species': Examining Racial Framing in Social Movements." *Sociological Focus* 51, no. 3 (July 3, 2018): 238–51. https://doi.org/10.1080/00380237.2018.1412233.

Macleod, Catriona Ida, and Tracey Feltham-King. "Representations of the Subject 'Woman' and the Politics of Abortion: An Analysis of South African Newspaper Articles from 1978 to 2005." *Culture, Health & Sexuality* 14, no. 7 (August 2012): 737–52. https://doi.org/10.1080/13691058.2012.685760.

MacroTrends. "China Fertility Rate 1950-2023." MacroTrends, 2023. https://www.macrotrends.net/countries/CHN/china/fertility-rate.

Manning, Christel J. "Women in a Divided Church: Liberal and Conservative Catholic Women Negotiate Changing Gender Roles." *Sociology of Religion* 58, no. 4 (1997): 375. https://doi.org/10.2307/3711922.

Marks, Jaime L., Chun Bun Lam, and Susan M. McHale. "Family Patterns of Gender Role Attitudes." *Sex Roles* 61, no. 3–4 (June 9, 2009): 221–34. https://doi.org/10.1007/s11199-009-9619-3.

Martin, David. *On Secularization: Towards a Revised General Theory*. London: Routledge, 2017. https://doi.org/10.4324/9781315247694.

Marx, Karl. *Capital*. Vol. 1. Harmondsworth, England: Penguin/New Left Review, 1867.

Masci, David. "American Religious Groups Vary Widely in Their Views of Abortion." *Pew Research Center*, January 22, 2018. https://www.pewresearch.org/fact-tank/2018/01/22/american-religious-groups-vary-widely-in-their-views-of-abortion/.

Mason, Carol. "Opposing Abortion to Protect Women: Transnational Strategy since the 1990s." *Signs: Journal of Women in Culture and Society* 44, no. 3 (March 2019): 665–92. https://doi.org/10.1086/701156.

298 BIBLIOGRAPHY

Master, Farah. "Factbox: How China Is Seeking to Boost Its Falling Birth Rate." *Reuters*, January 17, 2023, sec. China. https://www.reuters.com/world/china/how-china-is-seeking-boost-its-falling-birth-rate-2023-01-17/.

McCall, Leslie, and Jeff Manza. "Class Differences in Social and Political Attitudes in the United States." In *The Oxford Handbook of American Public Opinion and the Medias*, edited by R. Y. Shapiro and L. R. Jacobs, 552–70. Oxford: Oxford University Press, 2011. Http://Dx.Doi.Org/10.1093/Oxfordhb/9780199545636.003.

McDonald, Henry, Emma Graham-Harrison, and Sinead Baker. "Ireland Votes by Landslide to Legalise Abortion." *The Guardian*, May 26, 2018, sec. World news. https://www.theguardian.com/world/2018/may/26/ireland-votes-by-landslide-to-legalise-abortion.

Miller, Alan S., and John P. Hoffmann. "Risk and Religion: An Explanation of Gender Differences in Religiosity." *Journal for the Scientific Study of Religion* 34, no. 1 (1995): 63–75.

Minkenberg, Michael. "Religion and Public Policy Institutional, Cultural, and Political Impact on the Shaping of Abortion Policies in Western Democracies." *Comparative Political Studies* 35, no. 2 (2002): 221–47.

Mishtal, Joanna. *The Politics of Morality: The Church, the State, and Reproductive Rights in Postsocialist Poland.* Ohio University Press, 2015.

Parker et al., Kim. "1. Demographic and Economic Trends in Urban, Suburban and Rural Communities." *Pew Research Center's Social & Demographic Trends Project*, May 22, 2018. https://www.pewresearch.org/social-trends/2018/05/22/demographic-and-economic-trends-in-urban-suburban-and-rural-communities/.

Mitchell, Travis. "About Three-in-Ten U.S. Adults Are Now Religiously Unaffiliated." *Pew Research Center's Religion & Public Life Project*, December 14, 2021. https://www.pewresearch.org/religion/2021/12/14/about-three-in-ten-u-s-adults-are-now-religiously-unaffiliated/.

Mooney, Christopher Z. "The Public Clash of Private Values." In *The Public Clash of Private Values: The Politics of Morality Policy*, edited by Christopher Z. Mooney, 1–22. New York: Chatham House, 2001.

Mooney, Christopher Z., and Mei-Hsien Lee. "Legislative Morality in the American States: The Case of Pre-Roe Abortion Regulation Reform." *American Journal of Political Science* 39, no. 3 (1995): 599–627. https://doi.org/10.2307/2111646.

Moore, Laura M., and Reeve Vanneman. "Context Matters: Effects of the Proportion of Fundamentalists on Gender Attitudes." *Social Forces* 82, no. 1 (2003): 115–39.

Mosley, Elizabeth A., Elizabeth J. King, Amy J. Schulz, Lisa H. Harris, Nicole De Wet, and Barbara A. Anderson. "Abortion Attitudes among South Africans: Findings from the 2013 Social Attitudes Survey." *Culture, Health & Sexuality* 19, no. 8 (August 2017): 918–33. https://doi.org/10.1080/13691058.2016.1272715.

Mukaka, M. M. "Statistics Corner: A Guide to Appropriate Use of Correlation Coefficient in Medical Research." *Malawi Medical Journal: The Journal of Medical Association of Malawi* 24, no. 3 (September 2012): 69–71.

Murray, Nancy, William Winfrey, Minki Chatterji, Scott Moreland, Leanne Dougherty, and Friday Okonofua. "Factors Related to Induced Abortion among Young Women in

Edo State, Nigeria." *Studies in Family Planning* 37, no. 4 (December 2006): 251–68. https://doi.org/10.1111/j.1728-4465.2006.00104.x.

Myers, Scott M. "An Interactive Model of Religiosity Inheritance: The Importance of Family Context." *American Sociological Review* 61, no. 5 (1996): 858–66.

Nauck, Bernhard, and Daniela Klaus. "The Varying Value of Children: Empirical Results from Eleven Societies in Asia, Africa and Europe." *Current Sociology* 55, no. 4 (July 2007): 487–503. https://doi.org/10.1177/0011392107077634.

Nelson, Thomas E., Rosalee A. Clawson, and Zoe M. Oxley. "Media Framing of a Civil Liberties Conflict and Its Effect on Tolerance." *American Political Science Review* 91, no. 3 (1997): 567–83.

Nepstad, Sharon Erickson, and Rhys H. Williams. "Religion in Rebellion, Resistance, and Social Movements." In Edited by James A. Beckford & N. J. Demerath III, *The SAGE Handbook of the Sociology of Religion*, 419–37. 1 Oliver's Yard, 55 City Road, London EC1Y 1SP United Kingdom: SAGE Publications Ltd, 2007. https://doi.org/10.4135/9781848607965.n21.

Newport, Frank. "Abortion Moves Up on 'Most Important Problem' List." Gallup.com, August 1, 2022. https://news.gallup.com/poll/395408/abortion-moves-important-problem-list.aspx.

Ng, Weiting, and Ed Diener. "What Matters to the Rich and the Poor? Subjective Well-Being, Financial Satisfaction, and Postmaterialist Needs across the World." *Journal of Personality and Social Psychology* 107, no. 2 (2014): 326–38. https://doi.org/10.1037/a0036856.

Nie, Jing-Bao. *Behind the Silence: Chinese Voices on Abortion*. Rowman & Littlefield: Maryland, USA. 2005.

Nie, Jing-Bao. "Limits of State Intervention in Sex-Selective Abortion: The Case of China." *Culture, Health & Sexuality* 12, no. 2 (August 4, 2009): 205–19. https://doi.org/10.1080/13691050903108431.

Norrander, Barbara, and Clyde Wilcox. "Public Opinion and Policymaking in the States: The Case of Post-Roe Abortion Policy." *Policy Studies Journal* 27, no. 4 (1999): 707–22. https://doi.org/10.1111/j.1541-0072.1999.tb01998.x.

Norris, Pippa, and Ronald Inglehart. *Sacred and Secular: Religion and Politics Worldwide*. 2nd edition. Cambridge Studies in Social Theory, Religion and Politics. Cambridge: Cambridge University Press, 2011. https://doi.org/10.1017/CBO9780511894862.

NPR interview, "How China's One-Child Policy Led to Forced Abortions, 30 Million Bachelors", *The Aquila Report*, 2016. Accessed 10 September 2024. https://theaquilareport.com/how-chinas-one-child-policy-led-to-forced-abortions-30-million-bachelors/.

"NSFG—Listing P—Key Statistics from the National Survey of Family Growth." Centers for Disease Control. November 6, 2019. https://www.cdc.gov/nchs/nsfg/key_statistics/p.htm.

Nyarko, Samuel H., and Lloyd Potter. "Effect of Socioeconomic Inequalities and Contextual Factors on Induced Abortion in Ghana: A Bayesian Multilevel Analysis." Edited by Kannan Navaneetham. *PLOS ONE* 15, no. 7 (July 9, 2020): e0235917. https://doi.org/10.1371/journal.pone.0235917.

BIBLIOGRAPHY

Ogland, Curtis P., and Ana Paula Verona. "Religion and Attitudes toward Abortion and Abortion Policy in Brazil." *Journal for the Scientific Study of Religion* 50, no. 4 (2011): 812–21. https://doi.org/10.1111/j.1468-5906.2011.01602.x.

Ohlander, Julianne, Jeanne Batalova, and Judith Treas. "Explaining Educational Influences on Attitudes toward Homosexual Relations." *Social Science Research* 34, no. 4 (December 2005): 781–99. https://doi.org/10.1016/j.ssresearch.2004.12.004.

Ortiz-Ospina, Esteban, and Max Roser. "Economic Inequality by Gender." *Our World in Data*, March 21, 2018. https://ourworldindata.org/economic-inequality-by-gender.

Page, Benjamin I., and Robert Y. Shapiro. "Effects of Public Opinion on Policy." *The American Political Science Review* 77, no. 1 (1983): 175–90.

Pan, Po-Lin, Juan Meng, and Shuhua Zhou. "Morality or Equality? Ideological Framing in News Coverage of Gay Marriage Legitimization." *The Social Science Journal* 47, no. 3 (2010): 630–45.

Panopoulou, Giota, and Panos Tsakloglou. "Fertility and Economic Development: Theoretical Considerations and Cross-Country Evidence." *Applied Economics* 31, no. 11 (November 1, 1999): 1337–51. https://doi.org/10.1080/000368499323229.

Parry, J. "Chinese Migrant Workers Are Vulnerable to Abortion Risks, Expert Says." *BMJ* 343, no. oct04 2 (October 4, 2011): d6354–d6354. https://doi.org/10.1136/bmj.d6354.

Peffley, Mark, and Robert Rohrschneider. "Democratization and Political Tolerance in Seventeen Countries: A Multi-Level Model of Democratic Learning." *Political Research Quarterly* 56, no. 3 (2003): 243–57.

Perl, Paul, and Jamie S. McClintock. "The Catholic 'Consistent Life Ethic' and Attitudes toward Capital Punishment and Welfare Reform." *Sociology of Religion* 62, no. 3 (2001): 275–99.

Perlez, Jane. "Women Who Have Premarital Sex Are 'Degenerates': China Textbook." *Sydney Morning Herald*, June 29, 2016. https://www.smh.com.au/world/women-who-have-premarital-sex-are-degenerates-china-textbook-20160629-gpu68p.html.

Perlman, Francesca, and Martin McKee. "Trends in Family Planning in Russia, 1994–2003." *Perspectives on Sexual and Reproductive Health* 41, no. 1 (March 2009): 40–50. https://doi.org/10.1363/4104009.

Peters, Rebecca Todd. "I'm a Christian Minister Who's Had 2 Abortions. Here's How Faith Informed Those Decisions." *USA TODAY*, October 10, 2021. https://www.usatoday.com/story/opinion/2021/10/10/my-christian-faith-informed-my-decision-get-2-abortions-roe-v-wade/5945020001/.

Petersen, Kerry A. *Abortion Regimes*. Aldershot, UK: Dartmouth Pub Co, 1993.

Petersen, Larry R. "Religion, Plausibility Structures, and Education's Effect on Attitudes toward Elective Abortion." *Journal for the Scientific Study of Religion* 40, no. 2 (2001): 187–204.

Pew Research Center. "How Religious Commitment Varies by Country among People of All Ages." *Pew Research Center's Religion & Public Life Project*, June 13, 2018. https://www.pewresearch.org/religion/2018/06/13/how-religious-commitment-varies-by-country-among-people-of-all-ages/.

Pew Research Center. "Modeling the Future of Religion in America." *Pew Research Center's Religion & Public Life Project*, September 13, 2022. https://www.pewresearch.org/religion/2022/09/13/modeling-the-future-of-religion-in-america/.

Pew Research Center. "America's Abortion Quandary." *Pew Research Center*, May 6, 2022. https://www.pewresearch.org/religion/wp-content/uploads/sites/7/2022/05/PF_05.06.22_abortion.views_.fullreport.pdf.

Pew Research Center. "America's Changing Religious Landscape." Pew Research Center on Religion & Public Life, May 12, 2015. http://religions.pewforum.org/reports.

Pew Research Center. "Categorizing Americans' Religious Typology Groups." *Pew Research Center's Religion & Public Life Project*, August 29, 2018. https://www.pewforum.org/2018/08/29/politics-and-policy-2/.

Pew Research Center. "In U.S., Decline of Christianity Continues at Rapid Pace." Washington D.C.: Pew Research Center's Religion & Public Life Project, October 17, 2019. https://www.pewresearch.org/religion/2019/10/17/in-u-s-decline-of-christianity-continues-at-rapid-pace/.

Pew Research Center. "Measuring Religion in China." *Pew Research Center's Religion & Public Life Project*, August 30, 2023. https://www.pewresearch.org/religion/2023/08/30/measuring-religion-in-china/.

Pew Research Center. "The Age Gap in Religion around the World." Washington D.C.: Pew Research Center, June 13, 2018. https://www.pewforum.org/2018/06/13/the-age-gap-in-religion-around-the-world/.

Pew Research Center. "The Gender Gap in Religion around the World." Washington D.C.: Pew Research Center, March 22, 2016. http://assets.pewresearch.org/wp-content/uploads/sites/11/2016/03/Religion-and-Gender-Full-Report.pdf.

Pew Research Center. "Tolerance and Tension: Islam and Christianity in Sub-Saharan Africa." Washington, DC: Pew Research Center, 2010. https://www.pewresearch.org/wp-content/uploads/sites/7/2010/04/sub-saharan-africa-full-report.pdf.

Pew Research Center. "Religion in Latin America: Widespread Change in a Historically Catholic Region." *Pew Research Center*, November 13, 2014. https://www.pewresearch.org/religion/2014/11/13/religion-in-latin-america/.

Pflum, Mary. "'We Were Not Prepared for Any of This': Fertility Clinics Struggle with a Growing Number of Abandoned Embryos." NBC News, August 12, 2019. https://www.nbcnews.com/health/features/nation-s-fertility-clinics-struggle-growing-number-abandoned-embryos-n1040806.

Pitt, Cassady M. "'Thou Shall Not Kill': Abortion, Euthanasia, Suicide, and Religious Context." *Journal of Cultural and Religious Studies* 2, no. 4 (August 28, 2014). https://doi.org/10.17265/2328-2177/2014.04.007.

Pittman, Genevra. "Abortion Safer than Giving Birth: Study." *Reuters*, January 23, 2012, sec. Healthcare & Pharma. https://www.reuters.com/article/us-abortion-idUSTRE80M2BS20120123.

Planned Parenthood. "The History & Impact of Planned Parenthood." Accessed March 1, 2023. https://www.plannedparenthood.org/about-us/who-we-are/our-history.

Plotnick, Robert D. "The Effects of Attitudes on Teenage Premarital Pregnancy and Its Resolution." *American Sociological Review* 57, no. 6 (December 1992): 800. https://doi.org/10.2307/2096124.

PONARS EURASIA. "Abortion in Russia: How Has the Situation Changed since the Soviet Era?" February 12, 2019. https://www.ponarseurasia.org/abortion-in-russia-how-has-the-situation-changed-since-the-soviet-era/.

Popov, Andrej A. "Family Planning in the USSR. Sky-High Abortion Rates Reflect Dire Lack of Choice." *Entre Nous* 16 (September 1990): 5–7.

Popov, Andrej A, and Henry P. David. "Russian Federation and USSR Successor States." In Ed. Henry P. David, Joanna Skilogianis. *From Abortion to Contraception: A Resource to Public Policies and Reproductive Behavior in Central and Eastern Europe from 1917 to Present.* Westport, CT: Greenwood Press, 1999: 223–277.

Poushter, Jacob, and Fetterolf. "A Changing World: Global Views on Diversity, Gender Equality, Family Life and the Importance of Religion." *Pew Research Center's Global Attitudes Project,* April 22, 2019. https://www.pewresearch.org/global/2019/04/22/a-changing-world-global-views-on-diversity-gender-equality-family-life-and-the-importance-of-religion/.

Powell, John Joseph. *Abortion the Silent Holocaust.* Allen, TX: Tabor Pub., 1981.

Pruitt, Sandi L., and Patricia Dolan Mullen. "Contraception or Abortion? Inaccurate Descriptions of Emergency Contraception in Newspaper Articles, 1992–2002." *Contraception* 71, no. 1 (January 2005): 14–21. https://doi.org/10.1016/j.contraception.2004.07.012.

Psaki, Stephanie R., Erica K. Chuang, Andrea J. Melnikas, David B. Wilson, and Barbara S. Mensch. "Causal Effects of Education on Sexual and Reproductive Health in Low and Middle-Income Countries: A Systematic Review and Meta-Analysis." *SSM - Population Health* 8 (August 2019): 100386. https://doi.org/10.1016/j.ssmph.2019.100386.

Purcell, Carrie, Shona Hilton, and Lisa McDaid. "The Stigmatisation of Abortion: A Qualitative Analysis of Print Media in Great Britain in 2010." *Culture, Health & Sexuality* 16, no. 9 (October 21, 2014): 1141–55. https://doi.org/10.1080/13691058.2014.937463.

Quivering, No Longer. "Racism Drives Quiverfull - Nancy Campbell Really Fears Brown People." *No Longer Quivering,* February 11, 2020. https://www.patheos.com/blogs/nolongerquivering/2020/02/nancy-campbell-really-fears-brown-people/.

Ragin, Charles C. *The Comparative Method: Moving beyond Qualitative and Quantitative Strategies.* Berkeley: University of California Press, 2014.

Ranji, Usha, Karen Diep, and Alina Salganicoff. "Key Facts on Abortion in the United States." *KFF,* August 29, 2023. https://www.kff.org/womens-health-policy/report/key-facts-on-abortion-in-the-united-states/.

Rao, Prashanth, and Maite Taboada. "Gender Bias in the News: A Scalable Topic Modelling and Visualization Framework." *Frontiers in Artificial Intelligence* 4 (2021). https://www.frontiersin.org/articles/10.3389/frai.2021.664737.

Ravi, Anusha. "Limiting Abortion Access Contributes to Poor Maternal Health Outcomes." *Center for American Progress,* June 13, 2018. https://www.americanprogress.org/article/limiting-abortion-access-contributes-poor-maternal-health-outcomes/.

Raymo, James M., and Hiromi Ono. "Coresidence with Parents, Women's Economic Resources, and the Transition to Marriage in Japan." *Journal of Family Issues* 28, no. 5 (2007): 653–81.

Raymond, Elizabeth G., and David A. Grimes. "The Comparative Safety of Legal Induced Abortion and Childbirth in the United States." *Obstetrics & Gynecology* 119, no. 2, Part 1 (February 1, 2012): 215–19. https://doi.org/10.1097/AOG.0b013e31823fe923.

Reeves, Richard V, and Joanna Venator. "Sex, Contraception, or Abortion? Explaining Class Gaps in Unintended Childbearing." *Brookings Institute*, 2011, 14: 223–277.

Regnerus, Mark D. "Moral Communities and Adolescent Delinquency." *The Sociological Quarterly* 44, no. 4 (2003): 523–54.

Reis, Ben Y., and John S. Brownstein. "Measuring the Impact of Health Policies Using Internet Search Patterns: The Case of Abortion." *BMC Public Health* 10, no. 1 (August 25, 2010): 514. https://doi.org/10.1186/1471-2458-10-514.

Reisig, Michael D., Scott E. Wolfe, and Travis C. Pratt. "Low Self-Control and the Religiosity-Crime Relationship." *Criminal Justice and Behavior* 39, no. 9 (June 4, 2012): 1172–91. https://doi.org/10.1177/0093854812442916.

Remennick, Larissa I. "Epidemology and Determinants of Induced Abortion in the U.S.S.R." *Social Science & Medicine* 33, no. 7 (January 1, 1991): 841–48. https://doi.org/10.1016/0277-9536(91)90389-T.

Westoff, Charles F., Almaz T. Sharmanov, Jeremiah M. Sullivan, and Trevor Croft. *Replacement of Abortion by Contraception in Three Central Asian Republics.* 1998. The Policy Project and Macro International Inc.: Maryland, USA.

Rigdon, Susan M. "Abortion Law and Practice in China: An Overview with Comparisons to the United States." *Social Science & Medicine* 42, no. 4 (February 1, 1996): 543–60. https://doi.org/10.1016/0277-9536(95)00173-5.

Rigdon, Susan M. "Abortion Law and Practice in China: An Overview with Comparisons to the United States." *Social Science & Medicine* 42, no. 4 (February 1, 1996): 543–60. https://doi.org/10.1016/0277-9536(95)00173-5.

Robertson, Christopher J., and James J. Hoffman. "How Different Are We? An Investigation of Confucian Values in the United States." *Journal of Managerial Issues* 12, no. 1 (2000): 34–47.

Rohlinger, Deana A. *Abortion Politics, Mass Media, and Social Movements in America.* Cambridge University Press, 2015.

Rominski, Sarah D., Eugene Darteh, Kwamena Sekyi Dickson, and Michelle Munro-Kramer. "Attitudes toward Abortion among Students at the University of Cape Coast, Ghana." *Sexual & Reproductive Healthcare* 11 (March 1, 2017): 53–59. https://doi.org/10.1016/j.srhc.2016.10.002.

Rostosky, Sharon Scales, Brian L. Wilcox, Margaret Laurie Comer Wright, and Brandy A. Randall. "The Impact of Religiosity on Adolescent Sexual Behavior: A Review of the Evidence." *Journal of Adolescent Research* 19, no. 6 (November 2004): 677–97. https://doi.org/10.1177/0743558403260019.

Samman, Emma, Elizabeth Presler-Marshall, and Nicola Jones. "Women's Work: Mothers, Children and the Global Childcare Crisis." London: Overseas Development Institute, 2016. https://bettercarenetwork.org/sites/default/files/Women%E2%80%99s%20work-%20Mothers%2C%20children%20and%20the%20global%20childcare%20crisis.pdf.

Sandler, Danielle, and Nicole Szembrot. "New Mothers Experience Temporary Drop in Earnings." Census.gov, June 16, 2020. https://www.census.gov/library/stories/2020/06/cost-of-motherhood-on-womens-employment-and-earnings.html.

Sanger-Katz, Margot, Claire Cain Miller, and Quoctrung Bui. "Who Gets Abortions in America?" *New York Times*, December 14, 2021, sec. The Upshot. https://www.nytimes.com/interactive/2021/12/14/upshot/who-gets-abortions-in-america.html.

Sargent, Elena. "The 'Woman Question' and Problems of Maternity in Post-Communist Russia." In *Women in Russia and Ukraine*, by Rosalind Marsh, 269–85. Cambridge, England: Cambridge University, 1997.

Sarkissian, Ani. "Religion and Civic Engagement in Muslim Countries." *Journal for the Scientific Study of Religion* 51, no. 4 (2012): 607–22.

Scheepers, Peer, Manfred Te Grotenhuis, and Frans Van Der Slik. "Education, Religiosity and Moral Attitudes: Explaining Cross-National Effect Differences." *Sociology of Religion* 63, no. 2 (2002): 157–76.

Scheitle, Christopher P., and Amy Adamczyk. "High-Cost Religion, Religious Switching, and Health." *Journal of Health and Social Behavior* 51, no. 3 (September 2010): 325–42. https://doi.org/10.1177/0022146510378236.

Scheitle, Christopher P., and Amy Adamczyk. "It Takes Two: The Interplay of Individual and Group Theology on Social Embeddedness." *Journal for the Scientific Study of Religion* 48, no. 1 (2009): 16–29.

Schiappa, Edward, Peter B. Gregg, and Dean E. Hewes. "Can One TV Show Make a Difference? Will & Grace and the Parasocial Contact Hypothesis." *Journal of Homosexuality* 51, no. 4 (2006): 15–37.

Schmalz, Mathew. "Why Donald Trump Won the Catholic Vote." *Fortune*, November 9, 2016. http://fortune.com/2016/11/09/donald-trump-election-2016-catholic-vote/.

Schnabel, Landon. "Does Religion Suppress Gender Differences in Values? A Cross-National Examination." Accessed March 29, 2019. https://doi.org/10.31235/osf.io/k3qjr.

Schnabel, Landon. "Opiate of the Masses? Inequality, Religion, and Political Ideology in the United States." *Social Forces* 99, no. 3 (March 1, 2021): 979–1012. https://doi.org/10.1093/sf/soaa027.

Schwadel, Philip. "Individual, Congregational, and Denominational Effects on Church Members' Civic Participation." *Journal for the Scientific Study of Religion* 44, no. 2 (2005): 159–71.

Schwartz, Shalom H. "A Theory of Cultural Value Orientations: Explication and Applications." *Comparative Sociology* 5, no. 2 (2006): 136–82.

Schwartz, Shalom H. "A Theory of Cultural Values and Some Implications for Work." *Applied Psychology* 48, no. 1 (1999): 23–47.

Schwartz, Shalom H. "National Culture as Value Orientations: Consequences of Value Differences and Cultural Distance." In *Handbook of the Economics of Art and Culture*, edited by Victor A. Ginsburgh and David Throsby, 2:547–86. Oxford, UK: Elsevier, 2014.

Scudson, Michael. *The Power of the News*. Cambridge, MA: Harvard University Press, 1982.

Self, Robert O. *All in the Family: The Realignment of American Democracy since the 1960s.* Farrar, Straus and Giroux, 2012.

Shapiro, G. K. "Abortion Law in Muslim-Majority Countries: An Overview of the Islamic Discourse with Policy Implications." *Health Policy and Planning* 29, no. 4 (July 1, 2014): 483–94. https://doi.org/10.1093/heapol/czt040.

Shear, Michael D., and Eileen Sullivan. "'Horseface', 'Lowlife', 'Fat, Ugly': How the President Demeans Women." *New York Times*, October 16, 2018, sec. U.S. https://www.nytimes.com/2018/10/16/us/politics/trump-women-insults.html.

Sherkat, Darren. *Changing Faith: The Dynamics and Consequences of Americans' Shifting Religious Identities.* NYU Press, 2014.

Shi, Yaojiang, and John James Kennedy. "Delayed Registration and Identifying the 'Missing Girls' in China." *The China Quarterly* 228 (December 2016): 1018–38. https://doi.org/10.1017/S0305741016001132.

Shin, Doh Chull, and Russell J. Dalton, eds. *Citizens, Democracy, and Markets around the Pacific Rim: Congruence Theory and Political Culture.* Oxford: Oxford University Press, 2006.

Shleifer, Andrei, and Daniel Treisman. "The East 25 Years after Communism." *Foreign Affairs*, n.d.

"Shout Your Abortion—Normalizing Abortion and Elevating Safe Paths to Access, Regardless of Legality." Accessed June 29, 2023. https://shoutyourabortion.com/.

Silber Mohamed, Heather. "Embryonic Politics: Attitudes about Abortion, Stem Cell Research, and IVF." *Politics and Religion* 11, no. 03 (September 2018): 459–97. https://doi.org/10.1017/S175504831800010X.

Singh, B. K., and J. Sherwood Williams. "Attitudes and Behavioral Intentions about Abortion." *Population and Environment* 6, no. 2 (June 1983): 84–95. https://doi.org/10.1007/BF01362289.

Smith, Christian. *Soul Searching: The Religious and Spiritual Lives of American Teenagers.* New York: Oxford University Press, 2009. https://books-google-comez.lib.jjay.cuny.edu/books?hl=en&lr=&id=TubQCwAAQBAJ&oi=fnd&pg=PR9&dq=soul+searching&ots=c2FXAn3dWU&sig=uJWrZrpc2ZnWCz4kjiTRgov9JKw.

Smith, Christian, and Amy Adamczyk. *Handing Down the Faith: How Parents Pass Their Religion on to the Next Generation.* New York: Oxford University Press, 2021. https://doi.org/10.1093/oso/9780190093327.001.0001.

Sniderman, Paul M., Barbara Kaye Wolfinger, Diana C. Mutz, E. James, and Phillip E. Tetlock. "Values under Pressure: AIDS and Civil Liberties." In *Reasoning and Choice: Explorations in Political Psychology*, edited by Paul M. Sniderman and Richard A. Brody, 31–57. Cambridge, MA: Cambridge University Press, 1991.

Sommer, Udi, and Aliza Forman-Rabinovici. *Producing Reproductive Rights: Determining Abortion Policy Worldwide.* Cambridge University Press, 2019.

Spruill, Marjorie J. *Divided We Stand: The Battle Over Women's Rights and Family Values That Polarized American Politics.* First Edition. New York: Bloomsbury USA, 2017.

Stack, Steven, Amy Adamczyk, and Liqun Cao. "Survivalism and Public Opinion on Criminality: A Cross-National Analysis of Prostitution." *Social Forces* 88, no. 4 (June 1, 2010): 1703–26. https://doi.org/10.1353/sof.2010.0029.

BIBLIOGRAPHY

Stark, Rodney. "Physiology and Faith: Addressing the 'Universal' Gender Difference in Religious Commitment." *Journal for the Scientific Study of Religion* 41, no. 3 (2002): 495–507.

Stark, Rodney. "Religion as Context: Hellfire and Delinquency One More Time." *Sociology of Religion* 57, no. 2 (1996): 163–73.

Stark, Rodney, Daniel P. Doyle, and Lori Kent. "Rediscovering Moral Communities: Church Membership and Crime." In *Understanding Crime: Current Theory and Research*, Edited by T. Hirschi and M. Gottfredson, 43–52. Beverley Hills, CA: Sage, 1980.

Stark, Rodney, and Roger Finke. *Acts of Faith: Explaining the Human Side of Religion*. Berkeley: University of California Press, 2000.

Stark, Rodney, Lori Kent, and Daniel P. Doyle. "Religion and Delinquency: The Ecology of a 'Lost' Relationship." *Journal of Research in Crime and Delinquency* 19, no. 1 (1982): 4–24.

Steensland, Brian, Lynn D. Robinson, W. Bradford Wilcox, Jerry Z. Park, Mark D. Regnerus, and Robert D. Woodberry. "The Measure of American Religion: Toward Improving the State of the Art." *Social Forces* 79, no. 1 (2000): 291–318.

Stephenson, Emily, and Mica Rosenberg. "Trump Signs Order to Keep Out Some Refugees, Prioritize Syrian Christians." *Reuters*, January 27, 2017, sec. U.S. Legal News. https://www.reuters.com/article/usa-trump-refugees-idUSL1N1FH203.

Stevenson, Alexandra, and Zixu Wang. "China Needs Couples to Have More Babies: Can I.V.F. Help?" *New York Times*, January 22, 2023, sec. Business. https://www.nytimes.com/2023/01/22/business/china-birthrate-ivf.html.

Stewart, Katherine. "Eighty-One Percent of White Evangelicals Voted for Donald Trump. Why?" *The Nation*, November 17, 2016. https://www.thenation.com/article/eighty-one-percent-of-white-evangelicals-voted-for-donald-trump-why/.

Stewart, Meghan. "Curbing Reliance On Abortion In Russia." *Human Rights Brief*, 2004.

Stockmann, Daniela. 2013. *Media commercialization and authoritarian rule in China*. Cambridge University Press.

Strickler, Jennifer, and Nicholas L. Danigelis. "Changing Frameworks in Attitudes toward Abortion." *Sociological Forum*, 17, no. 2 (2002):187–201.

Štulhofer, Aleksander, and Ivan Rimac. "Determinants of Homonegativity in Europe." *Journal of Sex Research* 46, no. 1 (February 3, 2009): 24–32. https://doi.org/10.1080/00224490802398373.

Suiter, Jane. "Deliberation in Action—Ireland's Abortion Referendum." *Political Insight* 9, no. 3 (September 1, 2018): 30–2. https://doi.org/10.1177/2041905818796576.

Sun, Jiahong, and Andrew G. Ryder. 2016. "The Chinese Experience of Rapid Modernization: Sociocultural Changes, Psychological Consequences?" *Frontiers in Psychology* 7. doi: 10.3389/fpsyg.2016.00477.

Sutherland, Edwin H. *Principles of Criminology*. Chicago: JB Lippincott Company, 1947.

Tang, Longmei, Shangchun Wu, Dianwu Liu, Marleen Temmerman, and Wei-Hong Zhang. "Repeat Induced Abortion among Chinese Women Seeking Abortion: Two Cross Sectional Studies." *International Journal of Environmental Research and Public Health* 18, no. 9 (April 22, 2021): 4446. https://doi.org/10.3390/ijerph18094446.

Tappe, Anneken. "Child Care Is Expensive Everywhere. But This Country Tops the List." CNN Business, April 9, 2022. https://www.cnn.com/2022/04/09/economy/global-child-care-costs-us-china/index.html.

"The DHS Program - Demographic and Health Survey (DHS)." Accessed May 23, 2023. https://dhsprogram.com/Methodology/Survey-Types/DHS.cfm.

Center for Democracy and Governance. "The Role of Media in Democracy: A Strategic Approach." Center for Democracy and Governance Washington, D.C., 1999. https://www.usaid.gov/sites/default/files/documents/2496/200sbc.pdf.

The World Bank Data. "Fertility Rate, Total (Births per Woman) Kenya." Accessed June 3, 2022. https://data.worldbank.org/indicator/SP.DYN.TFRT.IN?locations=KE.

Thompson, Dennis F. *The Democratic Citizen: Social Science and Democratic Theory in the Twentieth Century*. Cambridge, UK: Cambridge University Press, 1970.

Thompson, Terri-ann Monique, Yves-Yvette Young, Tanya M. Bass, Stephanie Baker, Oriaku Njoku, Jessica Norwood, and Monica Simpson. "Racism Runs through It: Examining The Sexual And Reproductive Health Experience of Black Women in the South: Study Examines the Sexual and Reproductive Health Experiences of Black Women in the South." *Health Affairs* 41, no. 2 (February 1, 2022): 195–202. https://doi.org/10.1377/hlthaff.2021. 01422.

Tittle, Charles R., and Michael R. Welch. "Religiosity and Deviance: Toward a Contingency Theory of Constraining Effects." *Social Forces* 61, no. 3 (1983): 653–82.

Tong, Goh Chok. "Social Values, Singapore Style." *Current History* 93, no. 587 (1994): 417–22.

Tsui, Karina. "China Set to Discourage Abortion amid Concern over Birthrates." *Washington Post*, August 17, 2022. https://www.washingtonpost.com/world/2022/08/16/china-abortion-birth-rates/.

Tu, Wei-Ming. "A Confucian Perspective on the Rise of Industrial East Asia." *Bulletin of the American Academy of Arts and Sciences* 42, no. 1 (1988): 32–50.

Tuman, John P., Danielle Roth-Johnson, and Ted Jelen. "Conscience and Context: Attitudes Toward Abortion in Mexico." *Social Science Quarterly* 94, no. 1 (2013): 100–12. https://doi.org/10.1111/j.1540-6237.2012.00905.x.

"Turnaway Study." Accessed April 28, 2017. https://www.ansirh.org/research/turnaway-study.

Tyler, Patrick E. "Birth Control in China: Coercion and Evasion." *The New York Times*, June 25, 1995, sec. World. https://www.nytimes.com/1995/06/25/world/birth-control-in-china-coercion-and-evasion.html.

UNICEF. "Girls' Education." United Nations Children's Fund, August 19, 2022. https://www.unicef.org/education/girls-education.

United States Department of State. "2022 Report on International Religious Freedom: China (Includes Hong Kong, Macau, Tibet, and Xinjiang)." Office of International Religious Freedom, 2023. https://www.state.gov/reports/2022-report-on-international-religious-freedom/china/.

Upadhyay, Ushma D., M. Antonia Biggs, and Diana Greene Foster. "The Effect of Abortion on Having and Achieving Aspirational One-Year Plans." *BMC Women's Health* 15 (November 11, 2015): 102. https://doi.org/10.1186/s12905-015-0259-1.

308 BIBLIOGRAPHY

US Agency for International Development, *The Role of Media in Democracy: A Strategic Approach.* Center for Democracy and Governance, 1999. https://www.usaid.gov/sites/default/files/documents/2496/200sbc.pdf.

USCCB Committee on Pro-Life Activities. "Respect for Unborn Human Life: The Church's Constant Teaching | USCCB," 2023. https://www.usccb.org/issues-and-action/human-life-and-dignity/abortion/respect-for-unborn-human-life.

van den Akker, Hanneke, Rozemarijn van der Ploeg, and Peer Scheepers. "Disapproval of Homosexuality: Comparative Research on Individual and National Determinants of Disapproval of Homosexuality in 20 European Countries." *International Journal of Public Opinion Research* 25, no. 1 (2013): 64–86.

Vu, Hong, and Vu Van. "The View of Confucianism about the Importance of Men, Disregard for Women and Its Influence on Vietnam." *International Journal of Advance Research, Ideas and Innovations in Technology* 5, no. 3 (October 14, 2019): 1912–17.

Vu, Tien Manh, and Hiroyuki Yamada. "The Legacy of Confucianism in Gender Inequality in Vietnam." MPRA Paper, July 2, 2020. https://mpra.ub.uni-muenchen.de/101487/.

Wang, Vivian. "For China's Single Mothers, a Road to Recognition Paved With False Starts." *New York Times,* May 31, 2021, sec. World. https://www.nytimes.com/2021/05/31/world/asia/china-mothers-children-birth.html.

Warner, Jennifer. "Premarital Sex the Norm in America." WebMD, December 20, 2006. https://www.webmd.com/sex-relationships/news/20061220/premarital-sex-the-norm-in-america.

Westoff, Charles. "Recent Trends in Abortion and Contraception in 12 Countries". *DHS Analytical Studies,* No. 8. Calverton, MD: ORC Macro, 2005.

Westoff, Charles F., Almaz T. Sharmanov, Jeremiah M. Sullivan, and Trevor Croft, *Replacement of Abortion by Contraception in Three Central Asian Republics.* The Policy Project and Macro International Inc., 1998.

"WHO European Health Information at Your Fingertips." Accessed September 7, 2023. https://gateway.euro.who.int/en/indicators/hfa_586-7010-abortions-per-1000-live-births/visualizations/#id=19681.

Wilcox, Clyde. "Evangelicals and the Moral Majority." *Journal for the Scientific Study of Religion* 28, no. 4 (1989): 400–14. https://doi.org/10.2307/1386573.

Wilcox, Clyde. "Race, Religion, Region and Abortion Attitudes." *Sociology of Religion* 53, no. 1 (1992): 97–105.

Wilkie, Jacob, Pramuk, Christina. "Trump Declares National Emergency to Build Border Wall, Setting Up Massive Legal Fight." CNBC, February 15, 2019. https://www.cnbc.com/2019/02/15/trump-national-emergency-declaration-border-wall-spending-bill.html.

Williams, Daniel. "The Partisan Trajectory of the American Pro-Life Movement: How a Liberal Catholic Campaign Became a Conservative Evangelical Cause." *Religions* 6, no. 2 (April 16, 2015): 451–75. https://doi.org/10.3390/rel6020451.

Williams, Daniel K. "This Really Is a Different Pro-Life Movement." *The Atlantic,* May 9, 2022. https://www.theatlantic.com/ideas/archive/2022/05/south-abortion-pro-life-protestants-catholics/629779/.

Wind, Rebecca. "Concern for Current and Future Children a Key Reason Women Have Abortions." Guttmacher Institute, March 1, 2016. https://www.guttmacher.org/news-release/2008/concern-current-and-future-children-key-reason-women-have-abortions.

WIN-Gallup International. "Global Index of Religiosity and Atheism." WIN-Gallup International, October 16, 2012. https://web.archive.org/web/20121016062403/http://redcresearch.ie/wp-content/uploads/2012/08/RED-C-press-release-Religion-and-Atheism-25-7-12.pdf.

"Women Fault Soviet System for Abortion (Published 1989)," February 28, 1989. https://www.nytimes.com/1989/02/28/world/women-fault-soviet-system-for-abortion.html.

Woodruff, Katie, M. Antonia Biggs, Heather Gould, and Diana Greene Foster. "Attitudes toward Abortion after Receiving vs. Being Denied an Abortion in the USA." *Sexuality Research and Social Policy* 15, no. 4 (December 1, 2018): 452–63. https://doi.org/10.1007/s13178-018-0325-1.

World Bank. "Fertility Rate, Total (Births per Woman)—East Asia & Pacific Data." The World Bank Data. Accessed June 2, 2022. https://data.worldbank.org/indicator/SP.DYN.TFRT.IN?locations=Z4.

World Bank, 'World Development Indicators, 2.14 Reproductive Health', 2017. Accessed 19 June 2023] https://wdi.worldbank.org/table/2.14.

World Population Review. "Gender Equality by Country 2023," 2023. https://worldpopulationreview.com/country-rankings/gender-equality-by-country.

World Population Review. "Poorest Countries in the World 2022." Accessed September 22, 2022. https://worldpopulationreview.com/country-rankings/poorest-countries-in-the-world.

World Population Review. "Total Population by Country 2023." Accessed March 30, 2023. https://worldpopulationreview.com/countries.

World Population Review. "Out of Wedlock Births by Country 2024." Accessed September 9, 2024. https://worldpopulationreview.com/country-rankings/out-of-wedlock-births-by-country.

WVS. "World Values Survey: Aggregate File: 1981-2022." World Values Survey Association. Accessed June 3, 2022. http://www.worldvaluessurvey.org.

Xinhua News Agency. "More Care for Girls to Address Gender Imbalance," October 25, 2003. http://www.china.org.cn/english/2003/Oct/78355.htm.

Xu, Xiaohe, and Shu-Chuan Lai. "Gender Ideologies, Marital Roles, and Marital Quality in Taiwan." *Journal of Family Issues* 25, no. 3 (2004): 318–55.

Yam, Eileen A., Ingrid Dries-Daffner, and Sandra G. Garcia. "Abortion Opinion Research in Latin America and the Caribbean: A Review of the Literature." *Studies in Family Planning* 37, no. 4 (2006): 225–40.

Yang, Wen-Shan, and Pei-Chih Yen. "A Comparative Study of Marital Dissolution in East Asian Societies: Gender Attitudes and Social Expectations towards Marriage in Taiwan, Korea and Japan." *Asian Journal of Social Science* 39, no. 6 (December 2011): 751–75. https://doi.org/10.1163/156853111X619210.

Zakaria, Fareed, and Lee Kuan Yew. "Culture Is Destiny: A Conversation with Lee Kuan Yew." *Foreign Affairs* 73, no. 2 (1994): 109–26.

Zaugg, Julie. "Blood Smuggling in China: Why Pregnant Women Are Breaking the Law to Find Out Their Babies' Sex." CNN, October 14, 2019. https://www.cnn.com/2019/10/13/asia/hong-kong-blood-smuggling-nipt-intl-hnk/index.html.

Zhou, Min, and Wei Guo. "Fertility Intentions of Having a Second Child among the Floating Population in China: Effects of Socioeconomic Factors and Home Ownership." *Population, Space and Place* 26, no. 2 (March 2020). https://doi.org/10.1002/psp.2289.

Zhou, V. "'Shared Ignorance about Sex' in China Won't Change Any Time Soon." *South China Morning Post*, November 11, 2020. https://www.scmp.com/lifestyle/family-relationships/article/3109184/china-has-national-sexual-illiteracy-challenges-way.

Zhu, Wei Xing, Li Lu, and Therese Hesketh. "China's Excess Males, Sex Selective Abortion, and One Child Policy: Analysis of Data from 2005 National Intercensus Survey." *BMJ* 338 (April 9, 2009): b1211. https://doi.org/10.1136/bmj.b1211.

Ziegler, Mary, and Robert L. Tsai. "How the Anti-Abortion Movement Used the Progressive Playbook to Chip Away at Roe v. Wade." POLITICO, June 13, 2021. https://www.politico.com/news/magazine/2021/06/13/anti-abortion-progressive-roe-v-wade-supreme-court-492506.

Index

abortion
  culture, 167–169
  forced, 17, 103, 142, 229, 232
  rates, 200–211
  sex-selective. *See* gender inequality
Africa. *See also* specific countries, 4, 33–34, 40, 65, 119
African American. *See* race
Albania, 215–219
Americas. *See* specific countries
anti-ascetic hypothesis, 87–89
Armenia, 161–166
Asia. *See* Confucian and specific countries
Assisted Reproductive Technologies, 23, 193–194
atheism, 15, 241
authoritarian personality, 173–174

Bangladesh, 76, 250
behaving. *See* obedience
Biblical, 156
billboard campaign, 43, 154–155, 238
birth control, 36–37, 160–163, 207, 251–252
bloodlines, 133, 175
Brazil, 1–2, 4, 50, 191, 250
Buddhism, 14–16, 35, 38, 55–61, 241

Cambodia, 215–219
Cameroon, 215–219
Canada, 76, 107, 115, 117
capital punishment. *See* life ethic
case study, 13–17
Catholic, 36–37, 49–55, 51*f*, 118–119, 150, 241, 257
causal order, 33–35, 46, 170–171, 176–177, 217–218, 220–221
Center for Reproductive Rights, 10, 248, 257–258, 269
children, 176, 212, 215
China. *See also* specific topics, 55–64, 103–110, 119–122
Christian Orthodox, 38
Christian. *See also* Catholic and Protestant, 14–16, 51–52, 238–239

civil liberties, 68, 95, 112, 115–116, 118, 269
claimsmaker, 113–119
Clinton, Hillary, 148, 151
clustering techniques, 12–13
"Coming Out", 172
communism, 159–167, 206–208, 244, 270
Confucian, 55–61, 133, 140–141, 178–188, 240–241, 244–245, 257, 263
Cote d-Ivoire, 215–219
Covid, 18–19
Cuba, 162
cultural value orientations, 73–75

data, 11–14
democracy. *See also* communism, 16, 92–96, 191, 244, 257, 269
Democratic Party, 150–151
Demographic and Health Surveys, 211–219
Dobbs vs. Jackson Women's Health Organization, 100–101, 147–152, 193
doctors. *See* medical culture
Durkheim, 6, 41, 47

economic concerns, 57–58, 241–243
economic development, 7, 16, 73–84, 202–206, 242–244, 257, 261, 270
economic threat, 67
education, 66–84, 149–150, 202–206, 212–213, 217, 223–224, 243, 256, 261
effect sizes, 261–263
England, 79
English, 81, 113–114, 118, 189, 265, 267–271
Equal Rights Amendment, 151
ethnicity, 71–72, 149
eugenics, 153–154
Europe. *See also* specific countries, 50, 65, 86, 147, 163, 193, 249
euthanasia. *See* life ethic
Evangelical Christian. *See also* Protestant, 36, 39
explanatory sequential design, 13

Factiva, 265
family dissolution. *See* divorce

312 INDEX

family planning, 57, 58, 63, 103–110, 218, 227, 232, 236
family values, 173–176, 182–183, 184*f*, 212–213
feminism. *See* gender equality and inequality
fertility policy. *See* one-child
fertility rates, 82–83
fetus, 191–194
Finland, 2, 115
folk beliefs, 55–61, 63, 240–241
foreigners. *See* immigrants
France, 4, 98, 118
Freedom House, 116*f*, 269

gay. *See* same-sex relations
GDP. *See* economic development
gender equality and inequality, 61–63, 67, 81–82, 85, 98, 104, 123–158, 163, 176, 183–184, 202–206, 234–235, 242, 245–246, 257, 261
gender roles, 61, 126–127, 245–246
Germany, 1, 115, 238
Global North, 99, 247
God, 26
guilt, 59–61

health, 137, 145–146, 185–187, 191–194, 214, 226–228, 235, 242, 245
Hierarchical Linear Modeling (HLM); analysis of
Hinduism, 35, 38, 49, 213, 256
Hofstede, 73–74
homosexuality. *See* same-sex relations
human-rights, 54, 147, 155

immigrant, 67, 71–72, 135, 151, 177
In vitro fertilization. *See* Assisted Reproductive Technologies
In vitro. *See* Assisted Reproductive Technologies
income, 66–72, 155, 212, 217, 223–224, 243, 256
India, 136, 192, 207, 213, 215–219
Indonesia, 4, 215–219, 238, 250
infertility, 137, 186–187, 245
Inglehart, 73–74
International Social Survey Program (ISSP), 12, 195
internet, 16, 19, 81, 120, 141–142
intersectionality, 153–157
interview methodology, 17–19, 247
Ireland, 7, 53–54, 99, 117

Islam. *See* Muslim
Italy, 98–99, 118

Japan, 107–108, 140, 179–180, 187
Jesse Jackson, 54, 61
Judaism, 35–36, 38, 214, 256

karma, 40, 58–59
Korea, South, 107–109, 135–136, 179–180

Latin America. *See also* specific countries, 4, 50, 190–191
laws 7–9, 44, 46, 53–55, 67, 96–102, 115–117, 208–211, 246, 247–251, 257–258
LGBTQ. *See* same-sex relations
life ethic, 36, 176–177, 183–184, 184*f*, 193

macro religious climate, 40–52, 238–239, 257, 263
macro-micro link, 6–9, 41, 44, 47–48, 73–79, 261
marriage. *See* single.
media, 80–81, 110–122, 265–272
medical culture, 75, 243
Mexico, 6, 151, 210, 258
Middle East 200–201. *See also* specific nations
migrant, 72
missing data, 258
mixed methods research, 11–14, 247
mixed modeling techniques, 12–13, 246, 258, 270
monotheism, 14–16, 26–27, 49
moral communities, 47–48, 261
Moral Majority, 150
moral, 36, 54, 62, 85–88, 97, 115, 116*f*, 169–173, 191–192, 195–197, 226, 252
mothers. *See* parents
multilevel models. *See* mixed modeling techniques
Muslim, 8, 15, 26, 32, 35, 239, 256, 270

National Longitudinal Study of Adolescent Health, 220–221
nationalism, 52–55, 151–152, 160–161, 167, 244
newspaper. *See* media
Nigeria, 4, 130, 250*f*
Norway, 2, 53, 75, 130, 140, 227

obedience, 173–174, 182–183, 184*f*

INDEX 313

one-child policy, 16–17, 55–57, 63, 82, 84, 103–110, 132–136, 187–188, 232–233, 242, 245, 251
out-of-wedlock. *See* premarital and single women

Pakistan, 238, 250
parents and parenthood, 34, 201–205, 212, 214–216, 223–224, 228
patriarchal, 127–128, 144–146, 167
Pew data, 12, 191, 195–197, 269, 270
Planned parenthood vs. Casey, 150
Planned parenthood, 153–154
Poland, 20, 50, 53–54, 86, 99, 117–118, 152, 249
policies regarding abortion. *See* laws
polytheism, 14–16, 26–27, 49, 56, 240–241
premarital sex, 140, 221–225, 227–228
press. *See* media
prolife and prochoice. *See* social movement
prostitution, 169–172, 182–183, 184*f*
protest, 54, 91–93, 113–117, 141, 144
Protestant, 36, 39, 49, 51–52, 54, 156, 270

Quiverfull movement, 71

race, 71, 149, 151–158
racism, 71–72, 151–158
reincarnation, 60–61
religion, 22–64, 100, 113–118, 120, 148–149-150, 208–211, 213–214, 216*f*, 219–225, 230, 238–242
religious affiliation, 14–16, 35–40, 38*f*, 138–139, 213–214, 216*f*, 240, 256
religious contextual effects, 41, 44–47
religious freedom and regulation, 15–16
religious importance, 28–31, 31–35, 44–46, 45*f*, 219–225, 208–210, 239–240, 256–257, 261–263, 269
religious switching
Republican Party, 150–152
Roe vs. Wade, 99–101, 147–152, 193, 252
Romania, 158, 166*f*, 270
rural, 72–73, 80, 82–83, 109–110, 133–134, 194, 212–213
Russia, 4, 98, 160–169, 207, 250–251

same-sex relations, 151, 169–173, 183, 184*f*, 252
sampling, 18
Sanger, Margaret, 153
Schlafly, Phyllis, 151
Schwartz, 73–74
secularization, 85–86, 241–242

self-expression, 7, 88
sex education, 138
sexism, 127, 143
shame, 136–141, 222–223, 225–231
Singapore, 179–180, 185
single women. *See* unmarried women
social class. *See* income and education
social control theory, 30, 42–43, 239
social learning theory, 29, 42–43, 239
social movements, 54, 85, 98, 116–118, 143–152, 230–231, 242–244
South Africa, 111–112
South America. *See also* Latin America and specific countries, 1, 50
Soviet Union. *See also* communism and specific countries, 152, 160–169, 206–208, 244, 270
"sui generis", 6, 41
Spain, 4, 98, 125
stigma. *See* shame.
Supreme Court, 1, 9, 16, 99–101, 147–150, 152, 244, 251
survey data, 11–13
Sweden, 2, 53, 118, 130, 140, 227
Switzerland, 75, 99, 130

Taiwan, 108, 115, 130, 179, 180*f*, 187
Taoism, 55–61
traditional values, 67, 128, 152
Trump, Donald, 148, 151–152, 244
Turkey, 6, 108, 115, 265

Ukraine, 125, 160, 163
ultrasound, 134, 173
United States. *See also* specific topics, 147–157
unmarried women, 136–141, 184*f*, 227, 233
urban, 73, 80, 109–110, 194, 212–213, 217, 219, 234
Uyghurs, 72, 157

Vietnam, 93–94, 140, 164–166, 179–180, 187

welfare, 43, 54
Western influences, 80–82, 98, 141–142, 163
women's rights. *See* gender equality and inequality
World Values Survey, 3, 5*f*, 8*f*, 11–12, 16, 18, 23, 27, 31–32, 35, 37–38, 44–45, 51*f*, 68, 75, 77*f*, 78*f*, 79, 88–89, 97–98, 106–110, 125–126, 128–129, 131*f*, 164–166, 170–171, 174–185, 187–188, 190, 195–198, 200, 206–208, 241, 249–252, 254–264